Down from the Attic

# Down from the Attic

*Rare Thrillers of the
Silent Era through the 1950s*

JOHN T. SOISTER *and*
HENRY NICOLELLA

McFarland & Company, Inc., Publishers
*Jefferson, North Carolina*

**ALSO OF INTEREST:** *American Silent Horror, Science Fiction and Fantasy Feature Films, 1913–1929,* John T. Soister and Henry Nicolella with Steve Joyce and Harry H Long; researcher/archivist Bill Chase (2012); *Up from the Vault: Rare Thrillers of the 1920s and 1930s,* John T. Soister (2004; paperback 2010); *Conrad Veidt on Screen: A Comprehensive Illustrated Filmography,* John T. Soister (2002; paperback 2009); *Claude Rains: A Comprehensive Illustrated Reference to His Work in Film, Stage, Radio, Television and Recordings,* John T. Soister with JoAnna Wioskowski (1999; paperback 2006); *Of Gods and Monsters: A Critical Guide to Universal Studios' Science Fiction, Horror and Mystery Films, 1929–1939,* John T. Soister (1999; paperback 2005)

ISBN (print) 978-0-7864-9831-4
ISBN (ebook) 1-4766-2544-7

LIBRARY OF CONGRESS CATALOGUING DATA ARE AVAILABLE

British Library cataloguing data are available

© 2016 John T. Soister and Henry Nicolella. All rights reserved

*No part of this book may be reproduced or transmitted in any form or by any means, electronic or mechanical, including photocopying or recording, or by any information storage and retrieval system, without permission in writing from the publisher.*

Front cover: Fredric March in a publicity shot from the 1934 film *Death Takes a Holiday* (Paramount Pictures/Photofest)

Printed in the United States of America

*McFarland & Company, Inc., Publishers*
*Box 611, Jefferson, North Carolina 28640*
*www.mcfarlandpub.com*

For Nancy and Jake and Katelyn and Jeremy:
*Familia mea, lux mea, vita mea, anima mea*
—John T. Soister

To Katie, Lucas, Hillary and
my favorite son-in-law, Eddie O'Hagan
—Henry Nicolella

# Table of Contents

| | |
|---|---:|
| NOTA BENE | viii |
| INTRODUCTION | 1 |
| | |
| *Der Tunnel*; *Transatlantic Tunnel* | 7 |
| *Sherlock Holmes* | 20 |
| *The Sky Ranger* (*The Man Who Stole the Moon*) | 34 |
| First Looks: *Das grinsende Gesicht*; *Die Insel der Verschollenen* | 52 |
| *The Monkey's Paw*; *Sweeney Todd* | 62 |
| *The House Without a Key* | 76 |
| *Forgotten Faces* | 91 |
| *High Treason*; *Men Must Fight* | 99 |
| *Les Fantômes de Paris*: *Chéri-Bibi*; *The Phantom of Paris* | 110 |
| *Just Imagine* | 125 |
| *Fog*; *Terror Aboard* | 139 |
| *The Horror:* The Patchwork Cinema of Bud Pollard | 149 |
| *Return of the Terror* | 168 |
| *Death Takes a Holiday* | 176 |
| Hispanic Horrors | 188 |
| *Der Hund von Baskerville* | 202 |
| *Císařův Pekař a Pekařův Císař* (*The Emperor's Baker, the Baker's Emperor*) | 213 |
| | |
| CHAPTER NOTES | 225 |
| BIBLIOGRAPHY | 229 |
| INDEX | 231 |

# Nota Bene

Thanks are due Steve Joyce—our research and technology guru. We cannot possibly overstate the degree to which he contributed to this book.

Steve is an acclaimed expert on silent science fiction movies and it was he who not only told us about *Les Rôdeurs de l'Air*, but was also able to actually get the film for us *and* provide us with rare ads and articles.

Steve made many a trip to Emory University and came back with reviews of most of the films covered in this volume.

And if that's not enough, he took pity on our grey hair and technologically-challenged ways and spent days cataloguing the illustrations to be used herein.

You are a wonder, friend Steve! We are in your debt.

# Introduction

We were born within a week of each other at the outset of that signal year, 1950. Although we weren't to meet for some four decades, later discussions found us having lived lives so parallel, so similar, that a dime-novelist might have had us twins, separated at birth. With John in Brooklyn and Hank in upstate New York, we experienced (separately but together): Zacherley and Shock Theater, '50s science fiction (concentrated mostly on robots and bugs), the Hammer remakes of those Universal originals we had seen (mostly) while Zacherley putzed around with Gaspard and the remains of his wife, the Vincent Price/AIP Canon (which gave respectability—such as it was—to Roger Corman), the Mexican horror films that were also remakes of those Universal originals while simultaneously being bizarrely novel variations on them, and George Romero's *Night of the Living Dead*, the picture that ultimately led to innumerable movies and TV series that promulgated putrescence, evisceration, and mindlessness as absolute necessities for the modern take on Good vs. Evil. We (and countless others of our generation) much preferred the set of rules that kept the ghoulish predation of a Conrad Veidt or a Boris Karloff within a rational—if undeniably fantastic—realm and that abjured the überviolence of the "zombification" of our favorite genre.

We read *Famous Monsters* with awe for its stills and a steadily diminishing respect for its "facts." We read *Castle of Frankenstein* for its more eclectic treatment of the genre, although Henry shot off at least one indignant LoC when he perceived that Chris Lee— and not Bela Lugosi—was that publication's preferred Dracula. We attended sci-fi "shows" (anyone else remember the Americana Hotel?) where we shared oxygen with giants like Isaac Asimov, Lin Carter, and Robert Heinlein. We went to screenings of 8mm prints of *Der Golem* und der like held by Cal Beck at the McBurney YMCA, and home-oriented gatherings of fans that led to little except for a free meal for FJA and a passel of snapshots for the next issue of *FM*. We bought crap from Captain Company, made checks out to Cal Beck's mom, and scoured the newsstand for any offshoots of the aforementioned magazines that had us hooked via their subject matter, even if we were less than enthralled by their mangling of grammar, distortion of facts, or patronizing tone.

Like so many others, we spent a significant fraction of our youth taping the soundtracks of our favorite horror films on Wollensak reel-to-reel dinosaurs; in founding and/or contributing to "fanzines" even before they moved from being mimeographed to being offset-printed; to penning LoCs (letters of comment): highly opinionated avenues of debate and/or argument over the merits/inadequacies of a film, a performance, a technical difficulty, a directorial mistake, a production shortfall, or the possible sexual orientation of whomever in whatever setting. We were overjoyed at the publication of Carlos Clarens's *The History of the Horror Film*, the first "serious" book that dealt fairly with the impact of the kind of movies we enjoyed so much, and the one that sort of opened the floodgates to more and better scholarship on the less prestigious cinematic genres ... like horror, science fiction, and twisted mystery.

Well, that was "then." (And we *liked* "then.")

"Now" is sort of a mixed bag. While the bar on published "horror film" criticism has been raised ever higher, the availability of illogical, erroneous, and unsubstantiated genre-related BS has never been greater, what with the Internet machine (thank you, Rachel Maddow!) and its sundry fora, blogs, and "experts," whose only expertise may lie in touch-typing skills and a reliance on someone else's fora and blogs. Putting such as these aside, we have to thank a number of genuine experts and generous associates in any number of film-related fields. And so, in alphabetical order, allow us to render our gratitude to the following: Xochitl y Rogelio Agrasánchez, a wonderfully accommodating couple, Mexican national treasures, and founders of www.AgrasFilms.com, a splendid site on Hispanic films and filmmakers; the BFI Reuben Library, which gave us some of the skinny on the 1922 *Sherlock Holmes*; John Boles, biographer and our fellow gravesite searcher in the Old Jewish Cemetery; Kevin Brownlow, film historian extraordinaire, who helped (im)perfect strangers fill in more than the occasional blank, as well as for ... well ... *everything* he's ever done!; James Card for being James Card and for the wonderful Seductive Cinema; Jared Case and Bill Stratman of the American Film Institute, perennially dependable researchers; Bill "Cleveland" Chase, friend, colleague, librarian, and researcher par excellence; Cinefania—and nuestro querido amigo Dario Lava—for insights into unas películas Hispanas (please don't fail to check out www.Cinefania.com); Kristin Dewey, old friend; Robert Dickson, author, film historian, mentor—our friend who never fails to come to our aid; William K. Everson for incredible contributions to film criticism and film conservation; Kristýna Haklová and the Národní Filmový Archiv for some splendid illustrations of emperors; Rosemary Hanes (Library of Congress) for arranging screenings and patiently responding to our many requests for materials; Juan Heinink for background information from his splendid *Cita en Hollywood*; Dr. Robert Kiss, film scholar and master collector, who was willing to share his vast, in-depth knowledge on virtually every obscure film we tossed his way; Tim Lussier, webmaster of the absolutely requisite www.SilentsAreGolden.com website, for his help and support; Diane MacIntyre, mistress of the superlative Facebook site The Silents Majority; Nicholas Mazzanti, conservateur, Cinémathèque Royale de Belgique, for extant footage on *The Sky Ranger*; Bruno Mestdagh, Koninklijk Filmarchief, Cinémathèque Royale, for additional materials on *The Sky Ranger*; Michael A. Morrison for help given us in the past which served us well again in the present; Gary D. Rhodes, chronicler of all things Lugosi, film scholar, filmmaker, genius, pal; Matias Gil Robert, nuestro amigo Argentino, for providing some rare graphics from *Una luz en la ventana*; Jay Salsberg, friend and font of information on seldom-seen films at the LoC; André Stratmann, unser Freund (we're not going to attempt "ever-dependable" in German) who tracked down a few rare films—and supporting materials—for us—vielen Dank, André; Stan Taffel for his insights and support; U Golema Restaurant, Prague, for sharing photos, anecdotes, and really wonderful food with us; and Kip Xool, Tod Slaughter fan extraordinaire.

Back to the "now" in which we find ourselves—at that certain age when one would love to be called an *éminence gris*, but usually has to settle for "that old man." We're in an age where the term "oldies" refers to products and performances made before the new millennium and in which silent film is a medium virtually unknown to anyone born in the last decade or so of

# Introduction 3

the 20th century or later. Still, things could always be worse.

It's 2016: a great year to be alive! (Most are, no?)

It is also a great year for lovers of vintage films.

The commercial market has expanded exponentially and is pretty much in the niche category (with silent films being a niche within a niche), with the result being that even the humblest horror movie of yesteryear might expect an A-1 treatment on video. A restored *Death Kiss* with commentary and extras? *Voodoo Man* on Blu-ray? Multiple *Plan(s) 9 from Outer Space*? Such things have come to pass, along an endless stream of "new" editions of *Nosferatu*, *Caligari*, *Phantom of the Opera*, and *White Zombie*. Archives have put some of their holdings online and, by hook or by crook, incredible rarities have ended up on YouTube. Turner Classic Movies is still going strong, and film festivals in San Francisco, Rome (New York), and Los Angeles screen movies that have thus far eluded television and video. Occasionally, a picture that was thought to be lost forever (the game's afoot, Gillette!) unexpectedly turns up anywhere from Alaska to Australia. Film buffs who used to lament the absence of so many rare films can now pop them into their DVD players and lament their quality: It's the wrong sort of music! The ratio's incorrect! There are still some scratches! Etc., etc., and so forth....

The bad news, though, is that most lost films are going to stay lost. Only two films that were considered lost at the time of the publication of our *Up from the Vault* (McFarland, 2004) have since turned up: the sound version of *High Treason* and 1933's *The Monkey's Paw*. Numerous obscure—but worthy—titles still exist in archives somewhere, but their lack of *commercial* potential and their donor restrictions or copyright issues make it unlikely that they will be retrieved from the vaults anytime soon. Of the films in this book, only one, the Charlie Chan serial *The House Without a Key*, is still categorically a lost film. Some of the others are extant, but elusive, while still others are readily accessible via television or home video.

We've chosen some interesting films for discussion and for a variety of reasons, but—with one possible exception—there are no *great* movies in the bunch. While love of *film* is an objective obsession, love for *a particular film* is as subjective as can be. Thus, any given reader may find a picture herein she thinks is unworthy of our (or any) coverage, while another movie has always been a real favorite of hers. We feel that, no matter where they might stand on the Good-Bad-Indifferent-ometer, and no matter whether they are easily located or as hard to find as a convenient parking space in Manhattan, relatively little has been written about any of them, and—for one reason or another—they are all worth a closer look.

*Der Tunnel* (1915) was based on a best-selling novel that won international acclaim. Its plot—the digging of a transatlantic tunnel—may have seemed outlandish, but both the "Chunnel" that runs between Folkstone in Britain and Pas-de-Calais in France and the Seikan Tunnel in Japan have proved that such a feat *can* be accomplished (on a more reasonable scale, of course). In light of the ongoing discussions about high-speed rail in the United States, plus last year's "retirement" of US-Airways (merged into American Airlines)—leaving only four American carriers to service overseas transportation—the notion of extensive subterranean "tube" travel no longer seems totally ridiculous. The picture suffers from the limitations of moviemaking in that early era, but—of the four film versions—it remains the most faithful to its literary source, and it's instructive to contrast and compare its approach with the 1935 British adaptation.

The recent, surprising find of the 1916 William Gillette *Sherlock Holmes* serves to renew our interest in the 1922 John Barrymore version, which is also based on Gillette's play. The Goldwyn production—the last major film for The Great Profile before he repaired to the stage for his iconic Hamlet—was hailed as a great success by many and sloughed off as a major disappointment by many others, but the picture's backstory and the details of its own rediscovery and restoration are important bits of film history.

One of 2015's great cinematic hits was *The Martian*, and that, together with astronaut Scott Kelly's breaking the American record for days in space in late October of last year, led us to consider a passel of science-fictional movies that had (occasionally tenuous) ties with space travel. *The Sky Ranger*, a 1921 indie serial featuring an aircraft of remarkable capabilities, was long thought to be lost. While in the midst of our dealing with extant, studio-generated plot summaries, the chapterplay—albeit certainly missing some footage—was found to be in the possession of the Belgian film archive. We were able to take a first-hand look at what remains of the film and compare what remains with what, apparently, has flown the coop.

*Just Imagine* (1930) is an acquired taste, but it's a fascinating oddity with some strong visuals and amusing Pre-Code elements. Looking to put some distance between the economic catastrophe that was the Great Depression and the hopes for a bright and shiny future, not only does the ambitious Fox musical offer a mindblowing prediction of everyday life in 1980, it also features far-out aircraft and a side trip to the Red Planet. And El Brendel! (Come on! There's at least one El Brendel fan out there—and you know who you are.)

*Das grinsende Gesicht* (*The Grinning Face*) is the first feature-length version of Victor Hugo's intriguing novel, *L'Homme qui rit* (*The Man Who Laughs*). Though not the equal of the later Conrad Veidt version, it's a very good film in its own right. We have paired it with another 1921 movie, *Die Insel der Verschollenen*, a *very* loose adaptation of *The Island of Dr. Moreau* by H.G. Wells. While you may need to visit the Austrian film archive to see *Das grinsende Gesicht*, *Die Insel* surfaced a few years back and can now be seen as a DVD extra.

We were not able to view the surviving footage of the 1923 *The Monkey's Paw*, but it sounds like a fascinating film and may have been better than—and more faithful to—W.W. Jacobs's short story than the 1933 version. (Fun fact: According to the Tulane National Primate Research Center, monkeys have *hands*, not *paws*.) Filling out our double bill with *Paw* is the 1928 *Sweeney Todd* which we did get to see (at least most of it). When Christopher Bond wrote a play about the Demon Barber of Fleet Street in 1973, he couldn't have foreseen that, in 1979, Stephen Sondheim and Hugh Wheeler would have adapted his work into one of Broadway's most popular musicals. Several iterations of that masterpiece have since come and gone, and the BBC did a 90-minute TV version in 2006. The film we discuss herein is the cinematic ancestor of all (including, obviously, Tod Slaughter's barnstormer from 1936). Marriott Moore, the unlikeliest of horror stars, stars in both *Monkey* and *Sweeney*.

*The House Without a Key* (1926) is still MIA. Regrettably, despite their immense popularity, a handful of Charlie Chan films remain lost at this late date. Searching out information on this silent serial was quite frustrating, since reviewers and trade papers largely ignored chapterplays, but we have done our best to shed some light on Spencer Gordon Bennet's nod to Earl Derr Biggers. We hope our effort here, when considered with our *Up from the Vault* coverage of Paul Leni's *The Chinese Parrot* and *Eran Trece*—the Spanish-language version of the still-lost *Charlie Chan Carries On*—will signal our commitment both to the Honolulu Police Force and to seldom seen pictures, in general.

Our opinion on what is, perhaps, the best film covered in this volume is the 1928 *Forgotten Faces*, which we have hoped to see ever since reading about it in Ivan Butler's *Silent Magic* many, many years ago. When the picture finally turned up at Capitolfest, it did not disappoint. Spoiler alert! It's not a horror film, per se, or really even a thriller, but it *is* a melodrama dotted with eerie moments and filled with strong performances that make you forget the story's far-fetched premise. What's more, it provides quite a showcase for the talents of Olga (*Freaks*) Baclanova.

While the silent *High Treason* can be found in the grey market on DVD (and is discussed in *Up from the Vault*), the sound version (1929) is not likely to go that route; still, it has been shown at several film festivals (thank you, Capitolfest, once again). We have discussed in it tandem with a far more accessible film, *Men Must Fight* (1933), another futuristic tale dealing with war and peace at the "quiet time" before, once again, the world was divided into allies and enemies.

*The Phantom of Paris* (1931) is usually regarded as something of a snoozer (especially when contrasted with the pictures featuring other curious characters filling movie houses that year), but it highlights a Gaston Leroux character—the magician/detective Chéri-Bibi—who remains far less well-known than his Opera Ghost. In addition, we look at the Spanish-language version of *Phantom* that not only preceded it, but also—sorry, John Gilbert!—inspired it.

A trip to the Library of Congress yielded viewings of *Return of the Terror* (1934) and *Fog* (1933), two seldom seen, but enjoyably hokey programmers with a chill or two folded into the mystery. We've double teamed *Fog* with *Terror Aboard* (1933), another tale of mayhem on the high seas and one with numerous production problems. We also watched *The Horror* (1933)—or what there is of it—and this inspired us to do a career piece on its director Bud Pollard, exploitation director extraordinaire and teller of tall tales.

*Death Takes a Holiday* (1934) was thought to be more appealing to intellectuals than to hoi polloi back then, although the picture doesn't seemed particularly profound today. With the majority of today's cinematic offerings intimately tied with Death—specifically, with *violent* Death—a gander at the Paramount thriller does give us an excuse to ruminate on the varied ways Death has been personified in the movies.

While South of the Border horrors from the '50s and '60s have drawn much attention and been given classy treatment on DVD, their vintage predecessors have not been so fortunate and are available only in eye-straining prints that lack English subtitles. We analyze the background and stories of three "mad médico" epics: *El misterio del rostro pálido* (*The Mystery of the Ghastly Face*, 1937), *El baúl macabro* (*The Macabre Trunk*, 1936), and *Una luz en la ventana* (*A Light in the Window*, 1942). With the Azteca chillers—and the Paul Naschy thrillers from a decade or two later on—in the debt of these early genre efforts, it's time they received at least a modicum of the attention they deserve.

*Der Hund von Baskerville* (1937) was the third version of the Conan Doyle tale to be filmed in Germany and, while it deviates from the original story from time to time, it's rich in atmosphere and style. Like most films made during the Third Reich, it's free of overt Nazi propaganda, an odd situation, now that we think of it. In addition to discussing this particular Hund, we tried to give a brief background of the non-British Holmesian output prior to the late '30s and Basil Rathbone's ascension to the deerstalker.

The most recent film we cover is *Císařův Pekař a Pekařův Císař* (*The Emperor's Baker, the Baker's Emperor*, 1951), a bizarre blend of comedy, music, and Marxist propaganda that features a giant Golem, magic, science, scientific magic, magical science, con men, doublecrossers, and a doppelganger perhaps inspired by *The Prisoner of Zenda*. It's still fondly recalled throughout the Czech Republic and has a fascinating background. Like *Der Hund von Baskerville*, though, it's not always easy to find subtitled in English.

As was the case with *Up from the Vault*, the keyword here is "eclectic." We've tried to comment on a good mix of pictures that haven't been beaten into the ground, analytically, yet that are worth the attention of every true genre fan. It's our hope that these screeds may lead folks to seek out these hard-to-find films—would someone start looking for *The House Without a Key* in earnest, please?—and enjoy them for what they are, and not merely how they stand in comparison with something else entirely.

# Der Tunnel; Transatlantic Tunnel

***Der Tunnel***—Projektions-AG Union (PAGU)—August 17, 1915 (censorship); September 1915 (premiere)—6 acts (2,006 meters) **Cast:** Friedrich Kayssler (Kayßler) as Mac Allan; Fritzi Massary as Ethel Lloyd; Hermann Vallentin as Lloyd; Rose Veldtkirch as Maud Allan; Felix Basch as Hobby; with Hans Halden

**Credits:** *Director and Screenplay*: William Wauer; *Producer*: Paul Davidson; *Assistant Director*: Heinz Karl Heiland; *Director of Photography*: Axel Graatkjaer; *Production Design*: Hermann Warm; *Distributor*: Nordische Films; *Based on the eponymous novel by* Bernhard Kellermann (1913)

***Transatlantic Tunnel*** (alternate title, ***The Tunnel***)—Gaumont-British—October 27, 1935 (U.S. release); November 1935 (UK release)—8,578 feet/90 or 94 minutes **Cast:** Richard Dix as Richard "Mack" McAllan; Leslie Banks as Robbie; Madge Evans as Ruth McAllan; Helen Vinson as Varlia Lloyd; C. Aubrey Smith as Lloyd; Basil Sydney as Mostyn; Henry Oscar as Grellier; Hilda Trevelyan as Mary; Cyril Raymond as Harriman; Jimmy Hanley as Geoffrey McAllan; George Arliss as the Prime Minister of Britain; Walter Huston as the President of the United States; James Carew as Jim Bardon; Percy Parsons as Financier; Cyril Smith as Man; with Pat Fitzpatrick, Jacqueline Giovanni, Helen Hay, Bryant Hebert, Dennis Hoey, Alan Jeayes, Mary Jerrold

**Credits:** *Director*: Maurice Elvey; *Producer*: Michael Balcon; *Associate Producer*: S.C. Balcon; *Screen Story*: Kurt Siodmak; *Scenario and Dialogue*: L. DuGarde Peach; *Additional Dialogue*: Clemence Dane; *Original Music*: Hubert Bath; *Musical Director*: Louis Levy; *Cinematography*: Gunther (Günther) Krampf; *Editor*: Charles Frend; *Art Direction*: Ernö Metzner; *Costume Design*: Schiaparelli, Joe Strassner; *Sound Department*: Michael Rose; *Special Effects*: Phillippo Guidobaldi, A. Stroppa, Jack Whitehead; *Based on the novel*, **Der Tunnel**, *by* Bernhard Kellermann (Berlin, 1913)

Nineteen fourteen saw the completion of the Panama Canal, an extraordinary feat of engineering that had been begun by the French in 1881 and then completed by the Americans. The human cost of this endeavor was dreadful: It is estimated that over 27,000 workers—most of them from the Caribbean islands—perished from disease or accident while working on the Canal. The number of people hurt or maimed during the construction is not known, but there were no doubt many thousands. Fraud, political intrigue, and corruption were also part of the Canal's history. Nonetheless, it was a magnificent accomplishment and was at least part of the inspiration for Bernhard Kellermann's novel,

*Der Tunnel*, published one year before the Canal was finished. Kellermann's story concerns an endeavor far more grandiose than the building of a canal: a tunnel under the Atlantic, extending from New York to Europe. The idea had been the subject of science fiction years earlier; in 1895 Michael Verne—son of Jules—penned a short story, "The Express of the Future," which envisions parallel pneumatic tubes spanning the Atlantic from Boston to Liverpool. The narrator's underwater journey turns out be a dream inspired by his having read a newspaper article about such a project. Awakened, he dismisses the whole idea as fit only for dreams. Bernhard Kellermann, however, was no dreamer. World traveler, writer, journalist (and, later, war correspondent), he was fascinated by the technological progress of the early twentieth century. *Der Tunnel* celebrates man the doer and his power to reshape nature to his own ends.

Mac Allan, the hero of *Der Tunnel*, is an American engineer who has created a drill that can penetrate the hardest rock with ease. Mac, a former coal miner, is a no-nonsense technician and self-made man to whom work is a religion. His architect friend, Hobby, introduces Mac to Mr. Lloyd, a multi-millionaire, to whom Mac outlines his grand plan: a tunnel extending from France to New York with additional entrances in Spain, the Azores, and the Virgin Islands. Railway lines will be constructed in the tunnel, thus making travel from Europe to America possible in a matter of hours rather than days. Lloyd is impressed and convinces his rich pals to invest in the scheme as well, and soon the Tunnel Syndicate is a reality. Mac wastes no time in organizing a gigantic world-wide work force, and the digging commences. Mac is also delighted when the Syndicate offers shares to the public, as he believes that the Tunnel should belong to the people, not just a small cabal of millionaires. However, Lloyd's right-hand man, Woolf [alas, an anti-Semitic stereotype] is a crook who uses some of the Syndicate money for his own private investments.

The whole world is excited and fascinated by the mammoth project. Edison Studios buys exclusive rights to film progress on the Tunnel, and each week movie audiences are thrilled to see the latest step of the great undertaking. Large settlements—"Mac Cities"—house the workers and their families near the Tunnel openings. As the years pass, Mac's obsession with his work becomes all-consuming, and he has little time for his wife Maud and their little daughter, Edith. Maud is hurt by his lack of attention, but is still devoted to him and occupies herself doing charitable work in the Mac City in New York, which is also the Syndicate's headquarters.

Mac's estimate of 15 years to complete the Tunnel proves to be overly optimistic. Still, things go well for a long time even though conditions underground prove to be hellish for the workers. All this changes when a terrible explosion rocks the New York Tunnel. The fact that the workers are hundreds miles away from the mouth of the tunnel makes escape and rescue even more difficult, and several thousand lives are lost. Mac is out of town at the time, but Maud, hearing of the accident, rushes to the Tunnel with Edith. They are confronted by a mob of women on the same errand, and these blame Mac for the disaster that has claimed their men. The crowd stones Maud and Edith to death. Mac arrives to a scene of utter chaos, but takes control of the situation.

Albeit devastated by the loss of his family, Mac soldiers on with the Tunnel. When he confronts Woolf over his embezzling, the financier throws himself in front of a train rather than face arrest. This scandal reaches the papers and makes public trust in the Tunnel project erode still further. When the workers refuse to return to the Tunnel, Mac, calling them cowards, fires them all and looks for replacements. Worldwide economic disaster follows in the wake of the Tunnel shutdown, and Mac is transformed from hero into villain in the public eye; a mob even burns down the Syndicate headquarters. Mac himself is arrested on a trumped-up charge and, although he is convicted, he wins his case on appeal and the Supreme Court ultimately frees him.

Discouraged and with his fortunes at a low point, Mac is comforted by Mr. Lloyd's daughter, Ethel, who has always been attracted to him. After a couple of bumpy stretches on the road to romance, they marry and, inspired by Ethel's confidence [and her daddy's millions], Mac resumes working on the Tunnel. After a total of 28 years in the making, the project is finally completed, and Mac takes the first train ride from Europe to America; all goes smoothly, but the train arrives 12 minutes late. Mac, while realizing that air travel is faster, still finds comfort in the fact that airplanes are only for the rich, while the Tunnel is for everyone.

*Der Tunnel*—enormously popular and perhaps the first international best seller to originate in Germany—was translated into 23 languages and sold hundreds of thousands of copies. There was, of course, the occasional skeptic who viewed askance the feasibility of the Tunnel, and one of these was Hans Dominik—a well-known German engineer (and himself a sci-fi writer)—who offered the following observation:

> By boring and blasting with machinery of the kind actually employed in work of this sort, the daily advance would be ten meters, five at each end and it would take 1000 years to complete the tunnel. Perfected machines might double the amount of work, reducing the time to 500 years. By laying the route from Spain over the Azores to Halifax and dividing the work into four sections, the tunnel could be completed in 125 years.[1]

We're guessing that that's why they call it science *fiction*.

Credible or not, *Der Tunnel* captured the imaginations of countless readers and just a few months after the book was published, an article in the August 27 edition of *Variety* stated that a German film syndicate (presumably PAGU) was negotiating with Kellermann for the movie version. Unlike some other writers, Kellermann had no problem with film adaptations of novels and wrote the following in response to a 1913 questionnaire:

> I am by no means unaware of the risks a novel runs if it is made into a film, but I see no reason to exaggerate them. The knowledgeable viewer can in most cases reconstruct the original work quite well from a film and the unsophisticated one will benefit from the film as much as, if not more than he would have from reading the book. As for the economic aspect, movies are such a powerful advertising instrument that the filming of a novel can only work to the benefit of author and publisher.

It took quite awhile for PAGU's *Der Tunnel* to be filmed and make it to the theaters. Apparently there were numerous delays—perhaps the Great War, a catastrophe Kellermann did not foresee in his novel and one that made a bloody mockery of his hope for international cooperation—that slowed down the progress of what was no doubt an expensive picture for the time.

In any event, the delay presented an opportunity for Imperator, a relatively new company, to do its own, unauthorized five-reel feature based on *Der Tunnel*. The names of the characters were changed, but the premise—digging a tunnel under the Atlantic—was not; however, some adjustments were made to the story (including a conspiracy against the enterprise) that were no doubt intended to protect the producers from charges of plagiarism. Directed by Siegfried Dessauer and Kurt Matull, the picture starred Eduard Rothauser, Sybill Smolowa, and Magnus Stifter, who probably essayed the villain. We haven't any more plot information, but—years later—Eduard Rothauser recalled having to jump into the Baltic Sea fully clothed, as stunt doubles were an unknown commodity in those early days of the cinema.

The Imperator version beat PAGU to the theaters by some five months, and Imperator even had the temerity to entitle its film *Der Tunnel*. PAGU promptly hauled its competitor into court, and, although no attempt was made to halt screenings of the Imperator epic, it was ruled that the picture could not be named *Der Tunnel*. The title was thus changed to *Das Riesenprojekt—Der Schienenweg unter dem Ozean* (*The Great Project—The Railway Under the Ocean*), although it was sometimes shortened to either *Das Riesenprojekt* or *Der Schienenweg unter dem Ozean*.[2] None of this fooled reviewers who were, nonetheless, rather blasé about the blatant plagiarism.

Perhaps to bolster its own claims to legitimacy, PAGU's *Der Tunnel* opens with footage of Bernhard Kellermann himself, grinning at the camera and puffing away on a cigar like it's his last smoke. This is followed by a shot of director William Wauer—every inch the Teutonic professor—jumping up from his chair and gesticulating operati-

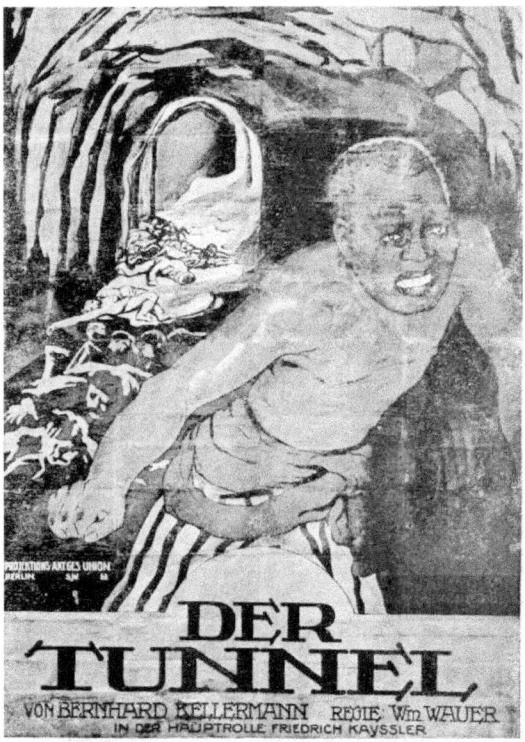

Ad for PAGU's author-approved version of *Der Tunnel* depicting a black worker fleeing the tunnel disaster. This character was part of the book and, briefly, turns up in the movie as well.

Another ad for *Der Tunnel*, this one depicting Mac (played by Friedrich Kayssler in the film though the drawing bears no resemblance to him) confronting the mob of angry workers who blame him for the tunnel catastrophe.

cally, although it's hard to say whether he's supposed to be directing actors or traffic. Wauer helmed a number of films in the 1910s, including *Richard Wagner* (1913; which is credited as being the first German film with an original musical score), but was more famous as an art critic and sculptor, with much of his work leaning towards Expressionism. (Fun fact: The Nazis later banned his sculptures.) In spite of this—*and* the presence of *Caligari*'s Hermann Warm as set designer—*Der Tunnel* is anything but Expressionistic and sometimes resembles an industrial film.

Wauer's screenplay is faithful to the plot of the book (though he omits the character of Woolf, perhaps for the better), but the focus shifts from Mac, the dynamic leader, to the actual process of putting the tunnel together and the manpower it involved in every aspect. We see railway lines being built, the workers massing, the dynamiting of the rock, the hauling away of the debris in trains, etc. There are numerous shots of crowds of workers walking toward the camera and shots of workers walking away from the camera. We see scores of brokers at the stock market and floods of customers cramming into the Syndicate headquarters to buy shares. At one point—when a sign advertising for 100,000 workers is hung—we see man after man shuffling along, and the viewer begins to fear that Wauer is going to show us each and every one of the 100,000 applicants pass by the camera. This emphasis on the labor required to build the Tunnel sometimes has the feel of a Soviet film, but without the rapid editing that catches the eye and distracts from the monotony. Curiously, little time is actually spent *in* the Tunnel; it never becomes a kind of character in its own right as in the book or the 1935 film version.

We are, of course, dealing with a 100-year-old movie, and the underdeveloped film grammar is very much of its time and place. The camera rarely moves and the only close-ups occur when actors walk directly toward the lens. There is very little cutting or change of perspective within scenes (one of the few exceptions occurs early in the film, when the characters observe each other with binoculars during a concert), and the actors usually gather in front of the camera in medium-shot, with the whole scene being played out that way. What's more, there are relatively few dialog cards even for some fairly long scenes, so the viewer is left in the dark as what everyone is chattering away about, although, again, this is not so unusual for a 1915 movie. (Or perhaps Wauer just assumed everyone had read the book.)

This simple technique does work well for the scene wherein Maud and Edith are

Imperator briefly tried to get its own version of *Der Tunnel* released with the same title as Kellermann's novel. Occasionally both film versions of the book appeared at the same time in the same city no doubt causing a bit of confusion.

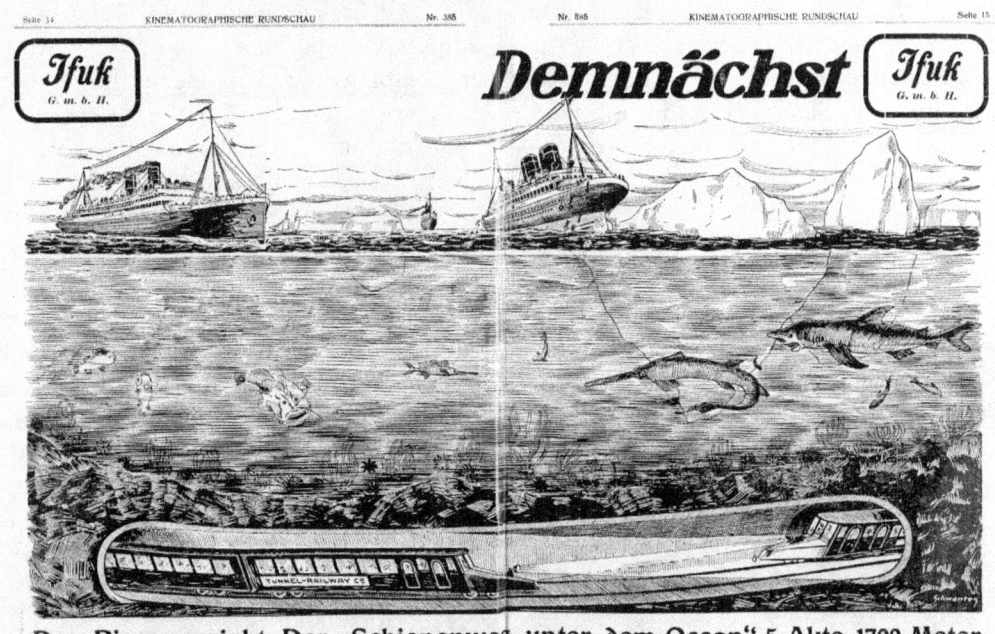

PAGU could not stop the showing of the Imperator version but the courts insisted that the film's title be changed. Imperator obliged and *Der Tunnel* became *The Great Project: The Railway Under the Ocean*.

killed by the mob (this is the only film version to contain that sequence). We watch as the crowd of women rushes along one side of the building, while Maud and Edith are running on the other. When the crowd subsequently sees them, they begin picking up stones. The camera shifts away from the terrified mother and daughter to the crowd hurling debris, and then back to the two victims, lying prone. The mob, suddenly realizing the enormity of what's been done, moves cautiously toward the bodies and then hurriedly withdraws in a pell-mell fashion. Here, the lack of close-ups makes the scene even more shocking, and even when viewed today, it is still startling.

Friedrich Kayssler was not well cast as Mac; he is much too bulky, slow-moving, and phlegmatic to suggest a robust man-of-action, although perhaps having such an uncharismatic hero suited Wauer's purpose. While Kayssler might have been done better playing Mr. Lloyd, he achieves real poignancy in the scene wherein Mac discovers his fallen wife and child. The camera is placed near their broken bodies, and we see Mac's car stop in the background. He rushes across the empty lot, backs away just for a moment when he reaches them, and then moves forward uncertainly. Slowly he bends over their still forms, and then kneels, gently removing some of the stones before bowing his head in grief. It's a superbly understated bit of acting. Kayssler made a number of movies (he turns up in the 1937 *Der Hund von Baskerville*; see entry), but his stage career was far more significant, and he remained a force in the theater throughout the 1920s and 1930s. Tragically, he was shot by the Russians in 1945 while trying to defend his wife during the last days of the Reich.

The rest of the performers barely register: Rose Veldtkirch pouts and does little else as Maud Allan, Fritz Massary's Ethel seems more Margaret Dumont than beguiling young heiress, and Hermann Vallentin's Lloyd sports a hairstyle that suggests he's been to visit the barber in *Genuine*. As in the book, Mac has a Chinese servant, but the unbilled Caucasian actor playing the part sports a ludicrous make-up job: a blob of dark greasepaint covers his face, but stops at his neckline!

The disaster in the Tunnel is fairly well done, with some tense shots of frantic workers climbing over each other as they desperately try to escape. On the downside, it appears that the same shot of the Tunnel ablaze is used again and again, and there's little to suggest that the deadly blaze is spreading or that its fatal fumes are following the workers as they flee. The burning of Syndicate headquarters is a bit more harrowing, though, as people leap from the front of the building into the nets below and, in the process, tear down some of the three-dimensional letters on the sign. There is one unintentionally funny moment: Mac continues to work away at his desk even as his office is filling with smoke.

Though set partly in the future, there is little in the way of sci-fi touches in the film (nor, admittedly, were there in the book). The one exception is the

**Maude Allan (Rose Veldtkirch) and her little girl are stoned to death by a mob of angry women.**

finale, when Mac and company triumphantly ride the Tunnel train on its maiden voyage (courtesy of the Berlin Underground), and we see the events unfolding as they happen on a giant screen set atop a building in New York City. There's a huge crowd below, presumably watching, but it looks more like they're marching around in circles and not really looking up at the screen.

*Die Lichtbild-Bühne* (September 11, 1915) gave the film a fairly good—though not uncritical—review:

> It is precisely the lofty song of labor, the poetry of machine technology and the imposing magic of industry on a mammoth scale that here are of primary moment. The scenes that are purely acting, for which director Wauer takes credit, are here an accessory, the passage between the individual battle scenes of labor. And if one discounts the photography, which is very bad in spots, there is still a great deal left to be getting on with, because the material is too absorbing and interesting. With billions one wanted to build a tunnel under the ocean, with thousands of marks, one has filmed the idea of the book, and hundreds of mark notes will flow into the cinema coffers, in order to follow the success of the experiment.

How many hundreds of mark notes it made, we don't know. Obviously the coming of the Great War and its frenzied nationalism prevented the film from achieving the international success of the book.

Perhaps, in passing, we should note the dubious story of one of Hitler's pals set during Der Führer's vagabond days:

> At Easter [in 1910] we did well and had a little more to spend so Hitler went to the movies. I preferred to drink some wine which Hitler despised. The next day I knew at once that he was planning a new project. He had seen *The Tunnel*, a picture made from the novel by Bernhard Kellermann. Hitler told me the story. An orator makes a speech in a tunnel and becomes a great popular tribune. Hitler was aflame with the idea that this was the way to found a new party.[3]

The scene in question only lasts a few seconds (at the exterior of the tunnel), and Mac doesn't really sway the crowd. There *is* such a scene in the 1933 versions of the story—made while Hitler was already in power—so maybe that's what Hanisch is muddling with the 1915 film. In any case, 1910 is three years before the publication of the novel and five years before the film, so perhaps Hamisch's preference of wine over cinema had clouded his memory.

The 1933 adaptation of *Der Tunnel* was done by Vandor Film, a company with studios in both Paris and Munich. The decision to make the film may have been influenced by the success of *F.P. 1 Doesn't Answer*, a 1932/33 picture (based on Kurt Siodmak's novel) about a mid–Atlantic platform built for refueling airplanes that becomes the object of much intrigue and sabotage. *F.P. 1* had German, French, and English versions, but Vandor decided to film *The Tunnel* only in French and German.[4] Gustav Gründgens appeared in both productions, playing the

In the 1933 film version of *Der Tunnel*, Paul Hartmann made a dynamic and forceful Mac. The insert shows Gustav Gründgens who played the crooked financier Wolfe in the German and French editions of the film.

crooked financier Woolf, who is portrayed as being even more villainous than he is in the book; he even tries to sabotage the Tunnel. Naturally he fails and then commits suicide, here by gunshot rather than train, although the latter fate befalls Mac Allan's hapless wife as she rushes to the site of the Tunnel disaster and is accidentally hit. Gründgens's Woolf is not the Jewish caricature of the book, but rather a suave and oily capitalist, replete with top hat and tails; the modern viewer might feel that the character just stepped off the Monopoly playboard.

After wrapping the French version in Paris, director Kurt Bernhardt, who was Jewish, was dismayed to learn that the producers expected him to return to Munich to helm the German edition as well. Even though Jews were being purged from the arts, the producers told Bernhardt that they had received assurances from Dr. Goebbels that he would not be harassed. The director was not convinced, but nonetheless walked back into the lion's den to complete his assignment. He was under close surveillance the whole time, but went unmolested until after shooting was completed, when he was unwise enough to make a disparaging remark about Nazi hero, Horst Wessel. This was reported and Bernhardt received a visit from the Gestapo, but he was able to bluff his way through and managed to escape first to Berlin and then Paris.[5]

The Ministry of Propaganda had no problem with Bernhardt's version of *Der Tunnel* and even provided a number of Storm Troopers to be used as extras. After all, the hero *is* a man of the people who overcomes great odds and—by sheer determination (and great oratorical skills)—achieves the impossible. Bernhard Kellermann on the other hand, faced harassment from the Nazis because of his 1920 novel *Der 9 November* (*The 9th of November*), which had been critical of the military. The book was publicly burned and Kellermann pilloried in the official press. The fuss abated, but Kellermann kept a very low profile thereafter.

Bernhardt's film follows the structure of Kellermann's novel and contains tense scenes of workers struggling against flood and explosions. After the main disaster, the movie makes no attempt to depict the world-wide cataclysm caused by the Tunnel's shut-down and Mac's calamitous fall from public favor (you would need an Abel Gance to pull something like that off). Instead we first see rows of coffins for the fallen workers and then a despondent Mac, who quickly regains the courage to go on. Cut to years ahead, with the completion of the Tunnel, both sides meeting midway, and somber Mac bidding everyone remember the many who perished to make it possible. Jean Gabin played the lead in the French version, and the role was delineated even more forcefully by Paul Hartmann in the German release, wherein the canny viewer can spot Max Schreck—Nosferatu himself—in a small role as one of the millionaires backing the Tunnel.

Vandor may have balked at an English language version, but in January of 1935 Gaumont-British announced a brand new production of *The Tunnel* that would be directed by Lothar Mendes, star Conrad Veidt (the two had teamed up earlier for *Jew Süss*), and be budgeted at a *very* impressive 150,000 pounds. Nevertheless, Mendes subsequently left Gaumont for London Films—where he directed *The Man Who Could Work Miracles*—and it appeared that Berthold Viertel would replace him. Kurt Siodmak—who ultimately wrote the screenplay for *The Tunnel*—later claimed that he had vetoed Viertel as director; however, since Viertel had achieved some success earlier with *Little Friend*, and Siodmak was, at that point, something of a nonentity, it seems rather unlikely that the studio would have valued his opinion so very highly. In any case, Maurice Elvey was given the job, and Gaumont-British would hire

Viertel to helm *The Passing of the Third Floor Back* (which was also to star Veidt) later that year.

Early publicity stated that Veidt would play the Mac Allan role, but when Richard Dix was added to the cast, it was announced that *he* would play the unstoppable engineer, with Madge Evans as his wife. Veidt was then apparently assigned the role of Hobby (here called Robbie, though it's hard to imagine Herr Veidt with such a name), who—in the novel—is in love with Maud Allen, but would never dream of betraying Mac and so is content to remain as Maud's devoted friend. The producers may have originally intended something of a romantic triangle involving the three characters, as early poster art depicts Veidt, Richard Dix, and Madge Evans eyeing each other ambiguously. In the end, Veidt left *The Tunnel* to do the penal colony melodrama *King of the Damned*, and his part was taken by Leslie Banks (who plays it very well), perhaps because the producers wanted a Briton to counterbalance the American action hero.

Maurice Elvey seemed an appropriate choice to direct *The Tunnel* as he had earlier done *High Treason* (see entry), another futuristic tale and one that had a tunnel linking England and France as one of its settings. The tendency of film historians to write off Elvey as a competent- but-uninspired director was challenged by the 1994 rediscovery of his *The Life Story of David Lloyd George* (which features appearances by Ernest Thesiger and Alma—later Hitchcock—Reville), made back in 1918 and thought lost for decades. The picture had been suppressed by the British government, which had then paid the producers not to release it. Following its restoration and several public showings, some critics found its style comparable to the epics of D.W. Griffith.

One serious problem facing a new version of *Der Tunnel* was that the increasing importance of air travel made the story's basic premise antiquated, if not downright Victorian. Air transport may not have been taken for granted in 1935 as it is today, but it was obviously the future of quick, international travel. Thus, the producers instead decided to emphasize the Tunnel as an exam-

**An early scene in the 1933 film depicts the arrival of the financiers who bankroll the tunnel. Gustav Gründgens was primarily a stage actor but his brief part as the elegant but deadly gangster chief in *M* was one of his most memorable film roles.**

ple of Anglo-American cooperation (here, the Tunnel stretches between America and England) that will serve the cause of world peace. What's never made clear is how any of this would lead to peace, although there is a reference to sinister Eastern forces in alliance against the English-speaking peoples. To underscore this message of British American ties and friendship, the Tunnel's virtues are extolled by the Prime Minister of England (Mr. George Arliss) and the President of the United States (Walter Huston, in England to do *Rhodes of Africa*; it is said that Huston and Arliss did their bits for *The Tunnel* gratis). Gaumont hoped that this emphasis on partnership—together with the fact that half of the film's cast hailed from Hollywood—would allow *The Tunnel* to crack the American movie market and pave the way for other solid hits that had originated in England.

Unlike other versions of *Der Tunnel*, Elvey's film wholeheartedly embraces a futuristic slant. The picture doesn't spell out exactly *when* the story takes place, and Elvey was coy about it in interviews:

> I have not attempted to date the film. So far as the period in which the drama is played, you can best say it is "tomorrow." But it is near enough in present time in which habits and customs and, above all human feelings, have not changed much from those we know and love; happiness, ambition, jealousy are the same influences as they are in our own time.[6]

There is, though, a reference to Mack having built the Channel Tunnel sometime "back in 1940," so 1950 would be a good guess for the time period. Television phones are ubiquitous—even in airplanes that can land on rooftops via gyroscopes—the high-speed rail cars in the Tunnel have a sleek bullet-like look, and the drill-vehicle resembles a tank, with an almost menacing, relentless quality. The Tunnel itself, which seems to stretch endlessly into infinity, has an otherworldly look and feel to it. Kurt Siodmak took credit for these aspects of the film:

> For the story *The Transatlantic Tunnel* I envisioned gigantic drills that would gnaw their way to America beneath the ocean floor. When the tunnel between France and England was recently built the machines that excavated the tunnel were very similar to those that I, as a trained engineer, had conceived. I also had the vision of gigantic television screens, unknown at the time but commonplace fifty years later. My conception of future video phones that replaced the telephone, showing the picture of the speakers was also premature as television was in its infancy.[7]

Well, Al Gore invented the Internet, and now we know Kurt Siodmak predicted FaceTime. Except that similar devices can be found in earlier films like *Metropolis*, *Up the Ladder*, and Elvey's own *High Treason*.

Siodmak might have given a little mention to set designer Ernö Metzner, who is actually responsible for the film's great visual strength. Like Siodmak, Metzner was a refugee from Nazi Germany, whence he had to flee because he was both Jewish *and* an ardent Social Democrat. He had worked on many outstanding productions for Ufa, including *Sumurun* (1920), *Pandora's Box* (1929), *Diary of a Lost Girl* (1929), and the avant-garde *Accident* (1930), which he directed. Metzner had also done

**Bad capitalist Basil Sydney and good capitalist C. Aubrey Smith Skype with Mac (Richard Dix) in *Transatlantic Tunnel*.**

the sets for *Kameradschaft* (*Comradeship*, 1931), the classic G.W. Pabst feature about a mining disaster that brings French and German miners together in a show of solidarity and brotherhood, a situation not wholly unlike *Der Tunnel*. Metzner's design for the Tunnel was inspired in part by the Mersey Tunnel (built under the Mersey River and connecting Liverpool with the Wirral Peninsula) which had just been completed in 1934, and which was the subject of the documentary *A Modern Miracle*. The Tunnel for the film was constructed on Gaumont's 75-acre lot at Northolt.

More than one critic pointed out that *The Tunnel*, for all its futurism, failed to show fashion and women's hairstyles keeping pace with all the changes in technology. It may be a valid gripe, but perhaps Elvey was restrained by memories of *High Treason* and the snickers engendered by the outlandish outfits worn by the fair sex in that epic. And can there be anything more ludicrous than the costumes donned by the characters in the last part of *Things to Come*?

*The Tunnel* starts out well with a witty and engaging introduction of all the principals at a musical event that precedes the meeting of the millionaires. This is taken from the book, although in the latter, it's a public and not a private concert. The names of the characters are changed, and Woolf seems to have been divided in two: the lecherous financier, Mostyn [Basil Sydney], and the arms merchant, Grellier [Henry Oscar], who thinks the Tunnel might have actually proven to be good for his business. We then jump ahead three years, when construction of the Tunnel is well under way.

Unfortunately, at this point, the story sags into the sort of hokum you might expect in a silent melodrama. Mack, who is already neglecting his wife and son, is obliged to leave England for America on a publicity junket to boost declining public interest in the great project. He is obliged to be photographed frequently with Mr. Lloyd's beautiful daughter, Varlia, who is enamored of him. Back in Old Blighty, Mack's wife Ruth decides to work in the Tunnel as a nurse and promptly contracts something called "Tunnel Disease," which renders her blind [which is still probably better than being stoned to death or hit by a train]. With Hobby's reluctant help, she retires to the countryside and refuses to let Mack know of her condition, thus leaving the engineer to suspect that something is going on between his wife and his best friend. It's all very contrived, and it's hard to believe Mack wouldn't simply seek Ruth out to find out what really happened. If that isn't cornball enough, poor Varlia must make the ultimate sacrifice and give herself to Mostyn so that he won't withdraw his financial support from the Tunnel.

This does, however, lead to a sequence that is handled with some subtlety. Having double-crossed Grellier by continuing to fund the Tunnel, Mostyn is cautioned by his partner to change his mind [albeit the financial machinations really don't make any sense at this point]. Mostyn gets into his limousine, eager for his tryst with Varlia, but Grellier asks him one last time to reconsider his position on the Tunnel. Mostyn refuses and drives off. We then see Grellier nod his head at some unseen party, and we hear another car promptly start up. Cut to the limousine arriving at Varlia's and the chauffeur opening the car door and finding his boss dead, the cigarette Grellier had lit for him still in his mouth.

The film gets back on track during its last third, when an active underground volcano

The poster for the Spanish release of *Transatlantic Tunnel* was far more imaginative than its counterparts in the U.S. and England.

impedes the work and costs hundreds of lives, including that of Mack's son, Geoffrey, who has chosen that inopportune moment to join his dad in the Tunnel. Mack, obliged to shut the emergency Tunnel doors so deadly gas won't spread, knows that his son is likely among the trapped workers. He can't quite bring himself to turn the fatal control and stands back in despair, allowing someone else to do the deed. Mack then has to face crowds of people looking for word on their loved ones, but they are silent when they realize what Mack has suffered as well ["My son, too," he says numbly]. Dix—very well cast as Mack—is particularly moving in these poignant sequences.

Once again, the ever self-effacing Kurt Siodmak takes a bow:

> Richard Dix, the burly American western star, did not know how to handle emotional scenes.... He asked me how to act [during those scenes] ... I told him it was the director's job to supply that answer. But Maurice Elvey cruelly told him, "You promised me to be an actor. I was told you are a top star in America. Find the solution yourself." I asked Dix whether he had children. Three months ago his wife had given birth to a son [actually twins]. I suggested he think of his son dying, to understand the impact of his decision. He found the solution logical and that scene lifted him above his artless macho appearance that had been the success of westerns.[8]

Whether Herr Kurt is full of sauerkraut or not, Dix's performance is certainly one of his best.

After a tense scene involving the last lap of the drive to by-pass the volcano and join the English and American tunnels, the film ends with everyone reconciled and looking forward to the world peace that will brought because of the completion of the great project. Perhaps a bit of irony would have been in order here, but that would detract from the uplift that is clearly the film's intention.

Elvey's film debuted on October 27 at New York's Roxy Theater under the title *Transatlantic Tunnel*; it did very good business. Canny publicity certainly helped, and Gaumont even organized a private showing of the film in the Lincoln Tunnel, where workers and engineers put down their picks and shovels long enough to watch on a special screen hung down the excavation. An RKO theater manager in Brooklyn, inspired by the film's pressbook, came up with a clever lobby display to promote the film:

> He had a 40 × 60 upright display showing a cross section of the Atlantic Ocean at a point where the crews from each side meet upon completion of the work.... Behind the opening made to give a view of the Tunnel inside was placed a shadow box with a glass front. Animated figures of several men working with pick and shovel are shown through the opening.[9]

The trade papers were very enthusiastic about the film. Abel's review in the October 30, 1935, *Variety* was typical:

> Gaumont-British after a number of false starts in its so called "invasion" of the American market has finally hit a good one. "Transatlantic Tunnel" has Julesvernish imagination, romance, bigness of thought, idea and production execution—and a couple of marquee names for the Anglo-American market.... Beside Elvey's capital direction, he has been well aided by the basic B. Kellermann story and the highly effective script by Kurt Siodmak, L. duGarde Peach and Clemence Dane. G. Krampf's photography is excellent and does much to clarify the presentation, particularly on the mechanical aspects. Charles Frend's editing was no small chore and he's turned in a corking job.... It's a big picture and will be big b.o.

Newspaper reviews, while mostly positive, tended to be a little more guarded:

> The technical or mechanical advancement is far greater than the human characters in the story.... Richard Dix fails to get his teeth into the tale and even when men are dying and his son is gone, this star, who scored mightily in *Cimarron* can't seem to get up the emotional steam to put the role anything above the average height of a fellow who has lost his wife because his work took up too much of his time.... This picture is recommended because of its great technical achievements rather than because Americans went over to Britain and conquered any histrionic foes which assuredly they did not do this time.[10]

In the October 29, 1935, edition of the *New York Post*, however, critic Iris Thirer was lavish in her praise of the film, calling it "imaginative, original, gripping, suspenseful, thrilling and enthralling." She was also very moved by the meeting of the American and British teams: "When this scene finally happens it 'gets' you in spite of the fact that it's just a movie. And it isn't yet 1950 and it's all a product of someone's else imagination-or foresight." Thirer also thought it commendable that the film had "an ideal as well as an idea." Norbert Lusk of the *Los Angeles Times* noted the enthusiasm of the crowds coming to see the film, but had his reservations:

> Its physical values are magnificent but the characters and their emotional problems are unimportant. They are never brought near enough to the spectator to matter much and are tolerated as an excuse for the tunnel scenes which they interrupt.... In spite of its defects it has imagination and vision and stimulates more than it dulls.[11]

Ellen Creelman of the *New York Sun* (October 26, 1935) found the film "stiffly constructed and occasionally old-fashioned," but with plenty of "sturdy adventure." Nevertheless, the central idea did impress her: "That idea is the tunnel, the tunnel itself. Somehow, before the picture reaches it last band-playing, flag-waving scene, the tunnel has achieved a very real personality of it own."

There were some doubts on the other side of the Atlantic as well:

> This is almost a good film. It is well acted and directed. Its photography shows imagination and the idea behind its story is interesting. But side issues are too often allowed to delay the working out of the main plot. The domestic unhappiness with which the hero is settled is the chief offender in this respect. I felt that it added nothing whatever to the film.[12]

And, despite good box-office, there was even more skepticism Down Under:

> The whole thing is synthetic, muddled and unconvincing. Somehow or other the building of the Transatlantic Tunnel will further the cause of peace. So much the audience is expected to gather from the grandiose speeches made in the House of Commons by a statesman who looks like [and is in fact] George Arliss and by an insignificant figure of a man who turns out to be the President of the United States. But the precise significance of the tunnel in building up international goodwill is never made at all plain. No one ever seems to consider the construction from a practical point of view as a thoroughfare for travel between the two countries. If people want to go from London to New York rapidly they go by aeroplane. Even when the national anthems of Britain and the United States crash out at the end, the inner workings of the plot remain wrapped in magnificent obscurity. The acting, as directed by Maurice Elvey, does little to lighten the general oppressiveness. Some of the more dramatic incidents have been represented in a style that can only be described as the quintessence of "ham."[13]

Flawed or not, *Transatlantic Tunnel* seems to have done very good business. Still, when push came to shove, it did not lead to British films taking America by storm. The Hollywood studios did not appreciate the competition, and their ownership of so many theater chains gave them the decided advantage. In the end, although Anglo-American friendship might have built a trans–Atlantic tunnel, it was trumped by the Almighty dollar.

# Sherlock Holmes

Goldwyn Pictures—May 1, 1922 (New York premiere)—8,200 feet/9 reels/c. 136 minutes; October 29, 1922 (general release)—c. 7,200 feet/8 reels/c. 120 minutes; January 29, 1923 (England)—8,000 feet/9 reels/c. 133 minutes (see note below)

**Cast**: John Barrymore as Sherlock Holmes; Gustav von Seyffertitz as Professor Moriarty; Carol Dempster as Alice Faulkner; Roland Young as Dr. Watson; Reginald Denny as Prince Alexis of Arenberg; William H. Powell as Forman Peg (alias Wells); Hedda Hopper as Madge Larrabee; Peggy Bayfield as Rose Faulkner; Anders Randolf as James Larrabee (alias C. Nevill Chetwood); Louis Wolhein as Craigin; Percy Knight as Sid Jones; Margaret Kemp as Therese; Robert Schable as Alf Bassick; David Torrence as Count Von Stalberg; Robert Fisher as Otto; Lumsden Hare as Dr. Leighton; Jerry Devine as Billy; John Willard as Inspector Gregson

**Credits**: *Producer*: F.J. Godsol; *Director*: Albert Parker; *Screenplay*: Marion Fairfax, Earle Browne; *Design*: Charles Cadwallader, John Barrymore; *Director of Photography*: J. Roy Hunt; *Based on the eponymous play by* William Gillette *and the stories by* Sir Arthur Conan Doyle

Note: Footage lengths/running times provided by the AFI and BFI. Still, as renowned film historian Kevin Brownlow, pointed out to us: "16 fps was once the speed at which cameramen endeavoured to crank in the early days, but thanks to the 'racing' of projectionists anxious to get home, the speed at which pictures were photographed had increased by the time this film was released. My educated guess would be 22 fps (12 mins per 1,000ft), which would lop roughly half an hour off the running time. MGM photographed their pictures at this speed and had them projected at 24, and since MGM was formed through a merger involving Goldwyn, one can assume the practice was already in place."

Sir Arthur Conan Doyle first introduced Sherlock Holmes to Victorian England—and thence, to the rest of the world—with *A Study in Scarlet* in 1887, and the American Mutoscope and Biograph Company was responsible for the detective's cinematic debut not long thereafter, with *Sherlock Holmes Baffled* in 1903. The title of the short[1] bears witness to the fact that, even during the cinema's extreme early childhood, viewers were familiar enough with Holmes to recognize the identity of the "man attired in a full-length dressing gown"[2] without being provided any additional information. *Baffled* was followed[3] by 1905's *The Adventures of Sherlock Holmes* (aka *Held for a Ransom*) which clocked in at about 10 minutes. 1908 saw Conan Doyle's masterful protagonist venture into territory more closely associated with C. Auguste Dupin (the one-reeler *Sherlock Holmes and the Great Murder Mystery* was inspired by "Murders in the Rue Morgue"), but he also found himself at the outset of a series of short films, produced by Nordisk Film's Copenhagen studios.

The next half-dozen or so pages herein might well be filled with details of the *abbondanza* of international output centered on the Great Consulting Detective within the next 15 or so years, but that would not only needlessly duplicate the meticulous work essayed by the Sherlockian researchers whose books pepper our bibliography, but would also deprive the tenacious Holmesian scholars out there of the pleasure of reading those volumes themselves.

Cinematically, it's interesting to note that from 1994 until 2009—that is, from Granada Television's *The Memoirs of Sherlock Holmes* to Guy Ritchie's steampunk'd *Sherlock Holmes*—there was a virtual black hole, television apart,[4] with respect to Holmes's screen adventures. Since the Warner Bros. release, though, Baker Street aficionados have had a trifecta of Holmeses and Watsonses with which to deal: Robert Downey, Jr., and Jude Law; Benedict Cumberbatch and Martin Freeman; and Jonny Lee Miller and Lucy Liu. Three different takes: Ritchie's, two features (so far) set in a Victorian Age like no other; Hartswood Films/Masterpiece Theatre's *Sherlock*, 90-minute-long adventures that play out in present-day Britain; and *Elementary*, the collaboration of Timberman-Beverly Productions, Hill of Beans Productions, and the CBS Television Studios: hour-long stories, also unfolding in the here-and-now—the "here" being New York City—with the added wrinkle of Watson's being an Asian woman. Quite a daunting spread, and, it would seem, one allowing little opportunity for further variation.

Prior to the production to which this essay is devoted, there had also been more than one noteworthy interpretation of the Great Consulting Detective available to interested parties. Neither was as radical as any of the three choices afforded to us Millennial viewers, and both portrayals were fairly ubiquitous while Conan Doyle was still penning his Holmes stories. Thus, in the late 1910s/early 1920s, fans of Doctor Watson's scribblings had a brace of Sherlocks readily available for perusal, onscreen and onstage: an American, William Gillette, and a Briton, Eille Norwood. Between them, the two had fairly cornered their respective nation's markets on performance-art renditions of "Conanical" adventures.

Gillette was a Connecticut Yankee whose association with the role of Holmes lasted almost a quarter-century: his four-act melodrama—written with what passed for a blessing (closer to a shrug, actually) from Conan Doyle—had premiered in late 1899 and was revived with fair regularity until 1923. It was Gillette who introduced the curved briar to Holmes's lips (he found that a "straight" pipe made line delivery awkward), who dismissed a deduction of his as being "elementary," and who donned the deerstalker favored by Paget in the pages of *The Strand*. He also made sure that the detective was seen with the violin nestled on his shoulder and the syringe cuddled in his hand. Gillette had had an extensive stage career before stepping into Holmes's shoes: besides acting, directing, and working to modernize old-fashioned stage mechanics, he authored or adapted almost two dozen plays. Still, it is said that he played the role some 1,300 times during the course of his lifetime. Per www.tcm.com, the actor's last performance as Holmes—at age 79—was given on March 19, 1932, and Sherlock remains the role for which he was best known/is best remembered.

Norwood—born Anthony Edward Brett—had originally adopted that stage name while *he* was at home under the proscenium arch, if only to avoid disappointing his father, who was hoping to have sired a lawyer.[5] In the legitimate end of the performing arts since 1884, Norwood's having been born in October 1861 meant that he was among the oldest—if not *the* oldest—to don the dressing gown and other, now-familiar accoutrements at the time of his debut in the role in Stoll's fifteen-part series *The Adventures of Sherlock Holmes* in April 1921. Per Sherlockian authors Robert W. Pohle, Jr., and Douglas C. Harte, the actor's contribution to the Silent Era's perception of the Great Consulting Detective lay in his talent—in Conan Doyle's words—for "doing nothing."

"Nothing" is indeed what Norwood is engaged in for long stretches of his films; Norwood's is surely the most understated Holmes ever. It is remarkable that someone who had spent so great a part of his life on the speaking stage could grasp so fully the technique of silent-film acting; that his mime could be at once so subtle and so eloquent.[6]

Norwood's marked capacity for making "doing nothing" seem riveting saw him through 47 celluloid renditions (45 shorts and two features) of Sir Arthur Conan Doyle's published tales, all of which were shot and released between the aforementioned and the mid- to late summer of 1923, while Sir Arthur was still "cranking them out." Unlike his American counterpart, Norwood made the detective something of a late-in-life cottage industry; following his prolific cinematic spurt, he starred in Harold Terry and Arthur Rose's melodrama *The Return of Sherlock Holmes*, which enjoyed a lengthy run at London's Princes's Theatre. Nonetheless, the reputation he had made for himself on the legitimate stage prior to all-things-Sherlock soon became lost in the shadow of his embodiment of Conan Doyle's bête noire. ("Embodiment" may prove to be an excellent choice of words. As illustrated on pages 48–49 of Peter Haining's *The Sherlock Holmes Scrapbook*, the play required that a life-size wax model of Holmes be crafted to confound Moriarty. The effigy, an eerily accurate likeness of the actor, subsequently became part of the Norwood Holmesian legacy.)

Come 1922, as John Barrymore was enticed to reinterpret the role in light of his own established persona, Gillette's take on the character had already come to be regarded as almost iconic in the Colonies, while Norwood's was the more pervasive portrayal throughout the Continent and the United Kingdom. Thus, The Great Profile (and most of Western Civilization) had to deal with two enduring, albeit competing, impersonations of one of the most unique literary inventions ever. The fact that he was initially unwilling to play the role probably

**A distracted Holmes, about to light his pipe the hard way. Barrymore studied Frederic Dorr Steele's illustrations closely in preparing for the role.**

did nothing to ameliorate the situation. Per director Albert Parker[7]:

> I went to see John Barrymore in his theatre dressing-room when he was appearing on the stage. I forget the play.[8] I told him that I wanted to make a film of the Gillette play and I wanted him to play Sherlock Holmes.... He didn't want to do the film, I had to talk him into it. He didn't like the part, because it was such a trade mark....

Inasmuch as Gillette himself had made a film of the Gillette play in early 1916,[9] we can only wonder whether Barrymore found Parker's idea less than enthralling for its essentially being a *remake*. When he had earlier taken his turn as Robert Louis Stevenson's profoundly schizophrenic scientist, Barrymore had set the bar for future interpretations; previous productions had never been more than a half-hour or so in length, and although 1920 would be *the* year for Jekyll and Hyde, contemporary rival efforts consisted of a comedy short, a foreign import that drew limited audiences, and a five-reeler that was markedly lower-shelf.[10] Barrymore's subsequent screen portrayals of Beau Brummel, Captain Ahab, and Don Juan would likewise be considered the standards against which other performances were gauged; not for *this* actor, stepping into someone else's boots (or dressing gown).

Our synopsis is based on viewing the result of the Brownlow/Parker collaborative effort, as coordinated by the George Eastman House and released by KINO (now KINO-Lorber) in 2009. This print has a running time of 85 minutes.

> Following a *very* brief aerial tour of the more renowned environs, the viewer is dropped off in "a little forgotten thoroughfare in Limehouse—the most mysterious quarter in all London." This grammatical quandary—is this particular thoroughfare forgotten because of its diminutive dimensions? or does it remain only slightly forgotten [and therefore mostly remembered]?—introduces Professor Moriarty, played by Gustav von Seyffertitz as a [what else?] shaggy goblin of a man; Moriarty's "chief lieutenant in crime," Alf Bassick [Robert Schable], whose chief duty as lieutenant seems to consist in answering any variety of telephones; and the professor's eccentric headquarters, pocked with multiple secret doors and staircases, at least one of which leads up to a floor-level trapdoor. Moriarty is first seen at the center of a spider web, a visual metaphor for his involvement in dastardly deeds throughout all of London and, perhaps, a nod to Barrymore's arachnid-like Mr. Hyde from a couple of years earlier.
>
> A cut to the professor's underground lair finds him working on the books as the shadow of a man, hanging by his thumbs, looms large in the background; when cut down, the man is ordered back into the field by Moriarty in order to "tell the others what happens when they disobey me."
>
> TITLE: "Let us look in on one particular case."
>
> Following a brief scene in which a young man is seen floundering about on the floor of a university office, obviously searching for something amidst the books and papers, we cut to one of Moriarty's presumably more obedient agents, Otto, who is currently acting as butler to Prince Alexis, a student at St. John's College in Cambridge.
>
> Prince Alexis has been accused of stealing "the Atlantic funds," an indeterminate amount of money that a Dr. Leighton kept stashed [large bills!] in his wallet. When Inspector Gregson reports "there is no doubt" that the prince made off with the funds, we shake our heads, cognizant that—at least per William Gillette and Sir Arthur Conan Doyle—there can be no doubt that Scotland Yard has blown yet another one. Why would anyone stealing bills from an unattended wallet also snatch the wallet, only to stupidly hide the same to be found amidst his own intimate apparel? Nonetheless, this sets the stage for the prince to mention his awkward circumstances—and his impending marriage to "Rose" in Switzerland—to fellow student, John Watson, who reveals, "There's a fellow in my year—Sherlock Holmes—he might help you—a marvel at digging out things—rather uncanny—he ..." and we cut.
>
> [The following reel or so is an exposition with respect to the personage of Mr. Holmes: fairly precious and therefore not a little tedious—anyone sitting through a picture entitled *Sherlock Holmes* in the early 1920s had no need of introductory materials—the scene does allow the Holmesian aficionado at least to marvel at the discrepancy between Barrymore's youthful interpretation and those of his more ... er ... *venerable* counterparts, discussed above.]
>
> Holmes is introduced while sitting against a tree in a pastoral setting, where he fastidiously jots down in a notebook his every observation [including a list of his own "limitations"], puffs away at his pipe, measures the length of a passerby's tread, and falls hopelessly in love with a young woman [Alice Faulkner, played by Carole Dempster] who just misses killing him with her pony-cart. When Watson helpfully shows up moments later, Holmes learns that the young woman is the sister of Prince Alexis's fiancée and that the prince is "in a devil of a fix." Finding all this to be serendipitous, Holmes takes on the prince as a client. En route to the prince's rooms, Holmes notices through a ground-level window the man who is still rummaging about that office, and when the same man intrudes while Holmes and Watson are conversing with the prince moments later, Holmes asks whether he might be searching for a cuff link the detective has found. The man—Forman Wells—withdraws and returns to his own rooms, whence he is immediately sent off by Otto to report back to Moriarty at "99." Holmes, who has followed the anxious Wells downstairs and into the street, jumps into a hansom cab after him.
>
> In the cab, Wells [a young William Powell, with an unkempt mop of hair and eye-liner that Theda Bara would have killed for] reveals that he was sent by Moriarty to Cambridge in order to "meet important people—to play his game later." Holmes, who has known nothing of the professor to this point, sends Wells away ["Do what I tell you and everything will come out all right"] and then heads to "99," a shop in Limehouse. Bassick follows Holmes into the shop and then admits Moriarty to a back room via a secret door in the wall. Moriarty agrees to meet the "queer duck" who has been asking about him, and the two icons of Victorian literature come face to face for the first time. Wells will soon be found "a sui-

cide," the professor snarls, as he warns Holmes to "be a good little boy and go back to your books."

Back at St. John's College, Alexis's uncle, Count Von Stalberg, has shown up bearing a telegram announcing that the prince's two brothers have both been killed in an motor accident. Now the Crown Prince, Alexis must return at once to Harlstein, so he pens a note about destiny and tragic events to Rose, telling her, "It will be impossible for me to see you again—ever." The next title announces, "Meanwhile—in Switzerland" and we see the lovely young woman from the picture in Alexis's rooms for a moment before we read, "Rose Faulkner—who now faces a future of ostracism and disgrace—waits for her lover."

Once again at Alexis's university rooms, Holmes enters with Wells's written confession. Alexis refuses it, stating before he leaves for his homeland that his uncle has arranged things "satisfactorily" with Dr. Leighton. Shown the telegram by Watson, Holmes muses for a moment on Rose's fate, before he turns and lets fly with three title cards that spell out the rest of the picture:

"At the beginning of the hour, I met love—At the end—I met most monstrous evil."

"I have just met a man—a force—a thing—as deadly as sin itself."

"I've been groping for my place in the scheme of things. I've found it. My life's work is to rid the world of that gigantic menace—Moriarty."

TITLE: "At 221 Baker Street, Sherlock Holmes found a way to help the weary and mystery-laden."

[Things may have gone awry here, sequentially, or missing footage may account for the somewhat awkward flashback in the midst of the opening vignette.]

Puffing away on his pipe—he will later refill same from the Persian slipper on the mantel—Holmes is nestled in what are unmistakably his Baker Street digs. [Missing from the above title and the salutation on the letter he reads is the "B" that normally follows his street number.] The letter, from Count Von Stalberg, mentions the service Holmes "rendered some years ago," cuing everyone to the fact that an appreciable period of time has passed. Here the detective reflects on Rose, who is seen, in flashback, receiving the note of dismissal from Prince Alexis. She reacts viscerally, as one might expect of silent-movie females, and—in the very next scene—unties a safety rope that attaches her to the end of a line of mountain climbers and leaps off the summit. Back to Holmes and the letter's conclusion, which speaks of the need to "obtain those letters." [Ostensibly, these are love letters written by the prince to his abandoned lover.]

Watson arrives a moment later, bearing a newspaper announcing Alexis's impending marriage to a "Princess Olga of Brünwald-Torbay." This leads to Holmes's famous set of deductions about Watson's own marriage, return to medical practice, and inability to shave meticulously unless the sun is properly aligned. Good show!

Anyhow, it devolves that Alice Faulkner is being detained at the home of Mr. and Mrs. C. Nevill Chetwood—actually Mr. and Mrs. James Larrabee [Anders Randolf and Hedda Hopper]—and Forman Wells, who has not "been found a suicide," enters the honestead in the guise of a replacement butler from the employment agency. Alice has Rose's letters from the prince, the Larrabees and Moriarty and the royal family have hitherto been unable to discover same on/about her person, and Wells has been sent by Holmes to keep an eye on the proceedings.

A cane-wielding Cockney dandy, Sid Jones, also shows up, delivering a message to Larrabee about Alice from Moriarty: "If you ain't got the letters yet, I'm to bring 'er down to 'im at once." While Sid is dropping his haitches, Holmes is ringing the Larrabees's doorbell; not moments after he is admitted, he and Larrabee engage in a series of glares and harrumphs, and Alice descends the stairs to converse in private with the GCD. Per a prearranged signal, Holmes feigns an exit, Wells sets the kitchen on fire[!], and Alice makes for the hiding place of her sister's correspondence. Holmes refuses to take the letters without Alice's permission—she is later seen to stash them behind a loose brick, conveniently located just outside her window in the exterior of the Larrabee mansion—and Larrabee is warned

**Holmes and Watson: Barrymore eyeing Roland Young, the "quiet, agreeable bastard" who stole the picture.**

by the departing detective to leave Alice Faulkner "very much alone."

TITLE: "Moriarty again feels the menace of his great antagonist."

Told about the fire, the criminal genius waves away any concern about the Faulkner letters: "It is Holmes we must think of now.... He is setting a trap for me." Following a bit of conversation at the Baker Street digs about Alice's remaining safe in the clutches of the Larrabees, we return to Moriarty, who solemnly announces "Sherlock Holmes is gradually completing a chain of evidence that will reach to me as surely as I stand here! Something must be done!" [This pronouncement is mind-boggling, and we must either assume that the picture's still-missing footage saw the detective in constant evidence-chain-completing motion, or that scenarists Fairfax and Browne didn't think that this sort of activity merited screen time.] The "something" of which Moriarty speaks consists of his decoying bobbies away from Number 221, getting Watson to hie to a fake medical emergency call, and then showing up, in person, to shoot his nemesis at point-blank range. This, of course, fails miserably, and, after an exchange of snarls and barbs, the professor exits, his dignity still somewhat intact.

The sequence that follows is jumpy, footage is obviously missing—Holmes expostulates sans titles while Billy [Jerry Devine] comes and goes; an obviously disheveled Wells stumbles along a corridor—and we cut to Bassick [*again* on a phone] setting up another attempt at doing Holmes in, this time at the Stepney Gas Chamber, with Alice Faulkner as the bait. Moriarty has Craigin [Louis Wolheim] and a handful of minions boobytrap the location, with the intention, it is supposed, of killing Holmes slowly. When asked why he just doesn't "knock 'im on the 'ead," Moriarty replies, "I want Mr. Holmes to be in full possession of those faculties that drove me into the earth—as I slowly drive him off it." Admirably said, but we've still no idea how either Holmes or Moriarty has come to this point.

Holmes—accoutered with deerstalker, riding crop, and revolver—meets Larrabee at the gas works and, in walking pensively about the room, notes through a slit in a door that Alice Faulkner is standing in the next room. A comment about the prince's letters causes Holmes to dash the only lamp in the room to the floor. A brawl ensues, Miss Faulkner is yanked through the door, and she and Holmes flee the chamber, locking Craigin and the rest of the villains in behind them. Sid subsequently informs his boss of this latest fiasco.

TITLE: "Moriarty utilizes every resource of his vast machine."

"Every resource" include a burning 221 Baker Street, as a news vendor's sign informs the viewer.

Soon thereafter, a rifle-wielding marksman is nestled in a flat across from Watson's office, and Mrs. Larrabee—instructed to signal the assassin as to whether Holmes is holed up with his amanuensis—pretends to be a lady with a medical emergency in order to gain entrance to the doctor's waiting room. [The successful outcome of this assassination is crucial to the villain; otherwise, as Holmes has told Watson, Moriarty will be arrested and over 40 "mysteries" will be cleared up "by tomorrow night."] In the street, a motor car and a hansom cab collide, and—out of the melee—an elderly clergyman is carried up to Watson's office. It is Holmes, in disguise, and Mrs. Larrabee—not fooled by the detective's rather baroque make-up job—dashes to the window to give the signal; the plan is for naught, however, once the shade is drawn[!] Forman Wells, who had caused the accident so as to give Holmes the means of safely entering the building, takes Mrs. Larrabee away.

Watson is then informed, "We've rounded up all of Moriarty's gang. But so far he has eluded us." and "Larrabee has turned King's evidence." [Missing and/or misplaced footage must be held to account for Madge Larrabee's continued support of Moriarty after her husband has copped a deal with the authorities.] Moments later, Holmes has the butler "call that four-wheeler on the corner—and bring a bag here at once." Moments after the cabdriver sets foot in the office, Holmes slaps a set of cuffs on him. It is Moriarty! [Said cabdriver wearing the most blatant of hirsute makeup treatments does take a bit of the edge off that revelation....]

Moriarty's curtain line [in the existing print]: "You don't think for a moment—that this is the end?"

Holmes: "I had rather hoped so. Professor—I am starting on my honeymoon tomorrow."

Watson, as Alice Faulkner appears suddenly: "Marvelous, Holmes. Simply marvelous!"

Holmes: "Yes, isn't she?" Holmes moves in for a kiss [and viewers shudder].

Finis.

Reviews of the "premiere" cut of *Sherlock Holmes* ran from the *Laudatio Deo* variety—"One of the greatest film successes that Mr. Barrymore has ever made and a superlatively fine motion picture"[11]—to those crafted to deny the movie's sails any and all wind—"It falls; it falls to pieces."[12] Once the discerning film fan discounts the hosannahs of the most blatant of the paeans, he/she notices that the majority of the contemporaneous critiques deplored the lack of, well, *action* in the unfolding narrative. The *New York Times*'s reviewer pretty much summed it up when he wrote: "Professor Moriarty ... is a master [criminal] only on the strength of verbal representations. He doesn't *do* anything [emphasis ours] to reveal his powers. Nor does Holmes." Indeed, the professor never seems to take the easy way out when some complicated—if not preposterously convoluted—means is available to him via evil-genius-level cogitation. The lion's share of film critics present at the Capital Theatre press preview must have thus wept for joy when Louis Wolheim's Craigin suggested that they just knock Holmes "on the 'ead," if only to be spared yet another instance of Moriarty's malevolent machinations that went nowhere except down the bunghole. Nor, as the *Times*'s reviewer noted, did the normally detail-oriented Great Consulting Detective well utilize the original print's 136-minute running time to clue the masses in on his own plans: "When the hero's final victory comes, it is not explained. Holmes states that the time has arrived when he can arrest Moriarty, but no one knows why." Would the depiction of the enormous enterprise of London's Forces of Righteousness leading up to this point have broken the budget?

Not long after its New York debut, the film was withdrawn, reedited, and cut by a reel[13]; it was sent out on general release some months later. Such drastic action being taken on a big-budget feature (top-name stars, location shooting) was hardly an everyday occurrence, and the comments made by the reviewer in the May 14, 1922, edition of *Film Daily* may be the most concisely stated *raison d'être* for the paring down:

> It is too long and it is not easy to follow the story. In an effort to clarify matters, numerous long titles are used that often confuse more than they explain. The result is a "talky" picture and if you happen in after the first half-reel you are about lost because it is not the kind of story you can pick up readily.

Following the surgery, the picture made the national rounds, garnering largely excellent press in markets that had not been represented during the May preview/premiere and good box-office returns. Typical of the enterprise was a piece (in the October 22, 1922, *Cleveland Plain Dealer*) anticipating the picture's being screened at that city's Allen Theater: "*Sherlock Holmes* is *said* [emphasis ours] to be intensely interesting, bringing in many exciting moments by means of nasty looking creatures who think only of death."

That most helpful (sarcasm ours) of notices was followed by another mention of the film in the Cleveland paper, some ten days later: "It is a strong mystery story, and with the exception of one rule it is excellently played. The Holmesian admirer will be disappointed in finding no true Watson, and not once does Sherlock call for the needle. For shame, our latter day salvation." The strongest mystery associated with the piece is that last sentence, and we must pause to note the sentiments of the *Plain Dealer* critic on the film's slant on Watson. The *Morning Telegraph*'s Suzanne Sexton (cited above) also found fault with Sherlock's righthand

**The poster that says it all.**

man, albeit more with the actor's personality than with his interpretation. Of Roland Young, Sexton wrote, "He is as out of place in this production as a flapper in a hug-me-tight." With this latter phrase now joining our passel of mysteries, we note that Sexton continued, "He is debonair and gay throughout, but hardly a confidante for a man of mystery." Although few critics found "a man of mystery" to be an apt description of Barrymore's detective, the actor himself had his own opinion concerning Young's presence in the photoplay: "That quiet, agreeable bastard," The Great Profile opined, "had stolen not one, but every damned scene."[14]

Despite October 29 being the "official" date given for its general release, extant reviews indicate that the picture was out and about at least a month earlier. The fact that it was a big-budget production based on a well-known and well-regarded stage play and featuring one of the biggest names in the performing arts as one of modern fiction's most beloved creations virtually mandated that the reviews streaming from the newspapers covering non–New York venues be overwhelmingly positive. Thus, the fairly odd position taken by the September 26 *Philadelphia Evening Ledger* ("Barrymore plays the part as if he enjoyed it more than anything he ever did") and the wishful thinking displayed in the November 21 *San Francisco Chronicle* ("All the thrills of melodrama are in the picture plus the touch of mystery and the added glow of romance"). With the melodrama evident only in short spurts (and the most potentially melodramatic sequence—set in the Stepney Gas Chamber—marred by being too dimly lit[15]), most of the mystery talked about via titles (see the *New York Times*'s review, above), and the romance—to fans—an unwelcome intrusion, the *Chronicle*'s assessment was really nothing more than an all-out effort to support the local exhibitor.

It's not certain as to whether Barrymore actually *enjoyed* the role, but the attention he paid to the character's eccentricities was fulsome, to say the least:

> He had studied Conan Doyle's Sherlock Holmes for months, poring over the drawings of Doyle's definitive illustrator, Frederic Dorr Steele. He had persuaded an old German actor named Gustav von Seyffertitz to play Moriarty. He had sketched the set for the great detective's famous sitting room complete with Persian slipper, cigars in the coal scuttle, and V.R. spelled above the mantel in bullet holes.[16]

The actor's artistic bent—a trait he shared with his older brother, Lionel—came to the fore in his preparation for Holmes's Baker Street digs, with his sketches earning him a "design" credit along with Charles Cadwallader. The location shooting for exteriors—which included Stepney, Limehouse, Scotland Yard, Hampton Court, and Torrington Square, standing in for Baker Street[17]—also appealed to Barrymore, although, as biographer Margot Peters relates:

> When Albert Parker ... arrived in London he couldn't find his star anywhere. Days later he tracked him down in a little attic room at the Ritz. Jack was sitting up in bed, blind drunk. The room was chaos; there were even gin bottles in his shoes.[18]

P-shots taken on the streets of Blighty offer evidence that the 40-year-old star ended up none the worse for wear. It was only when the company returned to New York to film the interiors that Barrymore's enjoyment/excitement/commitment took a bit of a dip; per biographer James Kotsilibas-Davis, "Jack was preoccupied with preparations for his forthcoming *Hamlet*."[19] *Hamlet*, of course, solidified The Great Profile's status as one of the greatest actors of his generation, and, as Kotsilibas-Davis concludes, "*Sherlock Holmes* can be remembered as the last John Barrymore performance to be evaluated out of the inexorable shadow of his next towering achievement."

With an eye to picking up a few quid in a timely fashion, M-G-M exported the feature to the United Kingdom, where it premiered in January 1923 as *Moriarty*, an intriguing title shift if ever there was one.

The late, great film historian William K. Everson reported, "It seems ... likely that the mediocrity of so many earlier Holmes films was the deciding factor in releasing the film in Britain under the title *Moriarty*!"[20] The canny performance of Gustav von Seyffertitz as the "Napoleon of Crime" may also have swayed the decision; more than a few Stateside critics felt that while his villainous machinations were ultimately foiled, the professor—his makeup modeled, so went a theory, on Barrymore's Mr. Hyde—*had* succeeded in making off with the picture.

Retired—as was every other film, silent or talkie—once the law of diminishing returns came into play, both *Sherlock Holmes* and *Moriarty*, along with the footage that had been expunged in mid–1922 and (presumably) stored on cores,[21] were sent off to a comfortable niche in the studios's storage facilities. If either version of the picture was dusted off and rereleased at any time before the coming of sound made the exercise pointless (and, more importantly, profitless), we haven't a clue; despite an extensive search, we've been unable to find any extant reviews that were written anywhere in these United States and dated subsequent to the year or so following its New York premiere that support the possibility of its having resurfaced.

Holmes and Watson made their return—*many* returns, if truth be told—once the technology had been perfected, and Sherlock's deductions and pronouncements could be given the aural weight they deserved. Conan Doyle's most renowned creation was impersonated by everyone from Clive Brook to Reginald Owen (in the States) and from Raymond Massey to Robert Rendel to Arthur Wontner (in Blighty) to Bruno Güttner (see *Der Hund von Baskerville* elsewhere in this volume) and others on the Continent, before Basil Rathbone and Nigel Bruce were signed on by 20th-Century Fox to bring what would be regarded as *new*, iconic, onscreen portrayals. Full details of this progression (and beyond) will be found in the sundry dedicated volumes listed in our bibliography. Our point is that—from 1924 or so—the silent M-G-M *Sherlock Holmes* might just as well gone off to keep bees on the Sussex Downs for all the notice it was given by anyone. And when it, along with the rest of the contents of Vault #7 in Culver City burned up almost 40 years later, no one—save, perhaps, the most fanatical of Baker Street Irregulars—mourned especially the loss of the Barrymore feature.[22]

That loss did not stand for long....

The most extensive published account of the recovery and restoration of *Sherlock Holmes* to date is to be found in the February 1976 issue of *Films in Review*, and said account is pretty much a near-verbatim reprinting of notes distributed at a screening of the picture by William K. Everson at the September 22, 1975, meeting of the Theodore Huff Memorial Film Society in New York City. This screening has come to be regarded by many silent film aficionados as the premiere of the "newly reconstructed" *Sherlock Holmes*, with said reconstruction

**Was this P-shot taken the morning after "the curious incident of the gin bottles in the night-time"?**

due to the efforts of fabled film historian Kevin Brownlow and the picture's director Albert Parker. Both men had set out to work with what Mr. Everson called "several cans of negative of the film, each can consisting of short unconnected rolls."[23] That this pithy statement is the absolute truth *is* the absolute truth, albeit the story of the process begins some years earlier—most likely, *before* the Culver City vault disaster—with the participation of Eastman House's legendary preservationist, author, and film historian James Card.

Mr. Card passed away on January 16, 2000, and thus couldn't contribute the details of his role in the restoration, but some background information found in his obituary in the *New York Times* starts the narrative:

**The Great Profile Meets the Great Brow: Gustav von Seyffertitz's makeup as Moriarty was a tad reminiscent of Barrymore's Mr. Hyde.**

> Mr. Card joined the Eastman House in 1948, bringing with him his personal collection of 800 films, which became the cornerstone of the institution's archive…. Paolo Cherchi-Usai, the curator who holds Mr. Card's former position at Eastman, said that the collection would not have existed without Mr. Card. He added that his predecessor ranks as a preservationist with three other major figures in the field, Jacques Ledoux from Belgium, Henri Langlois from the Cinémathèque in Paris, and Iris Barry of the Museum of Modern Art in New York.[24]

As limned by obituary writer Mel Gussow, Card

> was always in search of lost films. As he said, "From barns, abandoned warehouses, attics, basements, even from bedroom closets, these old nitrate prints are still being discovered, for every good silent-film historian is a film hunter as well."

Mr. Brownlow, who graciously and repeatedly responded to our requests for information on his participation in the "recovery" of *Sherlock Holmes*, expanded on the subject of sites where old nitrate prints were not only found, but also were, in circumstances that would cause weeping and gnashing of teeth among devotees of the silent cinema, sent off to their demise:

> [Some] M-G-M storage vaults were [are] in a salt mine in Kansas…. The distribution route had a cul-de-sac where it was no longer commercially sensible to send the film back. They piled up and, in most cases, no one knew what to do with them. Dawson City had an indoor skating rink which began to subside. "What can we do about it?" "Fetch some of those film cans." They were kept in the basement of a library. Hundreds of them. They were used to prop up the rink, which they did, most satisfactorily. Then, I presume, they demolished the rink and found all those film cans. Mostly from the teens—many lost titles, but often just two or three reels of a five-reeler.[25]

With Card having been renowned for panning incessantly for forgotten and/or discarded cinematic gold, and with the plethora of unlikely/downright bizarre locations in which he might strike a vein a given, might he have come into possession of random sections of the *Sherlock Holmes* camera negative even before the vault fire in California destroyed all extant prints of the picture? Or might we postulate that those negative segments had been stored in some other facility? Mr. Brownlow shared our speculation:

> It initially puzzled me how Card got those rolls, but MGM sent a great deal of material his way in various states of preservation. When I borrowed a print from the studio of *Conquering Power* to show to Alice Terry in the late 60s, it turned out

that it had also been pieced together from masses of tiny rolls of negative. [As a result the neg was incredibly scratched.] I wonder what other lost films are sitting in MGM's Kansas salt mines[26] in the same chaotic state?

The "whens" and "hows" of Card's acquisition may never be known, but—as early as 1972 (also in his *The Detective on Film*), William K. Everson elaborated on the "whats":

> Rochester's George Eastman House ... some years ago was able to salvage several cans of negative of the film, each can consisting of short unconnected rolls. They were printed up, spliced together for viewing purposes, and found to be most intriguing but virtually incomprehensible.
>
> There was a little of everything—but not very much of anything. Some scenes ran but a few seconds; others would reappear with variations at regular intervals.... All told, there were about 50 minutes of surviving footage, seemingly representing most of the sequences, but only about half of the total.

Everson wasted no ink on how Card and the Eastman House acquired the negatives—this was regarded as a *fait accompli*—but his account in *Detective* did reveal that positive prints were made from the 35mm negs. Each negative segment was printed as a 16mm reduction positive, assuring that the film could be transported, screened, and inspected more readily than could the larger gauge. In addition, the picture's "numerous long titles" (to use *The Times*'s critic's phrase) had been excised from the negatives—titles tended to decompose faster than other footage—and one-frame-long "flash titles" were the only verbal cues now available to help with any hoped-for restoration.

Even prior to the printing of the 16mm segments, Everson and Card were colleagues and fellow keepers of the Drive-for-Preservation flame. Both men were passionate film collectors, both firmly believed in the need to recover whatever they could of that enormous percentage of Silent Era motion pictures that had been left to rot/consigned to the fire, and both were among the first to be considered "teachers of film" at a time when that title meant virtually nothing in the field of academia. At least here we can use Card's own words:

> In 1966 I was recruited to become the University of Rochester's first-ever professor of motion pictures and charged to devise its intial course in cinema.... In those early days, Bill Everson, David Bradley and I were peons with no academic degrees advanced beyond the minimal bachelor of arts to support our names in the university catalogue. We were tolerated first because Bradley and I had made films, but mostly since the three of us possessed vast personal film collections. And, in my case, I also had available the gigantic Eastman House collection.[27]

When all positive elements of *Sherlock Holmes* were declared lost in the May 13, 1967, vault fire, we theorize that Card immediately saw that the negatives in his possession were now the only means available to bring the 1922 feature back from the dead. Aware that Albert Parker was still alive and kicking and running a theatrical agency in Blighty, the first-ever professor of motion pictures asked

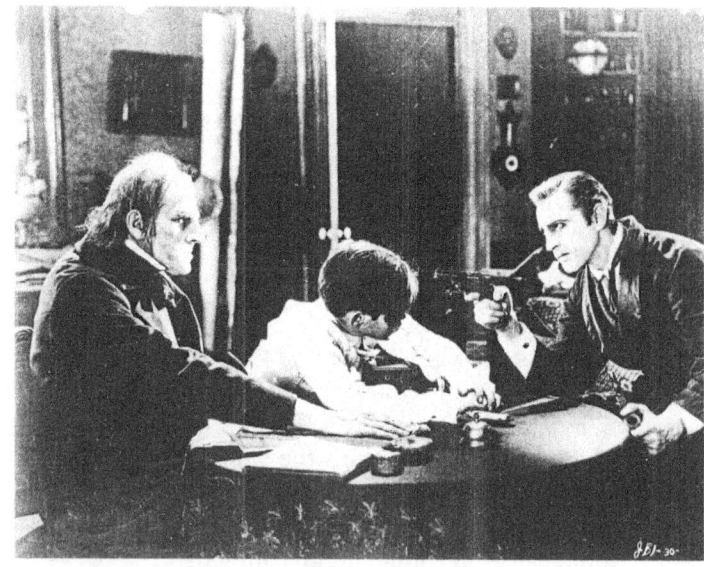

**Billy the page (Jerry Devine) finds himself in the midst of an awkward situation.**

Everson whether Parker might not be the ideal man to oversee a reconstruction.

It is at this point that Everson suggested that well-regarded film expert Kevin Brownlow work alongside the elderly director.[28] The suggestion was taken, the negs printed, and the game was afoot. Per Brownlow, "Bill Everson got the process under way, picked up the cans of l6mm print made from the jumbled rolls of neg, and brought them to UK in his luggage and handed them over. No work had been done on them." The restoration was now left to the Messrs. Brownlow and Parker, with the latter's chief responsibility being to recall the order in which the sundry segments originally appeared.

Alas! The best laid plans of mice and men…. In his notes that accompanied the Huff Society screening of the restored *Sherlock Holmes*, Everson wrote that

> with the limited help of director Albert Parker, who remembered but little of the film and who died while the reconstruction work was in progress, Kevin Brownlow in England did piece it together, replaced titles and generally made sense out of an impossible jigsaw….

The following account contains a bit more detail and is taken from a letter that Mr. Brownlow sent to Ms. Diane MacIntyre (founder of the splendid website *The Silents Majority*) in October 1996. We reprint it here with the permission of both the writer of the letter and its recipient.

> When we showed the jumble to Parker, the photographic quality—coming direct from the neg—was superb [J. Roy Hunt]. It looked like a spooky masterpiece. Parker couldn't remember the order in which the shots should go, but he found a few documents and photographs. I sat down with a viewing machine and tried to follow the story as outlined in reviews and synopses.
> Then I found that some of the shots were numbered, and this made the job fairly easy. The jigsaw was almost complete—and I found a place for every shot. But now the potential masterpiece was reduced to the banal level of a B picture. It was based not on Conan Doyle but on William Gillette's play. Although the Goldwyn company had come on location to London, the location work was minimal. The final result was a great disappointment.
> My job was to get the thing in order and send it back to Eastman House, where the rest of the work was to be done.

Both the reduction of the filmstock from 35mm to 16mm and the winnowing of the multiple takes of some segments left *Holmes* but a shade (more properly, a fraction) of its former self. Brownlow wrote to us, "The U.S. version of 8200 ft. had become 4594 ft. with flash titles when I got it." Following the regimen described above, he returned the print to Rochester, New York, without having had attended to the titles. We now know—per Jared Case, Head of Collection, Information, Research, and Access at Eastman House—"the intertitles on our Master were re-created by Jim Card in the simple black-on-white style so familiar from that time." Mr. Case went into more detail for us:

> [The] same nitrate produced both our Master element and Bill Everson's 16mm print. The nitrate neg was not in narrative order [possibly tinting order] and thus the resulting positives needed to be cut to fit the story. Our print was cut based on Kevin's work in the 70s, and more work was done to fine-tune it in the 80s.

**Holmes and Billy having a heart-to-heart. Charlie Chaplin played the page (beginning in 1903) in Gillette and Conan Doyle's four-act play.**

While Case did not specify what "more work" done in the '80s consisted of, his email to us did include a fascinating—and somewhat curious—statement:

> The Motion Picture Department of George Eastman House as a whole didn't know that Bill had a print until the collection came to us in the late 90s. When we realized that the print was there, and that Bill hadn't changed out the decomposing art titles, we proposed a new restoration that was completed in 2002. The titles were blown up from 16mm and rejuvenated digitally, resulting in what you now see on the [KINO] DVD.

Again, a bit of speculating. Might Jim Card have okayed that a 16mm print be struck from Brownlow's composite and given to William K. Everson as thanks for his help in getting the project underway? Inasmuch as the men were longtime colleagues, inveterate film collectors, and die-hard preservationists, this sort of *quid pro quo*—done quietly, without much hoopla—seems quite reasonable. But, then … did Everson just tuck away the print in his collection? Was the print shown at the Huff Society screening, then, *his* print, or one that was out on loan from the Eastman House? As for the "Master element," was it struck via reversal from Brownlow's work print and was thus in 16mm? Or were the nitrate negs themselves (which, per Case, have "since disappeared") cut and assembled and then printed for a 35mm master?

At this point we've cooked up the proverbial "tempest in a teapot," and we remain enormously grateful for the work of the Messrs. Brownlow, Parker, Card, Everson, et al. Critiquing a film and criticizing the process through which said film has survived all—including the Stepney Gas Chamber ambush—means walking down two disparate paths, and while both are well worth the attention, the latter still leads into the darkness. Let us, then, retrace our steps and deal with the more familiar twists and turns in the road.

Recounting the stage and screen career(s) of John Barrymore is a task better left to The Great Profile's many biographers and amanuenses, and we refer the interested reader to any/all of the pertinent titles listed in our biography.

The next biggest name at the time was that of Carol Dempster, made a star (to the intense displeasure of the Gish sisters, Mae Marsh, and others) by D.W. Griffith, who also pursued the young Minnesotan romantically while separated from his wife, Linda Arvidson. Discovered while a 14-year-old member of the Ruth St. Denis Dance Company, the ship captain's daughter would go on to play the female lead in almost every picture Griffith would make between 1920 and 1925. Following her turn as Sherlock Holmes's girlfriend, Dempster appeared in the inaptly named *One Exciting Night*, directed by Griffith for his own studios in Mamaroneck, Long Island, and adapted from "The Haunted Grange," a story he wrote under the *nom de plume* Irene Sinclair. After impersonating the title characters in *That Royle Girl* and *Sally of the Sawdust* (both 1925)—nowadays considered to be W.C. Fields films, when considered at all—she starred in 1926's *The Sorrows of Satan*, a supernatural thriller based on the eponymous Marie Corelli novel and helmed by Griffith for Famous Players-Lasky/Paramount. Choosing to end her brief film career with the Corelli adaptation, she was married (*not* to Griffith) three years later. Quite late in life, regretting not a whit her decision to leave the industry—in fact, quite amused that her films were still being enjoyed—the actress asked that her fans be told, "In real life, Carol Dempster had a happy ending."

(Even considering Griffith's romantic pursuit of Dempster, the act of turning Alice Faulkner into Sherlock Holmes's girlfriend must be blamed on William Gillette, who, as he was crafting the play reported on above, wrote to Arthur Conan Doyle for permission to marry off Holmes at the denouement. Conan Doyle's famed response—"You may marry or murder or do what you like with him"—led to Gillette's "infamous" climax, and, since the Goldwyn picture "*is* the Gillette play, amplified a bit,"[29] what better way to satisfy what was then the "boy gets girl" convention of the lion's share of 1920s motion pictures?)

For Roland Young and William Powell, *Sherlock Holmes* was the cinematic alpha, although both men—Young, an expatriated Londoner; Powell, a Pennsylvanian hailing from Pittsburgh—had started out onstage, and both were treading the boards in New York City in 1912. Powell first brought the character of Philo Vance to the screen (*The Canary Murder Case*, 1929), and yet, despite four subsequent appearances as S.S. Van Dine's quirky detective, became forever associated with Myrna Loy and the character of Nick Charles in the six features that comprised MGM's "Thin Man" series, beginning in 1934. Young, who appeared in the only Philo Vance movie to star Basil Rathbone (1930's *The Bishop Murder Case*), went on to famously impersonate Cosmo Topper, the perennially befuddled friend to the ghostly Kirbys, in a series of three films that began with *Topper* in 1937. Both men enjoyed cinematic success for some three decades, with Powell retiring from the screen following 1955's *Mister Roberts*, and Young's passing away "with his boots on," as it were, after completing *That Man from Tangier*, an American-Spanish coproduction released in 1953. (Powell went on to enjoy a lengthy retirement from the screen, passing away in Palm Springs, California, in early March 1984.)

Probably the most memorable portrayal in the film is Gustav von Seyffertitz's rendition of Professor Moriarty. The gaunt-visaged Bavarian was already in his forties when he debuted on the American stage in the late 1900s, and, following a spate of appearances on The Great White Way (and several—like 1910's fantasy *The Brass Bottle*—which he directed), he made the move to the movies, where he would spend much of his screen time scaring the pants off seatholders. Prior to *Sherlock Holmes*, he entertained contemporary genre fans with such titles as *The Devil-Stone* (1917), *The Whispering Chorus* (1918, as a "Mocking Face"), and 1919's *The Dark Star*, albeit in this last film—and for a brief time following the Great War—he was billed onscreen as "G. Butler Clonbough" in reaction to prevailing anti–German sentiments. Pursuant to *Holmes*, the actor also displayed his silent genre chops in *The Bells*, *Sparrows* (both 1926), and *The Wizard* (1927). Due to the fact that, as stated above, his make-up treatment for Moriarty was more than casually reminiscent of Barrymore's Mr. Hyde, *fama erat* (*very* briefly) that all von Seyffertitz was lending to the project was his name and that The Great Profile himself was doubling the leading roles.[30] The silent movies's gentle goblin died on Christmas Day in 1943.

Even with the film's secondary cast reading like a "Who's Who of Who's That?" to the interested viewer, *Sherlock Holmes* is more of a curiosity than a classic. The restored version is fairly talky, title-wise, except for the last reel where, apparently, the necessary explanatory flash-titles did not survive the sundry catastrophes that befell all original positive prints. Knowing what we do, we can reassess Barrymore's performance in light of his preoccupation with his impending *Hamlet* as well as agree (or not!) with William K. Everson's opinion on why the picture ended up being retitled in Blighty.

# The Sky Ranger
## (The Man Who Stole the Moon)

George B. Seitz Productions—May 1, 1921—15 chapters—A Pathé release

Released in France in 1923 as *Les Rôdeurs de l'Air* by Pathé Consortium Cinéma

**Cast**: George B. Seitz as George Oliver Rockwell; June Caprice as June Elliott; Harry Semels as Dr. Santro; Frank Redmond as Professor Elliott; Joe Cuny as Murdock; Peggy Shanor as Tharen; Charles "Patch" Revada as Bean; Thomas Goodwin as The Butler; with Spencer Gordon Bennet, Marguerite Courtot

**Credits**: *Producer and Director*: George B. Seitz

The following synopsis is taken from the copyright registration submissions filed at the Library of Congress between April 6 and June 7, 1921. Grammar, spelling, and punctuation have been left as originally printed. Several words on these registration documents are illegible, and these have been indicated by a series of five dashes (-----) in the text below. (The original text also occasionally includes a pair of dashes [- -], but the meaning and intent of these remain uncertain.) Intriguingly, the LoC summaries for chapters seven through fifteen are both significantly longer and in a different typeface than those of the first six chapters.

**Chapter One: "Out of the Clouds"**

George Oliver Rockwell, in accordance with the prophesy of a gypsy fortune teller, meets a beautiful girl, falls in love with her at sight, and follows her to her home. She is June Elliott, daughter of William Elliott, inventor of a powerful searchlight that will signal to Mars. Murdock, a rival scientist, wants a share of the invention.

Elliott's home is guarded day and night by armed men. George is warned to keep out, but the element of danger adds zest to his predestined courtship, and he perseveres until he sees June at a window.

She throws him a piece of paper which he thinks is a love note, but it is blank. He dips it in lemon juice and brings out an algebraic formula written in invisible ink. Murdock interrupts and demands the paper. Instead he gets a fight.

George returns the formula to Elliott, who thanks the zealous lover by imprisoning him. George is delighted over being forced to stay under the same roof with June.

Meanwhile, Murdock is visited by Dr. Santro, who has come from Buenos Aires in three hours by an airplane of his own invention. Santro is a scientist and a magician, and proposes to destroy Elliott's searchlight.

He and Murdock agree to work together. Santro appears before George and June, a mysterious figure in his flowing magician's garb, and commands them to follow. A compelling force makes them obey. Then suddenly there is a blinding flash and a cloud of smoke.

**Chapter Two: "The Sinister Signal"**

The explosion in Prof. Elliott's laboratory injures Santro and sends him screaming from the house. George rushes into the laboratory with a fire extinguisher and is intercepted by Elliott, who demands to know why he came to his house in the first place.

George says he wants to marry June. Her father consents if George will take her away, so that he can work uninterruptedly on his light. This cold-blooded procedure angers June. She refuses to marry him—says she hates him!

Seeing no reason then for his imprisonment, George plans to escape, but changes his mind when June slips a pentitent note under the doorway.

June is kidnapped by Murdock and Santro. Her ransom is the light. George learns of June's kidnapping, recalls having seen signalling from a schooner anchored on the bay, and rushes to her aid.

He encounters Murdock, overcomes him and rows to the schooner where he finds June in the clutches of a brute. A terrific fight ensues, with victory in sight for George when Dr. Santro and his niece, Tharen, appear, making escape impossible.

**Chapter Three: "In Hostile Hands"**

George is clever enough to escape Dr. Santro and return June to her father. His heroic actions alter Prof. Elliott's attitude and convince him that George is a friend, and not an enemy. June also forgives the young man for his audacity.

Santro's second attempt to kidnap June succeeds. He also kidnaps George, and after hours of maddening whirling through space, George and June find themselves, alone, on a wind-swept plain in an obscure little country in Asia.

In the darkened courtyard of an inn in a nearby town a pilgrim is murdered and robbed of his bag of silver. June's scream when she stumbles over the body awakes the inmates of the inn. June and George are soon surrounded by a howling, menacing mob, who grab them and hurry them through the dark streets to the temple of justice for trail [sic].

Santro, watching from a doorway, is satisfied with his night's work, but Tharen, whose sympathies are with George, becomes frantic when Santro tells her that the best that can happen is death—the worst is a life sentence to the chest.

**Chapter Four: "Desert Law"**

June Elliott and George Rockwell are the center of interest of an angry mob, jabbering in a foreign tongue. A man who speaks their language tells them they are being tried in the temple of justice for the murder of a rich merchant.

The situation is a hopeless one when Tharen, moved by sympathy for George, slips him a note telling him to ask their accuser what he buried under the wall after the murder. The man confesses to the murder, but June and George's plight is still serious, because as they cannot explain how they got there, they are taken for sorcerers. In spite of George's desperate struggles to fight off her adversaries, he and June are locked in a chest.

In the morning a cruel mountain man rides into town and invites the revelers to join him in a little sport with the prisoners. In the meantime, George has pried open the lid far enough for June to spring the padlocks with a hairpin. They have just climbed out of the chest when they hear the bloodthirsty crowd approaching. Where can they go to escape their enemies?

**Chapter Five: "Mid-Air"**

The revelers, unaware that June and George have escaped from the chest, shoot it full of holes. In their search for a horse with which to get away from danger, June becomes separated from George. She is captured by a stray member of the drunken band, but escapes when her horse becomes unruly and plunges her down a bank.

She seeks shelter in a hut, but is horrified to find that it is the home of a sheep-herder, who has been a particular enemy ever since their strange arrival among those cruel people. George traces June by the prints of her French heels in

**George and June. Trade ad.**

the sand, but before they can get away from the sheep-herder, the revelers arrive.

Their murderous designs are frustrated by the arrival of Tharen. In her magician's costume they believe her a supernatural being sent to chastise them, and they fall prostrate at her feet. She leads the two Americans to Santro's plane, and demands that he return them to New York.

Santro deliberately starts the airplane before June is in. Clinging desperately to a rod she calls George for help. He tries to pull her inside, but Santro interferes. Unseen by anyone, a ruffian is clinging to the wheels of the plane, making his way evil intent, with perilously toward June, whose strength is fast giving out.

**Chapter Six: "The Crystal Prism"**

June is rescued from her perilous position and she and George are returned home, wondering if their adventure has been real, or only a horrible dream.

Santro and Murdock overhear Prof. Elliott explaining the peculiar powers of his light to George. Its secret lies in a crystal prism, which is his own invention. He leaves George to guard the prism. Santro and Murdock attack, are tricked by George and taken prisoners.

Murdock makes a getaway, secures the crystal prism and, in fleeing from George, who has taken up the pursuit, throws the prism onto the roof of the area where Professor Elliott keeps his supply of chemicals and explosives.

George climbs onto the roof; also Santro, who has escaped. It is too dark to see the prism and Bean, not knowing the power of the searchlight, turns it on. It sets on fire everything its rays touch, the flames fast approaching the supply house. George finds the prism and throws it to June. The reflected light from the searchlight knocks George senseless. The fire creeps closer to the building, with its supply of chemicals and explosives.

**Chapter Seven: "Danger's Doorway"**
As the flames mount to the roof of the burning shed where George Rockwell lies dazed, Professor Elliott returns. His assistant, Bean, rushes into the laboratory and shuts off the deadly searchlight. Murdock escapes from the guards. George descends from the roof as he regains his senses, and with Bean searches for Santro. Murdock and Santro meet in a remote spot on the ground and decide to try again that night to obtain the prism.

Meanwhile, the guards have put out the fire, and June, who has been guarding the prism all during the encounter, finds to her great relief that George is alive and well.

Now George and June wait upon the Professor in his laboratory and upbraid him for the dangers he is subjecting his household to in his blindness to everything except his present invention. George maintains the house is not safe for June. Santro and Murdock, who feel they have a ----- make repeated efforts to obtain what they consider to be their rightful due. Furthermore, George is decidedly of the opinion that the professor would stop at nothing to protect his property. The professor laughs away their worries—but the events of the evening were to prove that George and June were right in their suspicion of him.

At Murdock's headquarters there is now in progress a conference between Murdock and a new lieutenant, Arty Carrigan. Murdock is informing Carrigan as to the value of the signal [sic] light, and his desire to obtain the secret parts of it. In the adjoining room, Tharen and Santro are waiting. Now from the first, Tharen has shown herself to be tenderhearted and entirely out of sympathy with the methods adopted by Santro and Murdock. As she overhears the stern instructions that Murdock is giving Arty Carrigan, she can stand it no longer. She rushes to the door to interfere but is halted by Santro. The two of them are in theatrical garb, as Murdock had planned of staging a supernatural demonstration at the Elliott house, but had revised his program and engaged Arty Carrigan to carry out his orders.

In halting Tharen at Murdock's door, Santro has whipped out a long knife, such as is used by vaudeville artists in so-called "-----" acts." Tharen knows this is a mere threat, and tells Santro he wouldn't dare throw it at her. Of course she is right in this. He dissembles, pacifies the girl and sends her outside to wait in the airship until he has finished his engagement with Murdock.

Carrigan now starts for the Elliott house to carry out his sinister orders. Tharen, waiting beside the great airplane, decides to take the initiative. She starts the silent motor. The great plane leaves the ground and speeds for the Elliott grounds.

Meanwhile Elliott has been demonstrating to Bean, his assistant, a new protective device he has installed. His iron laboratory door is charged with electricity, an automatic indicator registers the footsteps of anyone approaching the door, and should the door be touched while the current is switched on—well, it would mean a terrific shock.

Bean is instructed to warn the household about the door, but for reasons best known to himself he leaves ----- with a very furtive manner, and pauses outside as though weighing certain chances.

At this time, George is saying goodnight to June at the foot of the living-hall stairs. Bean passes through, and perhaps because he doesn't want to interrupt a love scene, says nothing about the door.

A moment later, Tharen appears, warns June and George about Arty Carrigan, and slips away. George and June start for the laboratory to warn Elliott. Elliott at this time discovers the skulking figure of Arty in the grounds, rushes to the telltale indicator and stands ready to switch the current on the iron door in case Arty approaches.

The indicator lights up, his hand trembles on the switch. Unknown to him it is June and

**June (June Caprice) and George (George B. Seitz), at the mercy of the Tibetan sheepherders.**

George who approach the door. Before they reach it they hear footsteps. George rushes out to find the marauder. Arty has entered the house and proceeded to the kitchen where he encounters Bean. They are very friendly and have a private understanding. George bursts in, starts a terrific fight with Arty. Bean enters, smiles, calls, "Time!" and explains that Arty is his brother-in-law, a detective who has gained Murdock's confidence and has come to tell Elliott all he has learned. Delighted, George starts for the laboratory with Arty and Bean. But poor June, who has listened in terror to the sounds of the battle, and now feels that the battle is over, with George the loser, rushes straight for the laboratory door. Unwitting of the identity of the one who is approaching the door, Professor Elliott switches on the current just as June puts her hand on the steel door knob.

**Chapter Eight: "Dropped from the Clouds"**

George Oliver Rockwell has just received inside information concerning an attack that Santro and Murdock have planned for that night, whereby they hope to get hold of the priceless Elliott searchlight. The gravity of this news warrants immediate action. With June, George attempts an entrance into Elliott's most private sanctuary, his laboratory, only to receive a terrific electric shock—which luckily does not prove serious. This disturbance attracts the irascible Elliott who, when he hears of the planned attack, cheerfully remarks that he has just increased his force by fifty extra guards—and therefore has no fears.

June is sent to bed, while Mr. Elliott and George call the guards together and assign them their posts about the estate. Scarcely have they taken these, when the heavens begin to rain down fiery torches. The guards become panic-stricken and flee,—even the house catches fire. June awakens to see all this and runs out in time to see George heroically extinguish an ignited torch that has fallen upon the roof. Unable to see in the pitchy black night from whence those burning torches are being hurled, June suggests using her father's all powerful light. George and Mr. Elliott immediately act upon her suggestion and the light is flashed through the sky revealing Santro's highly-powered plane,—as the base from which this bombarding is taking place.

At this discovery, the plane becomes the target for the Elliott guards and straightaway disappears from sight.

It is then decided that this is much too dangerous an abode for the lovely June. Whereby George gallantly offers the hospitality of his roof-top bungalow in New York [!] which boats [sic] of a chaperone, servants and every comfort that a millionaire bachelor could think of. Here perched on top of a sky-scraper office building June should surely be safely hidden from the treacherous Santro and Murdock.

Approving of this scheme, Mr. Elliott not only entrusts his daughter but also a duplicate set of plans of his inventions to young Rockwell's care until the fiendish Santro and Murdock are captured.

In due time, June and George arrive at the young man's unique dwelling place, and having carefully locked up Elliott's plans, bid each other "Good-Night."

While the wily Murdock, having been informed by one of his trusties [sic], arrives by aeroplane at the Rockwell bungalow,—in quest of the plans. Gaining entrance to June's room, he stealthily sneaks up behind the unsuspecting young lady, thinking it will be easy to force this young lady to reveal the hiding place of the Elliott plans—when a fade out occurs, keeping us in suspense until the next week ! ! !

**Chapter Nine: "The House on the Roof"**

Because of the frequent dangerous attacks of rival scientists, William Elliott has entrusted his daughter, June, with a duplicate set of plans of his priceless inventions to George Oliver Rockwell. This young man has a unique dwelling place upon a sky-scraper office building in New York,—apparently safe from prying eyes,—the only approach being by elevator. George feels that this will be a cinch to guard and therefore a safer abode would be difficult to find.

But the ever vigilant Santro has already spotted them and is now hoverying [sic] above their very bungalow in his aeroplane. In fact, the treacherous Murdock, also a rival of Mr. Elliott's and in league with Santro, has been let down by a rope ladder from his aeroplane and is now searching for the duplicate set of plans in the bungalow. Encountering June, he tries to force her to tell where the plans are—but June is adamant.

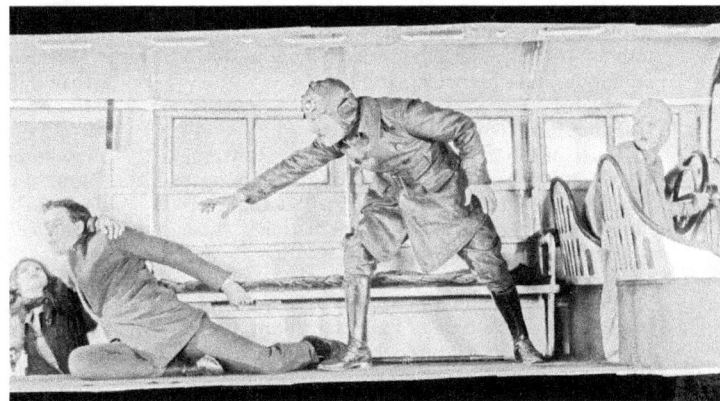

**On the (second) return trip from Tibet to New York. The interior of the "avion géant."**

In the meantime, Santro becomes suspicious of Murdock's lengthy absence and he sends Tharen, his fair assistant to spy upon him. Seeing this fierce struggle between June and Murdock, Tharen realizes the plans have not been found. Since her mission is to get the plans, she tries to get into the bungalow but only succeeds in raising the window a few inches. Her success must include outside help, so picking up a stick, she ----- through the window, and presses the elevator button. Meanwhile June has been forced to tell where the plans are and the wily Murdock has them in his hands, when, George, in response to the elevator signal, arrives on the scene of action. A horrible fight ensues—which results in Murdock's overcoming George. Not content with victory, he is about to push him over the railing into the street below—when Tharen who has become enamoured of George, arrives and rescues him. With Murdock as prisoner, who swears he will get even with Tharen for turning traitor, they go to June's aid. Tharen, then, beseechingly asks George if he will help her to escape from her dreadful Uncle Santro. George gladly assents to this, and tells June and Tharen he will return with the police for Murdock. They ring for the elevator, when the merciless Santro steps into their midst, and glowering with rage and unbounded hate, menacingly dares them to attempt to leave his presence!!

**George exercises some gun control, 1920s-style.**

**Chapter Ten: "Trapped"**
Professor Elliott has sent his daughter, June, to the city in the care of George Rockwell, a young millionaire. He entrusts Rockwell with a model of his invention. For safety, Rockwell has taken June to his bungalow on the top of a New York skyscraper.

Doctor Santro, and Tharen, his assistant, have brought Murdock, rival of Professor Elliott, to the roof in their airship. Murdock has made a murderous attack on George and June in an attempt to obtain the model of Elliott's invention. Tharen has assisted George to overpower Murdock.

Santro waits outside in his plane. Growing anxious, he descends, only to find his fears justified—Murdock is bound hand and foot—and Tharen has turned traitor. Loosening Murdock, the two rush out in time to interrupt George from leaving with June and Tharen. Santro commands Murdock to guard George and June and the Elliott blue-prints while he takes Tharen back to the plane. Murdock gives George three counts to escape by a window of his roof-top bungalow. June stands by mute with terror, sees George raise the window, preparatory to his leap—then suddenly turn, pull down the window drapery and envelop his adversary.

George then rescues the Elliott blue-prints and with June, he makes a dash for the roof, where they perilously rush from one building to another, at last finding an open door which they enter—in hopes of finding a passage to the street.

Meanwhile, the alert Santro, hearing the disturbance, leaves Tharen and goes to Murdock's assistance. They follow George and June in hot pursuit while Tharen rushes to rouse George's housekeeper who telephones for the police.

June and George find themselves caught in an elevator shaft. Rushing up to the roof again, they come face to face with their pursuers. Thus they are forced to turn back, their only means of escape now is to slide down the elevator cable to the floor below with the hope of finding an outlet. Arriving there, they find that the doors are locked!

Through a skylight above, Santro senses their predicament, orders Murdock below while he hurls missiles from above—to force George to drop the briefcase containing the coveted model of Elliott's invention. Santro succeeds in accomplishing his purpose, and Murdock who is below triumphantly picks up the briefcase and joins his master. Now for a speedy getaway—when a fiendish afterthought halts Santro and causes him to push the button for the elevator to descend upon the helpless ones below.

Meanwhile the police who have taken up the pursuit are attracted to the open sky-light by the terrifying screams of June. Rushing to her aid, they find the elevator doors locked,—the screams grow fainter. Then they notice the elevator indicator registers descend.

Meanwhile George and June cling to each other, terror-stricken and helpless as the descending cable lowers them to the bottom of the shaft, while the elevator comes closer and closer. Flattening themselves on the ground, they await the inevitable!!!

**Chapter Eleven: "The Seething Pool"**

Murdock and his ally, the mysterious Doctor Santro, have at last obtained possession of the models of Professor Elliott's searchlight. George and June have been trapped and locked in an elevator by those two who, to add to their terror, have pushed the button for the elevator to descend and crush them. June's screams attract the police who miraculously save her and George from being crushed to death.

The police take up the chase, run up to the roof, see a huge plane rise from an adjoining building with Murdock and Santro peering down at them.

Half an hour later, Jane telephones her father from police headquarters to say that Santro and Murdock have escaped with his models. Elliott leaves Bean in charge of the estate while he journeys to the city to join in the search for his plans. In the midst of narrating to the police what a menace to civilization his most powerful searchlight would be in the hands of an enemy, Elliott receives a phone call from Bean. He informs him that Santro has been there, and escaped with the vital parts of his mechanism and then destroyed everything else of value in the laboratory. Elliott is crushed by this catastrophe.

George offers his immediate service to the police lieutenant in charge who calls in Doyle. He proves to be an ex-service pal of George's. The facts of the case are stated and Doyle recalls having just seen an aeroplane of this description. Doyle and George are assigned to the case.

Arriving in the vicinity where Doyle saw the plane land, they spot a deserted foundry as the only sizable building that could house such a plane. They advance, see not only the plane but Santro in a heated discussion with Murdock, and manage to gain an underground entrance.

Santro grows desperate and calls Tharen, his assistant, aside, telling him to gather the plans together and prepare the plane for an immediate journey. Returning to Murdock, he appeases him in the most suave manner, and excusing himself for a minute, leaves with the most important part of the Elliott mechanism.

Suddenly Murdock realizes he has been tricked, and rushing after Santro, he meets the fate this fiend has planned for him.

George and Doyle arrive in time to see Santro preparing for departure. They plan a joint attack. Just then June, who has become impatient and followed them there, arrives on the scene of the action. Screaming to warn George of an imminent attack from behind, she proves to Santro that his fears are justified. This gives him a chance to prepare the same fate for them as he has for Murdock. George, now assisted by June, and Doyle are battering in different doors when Santro clips the bolts from George's door, the door gives way, hurling George and June into a steaming abyss below!!!!

**The mustached menaces: Murdock (Joe Cuny) and Santro (Harry Semels), who's chafed—and not just because of all that leather.**

### Chapter Twelve: "The Whirling Menace"

Dr. Santro, the mysterious scientist and aviator, who has stolen the models of Professor Elliott's searchlight, has been traced to an old foundry by George Rockwell, Sergeant Doyle, and June.

Santro, who is cornered between two doors which are being battered down, loosens the bolts of George's door, just as Doyle breaks through his door. Sizing up the situation, Doyle throws himself across the opening, forming a human bridge, thus saving George and June from the boiling vat below. A general mix-up ensues. George and Doyle, although outnumbered by Santro's gang, finally gain the upper hand. Santro seizes this opportunity to escape, not forgetting the briefcase containing the Elliott plans, and heads for the plane. June, not wishing to lose sight of the plane, follows him and jumps into the plane after him. Santro hasn't time to remonstrate with her, he is so intent upon making a speedy get-away. Realizing this, June picks up the briefcase and opening the door, throws it out just as Santro looks up. Beside himself with rage, he rushes back to June, while the plane, pilotless, begins a series of spinning nose dives which force him to assume his place at the wheel. Then it is that June spys the butt of his revolver and, sneaking up, snatches it out of his pocket. She commands him to turn around and head for her home in Long Island.

In the Elliott city home, are June's father, George and Doyle in close consultation with an officer of army aviation who has placed all his resources at their disposal for the capture of Santro and the recovery of June.

Meantime Santro, commandeered by June, arrives at the Elliott estate. With his usual cunning, he learns that there is a duplicate set of plans. By trickery, he manages to regain his revolver and then orders June to disclose the hiding place of the plans.

Encountering Bean and the butler, Santro overpowers them and locks them in a closet. June seizes this chance to telephone the Elliott city house and is caught in the act by Santro just as she gets her connection.

George answers the telephone, recognizes June's voice and the word "laboratory," and sensing trouble when the connection is cut off, he and Doyle jump into his roadster and start out for the Elliott estate.

Santro again demands to know where the plans are kept, but June is adamant. He goes through a file but with no success when June jumps up to close a cabinet and mashes her finger. Fainting, she sinks into a chair. Santro, rushing to find out what this ruse of hers may be, accidently turns on a devilish looking contrivance with great revolving arms which threatens her very life. Hearing a car drive up, just as Bean and the butler break through the closet, Santro rushes off, leaving June to her fate.

### Chapter Thirteen: "At the Last Minute"

In guarding from Dr. Santro a cabinet containing valuable scientific date, June Elliott, daughter of an inventor, has received an injury which causes her to faint. Santro, insidiously, has started a machine which places the unconscious girl in great peril.

Bean and the Elliott butler have just succeeded in breaking through the closet to go to the aid of their mistress when they encounter the fleeing Santro. A lively scuffle takes place in which Santro is finally overpowered and placed under arrest by Sergeant Doyle who with George Rockwell has come in answer to a mysterious phone call. Rockwell heads for the laboratory and saves June from the menacing contrivance which threatens her life.

Meanwhile Elliott arrives, greets June, and then rushes to the laboratory where he finds that his priceless searchlight can be repaired. Then Tharen, Santro's niece, arrives and requests to see her uncle before he is taken away. At sight of her,

"Cleverly fools" is code for "punches." Original lobby card.

**Original title card. That exposed bit of telescope is the most impressive prop in the serial.**

Santro feigns remorse and requests a few moments alone with his niece. June pleads for him and his request is granted, while ----- ----- leave to wander about the Elliott grounds.

Meantime a muffled figure prowls about, peering through the various windows. Finally we recognize the wily Murdock whom all think to be dead.

Santro's time is up, Doyle returns for him,— only to find that he has escaped while Tharen lies there, unconscious, another victim of her uncle's treachery. Reviving her, they call the guards to make a thorough search for him. Unknown to the Elliott guards, Murdock crazed with the desire for revenge, awaits his prey.

George and June in their meanderings have discovered Santro's plane, and spurred on by curiosity, enter. They, oblivious of the terrific struggle that is taking place outside between Santro and Murdock, are having a beautiful time turning levers, dials, etc. Santro overcomes his adversary, and jumping into his plane, discovers the young intruders whom he thrusts to one side without much ado, soars skyward at a terrific speed. Then he notices the torpedo dial has been tampered with. Growling savagely, he learns that June, unwittingly, has turned the dial so that the underslung torpedo will explode within twenty minutes. In his frenzied haste, Santro breaks the lever which would automatically release the bomb. "We are lost," he cries. George then volunteers his services and crawling out, at the risk of his life, he manages to cut loose the torpedo just as it explodes. The concussion of the explosion ----- the plane ----- at a terrific speed,—all are thrown from their seats in a downward drive to seeming destruction!!!

**Chapter Fourteen: "Liquid Fire"**

Professor Elliott, inventor of a powerful signal light, is in pursuit of Dr. Santro, the mysterious aviator who has made repeated efforts to obtain the secret of the light. The Professor does not know that his daughter and her friend, George Rockwell, were inspecting the plane when Santro, frantic to escape his pusuers, jumps in and drives off with them. Neither do any of them know that inadvertently, June Elliott has set the timing gear on an aerial torpedo, carried under the wings. Suddenly Santro discovers this, and it is only George's heroism in climbing out of the plane and releasing the torpedo that saves them from destruction.

Sergeant Doyle has just reported his failure to capture Santro when he and Elliott look up and,—a falling plane. As it comes nearer the ground, they recognize it to be Santro's plane. Suddenly two objects dart from the falling plane, and land in the treetops, then the plane rights itself and goes off.

Rushing over to the clump of trees, Elliott, to his horror, discovers the two objects to be the unconscious forms of his daughter, June, and her friend, George. The trees have broken their fall so, although they are badly shaken up, they are not seriously injured.

Seeking revenge on Santro, Murdock, whom all think dead, returns and offers to help Elliott repair his search-light. Convinced of his sincerity, Elliott sends Murdock to the top floor laboratory, where he assigns him several experiments to do. The noxious fumes from the chemicals forces Murdock to go up to the roof for air.

June is having troubled dreams that cause her to walk in her sleep, finally leading her to the top laboratory. Entering there, she, too, is overcome by the fumes and in falling to the floor she accidentally touches the lever which empties the ----- containing the chemicals. They drip through to the room below in which George is sleeping. Exhausted from his recent harrowing experience, the fumes do not rouse him and he gradually loses consciousness.

The butler of the Elliott household has not yet been won over by Murdock's sudden transformation, and has therefore been secretly watching him. Noticing thick clouds of smoke pour out of the laboratory and Murdock standing on the roof, he is about to rush up to investigate when Sergeant Doyle appears. He tells him his suspicions and together they start out on an investigation.

Meanwhile Murdock peers through the trap door down into the laboratory, and a horrible look comes into his face when he sees the unconscious form of Miss Elliott through the choking fumes while the burning acids creep nearer and nearer.

**Chapter Fifteen: "The Last Raid"**
In the capacity of a chemist, Murdock is now working for his former enemy, Professor Elliott. Because of the fumes in the laboratory, he has gone to the roof for fresh air. Unknown to Murdock, June Elliott has entered the laboratory and has been overcome by the fumes. George Oliver Rockwell has attempted to rescue June but has encountered the butler who believes him to be Murdock and suspecting his motives, engages in battle with him. It is Murdock who finds and rescues June, thereby convincing the Elliott household of the sincerity of his reformation.

In the two months that followed, the Elliott house was the scene of great activity. The mysterious Dr. Santro had disappeared utterly—and with Murdock's help, Professor Elliott had built a light that was even more powerful than the original one. George hasn't wasted any time and he and June have finally decided to stage their wedding on the night that June's father has chosen to display the wonders of his light to the leading scientists of the world.

The night of the double festivity arrives. There is a general undercurrent of happy excitement as the guests and scientists circulate about the spacious Elliott house. When Murdock, having occasion to go outside, is startled by a falling dart, containing a note from Santro whom all thought had disappeared forever. The note demands that Murdock destroy the light, giving him just five minutes to deliver the plans or Santro will act. Past dealings with Santro have taught Murdock that there is not a second to lose. Rushing in the house to warn Elliott, Murdock follows him from room to room, and before he has a chance to tell him, the strains of the wedding match ring out, and June advances toward the altar on the arm of her father. Murdock does not feel that he can interrupt this holiest of ceremonies. The minister has scarcely begun when Santro's threat is made good in the form of a terrific explosion. The panic stricken guests flee to the basement. George and Doyle rush out to find Murdock who points skyward and gasps, "Santro." Looking up, they see Santro's well-known bi-plane. Remembering the power of Elliott's light, George rushes to the laboratory where, after turning on the light, he soon spots the fiendish Santro. The intensity of the light rays set fire to the plane thereby causing the flaming plane to make its final nose dive to the earth.

George returns to June, and the marriage ceremony is completed. A final close-up shows these two happy young lovers, surrounded by baggage, in one of George's cars, honeymoon bound for SOMEWHERE!!!

The earliest motion pictures produced by anyone, anywhere were shorts: some, merely a few dozen feet in length and seconds in duration. As it became apparent that these briefest of depictions were fast winning a following—and a following willing to part with coin-of-the-realm for the experience—the length and complexity of the films quickly grew. Programs consisting of one- and two-reelers of all stripes followed soon thereafter, and, by 1913 or thereabouts, feature films were elbowing their way onto "select screens" fairly regularly. Granted, there had been a handful of lengthy offerings available now and again prior to that date, but most of those had been imported from foreign climes. Still, not every audience back then had the patience or time to sit still for an hour or more, and not every studio in those early days had the resources to invest in a lengthy production that would ultimately be a "hit or miss." Per film historian Kelton C. Lahue,

It was in this setting that one of the most interesting phenomena of the world of motion pictures, the American serial was born. A buoyant baby, it was to change its form several times during the years it reigned as a top money-maker. For the relatively short period of sixteen years, roughly 1914 to 1930, these weekly thrillers captured their audiences.[1]

Actually, the first silent American chapterplay we're aware of was 1912's *What Happened to Mary?*, a 12-part epic that starred Mary Fuller as the eponymous heroine and that featured Charles Ogle, unencumbered by his *Frankenstein* accoutrements. Pearl White's subsequent—and persistent—serial popularity was presaged by Miss Fuller, who carried six episodes of *Who Will Marry Mary?* the following year and then switched to a alliterative soubriquet for *The Active Life of Dolly of the Dailies* the year after that. Miss Fuller's heroic (heroinic?) perambulations and chases were choreographed at the Edison studios, also home to Mr. Ogle's memorable Monster.

To be honest, most of the earliest perambulations and chases of the chapterplay crowd were "heroinic" in substance. It would take a few years before titles like *The Adventures of Kathlyn* (1913), *The Perils of Pauline*, *The Exploits of Elaine*, *The Hazards of Helen* (all 1914; this last, with 119 one-reel episodes!), *Runaway Jane* and *The Ventures of Marguerite* (both 1915), and 1916's *The Adventures of Peg O' the Ring*, *Gloria's Romance*, *Lass of the Lumberlands*, *The Mysteries of Myra*, and *Perils of Our Girl Reporters* gave way regularly to nomenclature highlighting the Man of Action, the Menace, or the MacGuffin. Still, this lengthy list—by no means complete and minus all sequels and variations—shows that the lion's share of these most venerable of American serials were centered on how the titular Damsel in Distress would thwart the villain and thus succeed in her quest (shared by the hero, present chiefly to add needed muscle and for the romantic wrap) to attain/avoid some goddamned thing or another. This, of course,

Are we talking plans? Blueprints? A model? "You'll be confused!" General circulation newspaper ad.

would prove to be the essence of almost every American movie serial that was ever made, with the only difference being that the high(er) percentage of the attention—hitherto paid to the figure in the skirt/jodhpurs/prehistoric jeans—now shifted variously toward the hero, the villain, or the crucial gimmick on which the action turned. The Damsel would still be in Distress, but her personal peril would now be fairly sporadic and somewhat diminished in light of the imminent danger to be foisted by the villain (in pursuit/possession of the gimmick) on the country/Western Civilization/ the world.

Like virtually every other chapterplay, *The Sky Ranger* adheres fairly severely to this formula. If left solely to this Library of Congress summary, which we pored over more than once (in an effort to decipher the fairly substantial number of lines that were/ are near illegible), we'd conclude that this particular early serial would have been little different, stylistically, than any of those included above or omitted due to space. The participation of the murderous, sheep-herding revelers of the Asian plain in the plot of a serial entitled *The Sky Ranger* does provide an unexpected yet welcome departure from that norm, though. And the bizarre shift back and forth between "super-science" (Santro's plane) and sorcery (Santro and Tharen's wardrobe, promises of a "supernatural demonstration") must have made some viewers slightly dizzy; intriguingly, this odd mixture also fueled the Czech Golem movies, *The Emperor's Baker—The Baker's Emperor* (see essay).

Why? After a couple of reels of fairly sedate exposition (flashes of light, algebraic equations in invisible ink, "compelling" forces), the pro- and antagonists are basically constrained to running/climbing/leaping between rooms/onto roofs/into voids, or slamming shut/breaking down/kicking open lots of doors/gates/barriers. June's nonstop screams either help or hinder the righteous cause; Santro does his dirty work accompanied only by Murdock and Tharen or else is possessed of a "gang" that seemingly materializes out of nowhere and that apparently works only part-time; the evil doctor's "highly powered" airplane/aeroplane—which is as maneuverable as George's roadster, allowing the archvillain to run the gamut from "hoverying" to being able to "drive off" at a moment's notice at supersonic speeds— is (as we are shocked to learn in the Chapter 15 summary) a "bi-plane." A biplane?! *Really?!*

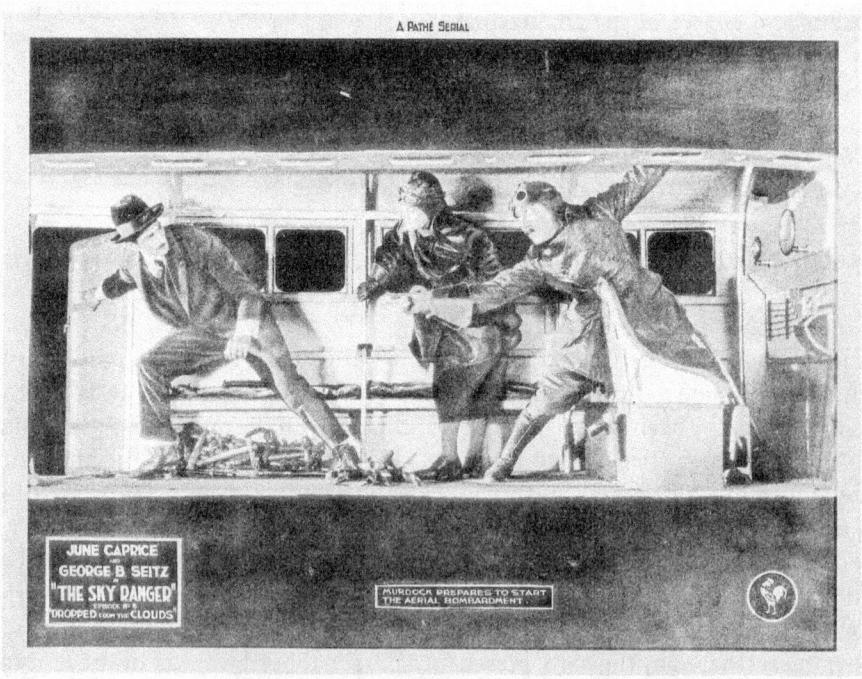

**Murdock (Joe Cuny), Tharen (Peggy Shanor) and Santro (Harry Semels) ... who's driving this thing, anyhow?**

Plus, the object of this particular serial's scientific lust is a briefcase full of secret information concerning a search-light/signal-light that—depending upon the particulars of any given episode under scrutiny—takes the form of blueprints, a model, or model(s) that will give away the show.

Then, too, already a mysterious scientist/aviator/prestidigitator—he is initially bedizened in "flowing magician's garb"—Dr. Santro also appears to be a master of hand-to-hand combat, seeing how he constantly "overpowers" anyone who runs into him (the real reason, perhaps, for his hiring only temps as thugs and goons). Unlike the other members of his malevolent fraternity—forever out to get their hands on the all-important whatchamacallit that will make mankind bow to their every whim—our Evil Genius spends his 15 chapters determined to destroy Professor Elliott's light, and thus ... *ummm*.... And while June's ongoing battle to remain conscious is really no worse than the similar struggles endured by the raft of serial heroines who aren't jungle goddesses, her scenario-driven propensity to trip switches, flip levers, and turn dials that lead always and everywhere to catastrophe did make the authors wish her role had required her to be unconscious longer and with greater frequency. (Unconscious! *Not* asleep!)

Finally—other than *The Vanishing Shadow*[2]—has there *ever* been a chapterplay in which the Forces of Good were so consistently suckered in by "acts of remorse and/or contrition" on the part of the Forces of Darkness?

Anyhow...

Originally titled *The Man Who Stole the Moon*, the story's leading characters had been Martians, but Pathé decided to remove the extreme fantasy from the plot and retitled it.... A kind of prologue opened the first chapter by showing a man clinging desperately to a huge globe which was being rapidly hurled through space while other heavenly bodies came perilously near. Showing this to be but the dream of a man, the serial then plunged at once into snappy action that was humorous and at times resembled a farce comedy.[3]

As none of the action recounted above involves even the *slightest* effort on anyone's part at stealing the Moon, what *was* the chief narrative thrust of Frank Leon Smith's first draft? Were the Martians were bent on appropriating Earth's satellite, à la *Despicable Me*, and Professor Elliott's search/signal light caught them, red-planet-handed? (Sorry.) Was Dr. Santro originally an Earthling turncoat, employed by our would-be overlords to destroy this scheme-revealing technology so that the Moon might become a Martian outpost, from which they would Rule the World!? Just how did Mars get demoted from playing *the* major role in the serial to being little more than the target of a light beam? And why was the Moon fired from the project?

Well, if we can trust the fidelity of those chapter summaries printed above, in its transition from pages yanked out of the typewriter to celluloid stock clattering through the gate, Leon Smith's original story was stripped of all vistas and occupants of Mars and everything conceivable regarding the Moon. But why? It's highly unlikely that Pathé removed the lunar presences or the "extreme fantasy" from that first treatment due the fact that the project ultimately devolved into something that "was humorous and at times resembled a farce comedy." The folks who flocked to movie houses to follow the serialized adventures of Pearl or Helen or Elaine were the same folks who flocked to see Chaplin, Keaton, Arbuckle, Lloyd, et al., whose one- and two-reel slapstick comedies shared the bill with the chapterplays. If both genres appealed to the same segment of the paying public, combining the two would surely not be out of the question to savvy movie moguls. Comic Moonmen? Funny Martians? Why not? With Orson Welles's radio broadcast still nearly 20 years in the future, it wasn't likely that said characters in the serial would suffer in comparison with other extraterrestrial personality types.

And given the fact that, during that era, studio backlots could be transformed into visions of heaven, hell, and anything/everything in-between via the usual combination of imaginative art director and monetary infusion begrudgingly acceptable to the bean-counters, it's doubtful that budgetary concerns would have precluded a couple of "other-worldly" vignettes.

Our theory: For quite a while there—"there" being America's Silent Era cinema—the more "recognizable" elements of our solar system were afforded very little coverage although shorts on comets and meteors were fairly plentiful: witness Kalem's *The Comet* (1910) and *A Bolt from the Sky* (1913), Thanhouser's *Cally's Comet* (1911), American Film's *The Comet's Come-Back* (1915), Keystone's *The Love Comet* (1916), and just plain old *Comets*, a 1919 documentary from J.R. Bray Studios. If nothing else, at the outset of the 1920s, Americans were concerned about objects hurtling about in the atmosphere; the Great War had shown that the most awful stuff could fall out of the sky. (North American Film's 1915 chapterplay *The Diamond from the Sky*—released a couple of years before the Doughboys were shipped "Over There"—tried to posit that not everything dropped from the heavens was the result of ordnance.) Given the outstanding success of the Rosetta Orbiter in putting the Philae probe on Comet 67P/Churyumov-Gerasimenko—which is traveling at 83,000 miles per hour while some four billion miles outside the Earth's atmosphere—our fascination with celestial bodies in motion has grown in direct proportion with our development of mindblowing technology.

But the Moon is also a celestial body in motion, no? And while we landed there a couple of times, decades ago, and uttered some memorable quotes, and took a few steps, and planted a flag…. *Pfffffft!* While all those one- and two-reelers centered on comets were part of 1910s' movie programs seen "at local theaters everywhere," Earth's little satellite got zilch in terms of attention from American filmmakers back then. Although Jules (*From the Earth to the Moon*) Verne and H.G. (*First Men in the Moon*) Wells had their following, and poets, songwriters, and astronomers from time immemorial had waxed romantically and scientifically about the heavens, people who frequented libraries and bookstores and concerts and observatories were not always the people who queued up for tickets at the local itch on a Saturday afternoon. (Nonetheless, it's possible that citing Arthur Conan Doyle's source story did indeed boost the box-office take on *The Comet's Come-Back*.)

Sure, the Moon *had* been a bit of grist for the silent cinematic mill; just not in this neck of the woods. Georges Méliès took moviegoers on *A Trip to the Moon* in 1902, Italy doubled down with a *Trip to the Center of the Moon* three years later, and even Pathé (the original French company) released *Moonstruck*, a 12-minute-long epic that included a dream featuring moonmen, in 1909. But that was "then," and none of those companies were American. In fact, following Pathé's effort, it took twenty years before anyone, anywhere took another shot at *la Lune*,[4] and that trip was led by the Germans—more specifically, Fritz Lang—in 1929's *Frau im Mond*. It's a bit startling to realize that one of the very first American films that tied the Moon to the genre we love so much was Universal's *WereWolf of London* in 1935. With there having been almost zero market for the Moon in the States come 1921, the Red Planet wasn't much better off. The same year (1910) the Edison studios had adapted Mary Shelley's signature work for the bedsheet, they also essayed *A Trip to Mars*. Said trip—the inventor of an anti-gravity chemical mix takes much of the five-minute running time to *float* up to the fourth planet from the Sun—

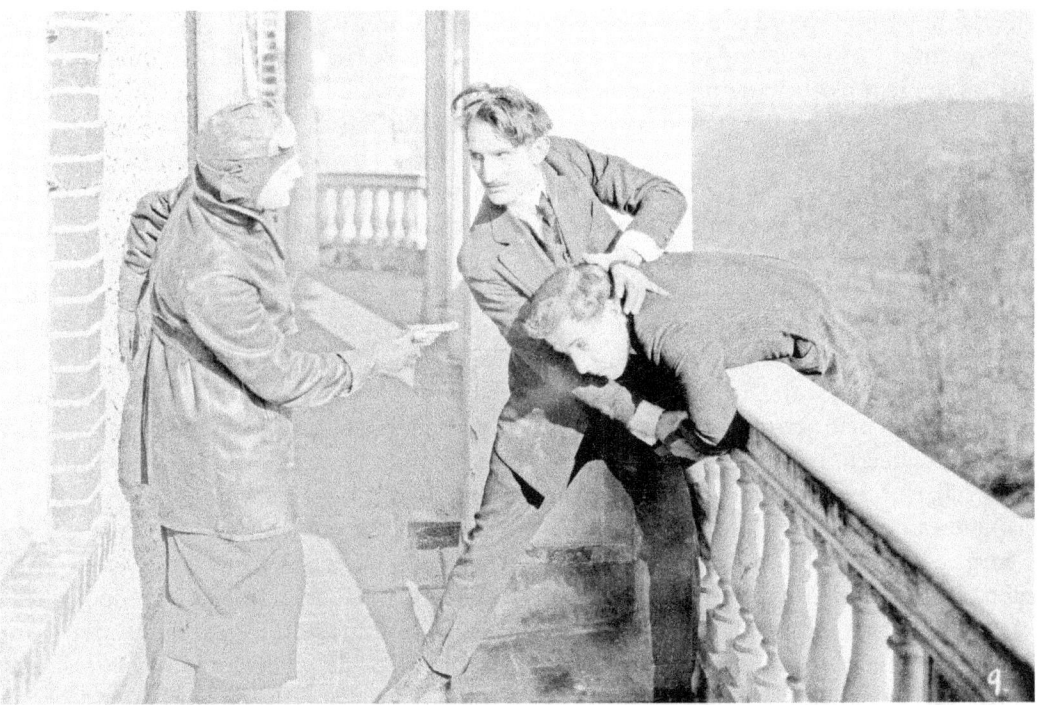

**Tharen (Peggy Shanor) advises Murdock (Joe Cuny) to hang on tight to George (George B. Seitz), although maybe not by the throat.**

more than anticipated the incredible speeds attainable by Dr. Santro's miraculous biplane. Feature-wise, though, the U.S.—and the world—would have to wait for Germany's *Algol* (1920), which marked the movies's boldly admitting that the universe extended beyond our Moon. Albeit the bulk of the film's narrative takes place on Earth, the notion (and depiction) of an interstellar junket by the inhabitant of a far-off star was downright revolutionary. Until *Algol*'s release, fantasy/science-fiction/horror films had been pretty much content to deal with witchcraft, hypnotism, adaptations of classical myths and literature, and tales of encounters with Death (in any of its myriad forms). Even within the increasingly popular German "slant" on the genre—hereto associated in the main with somnambulists and wide-eyed clay monsters—the Emil Jannings/Käthe Haack picture was regarded as a marked departure.

May we therefore infer that Pathé put the skids to Leon Smith's original Martian accents because of our national indifference to anything outside of Earth's atmosphere?

Not as easily as we would like. While *The Sky Ranger* was in production, rival studio Metro Pictures was engaged in bringing a six-reel feature, *A Message from Mars*, to the screen. Even then, at the outset of what would come to be called the Roaring Twenties, Metro would hardly have bankrolled a scenario with little box-office potential, and *Mars* had already been staged on both sides of the Atlantic *and* filmed twice, early on (c. 1902–1904) in New Zealand, and later (in 1913) in England.[5] Note: neither of the cinematic renditions had been American in origin. Metro's feature (released on April 11, 1921, just weeks before Chapter One of *The Sky Ranger* hit screens "officially") was *not* a critical success, although none of the lukewarm prose it received centered on the involvement of the Red Planet. Thus, we pause to note that, while two decades of silent fantasy film would come and go with zero mention of the outer reaches of the Earth's domain by the cinematic branch of the U.S. of A, 1921 hit the jackpot twice.[6]

Ah, well...

Thanks to the incredible efforts of our colleague—noted science fiction film historian and writer Steve Joyce—we were able to view the 10-chapter version of *The Sky Ranger* that had been released in France (as *Les Rôdeurs de l'Air*) and archived in the Cinémathèque Royale de Belgique. The totally silent print contains some wildly choreographed brawls (the very essence of the serial, *n'est-ce pas?*), unlikely-if-mundane sequences (when he initially meets June, George climbs out of the driver's seat of his car to walk alongside her; the now-driverless car accompanies the young couple as they amble down the road), and typical, early '20s movie-style overacting.

As one might expect, the abbreviated print takes quite a few (albeit relatively minor) departures from the Library of Congress summary. For example, we see Murdock pulling a gun on Prof. Elliott (in the first half of the first reel!), only to be socked by George Rockwell (who has vaulted over a wall) and then led off the premises by "Auguste," the head gardener who is also packing heat. June doesn't "throw" George a piece of paper; it is conveniently wafted out the window by the draft created when she opens the office door. And Murdock's fistfight with our hero apparently takes place in George's skyscraper "bungalow," so we're a bit disconcerted as to how George got home so fast (does he have a plane of some sort that was eliminated in the bowdlerizing of the 15-chapter serial?) or how Murdock managed to follow him. (George had fled the Elliott estate in his coupe; Murdock had run off—on foot, *naturellement*—in the opposite direction.) Still, after knocking Murdock into the next room three or four times, George watches the villain flee across the grass below from his window; unless that's a pretty awesome skyscraper bungalow, George has other digs in the neighborhood, as well. If nothing else, this is typical, early '20s movie-style indifference.

Tharen and Santro pilot their skyship in by looking out the *side* windows of the aircraft, which has no apparent cockpit; it's just a lengthy, cylindrical passageway. We note instantly that we are dealing with a biplane—no late-chapter summary surprises here—and one without glass in its windows, either. Santro—like Murdock, mustachioed—and Tharen are accoutered in '20's pilot attire: leather jackets and head gear with goggles (which they used not, while at the controls of the plane). They land at Murdock's place (in a "New York suburb," the French title informs us), where Santro reminds him "You forgot that I am a scientist. I have invented the fastest and quietest airplane in the world," and hands him a copy of a Buenos Aires newspaper—dated that very day—as proof.

The extant film continues on in this fashion: in the spirit of the summary, if not in every fact. Some of the French titles are risible, like the reference to the narrow-bodied biplane as "l'avion géant," the giant aircraft; many moments border on slapstick comedy, as the various instances in which George (and mostly everyone else, to tell the truth) is made to indulge in the sort of physically improbable movements that—at that point in time—hearkened *sideways* to Mack Sennett et al. (In their first-reel brawl, George and Murdock are punched and hurl through doorways like acrobats from Le Cirque du Soleil.) Come chapter two of the French variation, and Santro, having climbed through a window into Elliott's office, proceeds to sting both George and June with a ring containing a substance that saps their wills "pour la seconde fois," for the *second* time. Thereafter, they are spirited away to the desert, to fend for themselves among "une peuplade féroce du Thibet," a ferocious Tibetan tribe! Abandon all hope, ye who enter here.

*Les Rôdeurs de l'Air* begins—as did its English-language sire—with that man-clinging-to-the-globe vignette that we didn't much understand. The several feet of 35mm footage it probably took to reveal all this as a dream is missing from the French print, which abounds in jump cuts and has more than a couple of scene changes effected without a great deal of rhyme or reason. All the action took place happened the way the LoC document said, more or less, save that the back-and-forths with respect to the safety of the hero or the heroine or the plans or the whatever were as tedious when seen onscreen as they were when read on paper.

The footage of George and June's misadventures with the Tibetan hordes follows the summary quite faithfully, albeit we were a bit surprised to see that Santro and Tharen had changed from their flying gear into white gowns, caps and capes; we could only ask, *Pourquoi*? Devoting basically two and a half of the ten chapters in this abbreviated edition of *Ranger* to the mob violence in Asia struck us as being a sin of commission, as the plot is ultimately furthered not a whit. While the young Americans are busy escaping through the desert and fighting in the sheepherder's hut, we learn that Santro has flown back to Elliott's in the interim and—again in his pilot's garb—has just landed *back* in Tibet to inform Tharen that Elliott agreed to swap the secret of his light for his daughter. The chapter ends as written, although June's clinging to the plane appears to be solely her fault for hanging back while the others board.

Santro drops George and June at the Elliott estate and waits "prudently" at a distance. The professor doesn't so much as embrace the daughter who nearly died—these coldly scientific types—and the action picks up per Chapter Six, above. (It is worth noting that Santro is now in a suit, sporting a fedora; where in that "avion géant" does the man stow his wardrobe?) From this point—just as the action in most chapterplays begins to get "serious"—we have numerous instances of "farce comedy," as Murdock ducks the posse of watchmen surrounding him, Santro escapes and overpowers George on the rooftop, June flees, George and/or June are captured, then they escape, there are flames everywhere, more rooftops, the super-plane swoops, hovers, etc., etc. Considering that the principals are constantly grappling with each other, an awful lot of handwritten notes—some even a tad sarcastic—are exchanged. Every so often, Tharen pops up to reassure either George or June (or herself) that her heart is in the right place, despite all appearances to the contrary.

We weren't able to locate any contemporary Parisian critiques, but it appears that the science-fiction angles on which the chap-

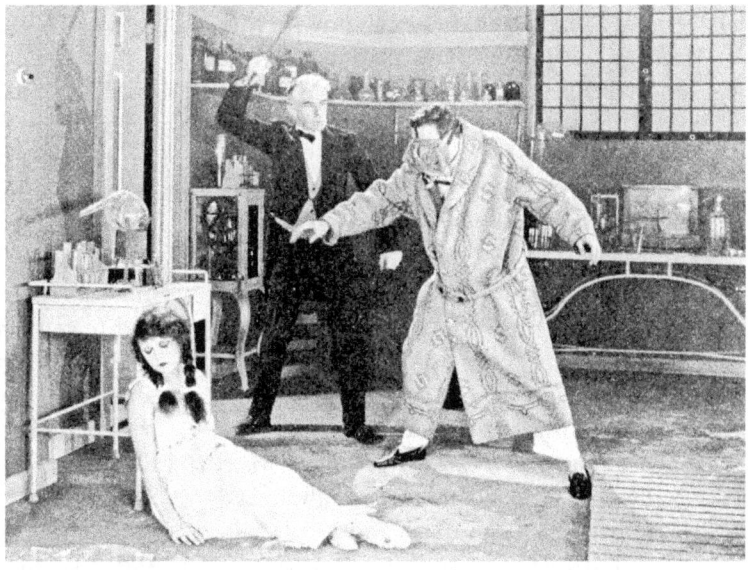

**The butler (Thomas Goodwin) about to take a swing at the man he believes to be Murdock, but who is really George. June, overcome by fumes, lounges in the lower left-hand corner.**

terplay turned were viewed by a good number of Americans as being as ludicrous as the farce comedy elements. This representative selection of comments from the *Exhibitors Herald* seem to show that the willful suspension of disbelief only carried the serial so far:

> It's a joke. Things very impossible. People going out of the theatre to wait for the feature, as they were disgusted with it. Starts good up to third episode, but after they discover the airplane, they go to Russia and South America in 10 minutes [Morgan Theatre, Henryetta, OK; September 24, 1921].

> First two episodes good, but the third was so poor fell flat from that on. They don't seem to like this one. Have shown 10 chapters and it's the first serial we ever ran that business fell off instead of picking up [Dreamland Theatre, Arcanum, OH; September 17, 1921].

Still, balance was achieved via movie theater owners's opinions such as "Very good serial. Liked by all my patrons" (Hippodrome Theater, Niagara Falls, NY; October 29, 1921), and "Started well, but is very slow. On seventh episode, improving. No kicks. Not many compliments" (Itasca Theater, Alice, TX; September 10, 1921). Please note: that's not many *compliments*, not *complaints*.

Santro was played by New Yorker Harry Semels, a veteran character actor with hundreds of credits (the majority of which were "uncredits"), including the 1933 end-of-the-world thriller *Deluge*; the 1934 romantic-comedy classic *It Happened One Night* (Gable & Colbert!); and 1939's *Swiss Miss* (with Laurel and Hardy). He interacted (usually without onscreen mention) with Garbo (*Ninotchka*, 1939) and Bogey (*They Drive by Night*, 1940); met Nick and Nora Charles (*Shadow of the Thin Man*, 1941) and Lord Greystoke (*Tarzan's New York Adventure*, 1942); and was confounded by The Three Stooges (*Three Little Beers*, 1935; *Movie Maniacs*, 1936; others). One of his bonafide credited appearances was in yet another serial—the still lost *The House Without a Key* (see essay); sometimes you just can't win. Semels, who stood 5'9" in his stocking feet, died with his boots on in 1946.

Peggy Shanor (Tharen) debuted in George B. Seitz's serial *The House of Hate* (1918), and the more than half of her film credits (she had but seven) were in silent chapterplays; between the two Seitz productions were 1919's *The Lurking Peril* and 1920's *The Mystery Mind*. The young actress made Tharen's ongoing crisis of conscience credible, even though the savvy audience knew there was no future for her with George Rockwell. The Virginia native died—too soon—in New York in mid-1935; she was 38 years old.

Frank Redman (Professor Elliott) was pretty much a Seitz regular, showing up, as he did, in eight of his nine credited appearances for George B. Apart from the serial under discussion, Redman's most interesting picture (to us) may have been 1919's *The Lighting Raider*, a Seitz chapterplay featuring Warner Oland and Boris Karloff. In *Ranger*, Redman's inventive professor is the least emotive in the cast, and one has to wonder whether it was Seitz's direction—and not Redman's natural inclination—to greet his daughter, June, so dispassionately mere hours after her escaping death at the hands of Tibetan sheepherders.

June Caprice was born Helen Lawson in Massachusetts in late 1895, and she took her nom du film from and just in time for her first role—she was Fox's *Caprice of the Mountains* in 1916—and while she was at Fox she worked for (and later married) studio director Harry F. Millarde. Caprice's film career wasn't much more extensive (she had fewer than two-dozen screen appearances) or lengthy (she called it quits in 1921) than Peggy Shanor's; in fact, *The Sky Ranger* was her last movie. June Caprice's June Elliott was a fairly typical silent B-film heroine, and not a typical silent serial heroine; the fault, though, is that of the uncredited and still unknown screenwriter.

Producer, director, and romantic lead George Brackett Seitz—like June Caprice, from Massachusetts—was a cinematic house afire. He started his lengthy career directing a number of serials starring Pearl White (1914's *The Exploits of Elaine* was the first) and wrapped by directing the Hardy family series (*Andy Hardy's Blonde Trouble* was last) forty years later. Another "four-tool" movie man (director, producer, writer, actor), he didn't appear onscreen after *The Sky Ranger*, but his presence in that one (and in nine other films, all of which featured either Miss White, Harry Semels, or both) is fairly effective, even if his George Rockwell gets as good as he gives.

We've left Spencer Gordon Bennet until last for two reasons: (1) we have no idea what role he played in *The Sky Ranger* and therefore could not pick him out of the sundry good and bad guys in *Les Rôdeurs de l'Air* for comment; and (2) Bennet was far more often in the director's chair than he was in front of the camera, and we're all enormously grateful to him for such popular *sound* serials as *G-Men vs. the Black Dragon* (1943), *Zorro's Black Whip* (1944), *The Purple Monster Strikes* (1945), *Daughter of Don Q* (1946), *Blackhawk* (1952), and a host of others. A four-tool veteran (like George Seitz), Bennet began his very brief acting career in a Pearl White serial (1914's *The Perils of Pauline*) and ended it in a serial—1925's *Sunken Silver*, which he also co-directed with Seitz. He helmed a number of silent chapterplays as well, like 1925's *The Green Archer* ... and 1926's *The House Without a Key*, and there's more on the wonderful Mr. Bennet in our chapter on that film.

With a few classy exteriors (Prof. Elliott's manse is quite impressive) offset by cheap-and-cheesy-to-serviceable interiors, *The Sky Ranger* must have indeed been the mixed bag the *Exhibitors Herald* comments indicated. From the surviving French print, we can attest to there being plenty of action, but—as was pretty much the norm for serials—most of this consisted in variations on the totally unrestrained fistfight. A number of decent props may be espied—the lower part of Elliott's telescope is quite realistic looking—and the cheek of asserting that Santro's biplane can make it from Tibet to New York and back based on Harry Semels's mouthing of words to that effect is likewise impressive. Still, the serial itself is as much a time machine as is *Back to the Future*—so celebrated October last—or as is *Just Imagine*, celebrated elsewhere in this volume.

# First Looks: *Das grinsende Gesicht*; *Die Insel der Verschollenen*

*Das grinsende Gesicht* (*The Grinning Face*)—Olympic-Film—October 22, 1920 (Trade preview in Vienna)—March 18, 1921 (general release) 6 acts (2,200 meters) **Cast: Prologue:** Joseph Moser as King James II; Robert Valaity as Lord Linäus Clancharlie; Suzanne Osten as Lady Dirry-Moor; Eugene Jensen as Barkilphedro; Arpad Kramer as Dr. Geradus; Fritz Strassny as Dr. Hardquardonne; Franz Weißmüller as Ursus **Main Drama:** Anna Kallina as Queen Anne; Nora Gregor as Duchess Josianne; Jimmy Court as Lord David Dirry-Moir; Armin Seydelmann as Lord Boilingborke; Franz Höbling as Gwynplaine; Lucienne Delacroix as Dea

**Credits:** *Director*: Julius Herzka; *Screenplay*: Louis Nerz; *Director of Photography*: Eduard Hoesch; *Production Design*: Ladislaus Tuszinsky; *Based on the 1869 novel*, **L'Homme qui rit** *by* Victor Hugo

*Die Insel der Verschollenen* (*Island of the Lost*)—Corona Film—November 21, 1921—1,739 meters **Cast:** Alf Blütecher as Robert Marston; Tronier Funder as Dr. Ted Fowlen; Erich Kaiser-Titz as Professor McClelland; Hans Behrendt as Pat Quickly, buyer of monsters for Barnum and Bailey; Hanni Weisse as Jane Crawford; Ludmila Hall as Evelyn Wilkinson; Umberto Guarracino Cimaste as the Product of the Professor's experiments; Nien Tso Ling as Fung-Lu; Desdemona Schlichting as the Sole native survivor; Fritz Beckmann as Paid patient; Herman Picha as Paid patient; Julius Brandt as Dixon, reporter for *The Daily Murder*; with Louis Brody, Leo Bell

**Credits:** *Director*: Urban Gad; *Screenplay*: Bobby E. Lüthge and Hans Behrendt; *Director of Photography*: Willy Hameister; *Production Design*: Robert A. Dietrich

The problem with watching the Lon Chaney *Hunchback of Notre Dame* nowadays is that it's hard not to compare it with the Charles Laughton version. The latter is vastly superior in every way (except, arguably, for the title performance). The great set pieces of Victor Hugo's novel—the Feast of Fools, the kidnapping of Esmeralda, the pillory, Quasimodo's rescue of Esmeralda from the gallows, the siege of Notre Dame—are treated magnificently in the 1939 film; the comparable scenes in the 1923 film don't begin to measure up. Of course if there was no Laughton/William Dieterle film—and all we had for comparison was the lousy Anthony Quinn version—then the Chaney *Hunchback* might not look so weak after all, and it probably would be judged more on its own merits and not in light of another production.

We have a similar reaction watching *Das grinsende Gesicht*, the first feature-film version of another Hugo novel, *L'Homme qui rit*, and *Die Insel der Verschollenen*, a very free adaptation of H. G. Wells's *The Island of Dr. Moreau*. The 1928 version of *The Man Who Laughs* is one of the great films of the late Silent Era, and *Island of Lost Souls* is a classic from the Golden Age of '30s horror. The earlier versions may have been first, but they are far from the best. *Das grinsende Gesicht* is at least an earnest and faithful—though somewhat uninspired—adaptation of Hugo, while *Die Insel* might be described—anachronistically—as a "B" horror film.

*Das grinsende Gesicht* was produced by

a small company, Olympic-Film, an Austrian concern. The film industry in Austria was very slow to develop, but it was given something of a boost by the Great War since the foreign competition was cut out and more homegrown product was necessary. Nevertheless, the best and brightest members of Austria's *Filmwelt* inevitably migrated to Berlin, attracted by the prestige of companies like Ufa and far bigger budgets. While Austria may have produced nothing comparable to German masterpieces of horror like *Nosferatu* or *Caligari*, the country displayed an interest in the macabre from the very first. The oldest surviving Austrian drama is the 1911 ghost story *Der Müller und sein Kind* (*The Miller and His Child*), but this was preceded, a year earlier, by another supernatural tale, *Die Ahnfrau* (*The Ancestress*; its 1919 remake is still extant). During the 1910s, Austria churned out no fewer than three versions of *Trilby*, *Hoffmans Erzählungen* (*Hoffmann's Tales*), the very bizarre 1918 *Der Mandarin* (in which the demonic title character turns into the head of a mental institution where the hero is incarcerated), and 1919's *Lilith und Ly* (script by Austrian born Fritz Lang), wherein a statue of a beautiful woman, brought to life by magic, becomes a vampire.

Olympic-Film's first production, *Die arge Nonn* (*The Evil Nun*), was very much in the horror vein and was based on a story by Karl Strobl (whose novel *Eleagabal Kuperus* was adapted for the 1920 Conrad Veidt/Paul Wegener film *Nachtgestalten*, which was directed by Austrian Richard Oswald). According to *Paimann's Film List*,[1] this early bit of nunsploitation—which ran into trouble with the censors—had a decidedly macabre plot:

> Master builder Anders is the head of a construction team working on the grounds of an ancient convent. Along with historian Dr. Holzbock, he

 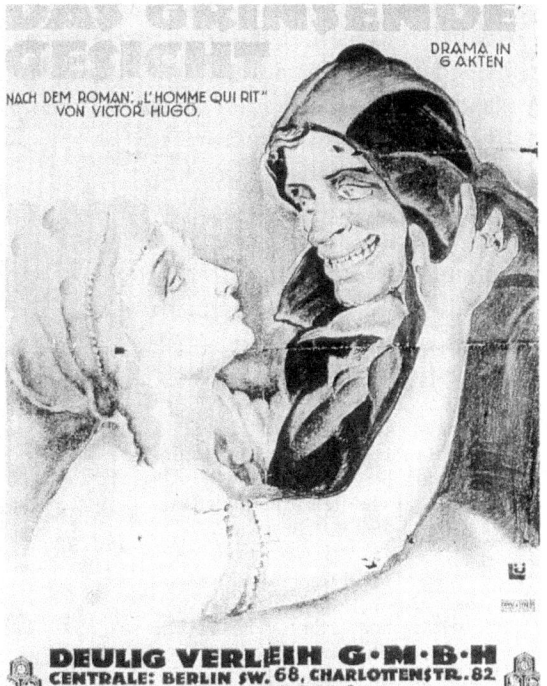

**Poster art for *Das grinsende Gesicht*. While the scene on the right certainly reflects the film, the one on the left does not.**

discovers an old chronicle of the convent's history. The chronicle describes the excessive lifestyle of the nuns, especially Sister Agathe, referred to as "die arge Nonne." They find an old map which leads them to the tomb of Sister Agathe. Anders begins to have strange visions. Eventually he goes mad and kills his wife, believing she has become Sister Agathe.

*Paimann's* felt the film was "very good."

*Paimann's* did not, however, get to review Olympic's next production, *Das Haupt der Medusa* (*The Head of Medusa*)—directed by Franz Höbling (who would go on to star as Gwynplaine in *Das grinsende Gesicht*)—as the film was banned by both Austria and Germany and was not even given a trade showing. Given that title, we presume it was a fantastic tale of some sort, but we have no information on the plot or on what could have so offended the censors. The picture was resubmitted to the German censors in 1921 and passed (though for adults only), but never seems to have played back in Austria.

*Das grinsende Gesicht* did not run afoul of *der Zensor* (though the picture *was* classified as only for adults), but of course it had a respectable literary source.[2] While the film follows the structure of the book—gradually revealing the title character's history in flashbacks—it does differ on a couple of plot points, and some changes were obviously made to accommodate the film's modest budget.

> The movie begins with a very grim prologue that introduces the comprachicos, a band of villains who buy children from poor families and then disfigure them so they can be displayed in fairs as freaks. Two of the scoundrels are seen negotiating with a poverty-stricken family for their baby. The older children are bribed with nice clothes, while the father, already tipsy, is given more money for alcohol. Only the horrified mother resists, but she is helpless to prevent the comprachicos from seizing her infant.

We then cut to Lord Linäus Clancharlie and his little boy, Fermain. Linäus is dying, but he has taken care to provide for the son who will inherit his father's title and lands. This does not sit well with Lady Dirry-Moore, Linäus's mistress, who has a child, David, by Linäus, and who wants him to inherit the estate. After Liänus's death, she enlists the aid of the schemer, Barkilphedro, to help bring this about. Barkilphedro, wearing a mask, visits the den of the comprachicos and makes a deal with one of their leaders, Dr. Geradus: Fermain is to disappear, but not be killed. Under cover of night, several comprachicos enters Linäus's house, tie up Fermain's nanny, and kidnap the boy [some nice shadow play in this sequence]. Fermain is spirited off to the house of Dr. Hardquardonne, chief "surgeon" for the gang—his quarters are lit and set like an alchemist's lair—where, fondling his victim, the evil doctor chortles, "I will give him a laughing face, an eternal laughing face! Laugh, little cat, laugh! Laugh forever!" Lady Dirry-Moore reports Fermain's abduction to King James II who declares that the boy must be found; however, after eight years, there is no sign of Fermain, so the king declares that, on the assumption that Fermain is dead, David Dirry-Moore shall inherit instead. [This is all a bit different from the novel wherein it is King James who has the boy disfigured in revenge for Linäus having defied him. Barkilphedro is a self-serving social climber at Queen's Anne's court in the book, but he has nothing to do with Fermain's disappearance. Interestingly enough, the 1928 film also turned Barkilphedro into the major villain.]

King James decides to outlaw the comprachicos,

**The disfigured boy (renamed Gwynplaine) and the blind baby girl find refuge with the philosophical mountebank Ursus (Franz Weißmüller).**

and Dr. Hardquadonne is subsequently arrested. The disfigured Fermain, now renamed Gwynplaine, is in the custody of Dr. Geradus, who flees along with a companion. The latter wants to kill Gwynplaine, but instead the two merely abandon the boy. Making his way through the mountains, Gwynplaine stumbles upon a sick woman and her infant daughter. The mother dies, and Gwynplaine takes the little girl with him. They both end up at the wagon of the mountebank, Ursus, who lives there with his pet, a wolf named Romo [Homo in the book]. Ursus, who's something of a philosopher and a kind of stand-in for the author, discovers that the girl is blind. He takes in both refugees and names the girl Dea. [This is actually shown later in the film when Gwynplaine gets engaged to Dea.]

[The 1928 film, with its generous budget, follows the book more closely for the following scenes: During a fierce storm, the comprachicos board a ship to escape, and the abandoned Gwynplaine has to trudge alone through a blizzard, when he encounters a corpse hanging from a gibbet before he runs across Dea and her mother [who's already dead]. These are powerful scenes, splendidly directed by Paul Leni, and the comparable sequence in the 1921 film—no ship, no storm, no blizzard, no hanging man—is threadbare by comparison. Again, the 1921 picture was not funded lavishly; crowd scenes are small, interior sets are no more than serviceable, and exteriors like the Tower and the Queen's palace are never fully shown. It is surprising, given the number of castles in Austria, that the director didn't press one of them into service for an exterior. The costumes, however, are quite imaginative though occasionally a little bizarre.]

Some years pass. Lord David Dirry-Moore is engaged to the haughty duchess, Josianne. Barkilphedro has risen to a prominent position in Queen Anne's court [Queen Anne, usually depicted as being horse-faced, is enacted by the *Burgtheater*'s lovely Anna Kallina]. The Queen and her entourage go on an excursion not far from where Ursus and his little company are putting on a show, in which Gwynplaine's grin, carved on his face by Dr. Hardquadonne, is the main attraction. Dea and Gwynplaine are in love, but Gwynplaine laments his disfigurement, although Dea tells him he is beautiful in her [sightless] eyes. Dea is accosted by one of the Queen's nobles who makes a pass at her. When Gwynplaine intervenes, the noble is too amused by his appearance to take offense. Gwynplaine asks Dea to marry him and she joyfully assents. Ursus tells the couple they will need money to marry, but the show will soon be in London where they expect to make a good profit.

Duchess Josianne complains to David that she is bored; even her black jester [played by a child] can't amuse her. David and his fellow nobles are also in need of distraction, and they all make their way to the fairgrounds where Ursus's show has just opened. The skit consists of Gwynplaine, decked out in a wig and costume, battling the forces of chaos, represented by Ursus in a bearskin. Josianne is both repelled and attracted by Gwynplaine's grotesque features, and even later, back home, she can't get the sight of him out her mind [via double exposure] and decides to send him a note. Meanwhile, David and his friends have gone to an inn to amuse themselves further. One of the tavern wenches reads David's palm and delivers a cryptic prediction: "Your destiny and fate will emerge from a bottle."

Sure enough, some fishermen at sea find a sealed bottle with a message inside and bring it to their admiral, who is so startled by the contents of the manuscript that he immediately goes to see the queen; it turns out to be a confession by Dr. Geradus. We cut and see Geradus and his companion struggling to survive in the wilderness. They empty a flask of wine and then Geradus seals a note in it [according to a title card, they are near Loch Lomond, though no water is shown]. The manuscript reveals Gwynplaine is of noble birth and that he is the rightful heir to Linäus Clancharlie. As Barkilphedro is named as a co-conspirator, the Queen has the discomfited courtier arrested and sent to the Tower.

Meanwhile, Gwynplaine receives Josianne's note in which she bids him come to her even though he is a monster and a nobody, while she is beautiful and a duchess [tact is obviously not her strong point; the wording of the note is right out of the novel]. Josianne's servant blindfolds Gwynplaine and conducts him to the Duchess's residence. Dea is both puzzled and hurt by Gwynplaine's absence. The Duchess seduces Gwynplaine and then sends him back home where Dea appears to be disappointed in him [though why exactly isn't clear, since she doesn't know about the note].

Soldiers arrive at Ursus's wagon and take the startled Gwynplaine away. Frantic with worry, Ursus follows them and sees Gwynplaine taken to the Tower where Barkilphedro has been tortured for days. Roped up on the dungeon floor, Bark-

The adult Gwynplaine (Franz Höbling) in costume for Ursus's show.

ilphedro confesses. When he sees Gwynplaine he says, "That's him" and dies. Gwynplaine, desperately protesting that he is only a poor clown and doesn't even know the man, is thunderstruck when he hears what has happened and that he is the heir to the manor. The body of Barkilphedro is put in a coffin and carried out. Ursus mistakenly thinks that it is Gwynplaine in the coffin and follows the soldiers who put him in an unmarked grave. The distraught Ursus brings the bad news to Dea who is overcome. Romo, however, continues to sniff around the Tower looking for Gwynplaine.

The Queen declares that Gwynplaine shall marry Josianne, and that he is to take his place in Parliament. Dressed in robes and without the traditional wig, Gwynplaine covers his grin with a handkerchief and is brought to Parliament [which has an oddly Expressionistic look] where the other lords immediately recognize him. His speech asking for justice for the poor is ridiculed, and the nobles burst into laughter. Only David is moved and, after the other lords have left, he embraces Gwynplaine and declares he has "spoken like a man."

Josianne is shocked to discover the identity of her new bridegroom, and when Gwynplaine arrives at her residence, she says she hates him, calls him a clown and a donkey, and angrily orders him to leave. Gwynplaine responds that Josianne is more wench than duchess and then departs.

Josianne convinces the Queen to dissolve her engagement to the new Lord Clancharlie, but David is disillusioned with Josianne and doesn't particularly want her back. In his palatial residence, Gwynplaine angrily glowers at his deformed countenance in the mirror and then decides he belongs back in the sideshow. He renounces his title and position in favor of David and, with Romo at his side, heads for the fairgrounds.

Dea is dying, but, as she expires, she declares to Ursus: "I can see, Father! For the first time I can see the sky." Gwynplaine arrives too late to share her last moments. As Gwynplaine mourns his love, a crowd outside demands to see The Man Who Laughs. Gwynplaine goes to the stage and declares that both Lord Clancharlie and the clown Gwynplaine are dead. He then stabs himself and collapses before the audience.

**Dea (Lucienne Delacroix) has a presentment of evil but Romo the wolf remains unperturbed.**

In the novel, Gwynplaine does see Dea just before she dies and afterwards drowns himself. In the picture, the manner of his death jibes perfectly with his being a tragic clown who makes everyone laugh despite his own suffering; however, unlike Pagliaccio, he can't take off his clown make-up. The 1928 film, of course, has both a happy resolution and an exciting and satisfying finale wherein Gwynplaine, with the help of the crowds and his actor friends, escapes the Queen's troops and is reunited with Dea, while the evil Barkilphedro meets his comeuppance at the fangs of Ursus's wolf. Some may find this climax too "Hollywood," yet one should remember that Hugo was not Zola, and his sympathy for the outsider and the outcast and his anger at injustice are—as in Charles Dickens—framed in terms of melodrama, and not realism. A contrived

**Josianne (Nora Gregor) is drawn to the clueless Gwynplaine (Franz Höbling) because of his deformity, not in spite of it.**

sad ending is really no more realistic than a contrived happy one.

Franz Höbling's Gwynplaine will not erase memories of Conrad Veidt in that role, but his is a respectable enough performance that's graced with a number of poignant moments. Höbling's grin is certainly less pronounced than was Jack Pierce's great treatment for Veidt, with his mouth only slightly distended and pulled back. The make-up in no way compares to the memorably grotesque "Joker look" one finds in the '28 version. Höbling, primarily a stage actor who occasionally turned to directing, did not have a particularly distinguished film career.

Gwynplaine finds a very different fate from the one he expected after being arrested by the Queen's guards and hauled off to a dungeon.

Nora Gregor (Josianne), on the other hand, made a number of important films, including Carl Dreyer's *Michael* (1924), *Impetuous Youth* (1926) with Conrad Veidt, the German-language version of *The Trial of Mary Dugan* (1931), and, most notably, Jean Renoir's 1939 *The Rules of the Game*, wherein her performance as Christine—the love object of a number of the other characters—was not without controversy. While she also scored triumphs on the stage and in opera, Gregor's personal life turned out to be far less happy. Although she married into Austrian nobility, she then had to flee into exile when her husband turned against the Nazis (his one-time allies, a quite ironic circumstance, given Gregor's Jewish parentage). With their lands confiscated, Gregor ended up in South America during the war. Impoverished and unhappy, she died (possibly a suicide) in Chile in 1949. In *Das grinsende Gesicht*, she isn't given the opportunities to be as wildly sexy as is Olga Baclanova in the '28 film (there is, for example, no nude bathing scene), but she does get Josianne's weirdly sado-masochistic attraction to Gwynplaine across in a few all-too-brief scenes.

Director Julius Herzka was a distinguished director of operas and plays in Vienna, but he helmed only a handful of films, most notably a 1923 adaptation of Shakespeare's *The Merchant of Venice* with Fritz Kortner as Shylock, and *Merista the Dancer*, featuring Nora Gregor as Lucrezia Borgia. Conversely, cinematographer Eduard Hoesch had a long career in the movies, and genre fans would be most interested in his work on *Drakula halála* (1921). Louis Nerz, scenarist for *Das grinsende Gesicht*, went on to do the script for what is probably Austria's most famous horror film, *Orlacs Hände* (*The Hands of Orlac*, 1924), with Conrad Veidt.

*Das grinsende Gesicht* seems to have done well and was widely circulated in Austria and Germany. *Paimann's* gave the film its highest rating.

Following the 1928 Universal version, filmmakers left *L'Homme qui rit* alone until a French-Italo production in 1966. Jean Sorel played the title role in a script that was a travesty of the original story, with the Gwynplaine character being renamed *Angelo* (!) and being cured of his macabre grin through surgery. Alas! He comes to an unhappy end anyway after becoming a henchman for the Borgias. Far closer to the mark was a 2012 French production with Marc-André Gardin as Gwynplaine and Jean Depardieu as a rather robust and randy Ursus. Though stylistically interesting, the film seemed closer to Tim Burton than to Victor Hugo, with Gwynplaine bearing a striking resemblance to Edward Scissorhands.

While *Das grinsende Gesicht* is very recognizably Victor Hugo, *Die Insel der Verschollenen* seems to want to disguise its source material, *The Island of Dr. Moreau*, perhaps to avoid paying royalties à la *Nosferatu* and *Der Januskopf*. The picture's premise—on a remote island, a sinister surgeon experimenting with animals has produced shambling monstrosities who turn on him in the end—is certainly taken from H.G. Wells's 1896 story; however, the titular isle is more Gilligan than Dr. Moreau and is full of clumsy humor and tepid romance. Sadly, the film is more akin to something like *King of the Zombies* than to any of the movie versions of *Moreau*.

> A newspaper reports a curious story: A note signed by Jane Crawford, giving the exact location of the island on which she's being held prisoner, has been found in a bottle floating at sea. The newspaper dismisses the note as a prank, but Robert Marston recognizes the handwriting as indeed being that of Jane Crawford, his fiancée who had disappeared from London three years earlier. Robert, now engaged to Evelyn, fears an awkward situation if Jane is rescued [Robert is quite the unlikeable jerk throughout the story]. His friend, Ted, an inept physician facing a scandal because of a silly publicity stunt involving the creation of an artificial man, is eager to leave town and suggests they go to the island to rescue Jane. The two caballeros board Robert's submarine [!] and head on out. Also on the sub is Robert's black valet.
>
> They find the island with little difficulty, and Ted and Robert go ashore only to discover a compound located in a marshland. Crossing a pond, Ted and Robert encounter the strange Dr. McClelland and his assistant, Fung-Lu. The doctor is conducting experiments with animals and has come to the island because it is bacteria-free; and, yes, Jane is indeed being held prisoner there. Ted and Robert free her, but they lose their guns in the process, and McClelland orders Fung-Lu to make sure they don't leave the island. In an ineptly directed scene, Fung-Lu blows up the submarine. Robert's valet, now sporting a top hat, somehow survives this and ends up on land. Jane tells her rescuers that she has no recollection of her abduction years before.
>
> We learn that Fung-Lu is an opium addict and that not only does McClelland keep him in thrall with the drug, but he also refuses to recognize Fung-Lu's contribution to their experiments. In addition, the doctor has a monstrous, animal-like servant who is actually more loyal to Fung-Lu than to him, and who sometimes tries to steal opium for Fung-Lu [!].
>
> Jane, Robert, and Ted begin a Robinson Crusoe–like existence. The entire native population of the island has been wiped out by plague except for one survivor: a woman, who is still there. She takes up with Robert's black valet who goes native, dons a grass skirt, and sticks a bone through his nose [typical of the film's juvenile humor]. When Jane learns of Robert's engagement, she switches her affections to Ted, at which point Robert becomes jealous and resentful. After failing to flag down a passing ship, Robert turns all his energies to building a raft.
>
> McClelland orders the monster-henchman to fire a tranquilizer dart at Jane and bring her to the compound. Jane collapses, but Ted gets to her before the slow-thinking Beast Man can complete his mission. Fearing Jane may have a fever, Ted goes to McClelland's compound to ask for quinine. At this point, McClelland reveals that he is the famous Dr. Thompson who had fled London years before. He has created monstrous animal-hybrids who are kept imprisoned in stalls, but his crowning creation is his artificial man who needs only a heart to become animate. Ted is horrified and flees the compound.
>
> Meanwhile, Robert has decided to leave on the raft and take the still unconscious Jane with him. Ted intervenes, the two former friends fight, and the Beast Man returns and carries Jane off. Robert knocks Ted out and goes after Jane, but the monster overpowers him, and thus both Jane and Robert become McClelland's prisoners.
>
> Meanwhile, Evelyn has tracked down the whereabouts of her fiancé and arrives on the island with Pat Quickly [described in the official credits, though not in the film, as a buyer of monsters for Barnum and Bailey]. Seeing the valet and his native girlfriend, Quickly immediately tries to sign them up for the circus. Evelyn learns from Ted that Robert has gone back to Jane, believing that he will never be able to see Evelyn again. Although tempted to leave then and there, Evelyn is curious to meet Jane and has the valet guide her to the compound.
>
> In the compound, McClelland reveals to Robert—tied up and behind bars—that he intends to use Jane's heart for the artificial man. He commands Fung-Lu to perform the operation, but his disloyal assistant is tired of the whole business and substitutes the heart of a tiger. [One might think that the great scientific genius, McClelland, would notice the difference between a human and animal heart. But, no.]
>
> The Beast Man then attacks the valet who stabs him to death. Evelyn, treading cautiously through the house of horrors in the compound, frees both

Robert and Jane. Meanwhile, the heart has been placed into the artificial man—McClelland proclaims "He's alive!" as the creature rises from the operating table—but McClelland at once realizes what has happened and angrily confronts Fung-Lu, who is too blissed out on opium to care. Evelyn sets the compound aflame and escapes with Robert and Jane. In the chaos, the monsters break their bonds and attack Dr. McClelland, and he and his creations perish together in the flames.

Ted and Robert—who resemble each other and who are both played by Danish actors—are certainly two of the most ineffectual heroes ever, even by horror-movie standards. It is the comic-relief valet who disposes of the main monster, and it is one of the heroines who comes to the rescue at the end, destroying the madman's lair as well. Evelyn and Jane should have headed back to civilization together and left their knuckle-headed lovers on the island to fend for themselves.

It's not likely H.G. Wells ever saw this version of his story, and, if he had, he probably would have disliked it even more than he did *Island of Lost Souls*. Aside from the animals-into-monsters angle, there are only a few very faint echoes of the original: at one point, McClelland threatens his monster servant with a whip and demands, "Who is your Lord?" That's literally the only reference to the cult that the beast men form around Moreau and his surgery, the House of Pain. Indeed, the monster in the movie identifies Fung-Lu as his master! While the novel gives Moreau a semi-alcoholic assistant, the film turns him into an opium addict, an admittedly interesting variation on the idea. And, as for the "artificial man," that steal from *Frankenstein* ends up being a cheat, what with all the build-up to his appearance and ... nothing.

*The Island of Dr. Moreau* and other works by H.G. Wells were published in Germany in the early 1900s, but failed to create much of a stir (Wells would become popular in The Fatherland, but only some years later). None of the reviewers who critiqued *Die Insel der Verschollenen* even recognized it as being taken from a Wells story; rather, the film reminded one critic of Maurice Renard's 1908 novel, *Le Docteur Lerne,* which concerned a mad scientist who—among other things—creates animal/human hybrids. Renard, better known for *The Hands of Orlac,* acknowledged his debt to *Island of Dr. Moreau* in his *Lerne* dedication.[3]

Some sources say that *Le Docteur Lerne* was also the basis for the 1913 French two-reeler *L'Île d'épouvante* (*Island of Terror*) which concerned a mad doctor doing some kind of (unspecified) surgical experiments on a remote island and the shipwrecked journalist who becomes his intended victim. Renard's book, however, takes place at a country chateau and not on an island, which suggests that *Moreau* certainly was one influence on this lost film. Available synopses do not mention any beast men (though the doctor's assistants are referred to as "half-wits"), but the film ends with the doctor and his lab going up in flames (according to one source, this is the doctor's

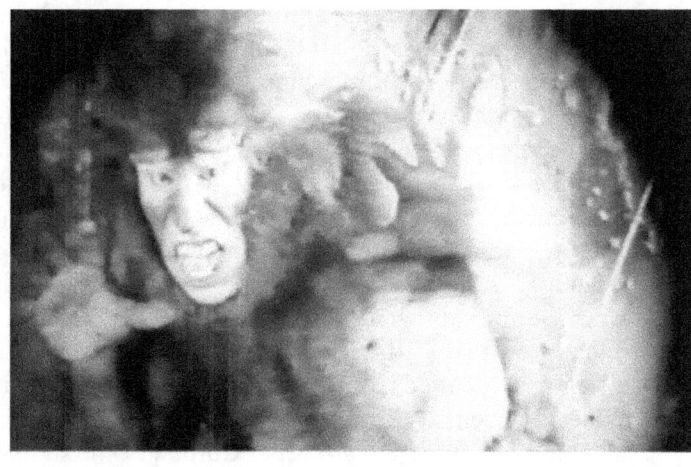

**The snarling Beast Man. The make-up artist for the film is not credited.**

own doing; in another, it's the work of his assistants after they turn on him). The journalist escapes on a raft in the company of the crazed surgeon's estranged wife. *L'Île d'épouvante* received wide distribution in a number of countries (including Germany and the United States), so it's at least possible the makers of *Die Insel der Verschollenen* had given it a look and later decided to come up with their own unauthorized version of *Lerne* and *Moreau*. After all, stealing from two sources is as easy as stealing from one, and it helps muddy the waters if anyone complains.

It's puzzling that director Urban Gad and his scenarists, Hans Behrendt and Bobby E. Lüthge—the three often worked together as a team—would be drawn to a horror subject in the first place. Gad rose to fame with the movies he made with his wife, Asta Nielsen, perhaps the world's first international film superstar. After his divorce from Nielsen in 1915, Gad still did some quite respectable work (although not to the same acclaim), but certainly nothing even remotely in the macabre vein, and the same is true of Lüthge and Behrendt (the latter also has the small role of Pat Quickly in *Insel*). Perhaps what appealed to Gad were the romantic and comic possibilities of urbanites stranded on an island and forced to revert to nature (think *The Admirable Crichton*). The business about the mad doctor and his creations is little more than an excuse to get everyone on the island. The film becomes somewhat surreal at times, especially with the loopy comedy at the beginning and odd bits of business like the heroes traveling in a submarine. As far as the latter goes, was it meant as a joke giving a new use for submarines as recreational vehicles now that a stipulation of the Versailles Treaty banned Germany from making them? Of course it's possible that the sub was simply left over from an earlier Corona film, the sea melodrama *Der vergiftete Strom* (*The Poisoned Stream*).

While Gad and his writers may not have had any background in horror, the same is certainly not true of *Insel*'s set designer, Robert A. Dietrich, and cameraman, Willy Hameister. Dietrich was the production designer for Paul Wegener's *The Student of Prague* and the serial *Homunculus* (another tale of an artificial man), while Hameister was the cameraman for *Caligari* and *Genuine*. Nonetheless, even though *Insel* was made while film Expressionism was at its height, neither settings nor photography show any Expressionist influence. The doctor's compound is strictly functional, and the photography of the marshy area around it is naturalistic and devoid of anything outré; compare that to the atmospheric and other worldly swamp settings of, say, *Fährmann Maria*. Also, McClelland's lab is barely glimpsed, and through some windows at that, although the tinting gives it a slightly creepy look, while the stalls the monsters are imprisoned in are strictly that—stalls that one might see in a barn—with no attempt made at distortion, albeit that would certainly be appropriate given the agony of the creatures.

McClelland's creations, though seen only briefly, are freakish enough to be unsettling. They really *do* seem like pathetic animals who have been subjected to cruel and crazy vivisection experiments (where's PETA when you need them?). In *Island of Lost Souls*, the monsters each tend to represent one animal (a dog-man, a pig-man, a goat-man, a panther-woman, etc.), but in *Insel* the creatures are a mixture of different animals (which is true both of *Moreau* and *Doctor Lerne*), among them, an ape with the head of a giant bird and some kind of walrus-fish combination. The more humanoid creatures of *Lost Souls* are pretty much represented in *Insel* by McClelland's monster-henchman, who can walk upright (though he sometimes goes about on all fours), can obey simple commands, and can even use a blowgun. Presumably, he is some kind of

Perhaps a walrus/ape hybrid? The mad doctor's monsters are seen only briefly toward the end of the film.

dog/ape-man (though he sports something like a lion's mane). Still, while the film seems to lean toward playing his behavior in a semi-humorous way, it's nice to watch him carrying the heroine away in the time-honored tradition of movie monsters since the earliest days of the cinema. This dog/ape-man with the lion's mane was played by Umberto Guarracino, the actor who portrayed the Creature in the lost 1921 Italian film *Il mostro di Frankenstein* in addition to having a couple of run-ins with Bartolomeo Pagano's Maciste in *Maciste in the Lion's Den* (1926; a circus film in which Guarracino played the bald-headed bad guy) and the totally crazy *Maciste in Hell* (1925; wherein he essayed the role of Pluto, King of the Underworld).

The performances in *Insel* are adequate. Erich Kaiser-Titz as McClelland resembles Irving Pichel with bushy eyebrows and seems more smug than maniacal. He *does* get off one good, sinister line (via title card, of course) when, observing the caged Robert, he remarks to Fung-Lu: "Do you not think the young man has wonderful eyes?"

Mention should be made of Louis Brody, who plays the valet. Brody, born M'bebe Mpessa in what is now Cameroon, came to Germany around 1915 and had a very conspicuous career in silent films. He can be seen in *Genuine* (where he plays the Malay), in Fritz Lang's *Destiny* (as the Moor), in *Armored Vault* (1926; wherein he played gangster Heinrich Georges's thuggish chauffeur), and in many others. Like Noble Johnson in Hollywood, Brody played Oriental parts as well. In the Sound Era, in addition to acting, he worked as a cabaret singer and a wrestler. He even continued to act under the Nazis, who gave him an exemption from the racial proscription laws that sent other German/Africans to concentration camps. Needless to say, the roles Brody was allowed to play were usually just stereotypes (though would he have fared much differently in Hollywood at that time?), and he even had a role in the infamous *Jud Süß* (1940).

A beautiful tinted copy of *Das grinsende Gesicht* (with Dutch titles) exists in the Austrian film archive, outside of which it is seldom seen. Chances of a DVD release are slim, though it's always possible that, should 1928's *The Man Who Laughs* ever get the Blu-ray treatment, its Austrian predecessor could be added as an extra. Something of the sort may have been intended for *Die Insel der Verschollen*. The film first came to public notice at the 2000 Berlin Film Festival (where the theme was artificial humans), and, years later, there was talk of adding it as an extra to the Criterion release of *Island of Lost Souls*. Nothing came of this, but a DVD of *Die Insel* was publicly screened several times and—not surprisingly—copies were made. While there's not likely to be an "official" DVD release, it was advertised for sale in the Dealer's Room of the last Cinefest (March 2015), with a still of Bela Lugosi from *Island of Lost Souls* on the cover. Those who bought the DVD expecting that the picture would be anything like the 1933 Paramount classic were in for a big surprise.

# The Monkey's Paw; Sweeney Todd

***The Monkey's Paw***—Artistic Films—February 1923—5 reels (5,194 feet[1]) **Cast**: Moore Marriott as Mr. White; Marie Ault as Mrs. White; Charles Ashton as Herbert White; Johnny Butt as Sergeant Tom Morris; Tom Coventry as the Engine Driver; A.B. Imeson as the Sailor; George Wynn as the Stranger; Montmorency as Tinker (the dog)
**Credits**: *Director*: Manning Hayes; *Script*: Lydia Hayward; *Producer*: George Redman; *Based on the eponymous short story by* W.W. Jacobs (1902)

***Sweeney Todd or The Demon Barber of Fleet Street***—QTS Productions—September 28, 1928—6 reels (6,167 feet) **Cast**: Moore Marriott as Sweeney Todd; Zoe Palmer as Johanna; Charles Ashton as Mark Ingestre; Judd Green as Simon Podge; Iris Darbyshire as Amelia Lovett; Philip Hewland as Ben Wagstaffe; Brian Glenny as Tobias Wragge; Harry Lorraine as Nick Todd; J. Blake as Sambo
**Credits**: *Director*: Walter West; *Producer*: Harry Rowson; *Scenario*: J. Bertram Brown; *Photography*: James Wilson; *Distributor*: Ideal Films; *Based on the play* **The String of Pearls** *by* George Dibdin Pitt (1847)

One of the most annoying "cheat" endings in film history is the *It's all been a dream* finale wherein the viewer discovers that nothing that has been seen on the screen actually happened in "real life," but was merely the product of the main character's unconscious or subconscious (we'll make an exception for *The Wizard of Oz*). In thrillers and horror films of yesteryear, the dream business was often a very lazy salvation for the writer who had painted his doomed characters into a corner and was in need of a *deus ex machina*. Even when the story—as depicted—was usually a by-the-numbers affair that didn't try to capture the disjointed, arbitrary, and/or impenetrable logic of real dreams, one was still expected to believe that it was all the product of someone's nap. Sometimes the device was used because it was assumed the audience would simply prefer a happy ending; other times it was utilized to avoid the demands of the Production Code. You couldn't get away with murder (or kill yourself), so films like *Woman in the Window* (1944), *The Strange Affair of Uncle Harry* (1945), and *Fear* (1946) were obliged to awaken their protagonists in the last few minutes and have them sigh in relief that all was still well. An ending like that wouldn't fly with today's audiences, but it's perhaps not so very different from what's become a *modern* movie cliché: the revelation that the main character is crazy and that the entire story has largely unfolded in his/her mind (cf. *American Psycho*, *Black Swan*). A major difference, of course, is that there's no happy resolution for these characters. *The Monkey's Paw* and *Sweeney Todd*—both hailing from England and based on tales originating in Old Blighty—employ the dream coda to tell their stories, although they do so in very different ways. Though horror as a film genre hadn't really come into its own in the Silent Era, American thrillers were full of evil hypnotists, old dark houses, fake ghosts, reincarnated lovers, spooky comedies based on stage plays, the occasional mad scientist, and a whole gallery of grotesques, courtesy of Lon Chaney. In Germany the shivers were even more full-blooded with films like *Nosferatu*, *Der Golem*, *Das Cabinet des Dr. Caligari*, and innumerable others. By comparison, in spite of its rich Gothic tradition, Britain's horror output during that period was pretty meager. There was the occasional ghost (*Dr. Trimball's Verdict*, 1913) or sinister mesmerist (*The Basilisk,* 1914), but most British filmmakers didn't find making their viewers shudder to be appealing, especially after two- and three-reelers were eclipsed by feature films. Producers with an inclination toward the macabre turned to established literary works for their inspiration, perhaps feeling that a distinguished pedigree would give their films a nobler purpose than merely trying to scare their audiences. Thus, we have film versions of *Trilby* (1914), *The Picture of Dorian Gray* (1916), *She* (1916 and 1925), *The Sorrows of Satan* (1917), and *The Suicide Club* (1914). Even though most of these are lost, one still suspects they were fairly timid as far as the horror element was concerned. This might not have been the case with *The Beetle* (1919), which was based on an 1897 novel that was briefly even more popular than another thriller published that same year, Bram Stoker's *Dracula*.[2] *The Beetle* features a shape-shifting sorcerer, a sinister cult that practices human sacrifice, and a quest for vengeance that follows its victim from Egypt to London. Nonetheless, although it had high praise for the acting, *Variety* (January 2, 1920) called the production "10th rate":

> The very things that grip in the novel fail to get anything but laughs in the film. For instance, the high priestess reincarnated in the form of a loathsome beetle is represented by a pantomime "prop" which does anything but inspire the horror hoped for but it will create more merriment than any screen comedy.

That kind of review may have helped convince the makers of *The Monkey's Paw* to keep their 1923 adaptation of the W.W. Jacobs tale more low-key. Jacobs was famous for humorous short stories about seafaring men and life in the dockyard district (where he had grown up), but he occasionally did a horror tale: "The Toll House" has a group of men agreeing to spend the night in a supposedly haunted house, and the Hitchcockian "The Well" concerns a murderer who is obliged to return to the scene of his crime to retrieve a jewel. "The Monkey's Paw," with its dire warning of "Be careful what you wish for," has certainly become his most famous story, has been adapted many times for stage, screen, television, and radio, and has been given dramatic readings by actors such as Christopher

**An unrecognizable Moore Marriott as the father in *The Monkey's Paw*.**

Lee and John Lithgow. Asked where he came up with the idea for "The Monkey's Paw," Jacobs replied that his study of a bearded old shoemaker in his small shop on the docks got his creative juices flowing. The story also owes an obvious debt to Robert Louis Stevenson's "The Bottle Imp," which likewise features an evil talisman that grants wishes but makes them come true in unexpected and cruel ways. In 1903, a year after it was published as part of a collection of Jacobs's short stories—published under the title *Lady on a Barge*—"The Monkey's Paw" was adapted for the stage by Louis N. Parker. A one-act play divided into three scenes— "The Storm," "Sunshine," and "Shadow"— the drama opened at the London Haymarket Theater and starred the great British actor Cyril Maude as Mr. White, and Lena Ashwell as Mrs. White. Still, it was another British actor, John Lawson, who took the play into his repertoire and toured with it throughout the United Kingdom and America. *Variety* (October 8, 1910) found the production disappointing when it reached New York in 1910 and thought that the climax— when the father and mother wish their dead son alive again and someone comes knocking at their door—lacked punch:

> Upon the mother flinging the door open, nothing is seen without. In England they say a ghostly figure appeared at the opening. This would not have been of aid here. To have gripped the house a breathed "Mother!" from the other side might have helped wonderfully but it is difficult to enforce the intensity of the moment if it does not come naturally. At any rate Americans are quite too skeptical about the uncanny and too practical for the supernatural.

There *is* a slight note of ambiguity in the story's climax: as no one actually sees the resurrected son, it's at least *possible* that a late-night caller is responsible for the knocking, though who it might be and how he could possibly skedaddle away so quickly down an empty path makes it very improbable. As in *Cat People* and *Curse of the Demon*, it's the supernatural that seems the most likely explanation for the strange events, even though the characters—and, perhaps, the reader—would prefer to believe otherwise. Arnold Daly, an actor usually associated with George Bernard Shaw's theatrical works, toured America with the play in 1911. At the same time, John Lawson—who had been shelling out $100 a week in royalties to perform the same play in the States— decided to take *Paw* and his other big success, *Only a Jew*, across the Pond and throughout the UK; he later moved his show to Australia. Lawson also starred in a three-reel version of *The Monkey's Paw* made in 1915 by Magnet Film Exchange and directed by Sidney Webber Northcote.[3] Ads for this lost film state that Lawson was supported by a "London company" without revealing any additional details. *Paw* became popular with small touring companies and local theaters, no doubt in part because it required only one simple set and a small cast; the original story has no scenes outside of the White's little cottage and only five characters. The climax, with the seeming return of the dead son, involved no elaborate special effects or intricate staging, but could be a real hair-raiser if done with panache. In 1922 Artistic Films began a series of movies based on W.W. Jacobs's stories, all scripted by Lydia Hayward and directed by H. Manning Hayes, and starring well-known character actors like Moore Marriott, Johnny Butt, Victor McLaglen, and Marie Ault. Most of the films were shorts, but *The Monkey's Paw* (1923) ran five reels and was likely given a more generous budget than the others. Changes made to the story apparently had to be approved by W.W. Jacobs, who gave his consent to what was—except for one thing—a reasonably faithful expansion of his brief tale. Our synopsis is courtesy of the Library of Congress:

> In a little country town live Mr. and Mrs. James White and their son Herbert. The only cloud in their sky is the mortgage on their cottage, and, now that Herbert has received a rise in salary, they hope to pay it off soon.
> One evening Sergeant-Major Morris, who has

just returned from India, has supper with them. The conversation veers to Hindu magic, and he relates the strange tale of the monkey's paw, which grants to its owner three wishes. But happy is he, continues the sergeant-major, who is content and asks for nothing, for the desires are granted by the monkey's paw in such a horrible way that the recipient would rather be without them.

Herbert persuades his father to ask the sergeant-major to sell him the monkey's paw. The old soldier at first refuses, but finally agrees to bring the charm with him next time he comes to see them. After he leaves, Herbert and his father play chess. It is Mr. White's move; the shadow of the monkey's paw shows on the board. There is a knock on the door. It is the sergeant-major with the monkey's paw. At Herbert's instigation, Mr. White wishes for the amount of money necessary to pay off the mortgage. He drops the monkey's paw with a shudder, insisting that, as he wished, it moved in his hand.

All that night and through the next morning Mr. and Mrs. White wait for the granting of the wish. By noon they have given up hope. There is a knock on the door and a stranger enters. He breaks the news to them as gently as possible that Herbert has been killed by an engine belonging to the company for which he works. The company disclaims all responsibility for the accident, but presents the old couple with the sum of money for which Mr. White had wished.

Weeks go by. The devoted mother is unreconciled to the death of her son. At last she has an idea: the monkey's paw shall restore him to her. She confides in her husband who is horrified, and tells her that poor Herbert's head had been horribly mutilated. She refuses, however, to listen to reason and forces the old man to wish that their son was alive again.

A wild storm is raging outside. Suddenly the latch on the cottage door moves up and down, and the thumps from the knocker reverberate through the room. Mrs. White rushes to draw back the heavy bar, and admit her dearly loved child. The bars stick, and Mr. White is too frightened to go to her assistance. He drops to his knees to pray and sees the monkey's paw. He grabs it up and wishes that his son may remain peacefully dead. The knocking stops. Mrs. White flings up the door. The wind howls and the rain hurls itself at her feet. No one is there!

Then just as one feels that the nerves can bear no more, the strain is relaxed and a thoroughly logical and satisfactory ending is achieved.

The logical—though not necessarily satisfactory—ending occurs when we discover than Mr. White had dozed off during his chess game with Herbert and had dreamt the whole horrible episode. When the sergeant-major subsequently knocks on the door with the monkey's paw, Mr. White wants nothing to do with it. This ending was not tacked on at the last moment, but was apparently planned from the beginning since it provides a rationale for the sergeant-major to make two visits to the Whites, and not just one, as in the story. The situation was summed up by the reviewer in the November 6, 1923, edition of *The Factory Gloucestershire Echo*:

> Mr. Jacobs's original story ends on a note of high tragedy but I doubt if many film audiences would like to see the thing end in such a grim fashion. The producers of the film were in a dilemma for undoubtedly this is the artistic way to end it. "But we didn't think any ordinary audience would stand it," a member of the firm told me, and so we made two endings, the Jacobs one and a happy one so that if any exhibitor did want to take a chance, he could do so. Personally, I thought the happy ending was splendid. That grim story of Jacobs always worried me and in the alteration I do not think the producer—whoever he is—has done the author any artistic violence.

The critic for the *Bohemian Burnley News* (January 12, 1924) concurred:

> Had the film stopped where the original story ends, cinema goers would have left the picture hall with a feeling that too much hair raising realism is bad for the nerves but this difficulty has been ingeniously surmounted and the final fade out is thoroughly justified by entertainment needs.

While it was not unknown in America for a producer to offer exhibitors two endings, one happy and one sad, this was less common in Britain. In an article entitled "Smiles Before Tears at the Cinema" in the February 20, 1924, issue of the *Yorkshire Evening Post*, the anonymous writer deplored the "happy ending" trend in movies. He called the dream ending of *The Monkey's Paw* a "dreadfully inartistic anti-climax" and was chagrined by the fact that most exhibitors showed that one over the tragic ending. No matter; reviewers in England were most enthusiastic about the film:

> It is a fact that in some places there is still prejudice lingering against British films but if ever there was one calculated to clear such prejudice

away this film, which has been successful both as a short story and a play is the one [*Yorkshire Evening Post*, September 29, 1923].

It would be difficult to imagine W.W. Jacobs's *The Monkey's Paw* pictured more successfully. The story contains a thrilling and well directed climax and the gradual building up of the situation where the mangled corpse of the son is willed by his mother to rise from the grave and the father's horror of such a ghastly reunion is so depicted that no audience could possibly avoid feeling the increasing tension and uncanniness and be carried away by it [*Bedfordshire Times and Independent*, October 12, 1923].

As is the case with Grand Guignol programs on the stage the tragic and dramatic incidents in the film are set off by witty subtitles and humorous scenes so that the story is not altogether grim and gruesome. It differs in many essentials from both the book and the stage play but is a great success [*Gloucester Citizen*, December 27, 1923].

An unspoken (yet perhaps telling) reason for the happy ending was that there were a great many couples like the Whites in England who had lost their only son, not to accident, but to the slaughter of the Great War. The loneliness and desolation of the old couple robbed of their son and their one joy in life was perhaps too heartbreaking a reminder of what many had just experienced.

Aside from the ending, there were some other changes from the original story. In the latter, the thunderstorm takes place at the beginning; the film wisely makes it part of the climax. There is more detail in the film about the modest but happy home life of the Whites: stills show Moore Marriott (Mr. White) playing the accordion and vainly trying to pump up a bicycle tire that is full of holes. Herbert has a little dog that rushes to greet him when he comes home from work. One still shows a couple of British soldiers talking to a Hindu fakir, indicating that the sergeant-major's tale was illustrated by a flashback though no doubt a pretty simple one (and thus no battle scenes, as in 1933's *The Monkey's Paw*). In Jacobs's original, Herbert is killed when he gets caught in the machinery at the factory of his employer, Maw and Meggins (What a great Dickensian name for a firm of heartless capitalists!), but in the film he is crushed by an engine at the factory. Since there is an actor credited as "engine driver," this scene may have been depicted in some fashion, and while episodes such as this opened up the story/play in an appropriate visual manner, they allowed the production to remain within budget. The exteriors—including a front for the White's cottage—were filmed at Bushey, a little town just outside of London which has, for decades, provided the rural scene for many movies and television shows. One review says the film's "fire scenes" were filmed there as well, but what exactly those entailed remain something of a mystery. *The Monkey's Paw* apparently also evoked a few shivers Down Under, at least if this article in Sydney's *The Sunday Times* (September 30, 1923) is credible:

There were muffled shrieks, half audible gasps and much groping in the dark for strong masculine hands when *The Monkey's Paw* was shown in Sydney last night.... The plot hinges on the danger of meddling with fate and is carried through with many shuddersome scenes to a most satisfactory and logical climax.

Coincidentally, the film played in Perth at the same time as did the stage version, thus drawing these comments from a writer for that city's *The Daily News* (April 8, 1924):

Perth will therefore have the opportunity of having concurrent and direct comparison between the spoken word of the stage drama and the appeal of the silent stage. There is no doubt that the latter is able to portray scenes in a far more spectacular and lavish manner than the stage but the question arises whether the screen can obtain that absorbing and thrilling effect that is so distinctive a feature of this dramatic story of "The Monkey's Paw."

Could the climax of the silent film have been as scary as the finale of the stage version? For the latter, there would have been that ominous knocking reverberating throughout the theater. On film, merely showing a hand pounding on a door wouldn't have worked nearly as well, even with effective musical accompaniment. Still, the description given in the February 1923 edition of

*Pictures and the Picturegoer* suggests the movie went one step further:

> The old lady wishes for the return of her son…. A fleeting glimpse of a terrible figure staggering along in the wind and rain. The door rattles and the old lady starts up in an agony. Then the old man seizes the mysterious relic and harshly cries out that he wishes for his son to rest in peace and the thing ends upon another swift vision of a grave disturbed. And more wind and rain. Eerie, very, but powerful and artistic.

And did Herbert's faithful little dog come running to the door? If anyone is going to complain that showing the revived son however briefly and indistinctly is too explicit and kills the ambiguity of the story, just remember: It's all a dream.

Unfortunately, we have no way of gauging the accuracy of this description of the climax. The prints of *The Monkey's Paw* to be found at the Library of Congress, the New Zealand Film Archive, and the British Film Institute are all incomplete, running 3040 feet out of the original 5194 feet. *And all are missing the last reel!* Sometimes you must wonder if the cinematic gods are in cahoots with the devil who, in *Bedazzled*, delights in ripping out the last page of Agatha Christie mysteries. In March 1923—during a time in which British pictures were *not* popular in the U.S.—producer George Redman and director Manning Hayes visited Hollywood, ostensibly to study American methods of filming. Having brought with them a stack of their W.W. Jacobs film adaptations (including *The Monkey's Paw*), the men were pleased when Selznick Distributing Corporation opted to buy the rights to *The Monkey's Paw* for distribution in the United States, Canada, and Australia. The film was subsequently advertised as having "a special cast," a phrase which American viewers immediately realized meant that the players were unknown to them. While it's not clear whether American exhibitors were offered the two different endings, the £200 Sterling that the old man wished for in Blighty was changed to $2000 for the American release; we can't comment on whether that was a particularly accurate exchange rate. The reviews were, for the most part, highly favorable, and there was certainly recognition that this film was not the usual sort of fare imported from the UK. The January 1924 *Photoplay* praised it as "an effort to stimulate thought and something of a relief after quantities of cinematic ice cream and lady fingers." *Harrison's Reports* (November 10, 1923) thought that the film "should prove fascinating to any audience," but also noted that the lack of romantic interest made it something of an oddity. The critic found the film both moving with its realistic characters and frightening because of the bizarre plot: "An air of mystery and weirdness pervades the picture; one continually tries [to guess] how, in the name of common sense, it will end." The *Exhibitors Trade Review* (January 19, 1924) was likewise enthusiastic though not sure about the film's box-office potential:

> Offering a plot steeped in weird atmosphere, alive with tense, melodramatic thrills but lacking the slightest suggestion of romantic interest, "The Monkey's Paw" figures as a unique production, something altogether different from the usual run of films…. It will fascinate many people with its odd haunting sense of the mystical and the unknown, its moments of pathos and terror. But what its commercial value may be in this country may be another question…. A grimly realistic bit of stuff, dramatically a gem and fairly loaded with suspense. And there is this to be said in its favor, although grewsomely [sic] tragic in spots there is no unhappy ending. An experiment that may do well in some places and flop in others.

Once again, *Variety* was a naysayer. After deploring the lack of a love interest in the movie, "Fred" spoke for the Bible of Show Biz as he castigated British filmmaking:

> The picture may be of the type that the English audiences like but it will hardly get over in this country, even in the smallest picture houses. The English director's idea of a good picture is evidently to have something moving on the screen and that is all. The picture is utterly lacking in action and is only carried along by the tritest of titles telling the story. With a mystery tale of this character to base a good screen story on it would

be rather a novelty in the hands of an American director who, with a lot of trick camera stuff, could turn out a picture that would be a real thriller. Its one outstanding feature is the fact that it has suspense but from the story rather than direction.

More than one American exhibitor agreed with Fred:

> I certainly got a roasting for showing this bunch of rot. Half of them walked out [Millen, GA].
>
> Some said terrible. Others walked out looking as if there had been a skunk at the party. The yessers tried to be nice but wouldn't commit themselves. Am saving the paper in case we have small pox or the measles [Waterbury, CT].
>
> A little bit too spooky to be enjoyed. Although a good picture [Deerfield, WI].

When the story was redone in 1933, filmmakers seemed to have taken *Variety*'s complaints to heart and gave Herbert a love interest; his father wishes on the paw so his son will have enough money to marry. Instead of the simplicity of the '23 version, there are complicated back stories and battle scenes to pad things out (but it still runs about the same brief length as the silent!). The '33 film does have one thing in common with its predecessor: It all turns out to be a dream.

While the sundry performance-art versions of *The Monkey's Paw* had an eminently respectable literary source, the same can't be said for *Sweeney Todd* (1928). Long before anyone could even have conceived that an award-winning Broadway musical could be based on the exploits of a throat-slashing serial killer, the "Demon Barber of Fleet Street" saw life as an 18-part "penny blood"[4] published between 1846 and 1847 in *The People's Periodical and Family Library* under the title *The String of Pearls*.[5] Even though the name "Sweeney Todd" didn't make the title (that would come later), the familiar characters are all there: Sweeney's accomplice, Mrs. Lovett, who turns the barber's victims into meat pies to sell at her pastry shop; the star-crossed lovers, Johanna and Mark (whose gift of pearls to his intended is what sets the plot in motion); and Sweeney's much abused apprentice, Tobias Wragge. Also appearing in the novel is the trick barber chair which, with the pull of a hidden lever, turns completely upside down, sending its occupant hurtling through a trapdoor onto the stone floor below. Should he survive the fall, Sweeney finishes him off with his trusty straight razor.

In the London of the mid–19th century—in addition to a craving for meat pies—there was a hefty appetite for lurid crime tales, even while real crime was rampant and ubiquitous. Some of these tales— "penny bloods"—were fictionalized versions of actual cases: the murder of Maria Marten by Squire Corder, popularized as *Maria Marten or Murder in the Red Barn,* was the most famous one, while others were cut from whole cloth (sorry). Sweeney Todd's career seems to fall into this latter category, even though unsuccessful attempts have been made to prove that the Demon Barber was an actual person. In any event, Todd certainly persisted as an urban legend: A 1924 excavation on Fleet Street revealed that a section of the wall of an old well had been cut away and was found to be partly connected to a cellar of an old house. The subsequent speculation that this was Sweeney Todd's lair was nothing new; his "lair" had been "discovered" any number of times. Decades later, the popularity of the Stephen Sondheim musical also revived interest in the "real" Sweeney Todd, but again investigations came up empty. Nonetheless, conspiracy theorists can take heart in that, after having revealed Todd's many crimes in *The String of Pearls*, the author insisted that the authorities insisted that the case be hushed up lest the gory details lead to a public panic.

The story of the killer barber and his pie-making accomplice may have originated in France, with some versions of the same perhaps going back to the Middle Ages.[6] Different variations on these tales and legends made their way across the Channel (possibly in the 1820s) and eventually inspired the account of Fleet's Street's most infamous tonsorial artist. Compounding this felony was the fact that, although much of the British public loved meat pies, there was some suspicion as to what exactly the "meat" therein was. With no requisite lists of ingredients or warning labels in those days, there was fairly widespread speculation that dogs, cats, and/or even rats may have been used by some of the less reputable establishments. In 1818 rumors of a corpse having being delivered to a London butcher shop caused the place to be attacked by a mob. (Perhaps one of them may have yelled, "Soylent Pie is people!") The source of the rumor, a writer for what might have been charitably called a "scandal sheet," later admitted the story had been pure invention. With the times, of course, being different, the writer—instead of making the rounds of the talk shows—went to gaol for six months. No doubt, though, but such stories buttressed the public belief that Sweeney Todd was indeed more than just a legend.

Sweeney made his first appearance on stage in 1847, before the serial *The String of Pearls* had even been completed. Such a circumstance wasn't unusual; Charles Dickens complained that his serialized novels were turned into (unauthorized) plays before he'd even written the last chapter. Plagiarism was commonplace and largely ignored by the courts, so it was not surprising that George Dibdin Pitt simply made his own adaptation of the plot of the blood penny—he freely acknowledged the source—and used the same main characters and even the same title, though he added *"The Fiend of Fleet Street"* as a subtitle. In doing so, he had to considerably simplify the story and leave out many secondary characters. He also claimed that his play was "founded on fact," a statement that, we suppose, was the Victorian equivalent of "based on a true story." In the serial, Todd poisons Mrs. Lovett when she becomes unreliable, but, in the play, he shoots her and tosses her body into a furnace. Also different from the serial is the courtroom finale of the play: Sweeney confesses all when he sees what he thinks is the ghost of Mark, not realizing that it's the young man in the flesh, his having survived Todd's attempt on his life. Of course, the most significant prop found in both works is the barber's chair. One of Dibdin Pitt's stage directions calls for "a revolving trap, which has a similar chair beneath, so that whatever side is shown to the audience, the position of the chair and its appearance are the same." The chair would sink beneath the stage with its occupant and then rise again empty. It's in *The String of Pearls* that we first find the line "I'll polish him off," which became Todd's catchphrase.

Dibdin Pitt's melodrama proved to be very popular and was often revived, although it had competition from numerous other stage versions, notably one written by Frederick Hazelton in 1865. The public's appetite for explicit gore on the stage was dismaying to the intelligentsia, who worried about the effects of such displays on the lower classes. Thomas Erle attended a revival of *The String of Pearls* (probably in the 1870s) and, after offering a somewhat tongue-in-cheek review of the performance, lamented the violence:

> If the Drama be "holding a mirror up to Nature," it should also be remembered that there is a thing, and a very real and common thing too, as holding nature up to the mirror. For the contemplation of an act of wickedness frequently, as is perfectly well known, inoculates weak minds with an irresistible impulse to do the same kind of thing.... Besides which, it isn't the pleasantest thing in the world to sit for an hour or two, looking at murders, although they are but sham ones, nor is it good to have too many of them on the stage.[7]

Later, of course, the guardians of the public welfare would say the same thing about the movies and, still later, horror comics.

Eventually, elements of self-parody began to creep into performances featuring the aging barnstormer, much to the horror of purists who felt the old chestnut should

THE GRAPHIC, February 18, 1928

## THE DEMON BARBER
How Sweeney Todd "Polishes 'Em Off" at the Elephant and Castle

THE BARBER'S FOUL VILLAINY
Todd—in "Sweeney Todd, Or The Demon Barber of Fleet Street"—sends the hero down into the gruesome cellar where, in the old melodramatic story, his victims were made into meat pies.

PISTOL AGAINST RAZOR
Mrs. Lovatt, Todd's criminal partner in the hearty melodrama which is drawing the West End to the Elephant Theatre, holds him off when they quarrel because she has fallen in love with the hero

"WHAT A WICKED WORLD IT IS!"
Dr. Lupin, the canting parson, uses this catch-phrase throughout the play. He is cursed by good Jasper Oakley for deceiving the women of the latter's household

FLOGGING THE APPRENTICE
Sweeney Todd's rascally accomplices, Dr. Lupin and Jonas Fogg, decoy Sweeney's apprentice into Fogg's lunatic asylum and flog him for having revealed the horrible secret of the murders by his master. Jasper Oakley then rushes in to the rescue

POLISHING HER OFF
Gory bloodstains appear on the throat of Mrs. Lovatt when Sweeney slits it in the cellar, while the hero and heroine lie helpless and unconscious. Sweeney's slogan when he confronts an intended victim is "I'll polish 'em off!"

SWEENEY AND THE SPECTRE
The demon barber, in the condemned cell at Newgate, gibbers before the ghostly apparition of Mrs. Lovatt, which appears on the wall and silently accuses him while he is preparing to escape

Scenes from the 1928 Elephant and Castle stage production of *Sweeney Todd* which had replaced an earlier version done by Tod Slaughter. Here J. Edward Martin plays the Demon Barber with Cicely Davis as Mrs. Lovett and Wilfred Lawson as the hero Mark Ingestre. Lawson went on to do villain roles in *The Terror* (1938) and *The Night Has Eyes* (1942).

be played absolutely straight. Still, the throat-slashing barber moved from the provinces onto London stages once again in successful revivals in the 1920s. Perhaps anticipating the audience participation in films like *The Rocky Horror Picture Show*, patrons got into the Victorian spirit of things and reacted very vocally to what was happening on the stage, hissing the villain and yelling shouts of approval when the lovers were reunited. Perhaps newer plays like *Dracula* could induce a shiver or two, but it was getting harder and harder to look at Sweeney Todd and Mrs. Lovett as anything other than campy icons from a bygone age of melodrama.

Could film put the cutting edge back on Sweeney's razor? The first attempt, a 1926 burlesque titled *Sweeney Todd* that ran about 1000 feet, was not encouraging. This picture, made "for the Kinematograph Garden Party" as some kind of in-house entertainment for a group of film exhibitors, apparently never had any kind of theatrical release. A "G.A. Baughan" reputedly played the title role, but there may have been some confusion between that name and E.A. Baughan, a film and drama critic who scripted the 1921 *The Adventures of Mr. Pickwick*. It's assumed that this short film did little more than depict a scene or two from the Dibdin Pitt play.

In 1928 a small company named QTS—with Harry Rowson as producer—did a movie version of *Maria Marten*, the aforementioned penny blood that had previously been filmed in 1902, 1908, *and* 1913, and that had recently enjoyed a successful 17-week run London's famous Elephant Theater. Veteran director Walter West was at the helm of the film, but the result was a rather lackluster and bloodless affair that was advertised as "a realistic story of a real life drama." Still, the receipts must have been impressive enough for Rowson and West to try again, this time with *Sweeney Todd* and with a stronger approach to the material.

*Sweeney Todd* was shot quickly and inexpensively and sent to the censor on the fourth of September 1928—only to be rejected. Censorship for movies was much stricter than for the "legitimate" theater, but even the latter didn't always escape the vigilance of the thou-shalt-nots. In April 1928, author Norman Lee complained that his play *Danger* was denied approval because of a scene in which a woman, stripped to the waist, is tortured with a hot iron. Lee pointed out that other plays featured equally grisly doings: electrocution in *The Monster* and onstage throat-cutting in *Sweeney Todd*, both of which played in London without interference. In any case, the censors informed Messrs. Rowson and West that there could be no mention of the real ingredients in Mrs. Lovett's pies in their film, nor could the demon barber be shown actually slitting his victims's throats.[8] The filmmakers complied even though they could have pointed out that the dream framework they used meant none of those awful deeds were actually happening.

Our synopsis comes from a viewing of the film:

> The credits proclaim that the film is "adapted from the famous Elephant and Castle melodrama and based on authentic facts."
> 
> A tired businessman comes home at the end of his work day and is dismayed to find that his dinner is not ready. "For man must work and woman must wait except for the wife who's always late" a title card informs us. The wife does turn up and is berated by her grumpy hubby and in turn scolds the maid. The husband settles down into his easy chair to peruse the newspaper and begins reading an article titled the "Death Chair," an account of the infamous demon barber.
> 
> The film tips it hand immediately and wants to make absolutely sure we know what's happening [or rather what *isn't* happening]. "Ever had the nightmare?" a subtitle asks. "Hobgoblins dancing on your chest and tailed and 3-horned demons tearing at your eyes with red hot pincers.... You shake yourself free.... You roll down a dizzy precipice—and then you wake up with a start to the pleasant reality.... Look at this fellow—He's so wrapped up in the tale of Sweeney Todd, the dirtiest dog ever that he fancies he is Sweeney. Don't disturb him! What does he see?" As the man dozes off, there's a clever close-up of a barber pole ripping through the newspaper like a dagger.

We then switch to Sweeney shaving a customer. Todd's manner is obsequious but beneath his bowing and scraping is a hot bed of envy and frustration. He takes his anger out on his hapless apprentice Tobias and even strong-arms the poor boy for his meager tips. Todd constantly dreams of "filthy lucre" and despises his well-off clients. However, things change when Todd receives a visit from his maniac brother, Nick [some sources mistakenly called him Mick], "an 'orrible criminal" hiding from justice. Nick attaches the barber chair to a trap door and rigs it so, with the pull of a lever located in the clock in an adjoining room, the trap opens and the chair catapults its occupant backwards into the basement below. Nick demonstrates with a dummy. Realizing the potential of this diabolical device Sweeney proclaims "Ha! Ha! My fortune is made." "*Our* fortune, brother," Nick responds, rather unwisely. As Nick sits in the chair, gloating over its perfection, Sweeney pulls the lever and his brother is sent hurtling to the basement. Todd opens another trap door to descend, pulls out a razor and menacingly approaches his half-conscious sibling. "And now to polish him off!"

"Business was brisk," a title card informs us. We see Sweeney with another customer, a farmer who tells the barber he just made a good profit from selling his oxen. The farmer mentions the sad fate of a friend who disappeared on his way back to town after going on a similar errand. Sweeney sends Tobias away and starts to shave the farmer, stopping when the man winces. "Such a stout beard! You'll want a keener razor," the barber exclaims. Sweeney discreetly locks the shop door and pulls the lever casting his customer down into the cellar. The scene fades.

Later Sweeney is in the basement, having just buried the farmer under the flagstones. Via double exposure, the images of his victims, all lying prone under the stones, appear to Sweeney. Todd seems not so much haunted by his crimes as frustrated by the lack of space for more corpses.

We switch to Mrs. Lovett's pastry shop, right next door to Todd's place. The pastry shop is dingy, dimly lit, and devoid of customers. Lovett, an attractive widow, is despondent over her failing business, but her spirits change when Todd pulls out a bag of money. She wonders what the barber is up to and the two converse. "And with your share of the money," Todd tells her, "We'll brighten up the place and attract rich folk. And once they are next door, you can leave them to me." Mrs. Lovett seems to react in horror to what Todd is saying, but she soon comes around.

Sometime later we find that business at the pastry shop has boomed and Mrs. Lovett has even hired two young women to help deal with the crowd of swells who crave her pies. Simon Podge, the beadle, remarks to Lovett, "Nothing has improved so much in this great city as your pies." Lovett credits her new recipe which is "a trade secret." Podge gets a considerably different greeting when he goes to the barber shop to complain to Todd that people have heard strange noises coming from his shop at night and even think the place may be haunted. Todd is indignant, throws the beadle out of his shop and even pours a pitcher of water on him from an upper window. Podge reports Todd's bad attitude to Ben Wagstaffe, sheriff's officer, who tells him Todd's behavior is indeed suspicious, but they presently have no evidence of wrong-doing.

We switch to the good ship *Star* and its captain, Mark Ingestre, who is looking forward to getting home to London and reuniting with his beloved Johanna. As Mark moons over a letter from Johanna, Sambo, Mark's "faithful follower in his adventures," takes over the wheel. In London, Johanna is excited about Mark's imminent return after so long an absence. She shares her joy with Mrs. Lovett who likewise has a romantic interest in the dashing sea captain. Sensing the pie maker's jealousy, Johanna makes it a point to refer to the young man as "*my* Mark."

As Mark's ship docks, Sweeney is gloating over all his loot. When he catches Tobias spying on him, the barber threatens to tear the boy's tongue out and polish him off if he goes against his master. Mark and Sambo visit the pastry shop where Mrs. Lovett flirts with the sea captain and insists that he lodge in one of her rooms. Mark agrees, but, while Mrs. Lovett is upstairs preparing the room, Mark tells Sambo—who's chowing down eagerly on meat pies—that's he going next door for a shave. Sitting in the barber chair, Mark tells Todd about his recent adventures and shows him some loose pearls he's acquired for Johanna. Giving Mark his usual line of needing a keener razor, Todd leaves the room and pulls the deadly lever. Mark plummets to the basement floor and is stunned. However, Mrs. Lovett, having learned from Sambo that Mark is next door, rushes to the basement of her own shop—which adjoins Sweeney's—and arrives in time to stop the barber from killing Mark. "Hands off!" she insists, "He's mine!" Surprised and rather cowed by her fury, Todd retreats. At this inopportune moment, Ben Wagstaffe and his men arrive to inspect the barber's premises [it's not clear what they're expecting to find; possibly this is the censor at work again]. Mrs. Lovett is able to help the injured Mark upstairs to his room before the authorities get to the basement. They uncover nothing suspicious though a huge vat of flour seems an odd thing to find in the cellar of a barber shop.

[At this point the copy we viewed is missing some footage, perhaps almost a whole reel.] Apparently there's a comic scene wherein Todd tries to dispose of Sambo who's come looking for Mark.[9] When Todd pulls the lever, Sambo hangs onto the chair and enjoys being turned upside down and then back up. He leaves the shop none the worse for wear and without realizing what Todd is up to.

While Mark recovers in his room at Mrs. Lovett's, Johanna becomes suspicious of the barber and, disguised as a rich young man, visits the shop pretending to look for a new wig. When Todd sees the fancy broach on her suit, he finds an excuse to leave the room. However, Johanna leaps out of the chair and hides in a closet. She looks on with horror as the trap door opens and the chair swings backwards. Todd comes back in and, peering down into the cellar, is dumbfounded when he doesn't see a body there. Images of Mrs. Lovett appear to the now frenzied Todd who is convinced she is cheating him of yet another wealthy victim. He confronts the pastry maker in the basement. Seeing that Todd is out of his mind, Mrs. Lovett tries to escape, but Sweeney drags her back downstairs and strangles her. Meanwhile, Johanna has gone for Wagstaffe. Todd ascends the stairs to Mark's room and tries to kill him with his razor. However, Mark's strength has returned and the barber is unable to overpower him. Wagstaffe and his police arrive and capture Sweeney. While the lovers embrace, the police bring Sweeney back to his shop as an angry mob forms outside. The officers force the barber to sit in his own chair as they interrogate him, but the ghost of Nick leaves its basement tomb and pulls the fatal lever. Sweeney is hurled to his death before the astonished eyes of the police.

At this point the businessman's wife tilts his chair back and awakens him for dinner. Still under the influence of his nightmare, the man frantically chases his wife around the room. Finally, looking at them both in the mirror, he calms down. Dinner is finally ready and it's his favorite: a meat pie! He's taken aback for a moment but then proclaims "I'll polish it off!" as he sits down to eat.

The dream-framing device serves to detach the viewer from the action and seems to invite him to sit back and chuckle at the melodrama, much like how playgoers at 1920s revivals of *Sweeney Todd* were sometimes urged by management to react vocally to the play (their Victorian counterparts apparently needed no such encouragement). It's a wink to the viewer not to take things very seriously, but still to try to get into the spirit of enjoying the horrible goings-on.

Thanks to the censor of course, said goings-on weren't *too* horrible. The play makes much of the human flesh meat pies; at one point, a character finds a human hair and then, later, a brass button in his pie. The film, of course, couldn't get that explicit, but, since Mrs. Lovett's famous pies were as familiar to Britons as Tom Sawyer's fence would be to Americans, there was no need to do anything more than hint. Londoners would no doubt groan a bit as characters chomped down enthusiastically on their pies, not knowing what they were really eating. And, of course, there's obvious racism afoot when Sambo wolfs down pie after pie as if his African nationality makes him particularly prone to cannibalism. Perhaps one reason the film never made it to America was that audiences there would not have known the story well enough to pick up on what was really happening. The Dibdin Pitt play had been done in the U.S.—including a brief stay on Broadway (where it was titled *Sweeney Todd*)—but it had not become a stage staple the way it had in England. When Tod Slaughter did his movie version of *Sweeney Todd* in 1936, the British censors subjected it to the same standards that had applied in 1928. Slaughter's film did make it to the States, but was promptly banned by the New York censor.

It's not known exactly how much footage Rowson and West had to cut to satisfy the censors. Presumably, the elimination of a few title cards in that early scene between Todd and Mrs. Lovett would have been sufficient to obscure any specific reference to the fate of Todd's victims. As it stands now, Todd seems only interested in sprucing up the pastry shop in order to draw a better class of clientele to his own establishment. There is no attempt at an explanation of what he plans to do with all the additional corpses once there's no more room in his basement. The throat-cutting is indeed soft pedaled; there's not even a close-up of Todd's razor (except when Mrs. Lovett knocks it out of his hand and steps on it). The murders linger less in one's memory than does Todd's brutal treatment of poor Tobias; he shoves the pathetic, cowering boy, slaps him, pulls his hair, and threatens him with a whip. This child abuse, while certainly Dickensian and true to the original stories, gives an unpleasantly realistic undertone to the otherwise outlandish tale.

Ads for *Sweeney Todd* promised "thrills and laughter in the story of the world's champion sinner." Some reviewers agreed:

> Mr. Walter West who was responsible for the photoplay production, has not stressed the pie making episodes, as was done in some of the stage versions, but has maintained much of the "meaty" flavor of the old drama. His presenting the matter as a dream of a man after reading a "thriller" tones down the atrocities and the spectator has a laugh at the end. Moore Marriott gives a gripping and powerful performance without "laying it on thick." Iris Darbyshire looks so pretty as Mrs. Lovett that one could hardly believe she had a hand in the making of those pies [*Yorkshire Evening Post*, October 10, 1928].

A writer for *The Lancashire Evening Post* (September 3, 1929) concurred:

> There are few people who do not feel a strange thrill of horror at the mention of Sweeney Todd for the story of the demon barber of Fleet Street is one of the classics of crime. The actual spectacle of Todd polishing them off in the revolving chair makes the film even more exciting than one could have expected. The trapdoor scenes are not faked though the chief actors used doubles one of whom broke a wrist and another severely hurt his head in falling through the trapdoor. In spite of the realism, the film is not revolting because of the director's skill in presenting the film as a man's vivid dream. Moore Marriott quickly changes from the affable barber to the gold-loving demon whichever the part demands.

*The Derby Daily Telegraph* (December 10, 1929) commented, "So excellent is the acting of Moore Marriott that the anti-climax ending was welcomed by the audience." However, *The Hull Daily Mail* (September 3, 1929) thought that Marriott's performance "was the only point of merit" in the film:

> Not that's it's not worth seeing. It only lasts an hour and holds the attention during that time—but the production has no subtlety and in consequence the attention it demands is purely superficial. The handling is at time[s] rather flippant thus toning down what otherwise might have been a very gruesome affair. What little money has been expended on the production has, for the most part, been devoted to the construction of the barber's fall den, the other settings being very simple. An opportunity for a good, hilariously dramatic climax has been lost by the deletion of the bake house sequences—in fact even the substance of Mrs. Lovett's pies is only suggested—but this perhaps is for the best.

The critic is certainly correct about the film's modest budget; it was probably comparable to the later, cheap Tod Slaughter barnstormers. There's no attempt to depict the crowded streets and turmoil of Victorian London; instead, we see just a few shops side by side on a small street setting, taken with the camera firmly rooted in medium shots designed not to give away too much. The cellars are near empty and nondescript with no shadows or eerie lighting. The creepy Expressionist touches we find in Hitchcock's *The Lodger* (1927) are nowhere in evidence here, no doubt for budgetary reasons as well as for a reluctance to makes things too spooky. If *Sweeney Todd* works at all, it is no doubt due to Moore Marriott's performance. In *The Monkey's Paw*, Marriott's make-up suggested some of the old codgers he was later famous for playing in the Will Hay movies, but, in *Sweeney*, he has a stout and dangerous look. His lips are usually clenched tight, but when he smiles, he reveals a set of snaggleteeth. (Marriott actually *had* no teeth and had several sets of false teeth to use for different characters.) Once he begins acquiring his filthy lucre, he does not need to adopt a fawning manner with his "betters" or people in authority; he may appear an 'umble barber, but his newly acquired hidden wealth gives him a feeling of superiority over the fools who can't see him for what he really is or how he longs to divest them of whatever they have. Marriott's restrained performance suggests a man barely able to maintain the façade of normalcy over his murderous impulses and unchecked lust for gold. This is in contrast to Harry Lorraine (his brother Nick, a character not in the play or blood penny), who puts in an over-the top-performance more appropriate for 1908 than 1928. Lorraine is constantly rubbing his hands, grimacing, rolling his eyes, laughing, and slinking about in a very stagey manner. It's hard to imagine how the men with the butterfly nets could possibly have missed him. Was this just a case of hammy acting, or did director West want a contrast with Marriott's more restrained and realistic villainy? In any case, Lorraine's role is mercifully brief and at least provides a ghostly revenge explanation for Todd's end. (In another version of the story, Todd does indeed die in his own barber chair, but we don't know what triggers the mechanism. The hand of God?) Marriott *does* have his maniacal moments: his leering down through the trapdoor reminds one of Bela Lugosi's Dr. Vollin, grinning at Boris Karloff from an upper window in *The Raven*. Marriott's all-too-brief scenes with Iris Darbyshire as a very sexy Mrs. Lovett work quite well (she also plays the businessman's wife in the framing story); their collusion has a queasy, erotic undertone. In one of the few well-edited sequences, the film cuts back and forth between Mrs. Lovett getting a bed ready for Mark and Todd preparing to kill him, perhaps suggesting that Todd's sexual impulses have been channeled into pure sadism. Mrs. Lovett's more normal sexuality trumps Todd when she's able to save Mark, but her victory is short lived. Darbyshire made very few movies, but she did a good deal of stage work, sometimes as a part of Sybil Thorndyke's company. Perhaps Darbyshire's most notable success was as the siren Tondelayo in *White Cargo* (the role played by Hedy Lamarr in the 1942 film version). Unlike the 1923 *Monkey's Paw*, *Sweeney Todd* did not get an American release. In addition to its questionable subject matter, it was a silent film at a time when *The Jazz Singer* had begun the process of relegating silents to a bygone era. It would take Stephen Sondheim to bring the murderous barber of Fleet Street back to throat-cutting life as a viable menace. And this time it wouldn't be a dream.

# *The House Without a Key*

Pathé Exchange, Inc.—November 21, 1926—10 chapters—c. 210 minutes

**Cast**: Allene Ray as Cary Egan; Walter Miller as John Quincy Winterslip; E.H. Calvert as Dan Winterslip; Betty Caldwell as Barbara Winterslip; Natalie Waterfield as Minerva Winterslip; Jack Pratt as James Egan; William Norton Bailey as Harry Jennison; Frank Lackteen as Dick Kaohla; George Kuwa as Charlie Chan; Harry Semels as Saladine; Charles H. West as Bowker; John Cossar as District Attorney; Scott Seaton as Detective; Clifford Saum as Kennedy; with John Dillon

**Credits**: *Director*: Spencer Gordon Bennet; *Screenplay* and *Adaptation*: Frank Leon Smith; *Based on the eponymous novel by* Earl Derr Biggers (Bobbs-Merrill: Indianapolis, 1925)

The following synopsis is taken from the copyright registration submissions filed at the Library of Congress between November 11 and December 26, 1926. To say that some of the phraseology found in these chapter summaries is "quaint" is to be charitable, and to describe it as "muddled" is to indulge in epic understatement. Still, inasmuch as the serial is lost, we have not attempted to alter the wording in any way, lest we inadvertently change the intent of the Pathé scribe who penned these things in the first place. (To be completely honest, the text reads as though it had been written by someone for whom English was a third language. Then again, the more-than-occasional dearth of definite articles and subject pronouns brings to mind Chan dialogue as articulated by the Messrs. Oland, Toler, and Winters.) In a couple of instances, though, we have adjusted the punctuation a tad when we felt it was absolutely necessary to do so in order to clarify expository phrases. In addition, there are several sentences to which we appended an exclamation point (!), indicating our momentary—yet total—bewilderment. Also, in true serial fashion, the first few sentences of each LoC chapter summary restate the last bits of action from the preceding episode. In order to avoid repetition—and in the interest of conserving the Amazonian rain forests—we have eliminated these redundancies.

**Chapter One: "The Spite Fence"**

Miss Minerva Winterslip, of Boston, visits in Honolulu. She alternates her stay between her two brothers. They live adjoining on the beach at Waikiki.

Amos, one brother, is partner with James Egan and part owner of the Reef and Palm Hotel. Between his home and that of his brother Dan is a "spite fence" erected twenty years before. The brothers have not spoken for this span of years. Amos is in rather lowly circumstances; Dan is rich.

James Egan is a hard-luck, lost nerve [sic] of the Pacific. He is fond of Amos Winterslip, but joins with him in hatred of Dan.

As the story opens, Minerva, who is past the bloom of youth but still beautiful, has failed in her efforts to reconcile Amos and Dan.

Dan is a big and important-looking man. He has a house that is a garden paradise. Kaohla, a Hawaiian, knows something out of the past of Dan and has been blackmailing the rich man.

There is an air of plots and counter plots: Saladine, a character of mystery flits in and out of the scenes. Amos and Egan in conversation hint at a crime Dan committed twenty years before.

\* \* \*

On the S.S. *Matsonia*, sailing from San Francisco for the islands, is John Quincy Winterslip, also of Boston, nephew of Minerva, Dan and Amos. He carries a heavy bag in which is a mysterious oaken box, containing something of vital importance in the life of Dan Winterslip and which he has been asked by his uncle to drop into the Pacific in mid-ocean.

Also on board the ship is Barbara Winterslip, daughter of Dan, and Cary Egan, daughter of James Egan.

John Quincy received the mysterious box on his arrival in San Francisco from Boston. It came from the attic of his Uncle Dan's old home there. Bowker, a steward, has information in his possession which makes him curious about the box. He would obtain it.

Barbara Winterslip is accompanied by Harry Jennison, attorney for her father. He plans to marry Barbara. He resents a cousinly kiss she bestows on John Quincy.

Cary Egan betrays and [sic] interest in John Quincy.

\* \* \*

In Honolulu Dan Winterslip is nervous in his great home. He sits and reads the papers anxiously. Mysterious men flit through the tropic growth surrounding the home. A knife is hurled and buries itself in the back of the chair in which Dan is seated. If he had not been leaning forward to pick up a piece of the newspaper it would have entered his body. It is an eerie time in the great mansion.

\* \* \*

On board the *Matsonia* John Quincy reads his instructions regarding the box. He is ordered by his Uncle Dan to throw it overboard "because his life and safety depend on it."

When they reach mid-ocean John Quincy departs from his stateroom to toss the box into the sea. Three men set upon him and they fight for the box. John Quincy tosses it aside and engages the men. Cary Egan rushes up and grabs the box, running away pursued by one of the men. The other two get John Quincy in a corner. They grab him by the legs, kicking and struggling. They heave him overboard. On a beautiful night John Quincy finds himself afloat in the Pacific with the *Matsonia* steaming away to Honolulu.

**Chapter Two: "The Mystery Box"**

John Quincy is ordered to throw the box overboard on reaching the deepest ocean lanes. Bowker, a steward, knows of the box and its contents. So does Cary Egan, daughter of James Egan, island neer-do-well.

When John Quincy attempts to toss the box into the sea he is set upon by three men. They throw John Quincy overboard and Cary Egan grabs the box.

Cary [sic] swimming in the wake of the *Matsonia* clutches at the rope that holds the rotating log propeller[!]. He is pulled along with the boat. Cary Egan struggling with the ruffians for possession of the box yells, "Man overboard." The ships officers hear the cry and the *Matsonia* is stopped. John Quincy is pulled from the sea.

Barbara Winterslip, daughter of Dan, watches the rescue and when she learns it is her cousin rushes to him and implants [sic] a big kiss on his wet cheek. This is not pleasing to Jennison, attorney for Daniel Winterslip who is aboard and would marry Barbara. John Quincy learns that it was Cary Egan who gave the alarm that led to his rescue.

Jennison comes to console John Quincy. Bowker the steward snoop around and would hear something [sic]. There is no doubt he desires to get possession of the box containing Dan Winterslip's secret.

\* \* \*

In Honolulu Dan walks forth and a hammer narrowly misses him as it falls from the hands of Kaohla, who places screening on the house at the direction of Dan. Dan accuses Kaohla of having thrown the knife meant to kill him on the night before. This the native denies.

Minerva tries again to reconcile the two brothers but her efforts fail. Saladine mysteriously comes in and out of the picture, listening here and watching there. He is under suspicion.

Because of the dealy [sic] to the boat in picking up John Quincy Winterslip who had been thrown overboard, the *Matsonia* is forced to lie outside all night on arrival in Honolulu harbor.

Bowker and his aides confer and steal from the room of Cary Egan the mysterious box. Cary takes John Quincy to get the box and learns this. She had planned to open it with him present.

Bowker by arrangement plans to deliver the box of [sic] Kaohla who comes out to get it in his outrigger canoe. On deck John Quincy and Cary plan to battle for the box. One of Bowker's henchmen goes aloft and drops a heavy block and tackle on the deck. It strikes John and Cary and the episode ends.

**Chapter Three: "The Missing Numeral"**

John and Cary are felled to the deck of the ship by a large block in the hands of one of Bowker's men. The box gets into the hands of Koahla [sic], a native who is in the employ of Dan Winterslip and blackmails his employer.

At this time the *Matsonia* lies at anchor in Honolulu harbor. Koahla comes from the shore in an outrigger canoe. Harry Jennison, attorney for Dan Winterslip is aboard. He learns by a nod from Bowker that the box is in the hands of the native. This is the first intimation he has of any knowledge of any plot, if there is one [!].

Jennison loves Barbara, daughter of Dan. John Quincy, on his way to visit his uncle, has fallen in love with Cary Egan. Barbara for the first time outwardly shows affection for Jennison on the deck of the ship.

Barbara produces a cable from her father which absolutely prohibits any thought of marriage to Jennison. Of course this does not please the young man who promises he will find a way to overcome the objection and is very significant in his wording of the statement to the girl.

John has his troubles here for Cary, because he made no effort to recover the box accuses him of being a true Winterslip, working only for the interests of his Uncle Dan, who hates Cary's father. John Quincy being rebuffed by the girl follows her to her cabin and standing at the porthole proposes marriage. Cary slams the porthole shut. John tells Barbara he plans to marry Cary Egan.

\* \* \*

In Honolulu, Dan Winterslip, the richest man in the islands, calls James Egan on the phone and demands he come to his house at once. Dan's manner is very brusque. On the telephone at first was his brother Amos whom he had not spoken with for twenty years. Amos had recognized his brother's voice. Egan makes his way toward the home of Dan.

At the Winterslip home, Minvera meets Cope. They have a very tender meeting. It is evident they have been something to each other in the past. When Cope leaves he flips away a cigaret [sic].

Minerva retires and is awakened in the night. She feels that something is happening. She hears a noise in the quarters of Dan. She summons a ntove [sic] woman and they enter. They see a dim figure and clearly the gloved hands of a man: on the man's wrists is a watch with a luminous dial. The figure THREE on the dial is missing. It is a few minutes past two o'clock. The figure disappears. Minervah [sic] finds Dan Winterslip dead. There is much evidence of a struggle. The floor is wet—the man had wet feet the servant ejaculates [!].

\* \* \*

The *Matsonia* lands. All is gay. Minerva is at the dock with Amos. Jennison pays money to Bowker the steward. Barbara learns her father had been slain. James Egan awaits his daughter who has a moment before promised, in a way to marry John Quincy when the two families end their feud. As Egan meets his daughter he is placed under arrest by Hallet, chief of detectives, for the murder of Dan Winterslip.

End of episode.

**Chapter Four: "Suspicion"**
Egan is arrested for the murder as the boat docks and in the presence of his daughter, who has just been asked to become the bride of John Quincy.

John Quincy, coming to visit his uncle is flustered. He stands between love and duty. Cary urges him to stick to his people.

Under suspicion is Amos Winterslip, brother of Dan. Dick Kaohla, a servant of Dan Winterslip, has been blackmailing the slain man for years. He is under suspicion. He is in league with a ship steward possesses a mysterious box which John Quincy was to have tossed overboard on ship.

Enter Detective Sergeant Charles Chan, of the Honolulu police, a Chinese and the shrewdest sleuth on the islands. He decides to find the slayer and takes to John Quincy, who would prove Egan innocent for he loves the daughter.

Harry Jennison, attorney for Dan, is mysteriously linked against him. He wants to marry Barbara, only daughter of the murdered man. Saladine, another mysterious character comes to and fro in the picture and is under suspicion of knowing about the crime.

At the investigation Minerva, aunt of John Quincy, takes sides against her nephew. She thinks Eagan [sic] is guilty, for he did have an appointment with the dead man. The slayer had wet feet, and Egan clothing had been found dripping water. Kaohla's clothing was also wet following the finding of the body.

A cablegram is revealed showing the police that John Quincy did have in his possession at San Francisco the mysterious box which told much of the past of Dan Winterslip. Where is this box?

Koaohla [sic] really has it in his possession. Jennison learns this and tells him to get rid of it. Amos Winterslip having decided to tear down the spite fence, now that his brother is dead, Kaohla decides to bury the box in one of the post holes of the uprooted fence. It also had developed that Egan had cabled his daughter to get the box from the hands of John Quincy.

Amos Winterslip, part owner of the Reef and Palm hotel with the man under arrests [sic] for some reason decides to leave the islands.

Kaohla goes to bury box. Hearing someone approaching he darts into cover leaving box. Cary Egan finds it. Kaohla fearful throws a blanket around her. John Winterslip coming near hears the girl's screams.

Kaohla is struggling with Cary as John Quincey comes up. The native tosses her over *a well*.\* The blanket catches on the barbed wire of the spite fence and holds the girl from plunging to her death.

The fence post starts to pull out. John Quincy runs up to the rescue. Kaohla trips him and he goes out into space as—the Episode ends.

\* \* \*

\* The typewritten words "the cliff" are crossed out in this spot and replaced by the handwritten phrase "a well." On the bottom of the page, the asterisk reveals more handwritten information: "West Coast advises Ray and Miller fall into well instead of over cliff."

**Chapter Five: "The Death Buoy"**
Cary Egan wrapped in a blanket, is dangling over a well, where she was tossed by Kaohla. John Quincy Winterslip also tossed into space by the native saves himself by grabbing at a fence post of dismantled spite fence.

Saladine lurking ever in shrubbery sees the mysterious box has momentarily been deserted by Kaohla. He grabs box, then changes his mind and replaces it.

John Quincy aids Cary. He makes her safer and Charlie Chan the detective arrives and sees the predicament of the two. He aids them to safety and then it is explained by both about the box. When they hunt for it the box is again missing, for Kaohla has returned and found it replaced and made away with it. Saladine sees this all.

Cary Egan then faints and they take her to the home of the slain man. There Jennison is called by Kennedy over the phone. Kennedy is one of the sailors who engaged in the fight with John Quincy aboard the *Matsonia*.

Kennedy demands money over the phone for placing a "can" in the harbor at a designated point. Jennison alarmed, signals Kaohla to meet him in the garden. There Jennison dictates a note and orders Kaohla to take it to the Reef and Palm Hotel where Kennedy awaits.

John Quincy and Chan escort Cary back to the hotel. Kaohla race there with the note to get to the sailor before he is recognized by John Quincy and Cary. Kaohla delivers the note.

Kaohla gets out of the hotel when John and Cary arrive. They recognize the sailor and John Quincy grapples with him. They fight outside the hotel.

Kennedy breaks free from John and makes his get away. The note that Jennison had dictated to Kaohla falls to the ground. Saladine picks it up. He takes it to the clerk of the hotel. Clerk gives it to John and Cary when they come up. The note says:

"In the morning the contents of the can you anchored off the reef will be replaced with money and a full letter of instructions."

In the morning off the reef Kaohla gets the anchored can. He replaces it with one containing dynamite controlled by a mechanism. If it is pulled free from the water it will explode.

Kennedy comes toward the can. He is in skiff. John and Cary in launch race for the can. They would get there before Kennedy but the sailor wins. He grabs the can. A great explosion and sailor goes into the air with his skiff. John and Cary in launch in head into the geyser caused by the explosion. Launch rises in the air but right itself scene of great confusion. The episode ends.

\* \* \*

**Chapter Six: "Sinister Shadows"**

Kaohla, who placed a deadly mine in the sea, watches from the shore as Kennedy, conspirator, is blown up. John Winterslip and Cary Egan in launch are racing toward the deadly buoy when explosion occures [sic]. They are near victims of blast. On the launch is Saladine.

Cary is thrown into water. John swims and grabs her. Launches put out from shore. Chan in one. John brings Cary aboard waterlogged launch. Saladine near sinking is rescued by John. Chan comes up and takes Cary aboard.

Chan starts for shore. Another launch comes up. On the shore Kaohla benches [sic] his canoe and another native coming along finds the can Kaohla had taken from buoy. Asks questions and is rebuffed.

On Chan's launch they question Saladine as to his presence. He resents questioning but says he is a wholesale grocer from Des Moines, Ia. John questions Saladine's explanation. He decides to cable Des Moines. In the meantime the other launch seeks for the body of Kennedy.

\* \* \*

Kaphla [sic] brings his canoe to a deserted dock. The dock shed is large gloomy and dusty. Huge sails hang from the rafters. A trap door is out of the floor. Kaohla meets Jennison. Kaohla comes on with the can buoy. Explanis [sic] to Jennison about the explosion, Jennison gives Kaohla directions of his plans for that night. He goes to attend to arranging the funeral of Dan Winterslip. They buried him in a tropical rainstorm.

At the Reef and Pam [sic] a telephone call summons Cary to come with John to 52 Harbor Street that night. It is a message from Saladine. Cary, who cannot get in touch with John goes to the address in the message. John leaves Jennison at the home and goes to the hotel where he gets the message that Cary answered. At the same time John gets an answer to his cablegram in which Deam [sic] Moines denies that saladine [sic] lives there. John takes a revolver and starts for the Harbor Street address.

Cary arrives at the rendezvous. It is raining. The interior is the dock shed with the hanging sails. A mysterious figure in long cloak moves about. Cary calls for Saladine. The mysterious figure is finally revealed as Saladine. John Winterslip rushes into the scene. Kaohla with henchman is there. Saladine seizes her and demand to now [sic] what she knows about it all.

John rushes into shed. Meets Cary and reassures her. It is very eerie there. Mysterious figure moves in back of hanging sails. Four men o [sic] come through trap door. Cary is given pistol by John. John is attacked by three men who would toos [sic] him through trap door into boat. John puts up a fight. Cary watches fight. One of the canvas sails is clung to by Cary. It comes down and buries the girl in the folds. The mysterious man stands revealed as the episode ends.

\* \* \*

**Chapter Seven: "The Mystery Man"**

The attempted kidnaping of John Winterslip and Cary Egan at the old dock shed is blocked by arrival of the harbor police boat and a large number of the kidnapers are captured. Saladine, who is in the shed, escapes arrest by crouching down and covering himself with his long coat.

Cary explains who she is and tells how she came to the shed expecting to get information that would establish the innocence of her father, held for the murder of Dan Winterslip. The note that was sent by Saladine is found. This character sneaks away.

The scene shifts back to the Reef and Palm hotel. In the lobby Charlie Chan, the detective awaits. Saladine snaeaks [sic] up to the hotel and crosses the verandah and gets into his own room without going through lobby. Furtively he packs his bag.

In the lobby gather Chan, Cary Egan, John Quincy and officer. The telephone message from Saladine is read and Chan says he wants to look into Saladine's room. They get pass key and start upstairs and Saladine creeps out and bolts verandah door.

Search of the room reveals false bears [!] and other disguises with small arms and shot gun. This bewilders the searchers. But they find nothing to add to the clews [sic] on the murder.

The next morning the search goes back to the Winterslip home. Saldine peering in shrubbery hears Jennison berate Kaohla for letting John and Cary escape the night before. He gives the Hawaiian boy some monty [sic] and goes into the home where all are assembled for going ----- the story of the slaying. Minervah [sic] states that she remembers the figure of the slayer wore a wrist watch with a missing number. In the shrubbery Saladine looks at his wrist. A white mark shows on his wrist where a watch had been worn. This clew gives John and [sic] idea and he rushes away. Chan is elated.

At the city prison James again meets his daughter and when she asks whom he suspects says he suspects Amos Winterslip. Cary gives clothing to her father and hurries away.

At the Reef and Palm Saladine comes into his room by the verandah. It is a shaky structure. He goes in and digs up a wrist watch that he had forgotten the night before.

John Quincy Winterslip comes to the hotel and rushes to the room of Saladine. He goes into the room and confronts the mysterious character; grabs his wrist and notes the mark made by watch strap.

The men fight all over the room. They sway to the balcony still fighting. Cary rushes upstairs. The porch sways as the men fight and then gives way.

Saladine and John Quincy go plunging down into the sea as the porch gives way. The water shows far below. They strike the sea. Other guests who have been watching scramble to safety. Cary is caught outside and grabs a railing and dangles above the sea. The board she clings to gives way and she swings downward as THE EPISODE ENDS.

\* \* \*

**Chapter Eight: "The Spotted Menace"**
Left dangling over the sea from the wrecked porch of the Reef and Palm hotel Cary Eagan [sic] falls into the sea. John Quincy and Saladine are in water swimming around in wreckage.

John sees Cary and swims toward her. Natives wade in and help John rescue Cary. Saladine catches floating box and putting his head under it swims away. Saladine disappears. John and Cary go to the hotel and Jennison and Barbara, out riding, hear the commotion and join them. John resents Jennison's attitude regarding Eagan [sic].

At Dan Winterslip's home Minerva has an interview with the detective Chan. Several boys come to the rear of the home and are given cakes by Kam the servant and grandmother of Kaohla. The boys announce they are playing pirates.

In a secluded glen the boys have unearthed the hidden box of mystery and are playing with it. Saladine, dripping wet, comes sneaking through the shrubbery. Kaohla finds the kids playing with the precious box.

Chan comes on the scene and grabs the box away. Chan makes way with it [sic] leaving Kaohla crestfallen. Saladine sees all this.

The box is opened in the home of Dan Winterslip. All the principals are present. It discloses the log of the Schooner Maid of Shiloh and written in Dan Winterslip's handwriting. The writing in the log book reveal that Anna Winterslip and James Eagan had delivered to Dan Winterslip money and jewels worth $100,000. This was twenty years ago.

Kaohla comes in. He was Dan's cabin boy on the Maid of Shiloh It is revealed that Dan was to have taken the box and its contents to Sydney, Australia But the ship wrecked.

Cary Egan reveals that the ship was wrecked [and] accused Dan Winterslip of having robber [sic] her father and his brother Amos. Jennison turns her words against her and says that furnished the motive for her father of murder Dan [sic]. Barbara says she will pay every dollar back. Jennison resents this, as he would marry Barbara.

They all ask where is Amos Winterslip?

Kaohla reveals that he is at the COVE. All decide to go there in a speed boat. Saladine hears all this. Kaohla loads the all aboard Dan's speedboat. They wear bathing suits for the sea is rough.

At the Cove Amos Winterslip is with the natives in their village. The native mothers fear for their children because the sea is filled with white sharks.

The speed boat with Kaohla, Chan, John and Cary comes near. They cannot make the beach. It is planned to swim ashore and return with a skiff. John and Cary jump into the water.

In the meantime another speed boat with a single man comes into view. Amos sees the two swimming in toward the beach. He rushes out with the natives to warn them of the white sharks.

Surface of waters cut by fins of sea monsters. John and Cary see the sharks and try to get back to the boat. Chan would help the swimmers aboard. Kaohla fells him with boat hook. Second speed boat comes up. Saladine is running it. Makes/takes/wakes [first letter of word illegible] Kaohla and rushes away.

The sharks reach the boat at the same time as John and Cary. Chan and Kaohla fight. The sharks are all around the swimmers as the EPISODE ENDS.

\* \* \*

**Chapter Nine: "The Wrist Watch"**
Amos Winterslip, with the aid of natives, frightens away [!] the white sharks that menace

John Quincy and Cary. They are brought into his launch.

In the meantime Kaohla and Saladine sepped [sic] away in the power boat that followed the others from Honolulu to the Cove. Saladine shuts down the boat and then covers Kaohla with a revolver. He makes terms with the Hawaiian boy whereby the plotter agrees to take him in on his "game." Amos, John, Cary and Chan in the launch give chase to this pair but are outdistanced. Chan promises the Honolulu police will get them.

At the home of Winterslip his daughter Barbara cancels her engagement to marry Jennison and decides to make restitution to her uncle Amos and Egan for the money her father stole.

At a river front Chinese shop that night Jennison goes to meet Kaohla. The boy is there with Saladine. Jennison announces to Kaohla that he is going to close up his affairs and clear out. He also announces he will get rid of John Quincy.

Jennison orders "everything" sold out for cash. A guard is placed in the rear room of the dive.

John Quincy Winterslip, lured to the place, is bound and gagged and placed under guard. Jennison has arranged with a ship captain to take him out to sea.

2.

Jennison boards a steamer that is to sail to the States. On the ship is Bowker, the steward in his employ. Jennison sends Bowker to the dive to clean up the cash.

In the meantime at police headquarters plans are being made to capture the conspirators. Chan gets the papers.

The sailing ship captain who is take John Quincy away comes to the shop and bargains for the tinned goods of mystery [!]. He is told only cash goes. Bowker runs into John Quincy, who recognizes the steward and hopes he will help him escape. The steward only ties him the more tighter [sic].

Cary Egan worried gets the address of the dive and shop and arrives there just as the men carry John out. Saladine then turns character [sic] and knocks up guards gun that conspirator fires at John. Saladine is wounded. He starts fight.

The police led by Chan descend on the dive. All are fighting. Cary is in the midst of the males. Suddenly she sees a wrist on which is the watch with the missing numeral. "The Watch, the watch," she cries out. Hands grab for her and she goes down in the crowd as the EPISODE ENDS.

* * *

**Chapter Ten: "The Culprit"**

Federal officers and Honolulu police cooperate in raid on Chinese dive and shop where John Quincy Winterslip are surrounded [sic] by a fighting mob of enemies [sic]. Jennison is aboard ship ready to steam away.

Saladine tries to help Cary Eagan [sic] who battles bravely. Chan leads his men on. Kaohla suddenly is grabbed by Saladine. The Hawaiian wonders at the sudden change of front [sic] by Saladine. John has been carried out to a skiff and tough men are ready to shove off for the ship. Harbor police boat sweeps in and grabs thugs. Some help John.

The fight at the dive continues. Saladine tries to grab Kaohla. Then John comes back and engages the Hawaiian. After the battle Saladine binds up his wounds. At the same moment he is revealed as the chief of the Federal narcotics squad in the islands.

It is also revealed that this the end of an organized band of dope dealers, led by Jennison. Saladine thought all the time that the Winterslip family was behind the band. Bowker was in the band it is shown. Cary comes in and tells about the wrist watch she has seen.

The watch is found on the arm of a native among the prisoner he says that he found the watch when diving the last trip that the steamer *Matsonia* made into the harbor. The diver says that Bowker is the man he saw throw it out of the port hole. Bowker, accused, points out that at the time of the murder he was miles out in the bay.

Bowker asked where he got the watch says it was given him by Harry Jennison. Bowker says that Jennison is aboard the ship now ready to sail and accuses him as head of the opium gang.

2.

John Quincy learning Jennison makes his getaway races for the ship. He finds the attorney. The men fight. The whistle blows for the ship to leave. Chan races aboard.

Jennison gets a revolver and is about to crush the skull of John Quincy when a revolver is thrust into his back from someone standing in the open port hole. Jennison releases John and turns to see Chan, the detective. They take Jennison to the police station.

Facing the prosecutor Bowker tells his story. This is repeated by the prosecutor who says:

----- [illegible] years before Dan Winterslip took the gold and jewels belonging to his brother and James Eagan [sic]. He also kept the box and the log book which told the story.

When his nephew, John Quincy, sailed from San Francisco he had gotten the box and log book back at his Uncle's direction and was to have thrown it in the sea. Cary Eagan [sic] had also been sent by her father to get the box.

Jennison knew of the box and arranged with the steward Bowker to get it away from John. He figured with the log he would be able to force Dan Winterslip to agree to his marriage to Barbara. But when he found that Dan was about to change his will—Jennison, when the ship anchored ten miles out, being once the champion swimmer of the islands, swam ashore, killed Dan Winterslip and would have gotten away with it had not Bowker, being on deck discovered him as he came aboard.

Jennison gave the wrist watch to Bowker and the steward threw it overboard the next morning as the ship docked.

So the mystery is revealed and it is presumed that Barbara was glad she was saved. John of course, must have married Cary, but at any rate the mystery and serial ends.

The most totally depressing aspect of researching that we—and our colleagues Steve Joyce, Bill Chase, and Harry H. Long—encountered while preparing our silent-horrors encyclopedia[1] was the frequency with which we had to tag a film as "lost." Along with their physical prints having disintegrated/gone missing/been purposefully destroyed, many of the pictures we discussed in our books seemingly had had all their attendant publicity materials go down the rabbit hole as well. Now, it's logical to assume that the extent to which a film was/is promoted was/is in direct proportion to its economic potential as perceived by its studio. Uncle Carl Laemmle certainly made that clear as films that were budgeted as "Super Jewels" (like 1923's *The Hunchback of Notre Dame*) or even "Jewels" (like 1927's *The Cat and the Canary*) received extravagant press materials and ubiquitous exposure that reflected their production costs and anticipated box-office returns, while for "Red Feathers" (like 1916's *A Huntress of Men*)—stuck at the bottom of the Universal heap—terse industry press alerts and the smallest of ad mats from the skimpiest of press-sheets in the Sunday cinema section of local newspapers were the rule.

Pathé Exchange was as aware of this economic tenet as was Carl Laemmle's frugal empire, if not almost exponentially more so. The Exchange was yet another iteration of the concern that had first appeared—as Le Société Pathé Frères—in France in 1896. Powered by the collective drive and genius of the four eponymous brothers, the company moved steadily from building phonographs to designing and manufacturing motion-picture equipment to becoming the largest production company in the world. In addition to producing thousands of films of various lengths, types, and genres, Pathé saw to their distribution as well as handling that task for numerous other smaller or independent studios, thus extending its influence and increasing its marketshare in the developing worldwide hunger for moving pictures.

Circa 1910, the company established its American base in Buffalo, New York; within a half-dozen years, studios were opened in Fort Lee, New Jersey, and the iconic serial *The Perils of Pauline* became the *bonjour* moment for Pathé Exchange. In 1921, the Pathé Exchange bid *adieu* to its French parent company, and the feature-length films subsequently produced were supported by a good hundred-and-a-half short subjects and dozens of 10-chapter serials. Many of these were the product of the collective talents of Spencer Gordon Bennet, Frank Leon Smith, Allene Ray, and Walter Miller, the principals of *The House Without a Key*, the motion picture debut of Charlie Chan.

Despite the array of comprehensive literature out there on the cinematic legacy of Charlie Chan, most volumes give comparatively short shrift to the productions that preceded the "mother lode" that ran from the discovery of the vein in 1931 (Warner Oland in *Charlie Chan Carries On*) to its petering out in 1949 with Roland Winters and *The Sky Dragon*. Those titles flanked a body of 44 feature films that included 22 starring Sidney Toler as the Chinese sleuth and a switch in the franchise's status from a modicum of "Shakey A"—"High B" prestige for the first few pictures at 20th Century-Fox to the barrel's bottom at Monogram.

The common denominator found in those 44 movies was the fact that the Chinese protagonist was portrayed by a Caucasian. This sort of thing was hardly an eye-opener in the first few decades following the emergence of the motion picture, of course; since the cinema's earliest days, bona fide Asians were normally found onscreen only in background shots, crowd scenes, and stock footage. There were exceptions—Japanese

Sessue Hayakawa achieved superstardom and imminent leading-man status in Cecil B. DeMille's *The Cheat* (1915), and 17-year-old Chinese American maiden Anna May Wong made her first resounding impact in 1922's *The Toll of the Sea*—but the common practice was for Oriental leads to be played by Occidental actors (the apex of which may have been Mary Pickford as 1915's *Madame Butterfly*). Come the mid-1930s, then, when Warner Oland was enjoying his greatest popularity as Biggers's detective, the lion's share of first or secondary cast Asian characters to be found on the beaded screen were played by the likes of E. Alyn "Fred" Warren and Leslie Fenton.

In 1929, though—before Fox was ready to commit to Chan or Oland or anything that resembled a series—the studio produced *Behind That Curtain*, a Movietone 10-reeler based on Biggers's eponymous novel from the previous year. Far from having his name grace the title—a practice that would start with 1931's *Charlie Chan Carries On*, the film version of the only one of the series of five novels to include the popular detective's name in the title—Inspector Chan saw his enactor relegated to 13th billing, virtually last in the cast scrawl. Profoundly little is known about E.L. Park who essayed the role in *Curtain*, although William K. Everson (*The Detective in Film*) and Ken Hanke (*Charlie Chan at the Movies*) maintained that Park was British and, based on such, John continued that assertion in his coverage of *Charlie Chan at the Opera* nearly two decades ago.[2] It is apparent nowadays, however, that Park was a San Francisco-born Korean American and was the third and last *Asian* actor to impersonate the Chinese detective.

In October 1927, Carl Laemmle's Universal had released *The Chinese Parrot*, a seven-reel "Jewel" based on the Biggers's series novel that had first seen print a year earlier.[3] Perhaps because Kamiyama (*The Thief of Bagdad*, *The Road to Mandalay*, *The Sea Beast*) Sojin was a fairly big name at the time, the Japanese-born actor was billed sixth, below Marian Nixon and Hobart Bosworth, but above Edgar Kennedy, Slim Summerville, and Anna May Wong. Intriguingly, Laemmle had originally bought the rights to Biggers's work to serve as a vehicle for German actor Conrad Veidt, who had ventured to LaLaLand earlier that same year to appear as Louis XI opposite John Barrymore in *The Beloved Rogue*. Laemmle, himself a German expatriate, then traded on their common roots, a multi-picture contract, and Paul Leni's behind in the director's chair on *Parrot* to get the lanky Veidt's John Hancock on a contract. Not long thereafter—having been convinced it was a mistake to waste the popular Veidt in a "Chinese" role—Laemmle moved his recent acquisition to another picture, and Sojin was signed in his stead. Thus, the second Chan to show his inscrutable face on the big screen was also Asian.

A year earlier still, in November 1926, with the film rights to the first "Charlie Chan novel" having been secured by Pathé Exchange, said company announced in the trade press the release of its movie version. Inasmuch as neither Biggers nor anyone else could have anticipated his readers's reaction to the canny—if self-effacing—Chan, the character was written to provide the solution to the mystery, such as it was, without intruding terribly much in the action. Adaptor Frank Leon Smith followed the author's lead, and so George Kuwa—who had been born Keiichi Kuwahara in Nippon and who was, in a literal sense, the movies's *alpha* Charlie Chan—found himself perched in the ninth spot on the thesp list. It was when Warner Oland assumed the role of the Honolulu detective-sergeant that the series went viral, of course, at which point the only Chans to be found being portrayed by Asian actors were Charlie's wives and children.

Back in 1925, though, it must have come

as a surprise to Biggers when letters about sequels to *House* began to arrive at his publisher, with most of the inquiries curious about the character of the Chinese detective. With all the brouhaha concerning Chang Apana (see below) as of yet undisclosed, Biggers admitted for the record that, in *House* at least, Chan was "a minor character, a mere bit of local color."[4] Depending upon the reader's personal proclivities, the light in which the Chinese detective was introduced may have ranged from being negatively stereotypical to mildly positive. Despite this, the character was found to be fascinating by the majority of the readership.

> As soon as Bigger's story ceased runing serially in *The Saturday Evening Post*, "Say—when are we going to have another Charlie Chan story?" became a popular cry, suggesting that Bigger's magazine excerpts had an electrifying effect on readers, in much the same way that earlier Americans had crowded the New York docks to get the next installment of a Dickens novel more than half a century earlier.[5]

Interesting point to consider: Did these three films feature Asian actors in the role only because—at that point in Biggers's series and cinematic convention—Charlie Chan was considered a *minor* character? It seems an unfortunate coincidence that two of these movie adaptations have gone missing, while the third—*Behind That Curtain*, interred for decades in the Fox studio vaults—has only recently (2007) finally been made available as a B-side curiosity in volume three of Fox Searchlight's "Charlie Chan Collection." (Of the three Asian portrayals, E.L. Park's is the briefest, clocking in at approximately four minutes on screen time.) As several of the earliest Oland entries (including his first, *Charlie Chan Carries On*) have likewise lammed it, we may attribute this collective tragedy to the casual attitude regarding/ill-thought-out decisions concerning film preservation during the earliest years of the Sound Era, as well as to Time's caprices.

The first installment of *The House Without a Key* appeared in *The Saturday Evening Post* in its September 24, 1925, issue. While there was clear precedent for the fairly speedy production of feature films derived from Biggers's literary properties—*Seven Keys to Baldpate* and *Fifty Candles* (the latter starring Bertram Grassby as "Hung Chin Chung"!) were also filmed within a couple of years of those novels finding a following—for some reason *House* was to follow the path set by the *Post* and be released in weekly episodes. Could this—the only Biggers's adaptation *ever* filmed as a chapterplay—have contributed to the film's ultimately becoming lost? All those short reels, coming and going, week after week…? When

**Not *what* or *where* was the key, but *who*? That alone kept everyone guessing.**

considered in tandem with 1927's *The Chinese Parrot*, *House*'s disappearance means that two-thirds of the silent Chan "canon" has gone missing. While both losses (particularly that of the Leni feature) are to be deplored, the concomitant dearth of publicity materials and related information concerning the serial is fairly easy to understand.

First off, let's be honest: *very* few moviegoers at any point in time plunked down the price of admission solely because of their interest in the latest serial episode. Like the newsreel, the trailer(s), and (from the late 1920s until the late 1950s) the nearly ubiquitous cartoon, the serial was just an addendum to the main feature. There was no conceivable reason for a studio to part with more than a few bucks on publicity materials or press promotions when—kids and a minuscule number of adult ticket-buyers apart—audiences almost never planned a return visit seven days down the road just to see how Tarzan had saved Jane's bacon yet again, or whether, that time 'round, Gabby Hayes had really been plugged by one of those goll-darned @#$%& varmints he was always going on about. Thus, other than the coverage they received (mostly from fans) years after the fact, chapterplays weren't afforded the sort of attention we researchers are always grateful for nowadays. The following, for example, is one of the very few snippets of attention paid to *The House Without a Key*.

> Judging by the first installments shown in the projection room Pathé serial followers are in for as good a time as they had with *Snowed In*, *The Fighting Marine* and others acted, directed and written by the same invincible co-operative organization assembled by Pathé.[6]

Both titles cited in that briefest of industry-press mentions were also 10-episode chapterplays directed by Spencer Gordon Bennet, written and/or adapted by Frank Leon Smith, and starring Allene Ray and Walter Miller. From 1925 through 1929, that team—more frequently than not supported by B-cast members Frank Lackteen, Harry Semels, et al.—cranked them out with gusto. The first of the lot—1925's *Sunken Silver*—saw the participation of co-director George B. Seitz, but the titles released over the next couple of years (*Play Ball* and *The Green Archer*, both 1925; the "MPN" titles above and *The House Without a Key*, all 1926) were the brainchildren of the forementioned quartet. Beginning the following year, Frank Leon Smith was supplanted by either George Arthur Grey or Joseph Anthony Roach, who joined with Bennet, Ray, and Miller for the rest of the run of the "team's" 10-chapter serials: 1927's *Hawk of the Hills* and *Melting Millions*; *The Terrible People*, *The Man Without a Face*, and *The Yellow Cameo*, all 1928; and 1929's *The Black Book*.

Of the four members of the "invincible co-operative organization," Smith was the first to jump ship. Per the IMDB, Smith "developed a hatred for the movies, especially movie serials." Nonetheless, in 1929, he penned the story for another 10-episode Pathé chapterplay that would prove to be his serial swansong: *The Fire Detective*, starring Gladys McConnell and Hugh Allan. Paramount's *Melody in Spring* (1934) marked the screenwriter's only post–Pathé credit, and his unfortunate demise from pleurisy followed shortly thereafter. *Bound and Gagged* from 1919 had marked Smith's entrée into the chapterplay field, with the 10-episode saga released in the U.S. by the Pathé Exchange and throughout the rest of civilization through Pathé Frères. This George B. Seitz effort marked the last time the Exchange's parent company would be involved in distribution of serials produced by Seitz, by any of the independent studios utilizing the Exchange, or by the Exchange itself. Six more Pathé-distributed chapterplays (including 1920's *The Phantom Foe*, starring Warner Oland, and 1924's *The Fortieth Door*, highlighted by the appearance of the sultry Anna May Wong) would come and go before Smith was assigned *Sunken Silver*, and we're back where we started, two paragraphs up.

Spencer Gordon Bennet (another of our gentlemen who insisted on using three names to endorse their paychecks) may be the most familiar of the fabulous four to such as us. Having seen his first light in Brooklyn on January 5, 1893, Bennet went on to be a jack of (most) all cinematic trades. En route to taking on the megaphone and jodhpurs, he acted a bit: his first of four onscreen appearances—in 1914's *The Perils of Pauline*—may be taken as career foreshadowing; his last—in his own (and George B. Seitz's) *Sunken Silver*—as a realization that his fortune lie *behind* the camera.

Bennet's being joined at the hip with chapterplays started with *Silver* (his only credit prior to that was 1921's *Behold the Man*, a New Testament snoozer) and reached up into the '50s. The episode-oriented Brooklynite was involved with dozens of sound serials, mainly for Columbia and Republic, before displaying a knack at working with eclectic crud like *Voodoo Tiger* (1952) and *Killer Ape* (1953), two efforts in the cheap and cheesy Jungle Jim series featuring ex–Tarzan Johnny Weissmuller; eight segments of television's 1953 Jungle Jim-rip-off *Ramar of the Jungle* (starring an embarrassed Jon Hall); and the under-appreciated and quasi-paranoid indie sci-fi feature *The Atomic Submarine* in 1959. Following the Pathé canon, but prior to/between/among this body of work, came such classic chapterplays as *The Masked Marvel* (1943), *The Tiger Woman* (1944), *Superman* (1948), *Batman and Robin* (1949), and *Captain Video* (1952).

In the '70s, Bennet sat down at the Columbia Pictures lot on Gower Street and chatted about the serial with author Jon Tuska,[7] who asked whether it had occurred to the director to cast Warner Oland—who was, even in 1926, renowned as a portrayer of Asian personages—for the role in *House*. Bennet admitted:

> Not to me, no. Of course, he specialized in playing Orientals, usually villains.... He was a splendid actor. The part in *House Without a Key* would have been too small for him, even if somebody had suggested he be cast for it.

Cognizant as to why Tuska had raised the question—for many "Chan-atics," Oland would go on to become the movies's definitive Chinese detective—Bennet explained:

> It was no Charlie Chan picture. Chan was just a detective. He wasn't that involved in the action. In fact, we were a couple of chapters into the story before he even made an appearance.[8]

Bennet, who enjoyed not only the approbation of the populace, but also a long run in life's venue, died in October 1987.

Walter Miller (1892–1940) had what might be termed a pretty conventional film career for an actor who made over 260 films between the early 1910s and, well, 1940. Starting out with a slew of uncredited bits in dozen of shorts (his film debut was 1911's *Tangled Lines*), Miller moved up the ladder, as it were, to credited bits (like 1915's *The Family Stain*), to secondary roles in features (Fox's *The Marble Heart*, 1916), to taking over as juvenile lead (1921's *The Shadow*),

**George Kuwa, the screen's first Chinese detective in the Honolulu Police Department.**

before back to the second cast (*Hill's Valley*, 1931), and then to uncredited bits (*The Man Who Cried Wolf*, 1937). Miller may have worked the last few years of his life without screen credit, but he worked often and everywhere: nine of the 1940 pictures in which he appeared were released posthumously, including *Island of Doomed Men*, *The Saint's Double Trouble*, and—most relevant to the discussion at hand—*Charlie Chan's Murder Cruise*. Among his 20–odd dozen jaunts before the camera were several he shared with Boris Karloff: the 1929 part silent/part talkie Mascot serial *The King of the Kongo*; Tiffany's *The Utah Kid* (1930); the 1931 Mascot chapterplay *King of the Wild*; 1931's *The Mad Genius* (unbilled); and, in 1936, he did one of his uncredited bits with both Boris *and* Bela, in Universal's *The Invisible Ray*. Another Miller appearance of interest to us (and for which he could read his name on the screen) was Universal's scientific claptrap 1934 chapterplay *The Vanishing Shadow*.[9] Betwixt and between all of this output were the Pathé serials listed above, a handful of Mascot serials in addition to those listed above, and B-pictures galore, many featuring the latest cowpoke to come down the pike and/or Rin-Tin-Tin.

With Bennet from Brooklyn and Miller a native of Dayton, Ohio, it just seemed geographically apropos that Allene Ray would have her roots in the Old West. Born in San Antonio, Texas, on January 2, 1901, Ray was up to her diapers in horses almost from day one. An accomplished equestrienne at an early age, she went on to local renown as the girl who (per the IMDB) "tamed wild broncos." In 1917 the Balboa Amusement Producing Company starred the 16-year-old in its short *Crossed Trails*, and it wasn't long thereafter that Tex O'Reilly—Western-oriented screenwriter and thespian—became something of a mentor to her. In 1919, Ray starred with Harry Myers in a trio of oater two-reelers and, the following year, she headlined as "Blue Bonnet" (we kid you not) in Bert Lubin's five-reeler *Honeymoon Ranch*. The next couple of years saw a couple more horse operas that clocked in at under an hour (including *Partners of the Sunset*, with future *White Zombie* star Robert Frazer) and, among other projects, a move from indies to the more established Fox Studios for seventh billing in 1923's *Times Have Changed*, a five-reeler whose plot introduced a dramatic change of venue for the young star: New York City.

Come 1924, Ray appeared in her first Pathé Exchange 10-reeler, *The Way of a Man*, in which she was restored to top billing and performed for the first time under the direction of George B. Seitz. Several more chapterplays followed—mostly for Pathé—until Ray starred in *Sunken Silver*, and we're again back to square one. The Exchange dropped chapterplays from its inventory in 1919, so Ray's last serial gasp came (in *12* chapters) courtesy of Universal: 1930's *The Indians Are Coming*, with Tim McCoy. Three more or less hour-long Bs followed (including 1931's *The Phantom*), and Allene Ray—pert, lovely, doer of her own stunts, possessor of a high-pitched voice not suitable to the talkies—called it quits. She enjoyed cinematic "retirement" for damned close to a half-century, passing away on May 5, 1979.

George Kuwa's cinematic résumé covers 60-plus appearances—in shorts, features, and (of course) serials, credited and uncredited in 15 years, beginning in 1916. It was some 30 years prior to his film debut in *The Soul of Kura San*, that the diminutive actor (at 5'3" he could look Allene Ray square in the eye) had been born in Japan; like so many of his Asian colleagues, he spent a good part of his career as background/in bits in scenarios of romance and/or corruption in Western civilization. Nonetheless, he did have featured roles in a few horror/thriller pictures of interest to us: *The Bottle Imp* (1917), *The Willow Tree* (1920), *Curlytop* (1924), *The Chinese Parrot* (1927), and *Chi-*

natown Charlie* (1928), plus a pair of uncredited appearances in Douglas Fairbanks's *When the Clouds Roll By* (1919) and 1931's *Daughter of the Dragon*, the third piece of the Warner Oland/Fu Manchu triad. The title of his last movie—1931's *Wicked* (directed by Allan Dwan)—was fitting, as Kuwa died (back home in Japan) on Halloween that same year.

Per film historian Hans Wollstein, the Japanese emigrant didn't make a beeline for the movies when he first reached American shores: "A former stock company actor for impresario Oliver Morosco, Kuwa had appeared on stage in both Japan and California prior to entering films in 1916."[10] Best known to non-genre movie buffs for his role in the 1922 Rudolph Valentino feature *Moran of the Lady Letty* (directed by George [*Drácula*] Melford), the actor got exactly zero's worth of ink in the very few pre-production write-ups on *House*, and Pathé opted to pass on the only maneuver that would have given the production a second shot at garnering some kind of press attention: changing its format.

Publicity-wise, if a silent chapterplay had been subsequently edited down and (re)released as a feature (like *Hawk of the Hills* in 1929), it might have seen some critical light of day; conversely, if it was *not* reconfigured thus, it usually saw its first run through the projector without press comment no matter how many chapters it had. Generally, a sparse handful of pre-production publicity puff pieces would alert both indie and studio-run movie palaces of serials on the cusp of emergence, but unless the gentlemen of the cinematic press added a sentence or two at the end of their reviews of the feature, any and all cogent commentary on the latest episode of the latest chapterplay was limited to casual conversation between and among ticket-buyers on their way out the theater door. One haphazard way, then, of searching out mention of *The House Without a Key* (or of any of the titles listed above, or of *any* silent serial, actually) would be to hunt down reviews of contemporaneous feature films and hie to the last paragraph, even with no guarantee whatsoever of finding that pertinent sentence or two at the end of same. Undaunted, we gave this hit-and-miss modus operandi a few shots, and came up empty.

One of the very few pieces of press coverage exceeding a sentence or two that we *did* find on the production was also printed prior to its general release. Other than several paragraphs of plot regurgitation, the salient bits of C.S. Sewell's commentary as set in stone in the November 27, 1926, edition of *Moving Picture World* are as follows:

> Here is a serial that, judging from the exceptionally good opening chapters, looks like a corker that will immensely please the fans.... There is no dearth of action and typical plotting and counter-plotting and scheming.... Allene Ray and Walter Miller are excellent in the leading roles and live up to their well-deserved popularity.... In addition to the popularity of the stars and the established reputation of Pathé as a producer of excellent serials, is the fact that the author is a very popular writer and the story on which this ten-episode play is based ran serially in *The Saturday Evening Post*.

Thus, the more cogent items mentioned in what was headed "Timely Reviews of Short Subject Productions." Please note that that very popular writer whose novel was the source of the serial is not named; Biggers must have been very popular, indeed. If, like virtually all other films, *The House Without a Key* involved a cinematographer or an art director, this notice demurred from acknowledging and/or identifying them: not major wellsprings of production credits, these publicity puffs. And, once again, George Kuwa earned nary a word, and, as for Charlie Chan ... who?

As it stands, we can't even vouch with certainty for the production's published release date. While *Motion Picture News* lists November 21 as "The Day" for *House* (headline: "New Serial on Pathé Schedule"), we've come across a couple of aberrations in our online newspaper-archive research: A minute box on the movie page of the February 18, 1926, edition of Indiana's *Hammond Times* revealed that the fourth chapter of the serial ("A Mystery of Modern Hawaii") had been unleashed on the viewing public. In addition, in the midst of its nondescript column, "In Movieland," *The Tipton Tribune* (also Indiana) alerted the squinting reader to the serial's existence and helpfully added, "In Hawaii." With both papers printed and circulated in the Hoosier State, our first, best guess is that we're witnessing the Roaring Twenties's equivalent of today's release scheme: "In select theaters on the -----, and in theaters everywhere on the -----."

The readily accessible secondary sources we checked mentioned *The House Without a Key* en passant if they mentioned the film at all. We quickly saw that most of the current books dealing with Charlie Chan's cinematic career limit details on the serial to the facts that it is lost and that George Kuwa was Asian. Several of these compendia also disclose that The Reef and Palm Hotel owed its literary existence to "Gray's by the Sea," the Waikiki Beach hotel Biggers and family vacationed at in April 1920, and/or that the character of Chan was based on a pair of real-life Chinese detectives—Chang Apana and Lee Fook—then on the Honolulu police force. And much of the time, Chang Apana is given 100 percent of the inspirational credit while Detective Fook gets … *errrrr* … left out. In a local newspaper article[11] reporting on a meeting held (finally) between Biggers and Apana, the novelist basically shrugs off these supposed real-life inspirations and admits, "Charlie's a storybook character.… He wasn't cut out after a pattern." (In another clipping we have on Biggers and Apana—dated March 22, 1931, but with no other source identification on it—the author again maintains, "The character of Charlie Chan, for better or worse, is entirely fictitious.")

In the decades between Biggers's Hawaiian holiday and our putting fingers to keyboard in the here and now, "Gray's by the Sea" metamorphosed into the Halekulani Hotel, which features a restaurant yclept "The House Without a Key." While this, too, is of interest to Charlie Chan-atics, it is *post hoc, ergo propter hoc* with respect to Pathe's 1926 chapterplay and really doesn't serve to explain or expand on anything concerning the production itself. Rendering any research on the nomenclature of the restaurant even more meaningless is Biggers's revelation (in the *Honolulu Star Bulletin* piece, referenced above) "I did not use any specific house in the story" and "There is no 'House Without a Key.'" Observing that the plot of the premier Chan novel and that of the eponymous movie version differed somewhat is useful, but doesn't provide us with much meat for the soup: most movies are adapted to fit the dynamics and requirements of the screen, and *HWK* was no exception.

Spencer Gordon Bennet: World-class serial director (and occasional actor).

One certainty—albeit not confirmable via studio press release or secondary-source attribution—is that *The House Without a Key* was *not* shot on location in the then–U.S. territory of Hawaii. Location shooting—virtually unheard of in U.S. productions during the Silent Era—slowly became more feasible with the coming of sound, and the second film to star Warner Oland as Chan—1931's *The Black Camel*, with Bela Lugosi—*was* shot in the Islands. (Intriguingly, the first film to star Sidney Toler as Chan—1938's *Charlie Chan in Honolulu*—was not only *not* shot in Honolulu, but, per film historian Ken Hanke, *Honolulu* "was going to be a 'B' picture and no mistake"[12] from the moment of its inception.) The *MPW* commentary (cited above) makes mention that "much of the earlier action takes place on shipboard and involving [sic] a rascally steward and the hero." That, together with the oft-semi-incoherent plot summaries setting most of the rest of the action in and around sitting rooms, bedrooms, lanai interiors, and the like, makes it fairly easy to infer that the only exposure *House* audiences had to any of the God's-honest Hawaiian Islands came courtesy of stock footage.

We don't know what the spread of critical reaction was to *The House Without a Key*. No one who saw the serial in its entirety left behind a public record of his impressions (that we could find, at any rate), and it's possible (some might say "probable") that Pathé Exchange, which liquidated in 1931, saw very little monetary advantage to storing silent serial chapters once sound held sway. Reedited feature versions might have novelty value, fill out a low-budget program, or serve as some sort of company record of an actor, an artisan, or a trend, but ... silent serial chapters? Aficionados of this subgenre maintain that the only such episodes that did survive time's ravages and studios's apathy were those either inadvertently overlooked by their owners or squirreled away by fans and collectors. Nonetheless, *House* did enjoy an initial exposure that was fairly international in scope, a condition shared by most productions shot, released, and distributed by the Pathé Exchange. While most export versions saw the carbon arc under a literal translation of Biggers's original title, some countries hosted the serial under a different banner; in Germany, for example, *House* was screened as *Die Opiumhöhle von Hawaii* (*The Opium Den of Hawaii*). As is clearly apparent from the Library of Congress chapter summaries, opium smuggling/dealing/whatever may have been a fairly important piece of explanatory revelation at the picture's climax, but the body of the serial was as opium-den free as were the Silent Era's ubiquitous "Farmer Al Falfa" cartoons. The sheer size of the area traversed via the distribution of *The House Without a Key*, though, may lead to the eventual discovery of prints of sundry episodes, perhaps out there in plain sight as we write this, albeit masked by a different title.

For the nonce, though, the serial, she is gone.

Considering some of the inordinate crud that has perdured, more's the pity here.

# Forgotten Faces

Paramount Famous Lasky Corp.—August 11, 1928—7,640 feet/8 reels/75–80 minutes
**Cast:** Clive Brook as Heliotrope Harry Harlow; Mary Brian as Alice Deane; (Olga) Baclanova as Lilly Harlow; William Powell as Froggy; Fred Kohler as Prisoner #1309; Jack Luden as Tom; Hedda Hopper as Mrs. Deane; J. Barney Sherry as Mr. Deane; with Francis McDonald, Crauford Kent

**Credits:** *Director*: Victor Schertzinger; *Presenters*: Adolph Zukor and Jesse L. Lasky; *Supervisor*: David Selznick; *Scenario*: Howard Estabrook; *Titles*: Julius Johnson; *Adaptation*: Oliver H.P. Garrett; *Cinematography*: J. Roy Hunt; *Film Editors*: David Selznick, George Nichols, Jr.; *Based on the story* **A Whiff of Heliotrope** *by* Richard Washburn Child (*Hearst's*, November 1919)

The plot device of purposely frightening someone in an attempt to drive them mad or cause their death is at least as old as *Gaslight* (1940 and 1944) and *Diabolique* (1955), not to mention such lesser efforts, like 1958's *Macabre*. A slightly less common idea has the villains conducting a campaign of terror with the aim of getting their victims to commit murder, a situation found in films like *Nightmare* (1964) and *Games* (1967). Far more unusual than either of these, however, is the set-up done in such a way that the perpetrator wants his victim to kill *him*. Such is the premise in Richard Walburn Child's 1919 short story "A Whiff of Heliotrope," which Hollywood liked enough to film four times.

Author Richard Washburn Child was a graduate of Harvard Law, a prolific writer, an editor for *The Saturday Evening Post*, a speechwriter for Warren Harding, a war correspondent, an ambassador to Italy, and a tireless promoter of Mussolini (he and Luigi Barzini ghostwrote Il Duce's autobiography). He was also fascinated by criminals of a more mundane sort—these served as the subject of many of his short stories—and even served on a national crime commission.

The hero of Washburn Child's "Heliotrope" is George Hasdock, a career criminal serving a life sentence for murdering a guard during a holdup. An exemplary prisoner and a man of honor, Hasdock is eligible for a pardon, but the warden is reluctant to grant it without the express approval of the governor, who is visiting the prison at the time. Hasdock's wife, Cleo, a hustler and sometimes dope addict, is threatening to blackmail their daughter, who knows nothing of her parentage, having been raised to be a proper young lady by a French governess, a situation arranged and paid for by Hasdock before he was imprisoned. Now that his daughter is about to be married to a society gentleman, Cleo—her hitherto hidden maternal instincts suddenly aroused—is planning to introduce herself to her daughter and future son-in-law and put the bite on them. Begging to be released so he can prevent this, Hasdock promises the warden and the governor that he will not lay a hand on Cleo or use any violence against her. As the warden considers the prisoner a man of his word, the governor grants his release.

While Cleo plans to visit her daughter—she has a letter proving that she's her mother—another letter, blank except for the strong smell of heliotrope, arrives in the mail. Hasdock always had the scent of heliotrope about him, so Cleo—learning that her husband is no longer behind bars—begins to fear for her life. She moves from one dive to the next, but the smell of heliotrope follows her everywhere. Frantic with fear, she arms herself with a revolver and, when Hasdock emerges from the shadows one night, she shoots him. But that was Hasdock's plan all along: he had earlier stolen the letter that was Cleo's only evidence of her motherhood and had come to meet his wife unarmed. Hasdock dies content in the knowledge that Cleo will certainly go to jail—probably for life—for killing him, and that his daughter will be free to marry without interference.

Provoking someone to shoot you knowing that the police are just in the wings provided the climaxes for both *Kiss of Death* (1947) and *Gran Torino* (2008), while, on the small screen, Victor Jory avenges the murder of his son by provoking the killers to shoot him in front of witnesses in "Death of a Cop," a 1963 episode of *The Alfred Hitchcock Hour*. The *Zane Grey Theater* screened a story more directly inspired by "Heliotrope": *Honor Bright*, in which Danny Thomas promises his dying daughter (played by real-life daughter Marlo) that he won't lay a finger on the philanderer responsible for her accidental death. Instead, he follows the man everywhere, delivering one rose at a time wherever he goes, while promising that there will be one last rose. The philanderer, thinking that the last rose will be given just before his murder, is frenzied with fear and shoots Thomas as he about to deliver it; however, Thomas is armed only with a rose—not a gun—and a roomful of onlookers makes the gallows a certainty for the scoundrel.

Though Washburn Child's later writings about crime certainly don't suggest that he was a bleeding-heart liberal, in "Heliotrope" his portrait of the criminal as a man with a strict code of honor seems more than a little romanticized and sentimental. Nonetheless, this was somewhat in keeping with the '20s' depiction of movie gangsters, who were usually shown to be elegant gentlemen, natty dressers, patrons of high-class establishments, and always with sophisticated, classy ladies at their side. It would take the grim '30s to bring more realistic portraits to the screen, with the likes of Scarface, Little Caesar, and Tom Powers. The image of the gentleman-crook *did* survive, though, in films about jewel thieves; presumably, Depression-Era audiences did not particularly care if someone lifted the luxury goods of the rich and powerful.

The first screen version of Washburn Child's story was a 1920 Cosmopolitan/Paramount production entitled *Heliotrope*. According to studio-generated publicity, director George Baker "selected the story,

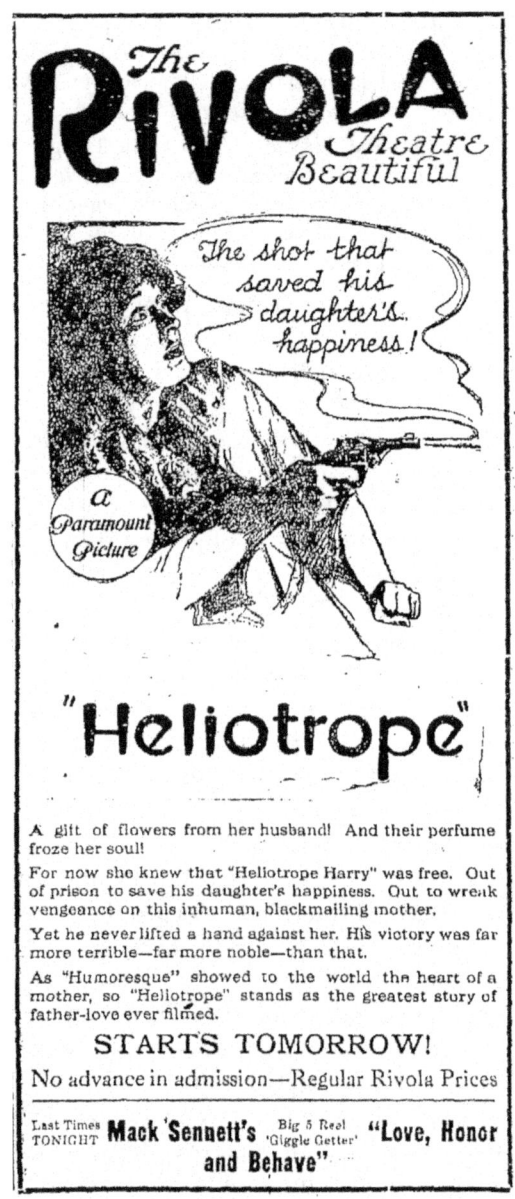

**The pistol packing blackmailing mama was played by Julia Swain Gordon who had been a major star at Vitagraph.**

wrote the scenario, directed the picture and titled it, thereby making it a 100% Baker feature." (He also edited it; truly an auteur.) Baker changed the name of the main character from George to Harry, obviously feeling that the nickname "Heliotrope Harry" would have more pizazz than "Heliotrope George." (Subsequent films went along with Baker's decision to call the protagonist "Harry," although each used a different surname for the character.) The February 1921 edition of *Picture Play* praised Fred Burton as Harry, but found much of the film mediocre, although "redeemed" by the climatic twist of Harry terrifying his wife into shooting him. Somewhat perversely, that's exactly what the November 28, 1920, *Wid's Daily* didn't like: "A corking good picture until the very finish … they plant an unnecessary murder and a lot of additional and unnecessary footage long after the story has been told and definitely closed." In any case, *Heliotrope* was the only version of the story to adhere faithfully to the ending of Washburn Child's tale.

Since the story had first appeared in a Hearst publication and since Citizen William Randolph himself was the force behind Cosmopolitan Pictures, *Heliotrope* received quite a bit of press. Many ads for the film stressed that it was not unlike another Cosmopolitan production, *Humoresque*, but while the latter dealt with the self-sacrificing commitment of a mother to her son, *Heliotrope* provided a parallel theme in the love of a father for his daughter. Of course, the ads could have promoted the film's depiction of the grasping, selfish mother as a *contrast* to the nice Jewish mama of *Humoresque*, but that wouldn't have sold many tickets. Melodramas about parents and children were very common in the Silent Era, and tales of parents shielding their true identifies from their offspring were also frequently filmed. (Tod Browning seems to have made a cottage industry out of pictures like these.)

Eight years later, during that period in which silent and sound films enjoyed a brief and uneasy coexistence, Paramount decided to emit "A Whiff of Heliotrope" once again. Hearst had taken his Cosmopolitan company to M-G-M, but Paramount still owned the rights to the Washburn Child story. During its five-week shoot, the film was known as *The Perfumed Trap*, a tag that actually makes a bit more sense than its release title, *Forgotten Faces*. Paramount's publicity department wasn't sure what to do with the new title, either, and offered the following: "Forgetting is perilous when sin makes the past ominous. Reason totters, chaos triumphs when Forgotten Faces find the victim of their hate." And, if *that* weren't obscure enough, there was also the description of the film as "A melodrama that defies forgetfulness."

While the 1920 *Heliotrope* is MIA and unavailable for comparison with the later version, at least one of the changes George Baker made to Washburn Child's story was retained by the writing team for *Forgotten Faces*: Harry is given a faithful sidekick who is also a crook and who helps Harry in his scheme to thwart his scheming spouse. *Heliotrope* also apparently devoted a fair amount of footage to the young lovers, but *Faces* wisely ignores them to concentrate on the game of cat and mouse going on between Harry and his ruthless wife. Our synopsis is based on a viewing of the film:

> The film begins as Heliotrope Harry and his pal Froggy hold up the patrons of a swanky casino. One of the socialites takes off her wedding ring, but Harry gives it back to her, saying, "Marriage is one of the few institutions I respect." No sooner have the crooks made their casual escape when a squad of police arrive and enter the casino. Harry realizes he's been double-crossed. [The *Variety* pan of the film comments that he surely would have been caught anyway, as neither he nor Froggy bother to wear masks or disguises during the robbery.]
> The scene shifts to Harry's wife, Lilly, and we see that she does not share her husband's reverence for marriage as she's entertaining a lover while her infant daughter cries, neglected, in her crib. Lilly tells her paramour that she can't stand heliotrope, but won't have to inhale its fragrance

ever again as she has turned Harry into the police. Much to her surprise, Harry promptly turns up, fatally shoots her lover and leaves with the baby.

Harry and Froggy come upon a house in a nice neighborhood that has a white slash on the door, indicating that the couple's infant daughter has died. Harry places his child on the doorstep and watches from hiding as the elated couple gratefully welcome the child. Harry makes Froggy promise to toe the straight and narrow so he can record the girl's progress over the years and keep knowledge of her new home away from Lilly. Froggy, whose loyalty to Harry makes Tonto look like Judas Iscariot by comparison, agrees. Harry turns himself in, thoughtfully letting a rookie cop who needs a break make the pinch.

Harry is sentenced to life, but he makes the best of it and becomes a trusty. Froggy dutifully sends him pictures of his daughter, named Alice by her foster parents, the Deanes. The years pass and after Mrs. Deane dies, Mr. Deane remains devoted to Alice who grows up to be a beautiful and poised young lady. The papers announce her engagement to Jack, a nice boy also from a wealthy family.

Meanwhile, Lilly has been trying for years to learn the whereabouts of her daughter. [This, obviously, not from maternal instinct, but how could she know the girl would be raised by rich people ripe for the plucking?] Froggy resolutely refuses to tell, but one day Lilly is hit by a car outside his room, and he reluctantly allows the medics to bring her inside. Told she's dying, Froggy takes pity on her and shows her the newspaper clipping about Alice's upcoming wedding. Surprise! Accident and medics are fakes, so now Lilly has the information she's yearned for.

Lilly goes to the prison and taunts Harry about how she intends to blackmail the Deane family. Harry flies into a rage and has to be restrained by the guards. He purposely hurts his hand so he can be sent to the infirmary to participate in an escape plan another convict is concocting; however, the warden stumbles into the scene and, after being trussed up, reminds Harry of his promise never to escape. Harry unties the warden and saves him from being knifed by the other convict. Harry is granted parole for his efforts, but he has to promise the warden that he will not harm Lilly.

Harry and Froggy blackmail the butler in the Deane home, thus causing him to skip town. Harry is hired in his place, giving him the perfect opportunity to keep an eye on things and to get to know his daughter. [In the original story, he never even attempts to meet her.] Lilly sends a note to Mr. Deane saying she will see him that evening with information about his daughter, but Harry gets the note first and disposes of it. When Lilly arrives at the appointed time, she is greeted by a sprig of heliotrope attached to the door knocker. She panics and flees the scene.

Knowing that Harry is free, Lilly changes apartments, but there's nowhere she can go without heliotrope sprigs or the fragrance following her. At one point she receives a package with a gun nestled in the flowers. This convinces her that Harry means to kill her, but she takes the weapon for her own protection.

Though increasingly unnerved, Lilly refuses to abandon her plan. She sends another note to Mr. Deane, telling him she will visit him Thursday. Once again Harry intercepts the note and is pleased that the Deanes are going out Thursday night to celebrate Alice's engagement. This means he will have the house to himself.

On Thursday night, Harry answers the door when Lilly calls, but his face is turned away from her and she does not recognize him. He leads her up to the dimly lit attic of the big house where she is frightened to see a light bulb dangling in a noose like fashion. Harry reveals himself and she promptly shoots him. She heads down the stairs, but finds there's a policeman in the hallway. Desperate to get out, Lilly sees an open window with a ladder propped up against it and tries to escape that way. However, one of the ladder's rungs has been sawed through, and she falls off and plunges to her death.[1] The cop turns out to be someone hired by Harry. The family returns in time for Harry to get one last loving look at his daughter before he expires.

Well, people don't go to the opera looking for a realistic story, either.

*Forgotten Faces* may not tell a believable tale; still, its emotions are true and valid. Gentlemen thugs like Harry may be rarely encountered outside the movies, but the idea that someone who realizes he has done one good thing in his otherwise useless existence and who will do anything to protect it and keep it pure, is not incredible. The cynical character of Lilly, who wants to bring everything down to her low level, makes the perfect foil for the world-weary idealism of Harry. It's all persuasive because Clive Brook and Olga Baclanova play their parts with absolute conviction, and Victor Schertzinger's imaginative and clever direction makes one overlook the story's many improbabilities. It's not surprising that, just a few years later, Brook said Harry was his favorite film role.

Olga Baclanova makes Lilly a particularly vicious character, especially in the sequence where she torments Harry in prison. She also etches a vivid portrait of

*Forgotten Faces.* Froggy (William Powell) and Harry (Clive Brook) plot their next move. Powell had to wait for the sound era to achieve stardom but Brook had already done major roles, notably in *Three Faces East* and *Barbed Wire*.

growing fear as Harry's heliotrope campaign against her drives her to the edge. Publicity for the film made much of Olga being "the Russian tigress" and even claimed that she had resorted to expletives in her native Russian for the prison scene with Clive Brook (and we don't know if any Russian-speaking lip-readers can verify this). Baclanova, a star in her native land, was a member of the prestigious Moscow Art Theater and had studied under the legendary Stanislavsky. On tour in America in the mid–20s, she decided to stay in the Land of Opportunity, no doubt preferring the fleshpots of New York and California to privation and decreasing artistic freedom back home.

While touring in a West Coast production of *The Miracle* (playing a nun!), Olga was recruited by Paramount who later signed her to a five-year contract to replace their other exotic star, Pola Negri, who was becoming increasingly volatile. After casting her in a couple of supporting roles, the studio announced she would be known only as Baclanova for *Forgotten Faces*, causing one of the trade journal writers to sniff, "Just why her name is featured is as unknown to me as the name itself."[2] That writer would become more familiar with the actress after her work in *The Man Who Laughs* and *The Docks of New York*, as the former gave her the opportunity to play one of the sexiest characters of the Silent Era while *Docks*, directed by Josef von Sternberg, contains one of her very best performances. Particularly memorable is the scene where Lou—a tough, cynical, tavern gal unhappily married to a rough neck seaman—helps Sadie (Betty Compson) get ready for an impromptu wedding ceremony to a tough, hard-drinking sailor (George Bancroft) in a waterfront dive. Lou embraces Sadie—there's a poignant close-up of Baclanova—and we see in Lou's expression a lifetime of regret and sadness mingled with the hope that by some miracle things will be different for Sadie. Baclanova later recalled that von Sternberg "harassed" her mercilessly to finally get the effect he wanted.

At one point it was announced that Baclanova would star as Catherine the Great in a Technicolor super-production to be directed by Roy William Neill, but that that did not come to pass. A "Life of Beethoven" project apparently got a little further along, but never made it before the cameras, either. The coming of sound marked the beginning of the end of Olga Baclanova's film career, as she had a very thick Russian accent which was hard to understand and was not pleasing to the ear. (Likewise, the great Russian actor Ivan Mosjoukine, a superstar in French films, became practically unemployable in the Sound Era because he couldn't master a comprehensible French.) At times, the actress also had a tendency to *over*act: she was reunited with Clive Brook for *A Dangerous Woman* (1929), but her shrill vamping, played off against Brook's stiff-upper-lip underplaying, resulted in something more campy than erotic. While horror fans remember her for Tod Browning's *Freaks* (1932), the picture was hardly a career enhancer. Baclanova did continue to do occasional stage work, as well as sing.

Clive Brook, of course, had no problem speaking English understandably, and he turns up in very early talkies as often as Conrad Nagel. Brook's first, *The Perfect Crime*, was released at about the same time as *Forgotten Faces*. The Briton had a long and fruitful career in the Silent Era, but he's probably best remembered today for his '30s films, like *Shanghai Express* and *Cavalcade*, as well as for a couple of turns as Sherlock Holmes.

William Powell makes for a likeable Froggy, although one critic was skeptical that the aristocratic Harry would be hanging out with a plebian petty thief. Powell played supporting roles—usually villains—in the Silent Era, but would soon be making his talkie (and talky) debut with *Interference* (1929, also with Clive Brook) before going on to essay *The Thin Man*, *My Man Godfrey*, and many other memorable roles in the '30s. Mary Duncan is a beautiful and appropriately fragile Alice, while Fred Kohler—looking even meaner than usual—snarls appropriately as the knife-wielding Convict #1309. Hedda Hopper's Mrs. Deane is barely a walk-on.

Victor Schertzinger, helped immeasurably by J. Roy Hunt's fluid camerawork, does a superb job on *Forgotten Faces*, even managing to introduce some subtlety into the melodramatic proceedings: when Harry shoots Lilly's lover, all that's seen is a medium shot of Harry facing the man and then smoke, wafting up to his face from his (off-camera) revolver. Lighting for the creepier moments are very much in the Germanic vein, and there is a good use of crane shots. The finale is splendidly tense and eerie as the traveling camera (in long shot) shows Harry leading the unsuspecting Lilly up one flight of stairs to another and then another before finally ending in the shadowy attic. Lilly's plunge to her death is like something out of *Vertigo*. Schertzinger, famous as a musician and composer as well as a film director, did one other genre film, *The Return of Peter Grimm* (1926). The picture is a gentle fantasy, and its ghost is benign, but it has some spooky moments, although nothing quite as unnerving as Lilly's ascent to her doom in *Forgotten Faces*.

Some reviewers were unimpressed with

**The poster for the Spanish release of *A Gentleman After Dark* was far more stylish than anything in the film.**

the film. *Variety* (August 8, 1928) damned it with faint praise, saying that the writers made "a fairly interesting picture out of a top-heavy yarn." The Bible of Show Biz also gave a rather tongue-in-cheek synopsis saying at one point that Harry tells his wife that if she ever lays hands on their kid again, "she will be given her celestial ukulele and an entire trip on the rumble seat of some cloud." Blissfully unaware of remakes yet to come, *Variety* concluded its review with the comment, "Even sound couldn't have helped this one much." The critic for the *New York Times* (August 6, 1928) shook his head at the positive portrayal of crooks and con men and decried a general lack of realism in the story:

> The theme is sentimental and old, but certain scenes and some good acting bring it up from the cellar, where it normally would be, to about the first floor. Many incidents are incredible, many others are overdone; some few are utterly impossible; yet on the whole, *Forgotten Faces* is average entertainment.

*Harrison's* (August 11, 1928) was much more positive: "Good. It is slightly morbid but there is much healthy sentiment in it." The reviewer also opined that the film did an effective job combining suspense and pathos, while "Mae Tinee" of the *Chicago Tribune* (July 25, 1928) was quite enthusiastic about the picture:

> *Forgotten Faces* is an alluring blend of fine acting, good direction and interesting story. Clive Brook is a fascinating "Heliotrope Harry" and Baclanova as the unregenerate Chloe [sic] is one whirlwind and make no mistake, she has an eye like a bronco's I knew once.... In addition to all this you are handed some unusually effective photography and are kept sitting on the anxious seat from start to finish.

Whitney Williams of the *Los Angeles Times* (July 22, 1928) concurred:

> In its seven reels of fast-moving action there are aspects of suspense and interest and intensity of feeling that cannot soon be effaced from memory.... Victor Schertzinger has done an excellent piece of direction. Not once does the situation get out of hand and he has allowed no incidental action to digress from the actual plot.... The picture has practically no let-downs in interest. It is enlivened, too by many clever touches, both from an acting and directorial standpoint, and an undercurrent of intense drama is ever prevalent.

Williams felt that Harry's heliotrope harassment of Lily worked particularly well: "The sense of fear is well established in these scenes. Back of it all too is a suggestion of menace, of a powerful mind striving to achieve a deadly purpose."

We don't have any hard statistics on how *Forgotten Faces* fared at the box office, but scattered reports from the trades suggested it held its own, no mean feat given the competition of the novelty of sound.

Determined to squeeze every last sou out of their investment in "A Whiff of Heliotrope," Paramount brought the story to the screen once again in 1936, this time with Herbert Marshall and Gertrude Michael in the leads. Known as *Something to Live For* during production, the title was changed to *Forgotten Faces* for its release.[3] The director, E.A. Dupont, had helmed the masterpiece *Varieté*, in Germany in 1925, but his subsequent career in England and the States was disappointing. Dupont was fascinated by show business (two of his other films, *Piccadilly* and *Moulin Rouge*, have theatre settings) which perhaps explains why the wife of "Heliotrope" is here transformed into a burlesque queen, and her motive for blackmail is to get money to keep the failing show going. Harry isn't a stick-up man but the proprietor of a casino, and he considers heliotrope his good luck flower. The film is unavailable for viewing, but—going by the reviews and the *AFI Catalog*—there were other significant changes as well. Harry is given a detective friend, and it is he who arranges for the baby girl to be adopted by a rich family. Harry's heliotrope campaign against his wife is meant to terrorize her into giving up her scheme, not provoking her to shoot him (Was there some thought that suicide by wife was still suicide and thus against the Production Code?). Still, shoot him she does, but in making her escape she tumbles off a balcony to her death.

Reviews of the film were respectful, but none of the critics seemed to actually like it. The leads were praised, as was Dupont's direction (especially his use of dueling close-ups during a verbal battle between the couple), but it was felt that the film was unrelentingly grim and scarcely a good choice for an evening's entertainment. Critics also complained about the total lack of humor.[4]

Paramount subsequently sold the rights to the Washburn Child story to United Artists who did another version of the film in 1942, this one given the puzzling title *A Gentleman After Dark*. Harry, played by Brian Donlevy, is now a jewel thief, and Miriam Hopkins is his hardboiled wife. The policeman pal (Preston Foster) is back, but he becomes a lawyer and eventually a justice of the New York Supreme Court. He is the one who adopts Harry's baby (Foster's wife is played by Gloria Holden, Countess Zeleska herself), and Hopkins enlists the aid of a sleazy lawyer (played by that master of sleaze Douglass Dumbrille) to put the bite on Foster. Donlevy escapes from prison to address the situation, but assures Foster he will not harm Hopkins. In a clumsy and unbelievable scene, Dumbrille is shot by the policeman guarding Hopkins, who mistakes the lawyer for Harry. Hopkins then goes on the lam with Harry's heliotrope following her at every step. Donlevy turns up in her apartment and menacingly approaches, causing her to retreat and fall backward through that ever helpful open window. Donlevy goes to the train station to watch his daughter leave on her honeymoon and then turns himself in.

The reviews were mostly unenthusiastic (*Variety* called the film "tedious" and Edwin Marin's direction "heavy handed"), with most not noting that the story had already been filmed several times. That fact did not escape Bosley Crowther of the *New York Times*, who mentions the 1920 and 1936 versions, but somehow overlooks the 1928 film. Per Crowther[5]:

> Brian Donlevy, who has quite a knack for playing hardboiled sentimentalists, does about as well as can be expected in this male Stella Dallas role, and Miriam Hopkins is unutterably poisonous [which she is supposed to be] as the wife.... Put them all together and they turn out for producer Edward Small some tasty mush.

Possibly because of the rights issue, both the 1928 and 1936 versions of *Forgotten Faces* disappeared from sight. Happily, the Library of Congress restored the 1928 version, and this was shown at Capitolfest in Rome, New York, in 2014. The picture looked great and was the hit of the weekend. The 1936 film is still MIA. Perhaps the release of *Varieté* on Blu-ray this past year will encourage someone to track down this missing piece of the E.A. Dupont's canon.

# *High Treason*; *Men Must Fight*

***High Treason***—Gaumont-British—September 20, 1929 (silent)—90 minutes; March 13, 1930 (American sound release version)—68 minutes **Cast:** Jameson Thomas as Michael Deane; Benita Hume as Evelyn Seymour; Basil Gill as Stephen Deane, the President of Europe; Humberston Wright as Dr. Seymour; Henry Vibart as Lord Sycamore; James Carewe as Lord Rawleigh; Hayford Hobbs as Charles Falloway; Milton Rosmer as Ernest Stratton; Judd Green as James Groves; Alf Goodard as the Tele-Radiographer; Irene Brooke as a Senator; Clifford Heatherley as a Delegate; Wally Patch as the Peace League Commissionaire; Raymond Massey as a Cabinet Member; René Ray as a Female Inductee; John Singer as a Boy; Kiyoshi Takase as a Conspirator

**Credits:** *Director:* Maurice Elvey; *Screenplay:* L'Estrange Fawcett; *Musical Score:* Louis Levy and Q. MacLean; *Photography:* Percy Strong; *Art Director:* Andrew Mazzei; *Costumes:* Gordon Conway; *Assistant Directors:* Fred V. Merrick and David Lean; *Sound Recordist:* Stan Jolly; *Special Effects:* Philippo Guidobaldi; *Assistant Cameraman:* Alan Lawson; *Musical Director:* Louis Levy. *Based on the eponymous play by* Noel Pemberton-Billing (1928)

***Men Must Fight***—Metro-Goldwyn-Mayer—February 17, 1933—73 minutes **Cast:** Diana Wynyard as Laura Seward; Lewis Stone as Edward Seward; Phillips Holmes as Bob Seward; May Robson as Maman Seward; Ruth Selwyn as Peggy; Robert Young as Geoffrey Aiken; Robert Grieg as Albert; Hedda Hopper as Mrs. Chase; Don Dilloway as Steve; Mary Carlisle as Evelyn; Luis Alberni as Soto; with Mary Gordon, Sherry Hall, Arthur Housman, Anderson Lawler, George Magrill, Bert Morehouse, Lee Phelps, Buddy Roosevelt, Richard Tucker, Byron Wells

**Credits:** *Director:* Edwin Selwyn; *Script:* C. Gardner Sullivan; *Cinematography:* George Folsey; *Editing:* William S. Gray; *Art Director:* Cedric Gibbons; *Costume Design:* Adrian; *Assistant Director:* Fred M. Wilcox; *Sound:* Douglas Shearer, Fred Morgan. *Based on the eponymous play by* Reginald Lawrence and S.K. Lauren (New York, October 14, 1932)

The synopsis of *High Treason* that follows was submitted by the producers to the New York State Censorship Board on March 13, 1930.

The year is 1940. The political forces of the world have been grouped and war is threatened between the Federated Atlantic States and the United States of Europe over a border incident. A syndicate of international financiers are deliberately agitating war for profit. They caused the border killing and they blow up the Channel Tunnel and bomb the Peace Building in London, making all these catastrophes seem the work of Atlantic States agents.

Since the Great War of 1914–18, twenty-five million people of all nationalities on both sides of the Atlantic have formed a Peace League to prevent war. The European leader of the movement is Dr. Seymour, whose daughter and enthusiastic secretary is in love with Major Michael Deane, of the European Air Force. While Deane prepares for war, Evelyn and her father fervently fight for peace.

The order to mobilize is given ... women as well as men. Evelyn makes a hysterical effort to the stem the war fever in a night club and, after Michael extricates her from an ugly situation, they part bad friends.

The European Council meets to decide the issue of peace or war. The vote is tied until the President's vote decides war. A declaration of war is to be broadcast to the world at midnight. Dr. Seymour makes a last appeal to the President while Evelyn goes to make an impassioned appeal to the conscripted women to prevent the airplanes from leaving. Deane has no option but to take stern measures to quell the mutiny, but, led by Evelyn, the women dare the men to fire on them ... and the men refuse.

Meanwhile, Dr. Seymour is rebuffed by the President, who invites him to broadcast and television a message of support from the Peace League. He agrees to talk, but when introduced he announces that there will be no war. Infuriated by this treachery, the President grabs a revolver to shoot Seymour, but the latter shoots first and the President falls dead ... sacrificed to save civilization.

At the airdrome Deane gives orders for the first squadron to take off, but Evelyn rallies the women and faces Deane with a bomb in her hand, ready to destroy men and machines if an attempt is made to carry out orders.

So the women and the Peace League triumph. War is averted, but Evelyn's father is arrested and tried for murder. Deane and his sweetheart are united in this crisis. The verdict is "Guilty." When the judge asks if the Doctor has anything to say why sentence of death should not be pronounced, the martyr simply answers "I am content."

*High Treason* was based on the 1928 play by Noel Pemberton-Billing, a rather unlikely advocate for pacifism. The flamboyant playwright was an aviator, soldier (Boer War), inventor, journalist, airplane designer, member of the British Parliament ... and major crackpot. Elected to the House of Commons in 1916, he became highly critical of how his government was conducting the Great War, insisting that air power was being unwisely neglected. As the war effort began to falter, his more reasonable observations took a bizarre turn and he claimed that the war was being lost because of "The Hidden Hand" and the "Cult of the Clitoris." The terms were meant to reflect his fear that many prominent Britons had been lured into homosexuality and were now being blackmailed by German agents to either sabotage the war or face exposure. He maintained that 47,000 such people were named in a "Black Book" held by the German Secret Service, and when he hinted that dancer Maud Adams—about to star in a private performance of Oscar Wilde's *Salome*—was part of said conspiracy, she sued him for libel. In the midst of this, Pemberton-Billing's enemies sent Eileen Villiers-Stuart, a young adventuress, to vamp the maverick MP and lure him to a male brothel, where he would be photographed. Intriguingly, he seduced *her*, and she testified in his favor at the Adams libel trial, during which she claimed to have actually seen the notorious Black Book. Pemberton-Billing, acting as his own lawyer, was found Not Guilty, an incredible verdict. After the war had been won, his conspiracy theories were exposed for the nonsense they were, and, certain of defeat, he declined to stand for re-election, claiming ill health.

The world of 1940. Or is it 1950? The producers couldn't decide.

Any of this would have made for far more engaging drama than *High Treason*. Set "sometime in the future," the play has nothing whatsoever futuristic about it, the notation apart: There is no mention of a Channel Tunnel, advanced gadgetry, outlandish fashions, or anything actually smacking of science fiction. The film's big scenes—the sabotage of the Channel Tunnel, the bombing of the Peace League, the standoff between the female draftees and the airmen—are not even hinted at in the play; instead, the audience is subjected to endless debates about war and peace, and an interminable trial sequence in Act Three. One of the play's main villains is Lord Raleigh (based on publisher and anti–German zealot Lord Northcliffe), a ruthless newspaper magnate who stirs up pro-war feeling; the character is almost invisible in the movie, where the war mongers are members of a secret society of profiteers. In the play, Dr. Seymour is a bishop, and his final confrontation—with Britain's bellicose Prime Minister—happens offstage, although we hear the broadcast and the fatal shot. Critics were rather amused by the quaint notion of a gunslinging prelate mowing down a Prime Minister. Such bad manners.... Unlike his counterpart in the film, though, the peace advocate doesn't come armed to the meeting, but rather picks up a revolver in the Prime Minister's office.

The play opened on November 7, 1928, at the Strand Theater in London, and while the critics found it dull, crude, intellectually shallow, and bad propaganda, some gave Pemberton-Billing points for at least being passionate about his subject. James Agate, for example, praised the acting and men-

**Benita Hume rallies the female draftees who support peace and attempts to prevent her country's war planes from taking off.**

tioned that "James Whale as a victim of shell shock had one disturbing moment." (Whale would be providing others with many disturbing moments just a few years later as director of Universal's *Frankenstein*.) On November 19, after the curtain had fallen on the final London performance of *High Treason*, Pemberton-Billing remarked on its failure: "I took in eight pounds the first night, 11 pounds the second and lost 1200 pounds the first week. I would lose thousands if it played in London for six weeks." He chose instead to send the play out on tour with two different companies: "I can spend the money beneficially by carrying the anti-war campaign throughout the country."[1]

We don't know how well *High Treason* did in the provinces, but the real mystery is why Gaumont-British picked a critical and commercial failure as a basis for an expensive film that marked the studio's first venture into sound. It's been said that *High Treason* was intended to be Britain's answer to *Metropolis*, but again, why choose a play that has virtually no science-fiction elements to mount an elaborate futuristic spectacle? There were certainly other futuristic tales they could have chosen to film, like H.G. Wells's 1910 novel, *When the Sleeper Wakes*. In 1927, L'Estrange Fawcett—who would go on to write the screenplay for *High Treason*—produced a scholarly study of contemporary movies, "Films; Facts and Forecasts," in which he expressed high praise for *Metropolis*. Fawcett, with only one scenario credit under his belt before *Treason*, may have viewed *Treason* as a sober, restrained, and veddy British antidote to the Teutonic excesses of the Fritz Lang film. Nonetheless, few then, and fewer still today, would place *High Treason* in the same league as *Metropolis*.

Director Maurice Elvey, with some fifty films already to his credit, shot the picture at Lime Grove Studio. The facility had to be quickly soundproofed in order to accommodate the new sound system provided by British Acoustic, Ltd., whose system involved the use of two synchronized projectors, one for film and one with sound on film. Assisting Elvey in this was David Lean—years away from *Oliver Twist*, *Lawrence of Arabia*, and so many others—who had been drawn to the movies because of *The Hound of the Baskervilles*, an earlier Elvey effort. Unfortunately, there were serious problems with the sound recording, and the silent version of *High Treason* was released some six months before its garrulous big brother. Thus *Blackmail* beat *High Treason* to the punch as the first British talkie (except in Australia where censorship problems temporarily derailed *Blackmail*).

**A determined Benita Hume tries to stop her lover from starting World War II.**

The sound version[2] received mixed reviews. While there was admiration for the film's visuals, many found the story lacking and its resolution both farfetched and morally dubious. In the June 7, 1930, edition of the *Motion Picture News*, the reviewer thought the film's time frame was a real disadvantage: "Audiences are going to refuse to believe so many changes could be wrought in ten years. If the producer had dated the film 1950 he would have stood a better chance of winning believers." (This critic would have been pleased with the silent version which, for some unknown reason, *does* set the story in 1950.) *Variety*, in reviewing a trade-show screening in October 1929, was enthusiastic about the film, while noting, "There are a lot of ideas the coupon cutters will think seditious in this picture but what of it?"

Apparently those coupon cutters occupied prominent positions in the New York Board of Censors because *High Treason* was denied a certificate allowing it to be shown in the Empire State. The film ran into occasional censorship problems elsewhere (Maryland nixed the shot of Benita Hume taking a shower and then drying herself off with a blow dryer), but only New York and Pennsylvania banned it outright. New York called the film "inhuman" and an "incitement to crime," two descriptors often used by the board when rationalizing its demand for cuts. This caused the film to be treated as something of a cause célèbre, with the National Board of Review vigorously objecting and calling the ban "censorship at its worst." The National Board of Review also sponsored a private New York showing for "500 prominent men and women who will be asked their opinion." Tiffany Productions, the U.S. releasing company for the film, made a few cuts and submitted it again, but it was still no go. To quote the board of censors:

> The few eliminations made in the picture did not, in the opinion of the Director, constitute a revision. A few episodes may have been omitted but when the film alleged to have been revised was submitted it portrayed the same story and retained the same objections from the standpoint of the statute namely that it portrayed government by assassination and the shooting of the President of a country by the President of a peace league as a means of preventing war and saving civilization.... If the picture can be revised in such a way to tell a different story, to show the Pacifists, by regularly constituted means, influencing the government to submit international conflicts to arbitration then I believe there is considerable which would become meritorious.

Presumably, had this been the silent version, a few title cards could have been rewritten to depict the President as willing to negotiate a peace at the last moment (Cue stock footage of cheering crowds); his murder and Seymour's trial could simply have been eliminated. In a talkie, of course, this was pretty much impossible. The censors also deemed as irrelevant the objections of the National Board of Review, which had been cited by the producers in their appeal. A *Variety* article headlined "*High Treason* Held Out as Propaganda" (March 1930) stated that New York Censor Commissioner Wingate "is awakening to a flock of propaganda films which have been slipping in from overseas.... While several glaringly -ism pictures from Russia are now being shown, Wingate indicated that the more violent will be re-investigated." This mini-Red Scare passed without much disturbance, but five years later the Board still banned *High Treason* when the producers optimistically submitted it again.

The film fared somewhat better on the West Coast, premiering on May 23 in Los Angeles's famous California Theater along with *Hungarian Rhapsody*,[3] a short directed by William Cameron Menzies who, in 1936, would helm another cinematic look at the future, *Things to Come*. Nonetheless, some problems arose in Seattle when one M.R. Bacon, a former Communist turned Red-baiter, denounced *High Treason* as Bolshevik propaganda. Per a brief mention in the trade press,[4] Bacon cited the RKO comedy *Loving the Ladies* as proof that "there were enough communist propaganda films on hand in Seattle to show one a week for six months." Although the producers of *High Treason* denied that the picture had been made due to subversive motives, in those days controversy wasn't a plus at the box office.

For years it was thought that the British Film Institute held the only extant copies of *High Treason*: the silent version and the talkie whose sound elements had totally deteriorated. It devolved, however, that a copy of the American-release sound version was in the collection of the Alaska Moving Image Preservation Association. The Library of Congress recently restored it and it has subsequently been making the rounds of different vintage film festivals, including the 2014 Capitolfest in Rome, New York. (There were no censors present this time 'round to stop the showing of the film, although some in the audience wish there had been.)

One might assume that the sound version of *High Treason* would likely be superior to its silent counterpart—which is a bit weighed down by the presence of many title cards—but, alas! That proves not to be the case. The sound recording comes across as being very unnatural, and the picture plays like a silent with sound simply and clumsily dubbed over (a bit like those late, cusp-of-sound hybrids that featured sound effects and crowd noises). Publicity for the film claimed that Maurice Elvey himself did the voices for nine of the minor characters, but perhaps he ought to have done the leads as well, since the performances of Jameson Thomas and Benita Hume—perfectly acceptable in the silent—come off as comical here. Thomas's delivery is sometimes so florid one might think he's parodying bad English acting, while Hume's shrill voice quickly becomes grating and there's no music track to drown her out. Basil Gill and Humberston Wright—Dr. Petrie in Stoll Productions's 1920s Fu-Manchu series—fare a little better.

The American talkie release is shorter than either the silent print or the original British version, and suffers from some peculiar editing choices. For example, the cleverest sequence in the silent has the American council debating the crisis for a few moments, only to have the scene end with cinematographer George Folsey pulling back to reveal that the council members are being watched by the conspirators via hidden camera. This shot is missing in the talkie although the plotters are heard to speak with French and Russian accents. (The chief conspirator later hums "Hail Britannia" while passing out blood money to his cohorts.) Gone, too, is the intense scene at the night club where Evelyn's outspoken pacifism causes the crowd—including more than a few men who clearly have rape on their minds—to turn on her; instead, all the dialogue and shouting from that sequence are heard over visuals of airplanes! The bombing of the Peace League is also less graphic: We see the destruction of the machine that tallies the increasing membership of the League, but gone is the close-up of its horrified operator as it falls on him. The shots of the wounded ladies, laying about in dishabille, are intact.

Despite the details of the synopsis submitted to the New York board, the confrontation at the airfield between pacifists and soldiers (with Evelyn brandishing a bomb) has been cut. So has Dr. Seymour's last line, "I am content," which was lifted directly from the play. In place of this last, we hear strains of the "Peace Song"[5] as Seymour stands there, his beatific lighting making it look as though he's either about to ascend bodily to heaven or get beamed up by a flying saucer headed for Metaluna. (Wright's make-up and costuming in *Treason* would fit quite comfortably into *This Island Earth*.)

Occasionally, the sound *does* work well. In the Channel Tunnel bomb sequence, the banal, everyday chitchat of the passengers makes for a poignant and suspenseful lead-in to the chaos of the deadly explosion (the silent has no title cards for those shots). The hum and buzzing of airplanes, dirigibles, and helicopters also give an appropriately futuristic feel to the skylines of London and New York. René Ray, playing a draftee dismayed by the ugly uniform she has to wear, gets a laugh with her sigh, "War is a terrible thing."[6]

The *Variety* review quoted earlier ends by saying, "With an anti-war feeling on a rising market this one is in the bag." The Show-Biz Bible may not have been accurate in predicting *High Treason*'s box-office potential, but it was quite on the money about the growing appeal of pacifism, at least among intellectuals and writers. Disillusionment with the War to End All Wars was widespread and cynicism had replaced jingoism when it came to treating war as a noble cause. *High Treason* was not alone in seeing the machinations of arms dealers and special interests working to reap profit from international conflict.

Plays with pacifist themes were to become quite common in the 30s, albeit only a few of them reached Broadway. Robert Sherwood's *Idiot's Delight* was the most successful of all and was made into a Clark Gable/Norma Shearer picture for M-G-M at decade's end. Irwin Shaw's *Bury the Dead*, on the other hand, was not a huge hit, but was certainly offbeat: Six soldiers slain in combat return to life and disrupt the war effort with their refusal to return to their graves; the play ends with a failed exorcism and the resurrected warriors walking off (a bit like the march of the dead at the end of Abel Gance's 1938 film *J'Accuse*).

Another anti-war play, Reginald Lawrence and S.K. Lauren's *Men Must Fight*, hit Broadway on October 14, 1932, and closed after just 35 performances. Like *High Treason* (and the opening scenes of *Things to Come*), the play is set in 1940. The United States is at odds with a confederation of Latin American states—which are allied with Japan—and ultimately war ensues. The young scion of a prominent family is torn between the pacifism taught to him by his activist mother and the call to arms supported by his father, the secretary of state.

In his critique for the *New York Times*, Brooks Atkinson praised the first two acts for "discussing the gravest of subjects intelligently," but opined that the third act ruined everything because it "begs the only question worth solving in such a play." In spite of his reservations, Atkinson ended his review by saluting the intentions and sincerity of the authors.

Even though the play was a flop, it was purchased by M-G-M where, in the course of production, it went through a couple of working titles—*What Women Give* and *Born to Kill* (!)—before being released under its original title. British star Diana Wynyard was under contract to M-G-M, and the play may well have been bought with her in mind, especially after her success in Fox's *Cavalcade* wherein she also played a devoted mother who loses a son to war. A *very* economical production by M-G-M's standards, the picture makes frequent use of newsreels as well as footage from 1931's *Hell Divers*, an earlier Clark Gable feature for the studio. For good or ill, *Men Must Fight* very much captures the gist of its source material, including its muddled message.

Synopsis:

In France during the Great War, Laura, a nurse, falls in love with airman Geoffrey Aiken. After their brief time together [there's a nice pre–Code moment showing the couple finishing up getting dressed, obviously after a tryst], Geoffrey is killed in action and Laura discovers she's pregnant with his child. Edward Seward, an officer who is in love with Laura, knows the situation and offers to marry her. She consents and gives birth to a son, Bob. Edward promises to treat him as his own and never reveal the truth of his paternity.

The year shifts to 1940. Edward has become secretary of state while Laura works tirelessly for peace. Bob is a chemist but also an aviator. Laura has instilled in him a hatred for war. However, the United States is at odds with Eurasia, a confederation of different countries, and war seems likely.

In their swank New York apartment, Bob announces his engagement to Peggy. Maman, his sarcastic grandmother, is delighted but Laura has reservations. Peggy doesn't approve of her intended's pacifism and her mother is shocked when she discovers her prospective son-in-law's convictions.

The situation between America and Eurasia worsens when the U.S. ambassador is assassinated and both sides mobilize. War now seems inevitable and Edward insists that Laura abandon her peace activities. She refuses and speaks at a mammoth rally during which she begs the mothers of the world not to sacrifice their sons [the camera shows women of different races and ethnic origins in the audience while superimposing clips of Nazi Germany and Imperial Japan; very surprising given the political reticence of most Hollywood films at this time]. Protestors disrupt the meeting and a riot ensues. Laura is badly shaken but, thanks to Secret Servicemen sent by her husband, she makes it safely back to their apartment. Waiting there are Peggy, Bob, Peggy's sister Evelyn, and her fiancé Steve, who has just enlisted.

The mob from the rally turns up outside the apartment and begins breaking windows. Edward, with Steve by his side, addresses them from the balcony, insisting that free speech should be respected until war is actually declared and if the latter situation does develop, he and his family will be behind it 100%. The crowd disperses but a reporter who has observed the scene interviews Edward who tells him Bob is going to enlist in the chemical division of the army since poison gas will be essential in winning the war. Bob objects saying he will never go to war.

Peggy breaks off their engagement and leaves. Bob and Edward argue and Edward tells him that he is part of the Seward family "only by courtesy." Bob is shocked by the revelation of his paternity and is angry at his mother both for not telling him the truth and raising him to be a pacifist. Nevertheless, he will not give up his convictions.

War is indeed declared and initially goes badly for America. We are told 300,000 soldiers have died in three weeks and another 100,000 perished unsuccessfully defending the Panama Canal. Though he still doesn't believe in the war, Bob begins to waver about not participating, especially as he contemplates how his real father died a hero.

Laura goes to see Peggy and explain Bob's convictions more clearly. A fleet of airplanes flies over New York and begins dropping bombs. The Empire State Building and the Brooklyn Bridge are destroyed. The cab carrying Laura and Peggy is overturned in the chaos and Laura is injured.

While his mother is recovering, Bob decides to enlist. Edward visits Laura in her sickbed and tells her that the Air Force has suffered terrible losses because of poison gas. Laura is still unyielding in her desire to keep Bob out of the conflict and, given the dire circumstances, even Edward wavers a little. However, directly after that, Bob informs them that he has joined the Air Force and that his squadron leaves in the morning. Laura is distraught but Bob tells her, "I've got to play the game.... There are certain things a man must do."

The next morning on the balcony, Laura, Maman and Evelyn watch the U.S. airplanes, Bob's among them, take off over the city. Peggy has had second thoughts about war and declares that if she has a son, he will not be sacrificed but Maman only snorts, "A fat lot you'll have to say about it. You'll be just another mother."

If the message of *High Treason* is "It's better that one man die than the whole people perish," *Men Must Fight* seems to promote the notion "A man's gotta do what a man's gotta do," whatever the womenfolk think. In *Men* Bob's embrace of war is also a way of cutting his mother's apron strings and countering the charge that he's a sissy whereas, in *Treason*, Diana remains her father's devoted acolyte right to the end.

The play *Men Must Fight*, much like the stage *High Treason*, makes little reference to its futuristic setting (other than the slightly loopy political context: War with Uruguay?). The film version has some mild futuristic touches, but nothing like those in *High Treason*. While the Sewards's apart-

**The play *Men Must Fight* flopped even though there was a strong anti-war sentiment in the thirties. Here Laura (Janet Beecher) and her husband Edwin (Gilbert Emory) greet their son Robert (Douglass Montgomery) and his fiancée Peggy (Erin O'Brien Moore).**

The last act of *Men Must Fight*. Edwin and Peggy congratulate Robert on his decision to join the air force but Laura didn't want her son to grow up to be an air cowboy. Edwin's mother (Alma Kruger) watches.

ment is somewhat Art Deco, it is hardly too outlandish for 1933. Publicity for *Men* stated that costume designer Adrian had to stretch his imagination to envision the sort of fashionable attire that women might be sporting in 1940. Nonetheless, he didn't come up with anything terribly unusual except— noted the *New York Times*—for the hats worn by the ladies, and these were still pretty conservative when compared with the bathing caps and racy female attire on display in *High Treason*. Both films also feature a television/telephone although *Men* limits it use to one conversation between Seward and Bob and thus does not suggest that, in 1940, it has become a common household device. Like *Treason*, *Men* has a scene set in a bar with a television, hardly a common sight in 1933 (especially as it's turned to Laura's speech, and not a baseball game). On the other hand, the airplanes in evidence are pretty much the type that gunned down poor King Kong, rather than anything newfangled. Still, the reference to the efficacy of small gas bombs—as few as ten of them can apparently destroy an entire city—at least suggests advanced weaponry.

In Lawrence and Lauren's original play, an enemy terrorist places a bomb in the subway, but there's no hint of any airplane attack on New York. In adapting *Men* to the screen, scenarist C. Gardner Sullivan (or someone at M-G-M)—very likely was inspired by *High Treason*'s scenes of New York being bombed— came up with a similar sequence, no doubt to alleviate all the talk that was threatening to turn the movie into little more than a filmed stage play. (As the *Variety* reviewer put it: "These scenes are the picture's only punchy moments, the rest being all gab.") When Seward grouses that America has fallen behind its enemies because of spending too much time seeking peace instead of preparing for war, his com-

Edgar Selwyn was a major producer on Broadway but the films he directed were largely inconsequential.

ments—and the attack on New York—are reminiscent of films like *The Battle Cry of Peace* (1915) and *Womanhood, the Glory of a Nation* (1917), which depict an unprepared America suffering invasion.

Publicity for the film insisted it was "a thrilling romance of 1940" and asked the question, "What will life be like in 1940?" while often making reference to the New York bombing scene. A rather peculiar ad depicts Laura hugging Bob with a caption that seemed to suggest something kinky was going on: "She who once gave love so freely—why did she now cling so fiercely to her boy?" Another ad shows Laura with arms outstretched over the words "You men who want our love, listen to our bargain." Perhaps this is a reference to a line in Laura's speech that seems to suggest that women will say no to the men who say yes: "War must stop or we'll stop making men for you." (A nod towards "Lysistrata?")

*Men Must Fight* did garner a few good reviews, but some critics were unimpressed and thought the film's message was too ambiguous to be taken seriously. Typical were these comments, found in the March 26, 1933, number of the *Philadelphia Inquirer*:

> The gravest faults of the film lie in its lack of both courage and conviction. It discusses pacifism and militarism at considerable length, vacillating between the two points of view and arrives at no conclusion that is either satisfactory or even especially intelligent.... As a document for peace it relies on emotional and sentimental reasons, basing its shrillest argument upon the aversion of mothers to having their sons slaughtered.

Generally speaking, high marks were given for the acting (though the brown wig and moustache worn by Lewis Stone in his early scenes were cause for some amusement), but there were a few reservations there as well. The 1933 edition of *Picture Play* observed:

> Diana Wynyard gives a dignified and tender performance but it's virtually wasted and certainly will not enhance her reputation. Phillips Holmes as the son has another thankless role and other players suffer the same handicap.

Indeed, the picture did little for Diana Wynyard, whose stay at M-G-M was brief. (Not helping her tenure at the studio was the fact that her part in *Rasputin and the Empress* had to be truncated because of a successful lawsuit against Metro-Goldwyn-Mayer.) Her

Laura (Diana Wynyard) prepares to deliver her message of peace on both radio and television. From the tens to the early thirties, Hollywood was fascinated by television and often included the device to represent a futuristic period. However, no one would have guessed that the Boob Tube would be Hollywood's main competition in the fifties and sixties.

film work would always run second behind her long and very distinguished stage career.

Nor did Phillips Holmes—as handsome as Adonis but usually cast as weaklings and dreamers (he's a bit of both in *Men Must Fight*)—have his M-G-M contract renewed. The actor had done good work in *An American Tragedy*, and Irving Thalberg had high hopes for him at M-G-M; however, Thalberg fell ill and had to absent himself from the studio for months just as Phillips was getting established there. David Selznick took over and had no interest in promoting Holmes. After M-G-M, Holmes's film career was largely undistinguished with parts in films like *House of a Thousand Candles* and *General Spanky*. When World War II broke out, Holmes followed the lead of his *Men Must Fight* character and became a pilot, enlisting in the Royal Canadian Air Force in 1941. He never saw any action, but instead was killed in a plane collision over Canada not long after he had completed his training.

# Les Fantômes de Paris:
## *Chéri-Bibi*; *The Phantom of Paris*

*Chéri-Bibi*—Metro-Goldwyn-Mayer—filmed January-February 1931—80 minutes

**Cast**: Ernesto Vilches as Chéri-Bibi/El Barón Max von Dyke; María Ladrón de Guevara as Cecilia; María Tubau as Vera; Juan Martínez Piá as Costaud; José Soriano Vosca as papá Duval; Eduardo Arozamena as Borrelier; Tito Davison as Juan; Manuel Arbó as Raúl; María Luz Callejo as María; Manuel París as Lacayo; Max Coll as Jaimito; with Luis Llaneza, Juan Duval, Monina Lamar, and Alida Vischer

**Credits**: *Director*: Carlos F. Borcosque; *Dialogue*: Edwin Justus Mayer; *Continuity*: Bess Meredyth; *Spanish version written by* Miguel de Zárraga; *Photography*: Leonard Smith; *Art Director*: Cedric Gibbons; *Film Editor*: Peggy O'Day; *Recording Director*: Douglas Shearer; *Assistant Director*: Bob Barnes

*The Phantom of Paris*—Metro-Goldwyn-Mayer—September 12, 1931—72/74 minutes

**Cast**: John Gilbert as Chéri-Bibi; Leila Hyams as Cecile; Lewis Stone as Costaud; Jean Hersholt as Herman; C. Aubrey Smith as Bourrelier; Natalie Moorhead as Vera; Ian Keith as Max, Marquis de Touchais; Alfred Hickman as Dr. Gorin; with (uncredited appearances by) Sidney Bracey, Tyrell Davis, Lloyd Ingraham, Claude King, Louise Mackintosh, Fletcher Norton, William H. O'Brien, Rose Plumer, Angelo Rossito, Douglas Scott, Philip Sleeman, and Elinor Vanderveer

**Credits**: *Director*: John S. Robertson; *Dialogue*: Edwin Justus Mayer and John Meehan; *Continuity*: Bess Meredyth; *Photography*: Oliver T. Marsh; *Art Director*: Cedric Gibbons; *Film Editor*: Jack Ogilvie; *Wardrobe*: René Hubert; *Recording Director*: Douglas Shearer; *Assistant Director*: Earl Taggart: *Based on the novel* **Chéri-Bibi et Cécily** *by* Gaston Leroux (Paris, 1916).

Popular magician/escape artist Chéri-Bibi is bound hand and foot in preparation for being lowered into a tank of water at the Cirque de Paris. With axe-wielding firemen at the ready, the audience as silent as the tomb, and Cecile Bourrelier, his great friend, a bundle of nerves in his dressing room, the dapper magus cheats death at the [seeming] last moment, to the enthusiastic amazement of the crowd.

Chéri and Cecile are in love, but Monsieur Bourrelier—Cecile's elderly and infirm father—would rather his daughter marry Max, the Marquis du Touchais. The marquis is all for this, especially when he learns that, as Cecile's husband, he will inherit a sizable sum upon the death of Bourrelier. When the future father-in-law discovers that Max is all title and no treasure, he informs his soon-to-be son-in-law that the bequest has been canceled. This does not sit well with the marquis, who is aware that Cecile has feelings for the dashing Chéri-Bibi. Soon after, M. Bourrelier also lets Chéri know that there's no way the magician is marrying Cecile, what with his being a common performer. This, in turn, does not sit well with the magician, and the two men exchange some words.

Within a short time, M. Bourrelier is found to have been murdered. When Police Chief Costaud interrogates the guests at the Bourrelier home, the marquis gilds the lily and tells him that the old man had found the magician threatening. The magus is charged with murder, tried and sentenced to death [all off camera]. However, he manages to escape by overpowering a guard and filching his uniform. Chéri seeks help from his friend, Herman, who hides the fugitive in the basement of his store.

Four years pass. Cecile, under the mistaken impression that it was her father's last wish that she marry Max, has wed the marquis and borne him a son. She is also not entirely certain of the magician's innocence. Chéri, weary of life in the dark basement, hears that Max is at death's door. Hieing to the marquis's home, the magician is at the point of having the dying man confess to having killed M. Bourrelier, but the man expires before pronouncing those fateful words.

Displaying the unbelievably creative thought processes of a master magician, Chéri brings the cadaver to the home of his friend, plastic surgeon Dr. Gorin, and asks that the doctor rearrange his [Chéri's] features to resemble those of Max. The surgeon, convinced of his friend's innocence of the Bourrelier slaying, agrees. Once the operation is successful, the magician announces to the newspapers the death of Chéri-Bibi, and embellishments as to how the magician had held the marquis prisoner soon follow. He tells Police Chief Costaud that he personally witnessed Chéri-Bibi falling to his death in a chasm but the policeman is skeptical. Still impersonating Max, Chéri "reunites" with Cecile and comes to the realization that Cecile does not love him [i.e., Max], but still loves him [i.e., Chéri-Bibi].

Chéri-Bibi also discovers that Vera, the house's social secretary, was Max's mistress and that she helped him with M. Bouurelier's murder. However, his questions cause Vera to discover his true identity and she goes to the police. Police Chief Costaud and some gendarmes arrive, and determined to get to the bottom of things, they fingerprint the marquis and discover that he is *not* the marquis—but Chéri-Bibi—and arrest him again. Again he escapes. Returning to Cecile's home, the magician causes Vera to admit to the crime. It turns out this last escape was done with the cooperation of Police Chief Costaud who is outside listening to the conversation. Chéri-Bibi is exonerated, and the magus and his true love are finally united.

A perusal of the titles we examine in our silent genre features encyclopedia will show that it took about a decade and a half for ticket-buyers to grow comfortable with pictures that dealt with depictions of "real" supernatural events, "genuine" grotesques, and "authentic" scientific impossibilities. During that span of time, last-reel revelations that any and all fantastic footage had been variously a dream, or the peregrinations of a diseased mind, or the result of a blow to the head became largely passé, giving way to the realization that a fairly large number of the movie-going public actually *liked* films with an outrageous premise. This period culminated in the death of the Silent Era and the ubiquity of Sound, and introduced—following a brief interlude in which pictures were "All Talking!" "All Singing!" "All Dancing!" "All Making as Much Noise as Is Humanly Possible!"—the first great horror film cycle.

Sound brought dialogue, and dialogue brought subtlety and comprehensiveness. The sense of novelty that had, years earlier, caused panic when a few seconds of film had shown a railroad train roaring to a halt or a desperado firing his pistol at the camera could only lead to heightened expectations, a drive for greater depth and detail, a demand for more substance *and* more style. As feature-length pictures became the norm (and serial chapters and short subjects were advertised as "added attractions"), earlier curiosities like Edison's *Frankenstein* would be "redone" with the benefit of an expository backstory, added characteriza-

**"Don't lose sight of this mysterious man arriving tonight!" … or leave before the stage show accompanying the gala presentation.**

tion, and the introduction of lengthier disquisitions on ersatz science. Foreign treatments like Murnau's *Nosferatu* were remade, albeit with the securing of rights and therefore along the lines of the authors' and playwrights's intentions, and in English, and with the introduction of achingly melodramatic religiosity.

Other familiar pieces of literature were also given the once-over, of course, often with extra doses of that same pseudoscience and potent religious symbolism, and almost always with second helpings of silliness. Somehow—for the first few years, at any rate—the added aural dimension gave a legitimacy to nonsense that would have given pause to the most shameless of intertitle writers. The brevity and silence of Rosenberg's "Murders in the Rue Morgue" (1914), for example, had led to a gorilla and a homicidal madman standing in for Edgar Allan Poe's razor-wielding "Ourang-Outang" and the world's most careless sailor. Given an hour's worth of screen time (62 minutes, to be precise) and the need to fill most of that with talk, Universal's 1932 feature massaged the story's most recognizable elements (the murders of the L'Espanayes and the musings of the "ear" witnesses) to fit a narrative heavy on bizarro-world dialogue about inter-species mating.

As time passed, then, facile explanations or *reductiones ad absurdem* due to time/footage constraints and the need to keep moving pictures moving and not focused on words posited on screens gradually all but disappeared. The explanations may not have become any more credible, but, for an ever-larger number of regular moviegoers, the hitherto outrageous or unbelievable had become a welcome relief from real life's miseries or mundaneness. Either via helping to expand more creatively treatments that had existed only in earlier (and more rudimentary) shorts, to deal more effectively with complex subjects ill-served by only a purely visual dimension, or to enable older (but still popular) projects to squeeze out more revenue until remakes could be planned and produced, the advent of sound also facilitated the acceptance of the horror film.

Sprinkled among those innumerable "explained away" titles found throughout the Silent Era was a handful of "genuine" genre goodies that brooked no facile justifications for what transpired onscreen. Again, these were usually literary adaptations, be they of an ersatz religious nature (1926's *The Sorrows of Satan*), science fictional (1929's *The Mysterious Island*), or purely fantastic (1917's *She*), although the occasional release of a fabulous yarn based on folktales (1924's *The Thief of Bagdad*) or popular poems (1925's *The Ancient Mariner*) added to the aggregate wealth. One had to be cognizant of stories that had first been introduced to audiences in media other than the cinema, though, in

**Chéri-Bibi (Ernesto Vilches) and Cecilia (María Ladrón de Guevara) in a rare happy moment...**

order to separate the genre wheat from the chaff. Relying on what would normally be considered a no-brainer term—like *ghost*—in a picture's title was of no value whatsoever to the '20s moviegoer looking for an incursion of the supernatural. Between 1921 and 1929, no fewer than seven American features were released that included *ghost* in their titles, and not a one was legit. If anything, that potential ticket-buyer learned that a ghost was the absolute *last* thing one could count on in a Western, no matter what its poster promised. And oaters advertising "haunted" whatever were even more profoundly disappointing.

But one's luck was rather better if a film title contained the word *phantom*.

That word *phantom*—so often bandied about on the printed page and any variety of screens—derives from the Greek φάντασμά, whence came the Latin *phantasma*, then the French *fantôme*, and, of course, the third word in this expository sentence. Genre stories featuring any and all forms of any and all of these iterations have to do—usually—with apparitions, sightings, specters, and the like. The incredible Georges Méliès was most likely the first to use a variation on the word in his 120-second-long masterpiece *Le Chaudron Infernal et les Vapeurs de Fantasmatiques* (1903), and in 1907 Pathè went for the gold with *La Légende du Fantôme* (*Legend of a Ghost*). Come 1913, Charles Ogle starred in Edison's two-reeler *The Phantom Signal*, and the following year the same studio released *Fantasma*,[1] a five-reel feature that took its name from the eponymous 1884 stage extravaganza performed by the Hanlon brothers: acrobats, magicians, and (above all else) showmen. Roger Karl—who would earn his genre nod as Chancellor Lang in Julien Duvivier's *Le Golem* (1936)—likewise appeared dans La Belle France in *Phantasmes*, a short released in 1917.

Thence and into the void, Phantoms/Phantasms/Fantômes gradually populated more and more film titles, as the definition

**Ernesto Vilches, the Spanish "Man of a Thousand Faces."**

of said word(s) grew correspondingly broader. Perhaps the most renowned variation of the term was *Fantomas*, the name given the super criminal in the dozens of novels initiated by journalists Marcel Allain and Pierre Souvestre in the Paris of 1911 and introduced to moviegoers by Louis Feuillade, who directed the "Genius of Evil" in a series of five feature-length films beginning in May 1913. Another journalist-turned-author, Gaston Leroux created literature's greatest phantom—*Le Fantôme de l'Opera*—and an actor renowned for his chameleon-like propensities—Lon Chaney—incarnated the Opera Ghost on the screen. It took 15 years for Leroux's novel to make the move from la bibliothèque to le cinéma, and Erik's horrific visage became, for many, the greatest of Chaney's thousand faces.

Leroux was a prolific author who had begun writing fiction about the sundry investigations of Joseph Rouletabille, an amateur sleuth drawn along the lines of C. Auguste Dupin and Sherlock Holmes. The first of his cases—*The Mystery of the Yellow Room* (1907)—led not only to a 1919 Mayflower feature film and eight more novels devoted to the detective, but also to four dealing with the exploits of our fabled practitioner of stage legerdemain, Chéri-Bibi, whose *Première Aventures* appeared in 1913. *Chéri-Bibi et Cécily* may not have impacted the City of Lights in 1916 the way the saga of the denizen of the Garnier Opera House had in 1910, but its title character—like the redoubtable Erik, a magician, an escape artist, and a figure ultimately notorious for his visage—soon won over a substantial portion of the local readership, and Paris took this "second phantom" to its collective heart. Ultimately, it also took 15 years for *Chéri-Bibi et Cécily* to appear onscreen, albeit renamed as the picture under discussion.

For today's moviegoer, the name "Lon Chaney" might bestir several levels of film-oriented unconsciousness, or it might not; at this point in time, most of us silent-film fans are fairly well weathered. For the average moviegoer at the tail-end of the 1920s, of course, the name was associated with macabre character roles and mostly offbeat offerings. Although the actor had pretty much freelanced until 1925, that average moviegoer back then might have been forgiven had he/she thought that Chaney was the property of Universal, as the Paris of both Erik the phantom and Quasimodo the hunchback was situated on that studio's back lot. In addition, Universal had poured beaucoup bucks into having ticket-buyers associate these most iconic of grotesques with Uncle Carl Laemmle's empire. Nonetheless, the fact of the matter was that, per Chaney biographer Michael F. Blake,[2] "Lon sign[ed] a one-year contract on January 6 [1925] with M-G-M that includes two yearly option renewals." Thus, every motion picture featuring Chaney after *The Phantom of the Opera* was an M-G-M production.

Perhaps encouraged by the profitable association of Chaney and Leroux in *The Phantom of the Opera*, M-G-M announced a slate of pictures for 1927–1928 release[3] that included *Seven Seas*, an adaptation of Leroux's Chéri-Bibi series. For reasons that remain unclear, *Seven Seas* never made it to the screen, but there *were* six Chaney features released during that time span, including *The Unknown*, *London After Midnight*, and *West of Zanzibar*, all directed by Tod Browning, and all offbeat offerings featuring macabre characters. In the midst of this wild windfall—and the rest of the newly released offerings by all Hollywood studios, major and minor—Warner Bros. released *The Jazz Singer*, viewers morphed into audiences, and the movies changed forever. Most minor-studio releases and "B" (or less) pictures from the majors were sent out to earn back what they could as last-gasp silents. Prestige productions and all pictures considered to be at least "shakey A's" were held back so that music, effects and dialogue sequences could be added; or, ultimately, were distributed in both silent and talkie versions, depending upon how far the installation of sound systems in studio-owned movie palaces had gone.

**Behind the scenes with director Carlos Borcosque (white arrow) and Ernesto Vilches (looking through view finder).**

Even without a string of movie theaters to call his own, Uncle Carl and company faced the same problems. Again, according to Mr. Blake,[4] Universal's original plan was to have Chaney reprise the role he had essayed in the studio's 1925 monster hit in a follow-up based on Gaston Leroux's *Return of the Phantom*. At casual glance, this was an undoubtedly clever plan; unfortunately, two rather large flies landed in Universal's ointment.

The first, *naturellement*, was Chaney's having signed that year-long contract (with options) with M-G-M just days after principal photography on *Phantom* had wrapped. What's more, any possibility that M-G-M might lend out their newly-signed star to Uncle Carl was pretty much quashed by the presence of the man whose personal genius and professional savvy had led him to cannily choose parts well suited for Chaney: Irving Thalberg. Producer of the three Browning/Chaney epics mentioned above (and others) *and* M-G-M supervisor of production, Thalberg had left Universal in a huff during the production of *The Hunchback of Notre Dame*, a "Super Jewel" that had been Thalberg's idea in the first place. With Thalberg's guidance and assistance, Chaney's career would take off and the actor would be allowed at times to display his skill in something other than the usual "offbeat offerings." And with Thalberg at the helm, Chaney wasn't budging from M-G-M.

Fly number two was the fact that *Return of the Phantom* did not exist. Even after all these years, it's uncertain whether Universal had de facto *commissioned* such a novel from Leroux, but the fact remains that the prolific

**Chéri-Bibi (John Gilbert) shows Inspector Costaud (Lewis Stone) that he's an old hand with handcuffs.**

**M. Bourrelier (C. Aubrey Smith) is not long for this world.**

Frenchman died on April 15, 1927,[5] without having added another word to the Opera Ghost mythos. Supposing for a moment—for the sake of argument—that Junior Laemmle (or the studio executive who had been hired to take Irving Thalberg's place at Universal) *had* negotiated with Leroux for a sequel to the 1925 cash-cow, it is fairly safe to speculate that, given the time frame with which we're dealing, Universal's follow-up Chaney/Leroux/Phantom project was at least initially to have been a silent.

And then Alan Crosland and Al Jolson screwed that up....

The most concise summary of the cinematic devastation wrought by *The Jazz Singer* must be attributed to writer/biographer Simon Louvish:

> [Nineteen twenty-eight] was the transition year, in which production dipped as the technical changes were made. Only ten all-talking and twenty-three part-talking movies were released that year, while there were 220 silents [counting feature films only], as against 216 part or wholly talking movies released in 1929 and only thirty-eight silents. By the end of 1929, silent movies were finished, artefacts, mere shadows of history.[6]

With the "original plan" not viable for the reasons stated, and everyone frantic to get with this latest "craze" and add sound wherever/whenever they could, Universal had little choice but to reissue *The Phantom of the Opera*—with talking sequences, a musical score, and sound effects—on December 15, 1929. To pull this off, the original film had to be modified a bit—had John Miljan's parents bought tickets, they would have searched in vain for their son's Valentin in the *Faust* sequence—but as the *raison d'être* for the revamped production was not only the need to catch up, technologically, but also to exploit the ever-increasing drawing power of The Man of a Thousand Faces, that mattered not at all. As it turns out, the actor himself was precluded from voicing so much as a syllable for Universal; truth-in-advertising—and the M-G-M legal department—required that publicity for the film state, "Lon Chaney's Portrayal of the Phantom is silent." That mattered little; the reissue was the best Universal could hope for. With Chaney's John Hancock on a contract that placed him among the group that consisted of "more stars than in the heavens," the actor's reprising his role as Erik in *Return of the Phantom* was nothing but a multi-level pipe dream.

By now, at least *some* of the readership are asking themselves, "What's with all the Lon Chaney stuff?"

*The Phantom of Paris* was originally slotted to be Chaney's second talkie. As the studio's dedicated movie theater chain was being outfitted for sound-on-film, the actor continued with a series of profitable silent features, like *The Big City, While the City Sleeps, Laugh, Clown, Laugh*, and more. Seeing Uncle Carl and raising him, M-G-M looked back at *its* 1925 Chaney hit, *The Unholy Three*, and—"talking sequences" be damned—remade the picture (which had, of course, been directed by Tod Browning and produced by Irving Thalberg) as a 100 percent talkie, with a mid–July 1930 release. Only Harry Earles (as Tweedledee)—and Thalberg, as producer—rejoined Lon for the sound version, and the film was successful not only for Chaney's faces, but also for his voice(s). Next up on the hit parade was to have been *Chéri-Bibi*—based on Leroux's *Chéri-Bibi et Cécily*—and the trades were advised of same in July 1930, just as *The Unholy Three* redux was being released nationwide. Just as that first proposed Leroux adaptation was to have been retitled back in 1927, so was this one: Chaney ... Leroux ... Paris ... Phantom ... anyone with an ounce of sense (and marketing savvy) could see this coming.

Unfortunately, what no one could see coming[7] was the fact that Lon Chaney would be dead on August 26 of that same year. Production on *Thunder*—Lon's last silent film, as it turned out—had been halted for a couple of weeks on April 30, 1929, when the actor came down with pneumonia. Come October of that same year, Chaney was diagnosed with lung cancer. A comprehensive overview of the end of the life of The Man of a Thousand Faces may be had by referring to the triad of biographical works by Michael F. Blake that can be found in our bibliography. Suffice it to say, the iconic actor passed away from a throat hemorrhage on August 26, 1930; he was 47 years old. His participation in the backstory of *Chéri-Bibi*—which may *not* have been retitled had he played the lead—obviously ends here.

For M-G-M, though, life went on. What to do with *Chéri-Bibi et Cécily*? Buying rights to properties that would then sit unused on shelves was not an efficient means of doing business. It did happen from time to time, of course, but novels, plays, and such were purchased for the sake of generating revenue, and not of increasing the amount of red ink in a ledger. It devolves that the answer was right under their *naríz*....

Under contract to M-G-M at that time was Ernesto Vilches, a Spaniard initially hired earlier in 1930 by Paramount, as that studio was set to film "international" versions of its musical revue *Paramount on Parade*. The American original, released on April 19, 1930, ran 13 black and white and Technicolor reels of songs, dances, and skits running the gamut from "I'm Isadore, the Toreador" (a *Carmen* pastiche) to "Murder Will Out," a travesty on detective films featuring Clive Brooks's Sherlock Holmes, William Powell's Philo Vance, and Warner Oland's Fu Manchu, all of which were Paramount properties at the time. Many of the original English-language sequences were retained for *la versión española*, *Galas de la Paramount*, but "Murder Will Out" was out, replaced by a trio of *fragmentos cortos* (short bits) from various sources, interpreted by Señor Vilches.[8] Intriguingly, instead of impersonating Fu Manchu, Vilches enacted a scene from Maurice Vernon and Harold Owen's drama *Mr. Wu*, which had served as the basis for one of Lon Chaney's five M-G-M features back in 1927. Although the "Oriental" picture had been apprised as

**Fingerprints do not lie (although plastic surgery might...). Inspector Coutard gets definite proof that the supposed Marquis de Touchais is really Chéri-Bibi.**

"not up to previous efforts" by the critical press in the aggregate, *Mr. Wu*'s international gross was second only to that of *Tell It to the Marines* in the Chaney canon that year.

Now M-G-M was no stranger to exporting movies to foreign climes; Hal Roach's two-reel Laurel & Hardy comedy *Night Owls*—distributed, like most of Roach's 1930s product, through M-G-M—had been the third such *rara avis* shipped overseas, and the studio would continue to do so with another 20 or so films from the "Lot of Fun" before Roach called an end to the practice. With the coming of sound, foreign markets were turning their backs on titled silents, and— with dubbing technology not yet perfected (the histrionics in hindsight of *Singin' in the Rain* notwithstanding)—the vastness and proximity of the revenue sources lying chiefly to the south of the continental United States demanded attention. A Spanish-language version of Buster Keaton's *Free and Easy* (released as *Estrellados*) was M-G-M's first such production,[9] filmed in Culver City in March 1930. In August 1930, during Lon Chaney's final weeks on earth, the Culver City studios started production on a seven-reel sound reworking of 1927's high-grossing tale of Mandarins and murder: *Wu Li Chang, totalmente en español*, with Ernesto Vilches in the role originally played by The Man of a Thousand Faces.

While there is no evidence whatsoever that a sound remake of *Mr. Wu* was in the cards for Chaney, what is very much evident is that M-G-M quickly grew to appreciate the Spanish/Hispanic markets. Happy to take its share for distributing foreign-language versions of other companies's products, M-G-M began producing the same for its own films, with *Sevilla de mis amores* (*Call of the Flesh*), *Su última noche* (a sound version of 1926's *The Gay Deceiver*), *En cada puerto un amor* (*Way for a Sailor*), *La fruta amarga* (*Min*

**Chéri-Bibi's impersonation of the Marquis of Touchais fools even Cecile (Leila Hyams).**

*and Bill*), and *La mujer X* (a remake of Lionel Barrymore's early talkie from 1929) all on reels and in cans before attention was turned to *Chéri-Bibi et Cécily*.

*La mujer X* and *Chéri-Bibi* were both filmed in Culver City—*Mujer* during December 1930 and *Chéri-Bibi* during January and February 1931—but while the Murcian José Crespo was thrilled to be enjoying a "Hollywood career" and a splendid Spanish/Hispanic reputation simultaneously, Tarragona-born Ernesto Vilches was bitching to the press about his struggles to find creative freedom and integrity in the American cinema.[10] Vilches had signed on for two years with M-G-M right after *Galas de la Paramount*, and he had apparently expected the royal treatment from the studio which he had regarded as *El Primero*. The actor complained that he was basically made to sit around while Spanish-language projects were found for him (à la *Wu Li Chang*, when he groused that the film had been edited "so as to make it appear that Vilches failed to give his work 'the correct ambience'"[11]) or were woven of whole cloth (as when Vilches had starred in *Su última noche*, which had about as much to do with the plot line of its supposed source—the 1926 Lew Cody epic

*The Gay Deceiver*—as it did with Caesar crossing the Rubicon). Illustrative of this profound change in the actor's perspective can be found in two articles that appeared in the Spanish-language newspaper, *La Opinión*, about three weeks apart. (We don't think any translation into English is necessary here):

> "Vilches está encantado con la ciudad maravillosa: Hollywood"—July 27, 1930
>
> "E. Vilches está desilusionado con Hollywood"—August 17, 1930

In light of this, he approached *Chéri-Bibi* more with skepticism than enthusiasm. What the actor could not know—what no one then could know—was that this would mark the only time that Hollywood made a Spanish-language film that would be neither a remake nor a knock-off of an extant English-language production, and which would actually *precede* its "English version." Still, Vilches felt that it was only because he was known in his native land as "El hombre de las mil caras"—and not for any God-given artistry he possessed—that he was being considered for such a plum part. He felt that he was making what was still, in essence, a "Lon Chaney film."

Nor could the proud Spaniard dare think that *his* "version"—again, the first of the two productions filmed—would ultimately make more of an artistic impact than would the 1931 picture. In *Chéri-Bibi*, Vilches (as the wrongly-accused magician) replaces *himself* (as el barón Max von Dyke), and an exercise in impersonation on that sort of level required more than a simple application of crepe hair and greasepaint. For a good portion of the film, Vilches had to enact for audiences two men who were distinct physically, vocally, emotionally, and behaviorally; when the dramatic pivot then turned on the transformation of Chéri-Bibi into Max, audiences watched the magician perform the ultimate escape from reality, create the ultimate illusion, as the actor playing both roles had to assume a third: that of the one impersonating the other. Some years later, Boris Karloff would "pull a Vilches" when, in Columbia's powerful melodrama *The Black Room*, he opened the picture playing dual roles—twins Gregor and Anton—and then was maneuvered by the clever screenplay into offering a third face to the viewers: Gregor *as* Anton. Karloff would deservedly win plaudits for his multi-faceted performance.[12]

*Chéri-Bibi* premiered in San Juan (Puerto Rico) on May 5, 1931, in San José (Costa Rica) on May 17, in Los Angeles on October 2, and then in Madrid at the end of January, the following year.[13] There is no record of its having played the usual "in neighborhood theaters" in the continental United States, and so perhaps Ernesto Vilches was justified in his lack of appreciation for American cinema: in his eyes, American cinema held him in little estimation. Following one more demeaning Hollywood experience—he took the lead in *El Comediante*, a seven-reel feature made by an inde-

**Box 5 of the Paris Opera House, where the city's original Phantom put his feet up...**

pendent studio and then distributed abroad by Paramount—Vilches left the United States. He continued in his film career, which took him from Mexico to Argentina and then, *finalmente*, back to Spain, and when he was not appearing on-screen, he could be found onstage, to great acclaim. We can only wonder whether, had Vilches won plaudits for his Hollywood-made films from people who spoke English as a first language, he might have reconsidered his move back to more comfortable surroundings.

Ernesto Vilches passed away in Barcelona on December 7, 1954, and he received only a brief mention in *Variety*. Nonetheless, the four-paragraph obituary[14] did note, "When news of Vilches' death spread throughout Spain, theatre audiences rose for one minute of silence and flags were flown at half mast."

Coincidentally, John Gilbert was not looking forward to *The Phantom of Paris* with great enthusiasm, either. It wasn't a question of stepping into Lon Chaney's shoes. Gilbert had been the romantic lead in two of Chaney's popular features—1923's *While Paris Sleeps* (for Maurice Tourneur Productions) and 1924's *He Who Gets Slapped* (for M-G-M)—and had enjoyed third billing both times. What irked Gilbert was his de facto "demotion," role-wise, at the studio where he had been under long-term contract since 1924. Since the year after he had signed his name for the ages, he had enjoyed being one of the studio's two leading men (the other was Rudolf Valentino), and had starred in such big-money hits as *The Big Parade* (1925), *La Bohème*, *Flesh and the Devil* (both 1926), *Love* (1927), and *A Woman of Affairs* (1928). These last three had seen him appear opposite M-G-M's megastar, Greta Garbo, and, happily, Gilbert and Garbo together were box-office sensations; offscreen, they were also apparently sensational together in the sack, and this led to some frightful confrontations for Gilbert with Louis B. Mayer. To some, this mishegas with the studio boss contributed to the actor's loss of prestige on the lot.

Another cause given for Gilbert's falling from grace involved the supposed poor quality of his voice. Not everyone recorded as well as he/she photographed in those heady early days, and for decades Gilbert's alleged faulty intonation or less than baritonal timbre were put forth to explain his quick exit from the talkies. (To be fair, the man did make pictures until 1934!) Also seeking to explain the actor's fade from cinematic fame is the theory that the roles he had played during his silent heyday had become passé with the coming of sound, and that the sort of syrupy pap that came across wonderfully so long as one had only to gaze at the screen didn't play so well when it was accompanied by the kind of dialogue that made one wince or grimace. Both "reasons" are listed here for the reader's consideration (and for the sake of comprehensiveness).

Gilbert's feeling that he had been occu-

On the run for years, Chéri-Bibi contemplates his future…

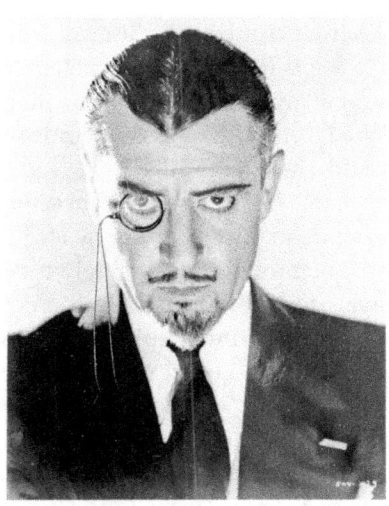

**Chéri-Bibi (John Gilbert) as Max, Marquis of Touchais.**

pying a lower-hanging perch for a while at M-G-M, though, might have been exacerbated somewhat by the realization that the role he was enacting here—indeed, pretty much the entire screenplay that was being shot—had been extruded from a *Spanish-language production* that had been planned and completed first. In the act of contextualizing *The Phantom of Paris*, film historian Harry Waldman mentions Chaney's death, only to add, "His replacement, John Gilbert, *wound up taking his cues from the star of the Spanish film*, who plays the magician Chéri-Bibi"[15] (emphasis ours). If Ernesto Vilches had had no clue that *Chéri-Bibi* was to be followed by an American "domestic" version, or that his film's being paired with *The Phantom of Paris* was to be unique in the annals of Hollywood production for foreign export, neither had John Gilbert. For all anyone knows, Gilbert might have felt that his being assigned to "remake" a film that had been solely intended for Spanish/Latino audiences was yet another public humiliation.[16] When push came to shove, *The Phantom of Paris* was released with the sort of gloss and glamour that most M-G-M "B" features received, and Gilbert earned more-than-decent notices. (Rob Nixon, writing on the film for www.tcm.com, averred that *Phantom* "earned John Gilbert his first good reviews in years," and that it was "one of the best of all his late films.") Still, 1933's *Queen Christina* apart—Gilbert was cast therein solely at Garbo's request—the only pictures remaining to the actor prior to his untimely death by heart attack were (to be charitable) unremarkable; the last, in fact, was produced by Columbia.

Gilbert may have felt like something of a fish out of water taking on a role once intended for Lon Chaney, but his *Phantom* co-star and supporting cast had or soon would become familiar names to genre fans. The lovely Leila Hyams, for example, had already been the skirt in Fox's *The Wizard*, a 1927 feature (based on yet another tale by Gaston Leroux!) that saw the beautiful New Yorker having to deal not only with Gustav von Seyffertitz, but also with pug-ugly George Kotsonaros in full ape regalia. In M-G-M's sound remake of *The Thirteenth Chair* (1929), she was one of the "two Helens" who had Bela Lugosi's Inspector Delzante posturing operatically under Tod Browning's direction, and a year later she marveled at Basil Rathbone's sole turn as Philo Vance in *The Bishop Murder Case*. Following *The Phantom of Paris*, Hyams appeared as Venus—also under Tod Browning's direction—in *Freaks*, and that same year (1932) saw her venture over to Paramount to be menaced by Charles Laughton and "manimals" of all sorts (and genders) in *The Island of Lost Souls*. Little wonder the actress opted to retire (at age 31) from the movies and tend to her personal life!

*Phantom*'s cast also included Jean Hersholt who, although remembered chiefly as the kindly Dr. Christian, had been featured in the silent thrillers *Black Orchids* and *The Terror* (both 1917), 1924's study-in-the-unconscious *Sinners in Silk*, and 1930's *The Cat Creeps*, the sound remake of the wildly popular *The Cat and the Canary*. Within a few years of sharing Paris with John Gilbert,

Hersholt would also share M-G-M's genre big-time with Boris Karloff (1932's *The Mask of Fu Manchu*) and Bela Lugosi (1935's *Mark of the Vampire*).

Lewis Stone—later the kindly Judge Hardy—had been in *Trifling Women* (the 1922 remake of *Black Orchids*), had impersonated Sir John Roxton in 1925's *The Lost World*, and would soon share the screen with Jean Hersholt (and Karloff, of course) in *The Mask of Fu Manchu*. Before the '30s were over, the actor would also grace *The Mystery of Mr. X* (1934), yet another remake of *The Thirteenth Chair* (still at M-G-M, this time in 1937), and—in a rare moment away from M-G-M—star that same year as the eponymous killer in Universal's *The Man Who Cried Wolf*.

Ian Keith, of course, had once been considered by Universal for its 1931 thriller *Dracula*, based to a large extent on his lean and hungry look. Prior to that, however, the Boston-born actor had appeared with Chaney in 1925's *The Tower of Lies*, shared major screen time with Conrad Veidt in 1927's *A Man's Past*, and assassinated fabled theater patron, Walter Huston, in 1930's *Abraham Lincoln*. It was as the decade shifted gears and the '40s pulled into view that Keith became less of a stellar character man and more of an onscreen "character." In the late '40s, he brought increasingly eccentric portrayals to the screen in such enjoyable (but decidedly minor) epics as PRC's *Fog Island* (1945, with Lionel Atwill and George Zucco), Republic's *Valley of the Zombies* (1946, as "Ormund Murks"), Monogram's *Mr. Hex* (1946, with the Bowery Boys), and RKO's *Dick Tracy vs. Cueball* and *Dick Tracy's Dilemma* (both 1947, Keith was "Vitamin Flintheart"). As had Gilbert decades earlier, Keith must have regarded this state of affairs as something of a come-down, for he, too, had appeared with Garbo in *Queen Christina*, had enacted Tigellinus in Paramount's *Sign of the Cross* (1932), and had played Octavian opposite Claudette Colbert in that studio's *Cleopatra* the following year. His last years

Original herald.

were spent mainly doing television (including the interesting study "Edgar Allan Poe at West Point"), although he did bring up the rear in 1955's *It Came from Beneath the Sea*, the very first of the Charles H. Schneer/Ray Harryhausen classics.

Appearing as the doomed killjoy, M. Bourrelier, was C. Aubrey Smith, the craggy old darling whom God had created as the stereotypical determined Briton with the stiffest of upper lips. Smith, who—like Gustav von Seyffertitz—seemed to have been born a senior citizen, so embodied the Raj-era British spirit that no matter his role, he might very well have slipped "This blessed plot, this earth, this realm, this England" into whatever was going on and have gotten away with it. While he might have been most people's absolutely last choice on earth to play an irascible Frenchman, the veteran actor did have an armful of genre credits on display throughout his lengthy career. In 1916, he was Jack Brookfield, the juvenile (sort of) in the first filmic adaptation of Augustus Thomas's *The Witching Hour*. Following *The Phantom of Paris*, Smith could be found onscreen in *Tarzan, the Ape Man* (1932), *The Monkey's Paw* (1933), *Transatlantic Tunnel* (*vid.*) and *The Florentine Dagger* (both 1935), the Spencer Tracy interpretation of *Dr. Jekyll and Mr. Hyde* (1941), and Julien Duvivier's Universal compilation *Flesh and Fantasy* (1945). An absolutely unique film presence, Charles Aubrey Smith died in 1948, and it's probably safe to say that *no one* has been as resolutely British as he ever since.

When all is said and done, *The Phantom of Paris* would probably have been an excellent choice for Lon Chaney's second sound film. It would have been child's play for The Man of a Thousand Faces to pull off the same identity switch as had El hombre de las mil caras, and it doesn't take much effort to see Chaney as the surgeon, either. Triple play! The narrative unfolds competently and well under the direction of John S. Robertson (he who had guided The Great Profile through his own identity-switch[es] in 1920's *Dr. Jekyll and Mr. Hyde*), even if the far-fetched-ness of the imposture demands more than the usual suspension of disbelief. Robertson had originally been slated to direct the Spanish-language version, too, but language difficulties resulted in Carlos Borcosque stepping in to take his place.

In 1938, Productions Charles Bauche shot and released the first *version français* of *Chéri-Bibi*. The film, which starred Pierre Fresney as a man "called" Chéri-Bibi, also featured international stars Jean-Pierre Aumont and Marcel Dalio. Inasmuch as the cast list did not feature a "Cécily," we must assume that the screenplay was not derived from the same Leroux novel as everything mentioned to this point, but possibly from the magician's *Première Aventures* (cited above), his *Nouvelles Aventures* (published in 1921), or even from his *Coup d'État*, which saw print the year before its author passed away. *Chéri-Bibi et Cécily* was the source for 1955's *Chéri-Bibi*, an Italian/French collaboration with Jean Richard escaping and disguising his way through Paris, and the character resurfaced in the eponymous French television series that aired in 1974. The magician's adventures were therein nothing if not brief, however, as the series was comprised of 46 episodes, each lasting 13 minutes.

*The Phantom of Paris* is out and about—it played on Turner Classic Movies as we were writing this essay—but the picture itself frequently falls victim to identity switch. From time to time, viewers gearing up to watch John Gilbert don hair appliances in order to become Ian Keith are puzzled to find themselves watching Patric Knowles trying to find out what happened to María Montez. Back in the very early '50s, Realart Pictures signed a deal to reissue many of Universal's classic (and some not-so-classic) horror films as double features, and 1942's *Mystery of Marie Rogêt*—due to be paired with *WereWolf of London*—was renamed *Phantom of Paris*. This was more than just an effort to achieve some titular symmetry; it probably was—as had been the case in the late '20s and early '30s, as outlined above—an effort to latch once again onto *Phantom of the Opera*, as the 1943 Technicolor remake (with Claude Rains) was also traveling the reissue circuit. Although *Rogêt* had been based on a short story by Poe, both stories's venue was Paris, both villains were accoutered in slouch hats and cloaks, and Realart's one-sheet neatly tied into Rains's character *and* the reason for his altered face by promising a "Phantom mangler."

How many phantoms can one city support, anyhow?

# Just Imagine

Fox Film Corporation—October 17, 1930 (world premiere); November 23, 1930 (general release)—10,200 feet/12 reels/113 minutes

**Cast**: El Brendel as Single O; Maureen O'Sullivan as LN-18; John Garrick as J-21; Marjorie White as D-6; Frank Albertson as RT-42; Hobart Bosworth as Z-4; Kenneth Thomson as MT-3; Wilfred Lucas as X-10; Mischa Auer as B-36; Joseph Girard as Commander; Sidney De Gray as AK-44; Joyzelle (Joyner) as Loo Loo/Boo Boo; Ivan Linow as Loko/Boko; with J.M. Kerrigan (uncredited) as the 1980's Traffic cop

**Credits**: *Director*: David Butler; *Producers*: (uncredited) Buddy De Sylva, Lew Brown, Ray Henderson; *Story, Dialogue, Songs*: Buddy De Sylva, Lew Brown, Ray Henderson; *Continuity*: David Butler; *Musical Numbers Staged by* Seymour Felix; *Music*: (uncredited) Hugo Friedhofer; *Photography*: Ernest Palmer; *Sound Recording*: Joseph E. Aiken; *Film Editor*: Irene Morra; *Settings*: Stephen Gooson, Ralph Hammeras; *Assistant Director*: Ad Schaumer; *Musical Director*: Arthur Kay; *Costumes*: Alice O'Neil, Dolly Tree, (uncredited) Sophie Wachner; *Songs*: "The Drinking Song," "The Romance of Elmer Stremingway," "Never, Never Wed," "There's Something About an Old-Fashioned Girl," "Mothers Ought to Tell Their Daughters," "I Am the Words, You Are the Melody," "Dance of Victory," "Never Swat a Fly"

Toward the tail end of the 1960s, just when it seemed like Western civilization was bottoming out, Stanley Kubrick and M-G-M offered a hopeful divertissement to the collective American consciousness: *2001: A Space Odyssey*. The much pre-publicized picture took us back to the earliest days of what we call "50s' sci-fi," when films like *The Day the Earth Stood Still* dealt creatively with crucial socio/political themes. Kubrick showed us how—if we managed to survive the next few decades—we'd find ourselves at a time when man could navigate the universe much as he had the Earth, when space flights and weightlessness would be commonplace, and when tranquility would reign (except, of course, for those instances wherein man was closeted with a paranoid computer). Said journey to tranquility got off to a profoundly bumpy start, though. The day after *2001* opened (on April 3, 1968), Martin Luther King was assassinated in Memphis, Tennessee, and less than three weeks after the film had its UK premiere (on May 15), Robert Kennedy was murdered in Los Angeles. America was finding itself ever more deeply enmeshed in Southeast Asia, and not even Nostradamus could have predicted that *Space Oydessy*'s iconic black monolith would find its counterpart in the Vietnam Veterans's Memorial in Washington, D.C., scarcely a dozen years later.

Roughly four decades earlier, just as the tail end of 1930 was within spitting distance and most stock-market-driven defenestrations had already taken place, David Butler and the Fox Film Corporation offered a hopeful distraction to the collective American consciousness: *Just Imagine*. Audiences were shown just what the future of America had in store for them, assuming they managed to weather the intervening fifty years. Unlike those of us who had gazed—completely puzzled—at the space child's debut at our local theater between assassinations, the ticket-buyers of some 85 years ago did not have to contend with myriad murders and U.S. involvement overseas. For a while there, as the victims of the Great Depression (and the leadership of Herbert Hoover) underwent a messaging via the New Deal and the fireside stroking by FDR, things were looking up. (We hasten to acknowledge how quickly things began to look w-a-y down in the second lustrum of the '30s.) The cinematic benchmarks of the first half of the '30s would consist of musicals—the very antithesis of the Silent Era; horror pictures—for those who felt that nothing in life could be worse than bank holidays and bread lines; and gangster films—a vicarious means of getting back at the system that had screwed one over.

In *Just Imagine*, David Butler guided his principals through a reasonably melodic, futuristic scenario concocted by famed tunesmiths De Sylva, Brown and Henderson. The picture, albeit popular, was even then a tough nut to crack, as the meld of its various elements—the traditional romantic triangle, topical musical interludes, science-fictional gizmos and venues, comic underpinnings—did not guarantee a winning combination. More than one critic found the picture tedious despite its array of obviously appealing elements. Another wondered why the movies seldom offered "fantastic features" like this one (or *The Thief of Bagdad* or *The Lost World*). As Edwin Schallert put it, "It is only a kind of superstition that the highly imaginative film output must be so limited."[1] Mr. Schallert seemed to have forgotten that M-G-M's 10-reel, Technicolor epic *The Mysterious Island* had premiered but a year earlier, an event that made the release of "highly imaginative films" ever so slightly less rare. Still, "space" had been on man's mind even before Copernicus and DaVinci assumed serious postures, and the pre–1930 Ür-cinema *had* dealt, albeit seldom, with what was indeed up there, and how it was, verily, a danger for all of us down here. Other than the earliest of imaginative shorts (mostly à la Méliès, dans la France), the few "fantastic features" that took us beyond the earth's atmosphere hailed from foreign climes. In 1918, Denmark's Nordisk Films came out with *Himmelskibet* (released a couple of years later in the U.S. as *A Trip to Mars*). Metro *did* produce *A Message from Mars* in 1920, but that was essentially a remake of a 1913 British picture. In 1923, though, dreams of communicating with the Red Planet served as the basis for *Radio Mania* (aka *M.A.R.S.*, aka *Mars Calling*, aka *The Man from Mars*),[2] a sci-fi comedy developed and produced in these United States. From that point on,

**The Big Apple in 1980. Not a plane to be seen, but loads of cars going ... where?**

**LN-18 (Maureen O'Sullivan) and J-21 (John Garrick) share a quiet moment together, hovering above mid-town Manhattan.**

though, until *Just Imagine*, the only major movies that dealt with extraterrestrial situations were from abroad: Russia's *Aelita* (1924) brought Mars back into the picture, and Fritz Lang's fascinating *Frau im Mond* (*The Woman on the Moon*) was imported from Germany in 1929.

The end of the Second World War and consideration of the awesome nature of atomic power led to our beloved '50s sci-fi, a genre that kept us enthralled—and amused—right up through the early '60s.[3] For all that, it took until 1957, when Sputnik was launched, for our nation—and not just the movies—to take giant steps, space-wise. *In ictu oculi*—in the twinkling of an eye—the U.S. government left Aeneas and Odysseus to find their own way—*Vale*, classical education!—and began emphasizing mathematics and science in the classroom. (Fast forward to 2016: liberal arts degrees be hanged; STEM, everyone?) The proposed "conquest" of outer space quickly moved from being the provenance of occasionally delirious science fiction to the realm of viability for America.

From JFK's call to put a man on the moon, to the successful achievement of that challenge, to the average American's almost humdrum reaction to a good 10 dozen of the 137 space shuttle missions, it became obvious that nothing diminished the titillating promise of the future than did the prosaic nature of the present. Naïveté is quickly replaced by ennui, creativity by indifference, novelty by replication, and charm by over-familiarity. Such is life.

Our picture starts with a quick succession of titles—read aloud in the sort of brash tone one might well associate with New Yorkers—and a couple of brief vignettes.

> "*Just Imagine* what a difference fifty years can make! Take a look at New York in 1880" offers the first title. We see pedestrians leisurely strolling along what is supposedly Fifth Avenue amidst horse-drawn vehicles, pedestrians and equestrians, and bicycles built for four. Gentility and calm rule the day.
> 
> "*Just Imagine*! The people in 1880 thought they were the last word in speed! Take a look at the same spot today." Number the second. A vintage-1930's jaywalker is hard-pressed to dodge whizzing Dodges and sundry coupes as he attempts to make his way across the avenue.

[And, no, he doesn't quite make it.] Nerves are frayed, courtesy is defunct, and it's worth one's life to traverse the City.

"If the last fifty years made such a change, *Just Imagine* the New York of 1980.... When everyone has a number instead of a name and the Government tells you whom you should marry. *Just Imagine* ... 1980!"

J-21 is in love with LN-18—and she with him—but she [hereafter L] had consented to MT-3's "filing an application" [she blames her father] and now J-21 [hereafter J] is in danger of losing his girl, as the Marriage Tribunal has found M [you've got that, don't you?] to be more "worthy." J has four months to prove he is the worthier of the two by accomplishing something really special. J immediately picks up something that vaguely resembles a guitar and sings—he sings every once in a while, alone or with others—about worth and love and such.

Meanwhile, J's flatmate, RT-42 and his girl, D-6, are headed off to see the result of a scientific experiment: Dr. X-10 is looking to resuscitate a man who was struck by lightning while playing golf in 1930. J accompanies them to the laboratory where the good doctor succeeds in reviving a certain Mr. Ole Peterson—hereafter known as "Single O"—from a half-century of death. J and R(T-42) offer O their apartment until he gets on his feet and the trio heads out into 1980's New York. O is astonished to learn that food and drink are now ingested in pill form and that babies are to be had for slipping a coin into a machine slot. "Give me the good old days," he says over and again, and that proves to be a song cue.

That night, as J is trying to sneak in to see L—R and D will be there, too—M and L's father [the interfering old So-and-So is letterless] are off to the theater. [L, feigning a headache, stays behind.] Not long after—although long enough to allow J to warble another song—M and his future father-in-law return unexpectedly. Thanks to the antics of the drunken O, J's presence is discovered, and M forces L to bid adieu to the man she really loves. The despondent J is approached by a man wearing a black hat and cape, who leads him into the presence of Z-4, the great inventor. Hearing of J's plight—and satisfied with his credentials—Z offers J the opportunity to fly a rocket-plane to Mars. "If you successfully make this trip," the inventor intones, "you will be the most distinguished man in the world." J accepts and later agrees to take R along with him.

Some prolonged singing and dancing follows as (1) "His buddies give J-21 a farewell party on the Air Liner Pegasus"; (2) R and D perform a protracted song-and-dance number together; and (3) Single O concludes with a comic bit in which

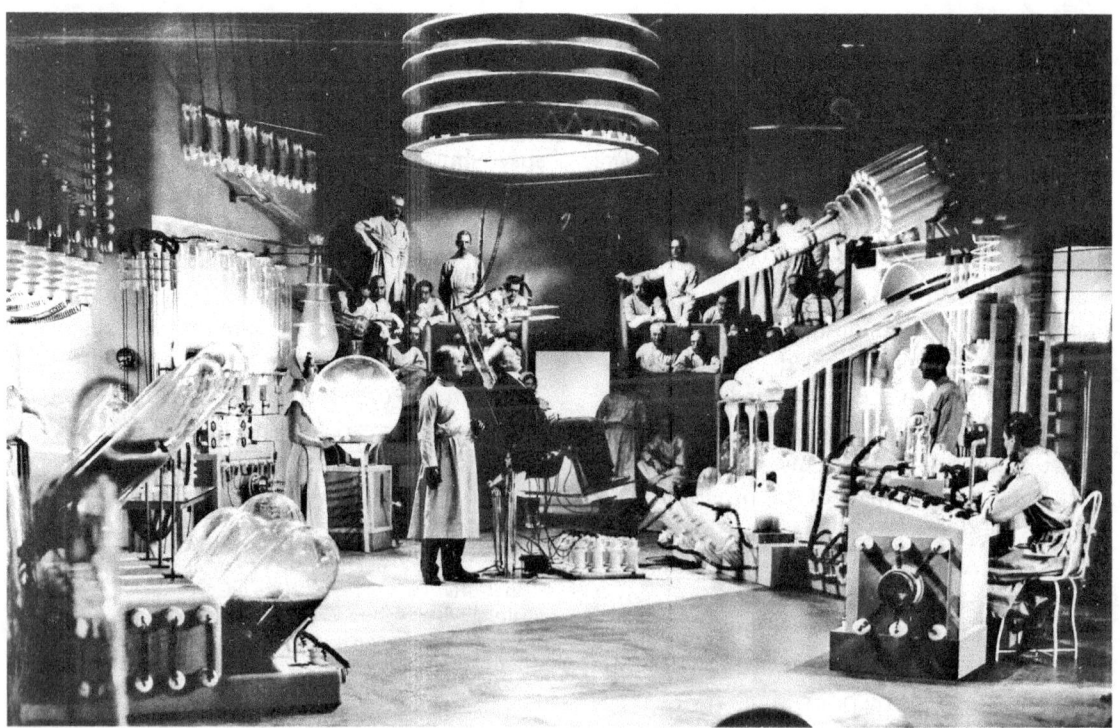

"No, this is not an outtake from Frankenstein." Once Single-O (El Brendel) has been revived from the dead, all those doctors and the awesome futuristic set disappear ... errr ... in a heartbeat.

he changes hats and attitudes quickly enough to keep the crowd amused. The days pass, and as J and R prepare to blast off, Z-4 shows up [in a black hat and cape] with some last-minute instructions, and L flies quickly to the launch site to see her love; however, she is moments too late and is left in the lurch [in the rocket-plane's exhaust, actually], unconscious and in the arms of an archly smiling M.

En route to Mars, it is discovered that Single O has stowed away. This matters not at all. A month later, the three men land on Mars, the rocket-plane being brought to a stop on a ground as flat and smooth as a pool table.

The newly resurrected Single O (El Brendel): ignored by medical types, but of interest and amusing to RT-42 (Frank Albertson), J-21 (John Garrick), and D-6 (Marjorie White).

Within moments, the men are led by a female Martian to the throne room of Queen LooLoo, who—via a wild series of gestures and eyebrow movements—attempts to communicate with the Earthlings. She is not terribly successful. The massive and muscular BoKo, who seems rather attracted to O, leads O and R into an area where the men are stripped and maneuvered into taking a bath. Rejoining J, the men witness the beginings of a production number featuring dancers clad as monkeys when—suddenly—the area is overrun by other, snarling, spear-wielding Martians. A battle ensues and the three Earthlings are carried off.

Only after the men find themselves in the throne room of a hissing, snapping, wildly gesticulating LooLoo doppelganger [yclept BooBoo] and a feisty, violent double of Boko [Loko] do they come to the conclusion that all Martians have identical, albeit evil, twins. The men are rescued from their cell by Boko, but pandemonium ensues, one cannot tell Boko from Loko, and it is left to O to get his two comrades—both of whom have been drugged—back to the ship. Onboard, O reveals that he has captured Loko and has stashed him away as proof that the trio did, in fact, make it to Mars and back.

On Earth once again, J makes it to the Tribunal in time to win a judgment in his favor. He and L are to be wed, R and D are likewise ecstatic, and O finds himself face to face with an elderly, goatee'd man who claims to be his "little son, Axel."

Every so often, a thriller is released that is publicized as being so upsetting that the audience needs be reminded, "It's only a movie!" With *Just Imagine*, we need remember, "It's only a musical comedy"—and an 85-year-old one, too—and allowances must be made. *Ooooops!* Hang on a second; the November 29, 1930, edition of the *Exhibitors Herald-World* begs to differ: "Do not judge for a minute ... that this is of the musical comedy variety for it is not. There are songs in it, and there is dancing, but these are but a minor factor in the film." Uh-huh, and there are puns and sophomoric physical humor and topical jokes about the Volstead Act and Henry Ford's anti–Semiticism, too. And while these (and the songs and dances) may be dismissed as ultimately being incidental to the plot, said plot *is* the inevitable Boy Has Met Girl—Boy Loses Girl—Boy Gets Girl, gussied up with some decent futuristic miniatures, some headache-inducing other-worldy sets, and unmitigated silliness. A respite of Godsend proportion from Depression-oriented depression, the film made audiences forget 1930 for a bit and made a goodly number of the usual critical suspects downright enthusiastic. It made money, too.

Where to begin?

First off, the traditional romantic triangle. Okay, in 1980, young swains can no longer rely upon gym memberships, fantastic genes, or unbridled sexuality to win the object of their affection; the government now interferes, adjudging the worth and distinction of any and all presumed beaux so as to award the belle—much like a prize—to the "best man," no marriage wordplay intended. At the outset of the film we were a trifle confused as to whether it's the United States government or the New York government (both "tribunals" apparently have reams of letterhead to spare) that's doing the interfering in the case of LN-18, J-21, and MT-3. We reached the conclusion that we're dealing with New York, if only because, other than that peculiar junket taken to the Red Planet, the action is confined to the isle of Manhattan.

By design, and despite its fairly lengthy running time, *Just Imagine* ignores the distaff side of this arrangement: Is the woman always to be the trophy won by the man? Will there be no Sadie Hawkins Day in 1980? Will no male ever be the prize dangled before two or more female aspirants? Judging from the way working women are under-represented or stereotyped à la 1930 in the movie— to say nothing of how the average woman will no longer even participate in that crucial-to-the-race activity yclept childbirth—that ain't ever gonna happen. Moreover, even well-intentioned young gals who know their own hearts may be coerced into opening the field for their hand against their best judgment. L reveals that MT (empty?) is currently in the lead, tribunal-wise, only because her father convinced her to allow the musically-challenged older man (who does, admittedly, go to the opera with L's dad) to "file an application."

The topical musical interludes still have a certain charm to them. Musical entertainments have obviously come a long way since husky tenors and hefty sopranos would pose immobile while singing at each other from opposite sides of the operatic stage. As did most other movie musicals of this early sound period, *Just Imagine* offers everything from the love-sick hero warbling (to guitarish accompaniment) directly at the camera to sparkling duets Foleyed in

The only musical number that is reprised during the picture.

Just imagine … a full-page ad in *Screen Play Secrets Magazine!*

over some high-energy hoofing to Busby Berkeley-esque production numbers.[4] The credits for the picture list eight of De Sylva, Brown and Henderson's tunes by name, and "I Am the Words, You Are the Melody" enjoys something of a reprise late in the proceedings. The print we viewed has only seven songs, though, and the absence of one struck a chord with *Variety*'s "Sid" in his appraisal of the film:

What may have been the best melody in the picture, "Never Swat a Fly," has been cut out altogether, and surprisingly enough, Seymour Felix has only one dance number in the entire film. The lone Felix contribution is also the result of a slice on his second number which abruptly cuts away from a chorus monkey routine soon after the start during the Mars sequence.[5]

The picture, which had been screened as a private preview for the delegates to the Motion Picture Theater Owners of America prior to its world premiere at Los Angeles's Carthay Circle Theater, had been thought to be much too long at one hour and 55 minutes and was subsequently trimmed. While the fact that the picture needed a bit of editing was no secret—*The Daily Reporter*[6] admitted that

> Dave Butler and De Sylva, Brown and Henderson made some retakes yesterday to bolster up a few minor weak spots in *Just Imagine* before shipping the negative to New York for general release.

It's apparent now that the lion's share of the footage excised was musical in nature. In fact, a month after the notice on retakes, the *Reporter* published a selection of brief comments from the New York papers, and most made mention of the music: "In the musical comedy style, with very little music. And not much else either"—*Post*; "Fantasy, fun and melody are shrewdly linked"—*Times*; "Its mood of Jules Verne gone musical comedy palls"—*Sun*; "A pictorial extravaganza and a fair screen musical"—*Journal*.

It seems odd, though—what with the rather protracted displays of extraterrestrial gibberish and ethnic shtick on hand[7]—that it was the work of the men whom the contemporary press called the "Three Musketeers of Music" that was bowdlerized. The year before *Just Imagine* opened, the Messrs. De Sylva, Brown, and Henderson had four (4) shows operating simultaneously on Broadway: *Three Cheers* with Will Rogers, George White's *Scandals*, *Hold Everything* with Bert Lahr, Victor Moore and Ona Manson, and *Follow Thru* with Jack Haley and Eleanor Powell. As a team, the men wrote such hits as "Sonny Boy"—immortalized by Al Jolson—while individually they were responsible for perennial favorites like "April Showers" (De Sylva), "Yes, We Have No Bananas" (Brown), and "Bye, Bye Blackbird" (Henderson). Seymour Felix, whose terpsichorean extravaganzas were—as noted by "Sid" at *Variety*—cut short and/or cut *out* of the production, was a choreographer of international renown not only onscreen, but also onstage. Felix's Broadway triumphs within a couple of years before and after *Just Imagine* included *Simple Simon* with Ed Wynn, *Rosalie* with Frank Morgan and Marilyn Miller, *Whoopee* with Eddie Cantor, and *Strike Me Pink* with Jimmy Durante.

We would venture to guess that, nowadays, most audiences would regard *Just Imagine* as being "quaint" as the sundry science-fictional gizmos found everywhere are not a little simplistic despite their being picturesque. The picture's overview of '80's New York—just like that 1968 view of the world to come in *2001*—was predicated on the belief that the pacing and scope of the sundry technological advances immediately impacted everyone; how else to explain the fact that the venerable scientist, Z-4 (Hobart Bosworth)—easily on the wrong side of the half-century mark—no longer bears the name he had been born with? Were 1930's audiences asked to swallow that the abrupt change in nomenclature might have started in 1931? Or the following year? From our vantage point, we can assert that the real-life permeation of technology—at least initially—is much more selective: thems with the cash gets the latest model smartphone first, no?

As for the accuracy of some of those technological predictions ... well, during the World's Fair held in Flushing, Queens, New York, in the early 1960s, Bell Telephone's exhibit featured a TV-screen set-up, much as is depicted in *Just Imagine* or in Great Britain's *High Treason* (see essay), which had been released as a silent over a year earlier. As the readers of this essay can attest, phone technology skipped right over the public forum—that wall-mounted (or desktop) TV-screen stage—and right into the intimacy of one's pocket, where its presence was quickly taken for granted. It is the person who does *not* have a smartphone who is regarded as "exceptional," and the features which make that particular gadget novel and charming soon do little other than mark

Not sure whether that's the Woolworth Building or what, but we'll take that city traffic any day…

department in dealing with De Sylva, Brown and Henderson's prognostications, and revelations of pill-cocktails that pack a punch, vending machines that dispense infants, and streets illuminated by hovering light patterns dot many of the extant critiques. If anything, 1980 is 1930's Art Deco gone wild.

With babies to be had for a shekel, the comparatively *meh* changeover from names born of heritage to initial-and-number combinations certainly seems more do-able, if still unrelentingly improbable. In rereading our plot summary, we found it a bit of a trial ourselves to keep track of who and whom while using initials instead of names, yet our "shortening" of the nomenclature reflects the dialogue in the film, wherein folks refer to each other by a single letter (sort of a "nickletter"). Going from bad to worse, we can *just imagine* the problems encountered everyday in 1980 by countless folks forced by alphabetic limitations to share "F-16" or some such. With a burgeoning worldwide population, do the names sooner or later become a tad complex of necessity? Will acronyms thus never make it into the lingua franca? Will there be no ROTFLMAO-5 or LSMFT-12?

its place in line as its owner waits for the latest, more distinctive model. (*Plus ça change, plus c'est la même chose.*) Still, Mordaunt Hall[8] was sufficiently impressed with all the technological trappings to spill some ink on the miracles that would come as a matter of course with the passage of a half-century:

> In the Gotham of the future there are all manner of novel ideas, including a city with nine levels, landing places for dirigibles and airplanes, which rise and descend like helicopters. It is a poor man, indeed who cannot afford an airplane. The television works to perfection…. Then there are strange circles of light instead of doorbells, and elevators that shoot up or down in the 200-story structures with amazing rapidity.

Hall was not the only critic to raise his eyebrows at the ingenuity of the uncredited art

As for science-fictional venues, the sets are as blatantly fake as they are imaginative, a factor that does *not* detract from one's enjoying the film so long as the viewer indulges in that same suspension of disbelief required to accept today's vampires with gym-hardened abs or zombies working toward an apocalypse. The sheer scope of the New York City skyline is breathtaking, and the opening scene—in which cars zoom along the streets far below a pair of flirts darting back and forth between hovering airplanes—does take the breath even if it also refutes a later claim that almost no one uses a car in 1980. Apart from the crowd scenes demanded by the narrative, the streets are strangely underpopulated—perhaps the citizenry stays in at night, watching television—and only a profoundly inebriated Single O adorns the sidewalk while J and L are meeting on the sly.

The Martian vista in evidence as the rocket-plane lands on that planet's surface is clearly—and brazenly—unreal, and the interiors into and through which the three Earthlings run apparently have no function or purpose, merely serving as an "otherworldy" design. Several commentators were most impressed with Z-4's rocket-plane. Edwin Schallert, for example, writing for the *Los Angeles Times*,[9] was fairly effusive: "From the time that the rocket plane leaves the earth ingenuity is at its peak." Douglas Hodges, reporting on that same date for the *Exhibitors World Herald*, went a step further:

> The rocket sequence in the picture is the finest and most impressive part of the film. The rocket is designed like the shell from a gun and is built somewhat on the principle of the shells used in the Big Bertha of the World War. Developing its own power after it leaves the surface of the earth it depends on the throw of the earth to propel it from the earth to the planet, Mars. Its departure is pure theatre.

Even allowing that Mr. Douglas's paucity of scientific terminology was due to his being a product of his generation, we can't see the pure theatricality of the launch scene for the life of us. Nor could "Sid" over at *Variety*:

> Besides the thin plot what undermines the picture is the failure to realize the possibilities in the Mars sequence. Takeoff is a quick flash of the rocket plane roaring away, after which the supposed month spent hurtling through the ether is merely an interior of the ship with the three men. A lingering look at this hemisphere dimly outlined, and Garrick's later glance through a Mars's telescope reveals a repeat shot of the same thing upon which is double exposed Miss O'Sullivan's head as she talks a reprive [sic] chorus of a melody—deadly to the pace and illusion.

Granted that *Just Imagine* was designed to be a delightful flight of fancy and not to be taken seriously to any degree whatsoever, might not the interior of the rocket plane—the design that so enthralled Mr. Douglas—have included some seats? If one is to stand for a month or so, might there not be, at least, a pole or some straps to hang onto? Or some windows that might actually jibe with the sightlines of the astronauts? And even with comestibles in handy pill form, might there not be the need of a loo? Or a change of clothes? There *is* a coffin-sized box that apparently has no function other than to conceal Single O at its launch and contain Loko during its return to Earth. *Ummmmm* … upon further consideration….

The fantasy element that is more peculiar than any of the gadgets and optics discussed so far is the conceit that Single O—born Ole Peterson and then killed by lightning back in 1930—would be raised from the dead so easily, and then left for dead, as it were, moments afterward. The operating theater in the picture is similar to those seen in a couple of the more classic horror films of the '30s—rows of surgically-garbed medical types watch earnestly as Dr. X-10 does whatever it takes (it doesn't take much) to restore life to that inert body clad in morning clothes. Once Mr. Peterson rises from the dead, the physicians mob X-10, congratulations fill the air, and not a solitary soul requests that the revivified golfer have his heartbeat monitored or his blood pressure checked. "What are you going to do with me?" X-10 is asked in Swedish-ized English. "I'm through with you," Dr. X coldly replies. "To me, you were just an experiment." Taken together with vending machines stocked with newborns, this scene—and the idea behind it—betrays a cynicism about America's future that the rest of the hoopla fails to counteract.

The unmitigated silliness is what dates the picture more than anything else. The lovey-dovey stuff—set to music or just expostulated via posture or tone of voice—is tolerable, even though the intervening years have put an edge to cinematic love-making. The gadgets and sets bring a smile to one's face, and the music is hummable and foot-tappable. But the humor?

The humor came from the pens of De Sylva, Brown and Henderson, with director David Butler aiding and abetting via continuity. Butler, born in San Francisco in late December 1894—and a survivor of that city's infamous earthquake—entered films as a thespian, moving and thesping à la the vision of such big names as John Ford, D.W. Griffith, and Frank Borzage. Apart from small or uncredited roles in a couple of big titles (*The Birth of a Nation* saw him, but not his name, on the screen), Butler did play bigger parts in films that only the most driven of completists might ever have heard of. Along the way, he moved into writing and directing—1927's *High School Hero* marked his dual debut in those areas—and comedy and music and he became frequent partners. It was he who helmed 1931's *A Connecticut Yankee*, starring comic legend, Will Rogers; 1936's *Captain January*, starring kid legend, Shirley Temple; 1942's *Road to Morocco*, starring twin legends, Bing Crosby and Bob Hope; and 1953's *Calamity Jane*, starring musical-comedy legends, Doris Day and Howard Keel. During the '50s and '60s, Butler became involved heavily in television. He directed *Captain Z-Ro*, an early '50s TV series that no one we know ever saw (unlike *Captain Video*), and worked on episodes of *The Twilight Zone, Wagon Train, The Patty Duke Show*, and numerous others; he oversaw the entire run of *Leave It to Beaver*. The man knew comedy and music and westerns and fantasy and television, and his knowledge grew over the years, so the silliness on display in *Just Imagine* might be excused as being a tad puerile.

Butler, who died in mid–June 1979, was active up until 1967, when he was talked into directing *C'mon, Let's Live a Little*, a malt-shop musical with Bobby Vee and Jackie DeShannon. Although our mini-biography would end on a true grace note had that film capped his career, it would probably be more correct to say it killed any desire he had to keep on working in the industry. As quoted on the International Movie Data Base (www.IMDB.com), Butler confessed: "I don't even want to talk about that. I tried to do a favor for somebody, and we made it so fast that I don't know what happened.... I never got paid a quarter for it." Coming from his Silent Era days, when he made $5 a day for emoting amid crowds of extras in fare like *The Birth of a Nation*, that sort of pay-off was a definite step down.

*Just Imagine*'s chief comic perpetrator, of course, was El Brendel, the movies's "Synthetic Swede." Born Elmer Goodfellow Brendel in Philadelphia, he early on decided to mine the operatically ethnic-rich veins of Vaudeville before entering the bastard art. Per an article by Cedric Belfrage[10] that was published shortly after *Hot for Paris*, a Fox musical released on December 22, 1929, "When the war came, El Brendel decided it would be healthier to abandon his German characterization and give the public a bit of dear old Sweden." Following a dozen years or so touring with faux German[11] shtick, El and his wife, Flo Bert, were signed by the Schubert organization in 1921, and he made the move to the movies with Paramount in *Wings* (1926); most of his role in that one ended up on the proverbial cutting-room floor. He signed on with Fox in 1929 (with *The Cock-Eyed World*), after which—according to Mr. Belfrage's screed—the comedian

blandly and almost unconcernedly deplore[d] the fact that it [was] no longer possible to be funny in a clean way and make 'em laugh.... In talkies, he's already become identified with racy drama of the—well—rather bawdy kind.[12]

There *are* a few lines/situations in *Just Imagine* that were probably viewed through purple glasses by some back in 1930, but neither Brendel nor any of the others should take the heat for the scenario. Just as the picture itself was aimed at an adult market, so was the humor directed; it was presumed that some of the jokes and references would be above the heads of children taken to watch the film. Maybe the tone *was* a tad suggestive at times—God knows, the only eyebrows that would be raised nowadays are those on the Martians's faces—but the fact that only *Harrison's Reports*[13] dwelled at length on them must mean something:

> It is unsuitable for children, for the reason that many of the things that are said have a double meaning, [the one, dirty] and some of the scenes are objectionable…. Most of the girls are in a state of undress, and one dance in particular, done by a group of people residing in [sic] the planet Mars, is vulgar. There is a good deal of vulgar humor throughout.

Mom and Dad (Dad, especially) might have had to explain the sundry references to Prohibition to their impressionable children; Single O has a propensity to get ossified, and the Volstead Act is apparently still the law of the land in 1980 ("It looks like in a year or two we're going to get light [sic] wines and beer"). Still, it would had to have been singularly dull American children who were *not* aware, even then, of the state of liquor in the States. We, in a world of craft beers and bacon-flavored brandies, can only smile knowingly and shrug.

More disturbing—and, perhaps, ultimately more unsettling—is the exchange that occurs an instant before O is given a cocktail-pill. The revived Swede is told that almost no one uses a car in 1980 (a statement undone by an earlier scene in which the audience sees dozens of cars on the vast streets in the "background" while J and L are idling and flirting in the sky), as "they all have planes." J is revealed to be a pilot on the Air Liner "Pegasus," while all the other airliners are "Goldfarbs." Brendel then mouths one of De Sylva, Brown and Henderson's less-than-deathless lines, "Somebody got even with Henry Ford," a statement greeted with laughter from his 1980 flatmates. Nestled here in the 21st century, most of us would have no clue as to what had set the two juveniles into chortling. The background on the "joke" casts an American Icon in an unflattering light.

> In the period from 1910 to 1918, [Henry] Ford became increasingly anti-immigrant, anti-labor, anti-liquor, and anti–Semitic. Ford wanted to assert that there was a Jewish conspiracy to control the world. He blamed Jewish financiers for fomenting World War I so that they could profit from supplying both sides. He accused Jewish automobile dealers of conspiring to undermine Ford Company sales policies…. In 1919, he purchased a newspaper, the *Dearborn Independent*…. In 1920, [the newspaper] printed the first of a series of articles titled "The International Jew; The World's Problem."[14]

If only because most jokes are effective only when one is aware of/can relate to the circumstances leading up to the punchline, a good deal of what was undoubtedly quite witty in 1930 has become quite flat in 2016. While Mr. Brendel's Swedish bumpkin doubtless still has his followers—we currently categorize comics and humorists in terms of ethnicity, vulgarity, sexuality, and the like—for many, his character is as strange and "foreign" as LooLoo, Boko, and B-36, the inscrutable messenger portrayed by Mischa Auer.

Filling out the picture's principal cast was Maureen O'Sullivan, a year and a bit away from making her own the character of Jane, soulmate to Johnny Weissmuller's Tarzan. Miss O'Sullivan hasn't much to do in *Just Imagine*, other than react to the goings-on around her, but she would get into the thick of things throughout the decade. Prior to hanging about M-G-M's jungles in loin clothing, the lovely young Irishwoman appeared opposite Frank Albertson and a pre–*The Mummy* Bramwell Fletcher in *So This Is London*; shared the screen with William Powell and Myrna Loy in 1934's *The Thin Man*; was spooked by

Lionel Barrymore in *The Devil Doll*; and survived the Marx Brothers in 1937's *A Day at the Races*. The '30s saw the actress positively awash in big productions for M-G-M, that biggest of studios. Some decades later, as she began to add television credits to her mix, she enlivened 1976's *The Great Houdini*, in which she played Lady Conan Doyle, wife to you-know-whom, played by Peter Cushing. She was also seen in 1986's major hits, *Peggy Sue Got Married* and *Hannah and Her Sisters*, and the '90s found her hither, thither and yon on the small screen. O'Sullivan died in June 1998.

Minnesotan Frank Albertson had begun gracing screens in 1922 and an interesting (and coincidental) title in which he appeared prior to *Just Imagine* was 1929's *Words and Music*. Albertson, too, cavorted with the Marx Brothers, albeit in RKO's *Room Service* (1938), and also participated in both gentle and brutal ends of our favorite genre, having appeared opposite Will Rogers and Miss O'Sullivan in 1931's *A Connecticut Yankee* and as far away from Lionel Atwill and Lon Chaney, Jr., as he could get in 1941's *Man-Made Monster*. Albertson died far too young—at 55 years of age—in 1964.

John Garrick was a Brit, born Reginald Dandy (what would Monty Python have made of *that*?) in Brighton in 1902. Music and flying machines marked his early film appearances, as he (and others) enchanted audiences in the melodically-heavy *Married in Hollywood* while dealing in dirigibles along with a pre–*Dracula* Helen Chandler in *The Sky Hawk* (both 1929). Before falling for her again in *Just Imagine*, Garrick chased Maureen O'Sullivan in *Song o' My Heart* and later did likewise with a pre–Nelson Eddy Jeanette MacDonald in *The Lottery Bride*, in which the comic relief was provided by Joe E. Brown and ZaSu Pitts as Hake and Hilda (and not as Double H). Apart from his turn as J-21, Garrick's best role (IOHO) might have been that of Mark Kennaway in 1931's *Charlie Chan Carries On*, a film that remains lost to this day. Garrick died in San Francisco in October 1966.

Marjorie White was also in *Charlie Chan Carries On*, as Sadie Minchin, wife of the character essayed by Warren Hymer. White, a 4'10½" bundle of energy, had debuted in Winnipeg, Manitoba, Canada, in July of 1904 and shuffled off this mortal coil following a car accident at the tender age of 31. She didn't amass many film credits in that brief time among us, but they did include a second Charlie Chan epic—1931's *The Black Camel*—*Diplomaniacs* (1933) with Wheeler and Woolsey, and a turn as Larry Fine's wife in the 1934 Three Stooges short, *Woman Haters*. In *Just Imagine*, the pert actress provides a hyper-level of energy that offsets perfectly the laid-back yokelism of Mr. Brendel.

Ivan Linow is best remembered, of course, as Hercules in the 1930 sound remake of Lon Chaney/Tod Browning's *The Unholy Three* and, intriguingly, the Latvian-born actor's first film was 1921's *Cappy Ricks*, in which he portrayed Ole Peterson, the name Single O had been saddled with while being struck by lightning, 50 years prior to the antics of *Just Imagine*. More of the same: Linow was featured in W.C. Fields and Allison Skipworth's 1933 classic comedy, *Tillie and Gus*. His role? "The Swede." Move over, El Brendel. Linow died in London in late November 1940.

Mischa Auer, the Russian character man who contributed to comedies and thrillers with over 175 films to his credit, is barely noticeable in *Just Imagine*. Still, the lanky Russky can be seen in *The Monster Walks* (1932), in *Tarzan the Fearless* (a serial with Buster Crabbe and Jacqueline Wells standing in for Weismuller and O'Sullivan), as "Zan, the Hunchback" in 1935's *Condemned to Live*, as well as in films that might be regarded as less esoteric and more "mainstream" like 1938's *You Can't Take It with You*, *Destry Rides Again* (1939), and *Hold That Ghost* (1941). In the midst of all this, the actor received an Oscar nomination for his outstanding performance as Carlo in 1936's *My Man Godfrey*. Auer passed away in Rome on March 5, 1967.

In July 1933 Fox would once again release a crazy sci-fi musical—*It's Great to Be Alive*—a remake of that studio's 1924 seven-reeler *The Last Man on Earth*. *Alive* saw broken-hearted aviator Raul Roulien returning from a flight to the South Pacific only to discover that, while he was out of town, every other male on earth had contracted "Masculitis," a condition that rendered them all sterile. Constructed along the lines of *Just Imagine*, the cast featured Gloria Stuart, Edna May Oliver, and Edward Van Sloan, the latter two playing Drs. *Prod*well and *Wilt*on, respectively.

It would take decades before the movies again attempted a mix as eclectic and peculiar as either Fox feature, although the Spanish cinema had taken a shot at the theme a lustrum earlier. In *Madrid en el año 2000* (*Madrid in the Year 2000*, 1925), the Manzanares River has somehow become a major waterway affording passage to enormous ocean liners through the heart of the Spanish capital. Definitely not as glitzy as the De Sylva, Brown and Henderson construct, *Madrid* did open wide Iberian eyes to the possibility of a fantastic future. And, as mentioned en passant in our essay on Hispanic Horrors, 1945 saw Juan Bustillo Oro craft fantasy *Lo que va de ayer a hoy* (*What Goes from Yesterday to Today*) in which the protagonist is in suspended animation for a half-century. Upon snapping out of it, though, his biggest adjustment is not to the then-current "technology," but rather to the loose morals found in the "future."

A fascinating yet somewhat creaky picture, *Just Imagine* is worth a look, if only for its unique meld of what were then disparate elements. *Harrison's Reports*, cited above, found that "the picture is too long, drags and becomes boresome [sic] most of the time." In one of his many mentions of the picture in his column for the *Los Angeles Times*, Edwin Schallert took a moment to depart from the multiple compliments he had in a half-dozen editions of the paper to grouse that most fantasy films smacked of "childishness, without that ethereal quality that fantasy should possess."[15] Writing in the January 1931 issue of the *Theatre Guild Magazine*, critic Evelyn Gerstein was likewise unimpressed.

> Despite its backdrop of helicopters and sliding panels and Martian interludes, manages to be pretty dull fare—a musical piece in which the perennial El Brendel with his mauve decade gags moves against a succession of fantastic modern backdrops that suggest both the old silent version of Fritz Lang's *Metropolis* and the more recent English *High Treason*, which the censors banned some months ago, in an attempt to portray a mythical 1980.

Still, for every finger wagged at the production, its theme, or its execution, there was a plethora of compliments, like the one found in the January 4, 1931, issue of the *Kansas City Star*: "[*Just Imagine*] is one of the most genuinely entertaining screen productions we have seen in years."

In this, the Age of Netflix and Ebay, very few pictures remain unavailable to the interested viewer possessed of tenacity and the Internet. We'll venture to say that, even after well over a century of cinematic science fiction, *Just Imagine* remains fairly unique. That last qualification may be grammatical gibberish, but the ultimate arbiter is you, the viewer. As they say (and said far more frequently in those pre–Sputnik days): *De gustibus non disputandum est*. (This is *also* the Age of Google.)

# Fog; Terror Aboard

*Fog*—Columbia Pictures Corp.—November 22, 1933—69 minutes **Cast:** Donald Cook as Wentworth Brown; Mary Brian as Mary Fulton; Reginald Denny as Dr. Winstay; Robert McWade as Alonzo Holt; Helen Freeman as Madame Alva; Samuel S. Hinds as Dickens; G. Pat Collins as Mullaney; Edwin Maxwell as the Captain; Maude Eburn as Mrs. Jackson; Marjorie Gateson as Mrs. Bentley; Montague Shaw as Dr. Alloway; with Eddie Fetherton, Merrill McCormick

**Credits:** *Director*: Albert Rogell; *Assistant Director*: Arthur Black; *Associate Producer*: Robert North; *Supervisor*: Sid Rogell; *Screenplay*: Ethel Hill, Dore Schary; *Cinematography*: Benjamin Kline; *Film Editor*: Richard Cahoon; *Sound*: Edward Bernds; *Based on the eponymous novel by* Valentine Williams and Dorothy Rice Sims (1933, Boston)

*Terror Aboard*—Paramount Productions, Inc.—April 14, 1933—69 minutes **Cast:** John Halliday as Maximilian Kreig; Charlie Ruggles as Blackie Witherspoon; Shirley Gray as Lili Kingston; Neil Hamilton as James Cowles; Jack LaRue as Leslie Cordoff; Vera Teasdale as Millicent Hazlitt; Stanley Fields as Captain Swanson; Leila Bennett as Lena Klein; Morgan Wallace as Morton Hazlitt; Thomas Jackson as Captain Allison; William Janney as Edward Wilson; Paul Hurst as the Boatswain; Frank Hagney as the Mate; Clarence Wilson as the Ship's doctor; Paul Porcasi as the Chef; Bobby Dunn as the Cross-eyed sailor; Kit Guard as Larson; Peter Hancock as Mate on yacht; Marty Faust as Reynolds; Clem Beauchamp as the First seaman; Eddie "Rochester" Anderson as Seaman; James Dime as Seaman

**Credits:** *Director*: Paul Sloane; *Assistant Director*: Russell Matthews; *Supervisor*: William LeBaron; *Screenplay*: Harvey Thew, Manuel Seff; *Story*: Robert Presnell; *Cinematography*: Harry Fischbeck; *Art Director*: W.B. Ihnen; *Editor*: Eda Warren; *Sound*: M.M. Paggi

One of the most terrifying episodes of Bram Stoker's *Dracula* is the sequence set aboard ship wherein the evil Count stalks and kills the entire crew. None of the many film versions did justice to these scenes, though Murnau's *Nosferatu* came closest. This conceit—being trapped with a killer in a confined space and with nowhere to run—did, of course, become standard horror-movie fare; so did the same concept, when situated in an old, dark house. Still, if you're stuck in an ODH, you can at least call the police (assuming the wires haven't been downed yet) or run out into the storm. At sea, though, no one (save for your fellow passengers) can hear you scream, and the turbulent waters of Neptune's realm seldom provide a safe haven.

*The Last Moment* (1923), which dealt with an ape-creature that escapes from its cage during a storm at sea and begins dispatching passengers and crew, illustrates our point. According to contemporary reviews, the claustrophobia and terror of the death-ship were captured very effectively by the camera; unfortunately, with the film MIA, we have no way of judging for ourselves. Ten years later, at the height of the first horror cycle, two pictures dealing with mayhem on the high seas were "launched" onto hapless audiences. And although *Fog* and *Terror Aboard* approached the premise *very* differently, they did have one thing in common: both sank at the box office.

Valentine Williams and Dorothy Rice

Sims's *Fog*, serialized over the course of several issues of *The Saturday Evening Post* (December 24, 1932–February 4, 1933), subsequently saw print as a novel. Williams, a journalist and war correspondent, was an old hand at thrillers and is probably best remembered (when he is, at all) as author of *The Clubfoot* mysteries. Dorothy Rice Sims—one of the first woman aviators *and* an early motorcycle racer—was renowned in the '30s as an expert at bridge; she was also the author of *Psychic Bidding*, a popular book on the game. Sims later said that the title was a misnomer—she meant "psychological," not "psychic"—and her game tactic involved "psyching out" her opponent, rather than using mental telepathy. Nonetheless, *Fog* contains both a psychic *and* a good deal of psyching out that is directed mainly at the reader. The magazine serial was quite popular and was often mentioned in conjunction with publicity for Columbia's film version, which was a reasonably faithful adaptation.

Since the film is not readily available (we had to go to the Library of Congress to see it), we offer a detailed synopsis:

> As the luxury ocean liner *Barbaric* prepares to disembark for England on a foggy night, scores of passengers say their farewells and board the ship. Among them is Wentworth Brown, a noted criminologist. He runs into a casual acquaintance who is seeing Mary Fulton off on her first cruise, and who introduces her to Brown. The criminologist seems more interested, though, in the arrival of the cantankerous, elderly, ailing millionaire, Alonzo Holt, who is helped aboard ship by his two aides, Dickens and Mullaney. Another passenger is famous psychic, Madame Alva, accompanied by her sharp-tongued German maid, Minna. Dr. Winstay, Holt's personal physician, arrives at the last minute.
>
> Holt treats Dickens and Mullaney miserably. Both men have criminal records, and, while Dickens is devoted to his boss, Mullaney is increasingly irritated by his employer's abrasive ways. We learn that Holt, who finds the fog unnerving ["It gets its dirty, slimy fingers in your brain. Makes me think of death"], was one of Madame Alva's former clients and had planned on leaving her one million dollars in his will. Because Dickens had exposed Alva as a fraud, though, the millionaire now intends to leave his money to a child from his first marriage: a child he has never seen and whose identity he does not know. Holt has made out a new will, but only Dickens knows about it, and private detectives have been hired to search for the unknown heir.
>
> Dr. Winstay visits Holt, who is surprised to find that his doctor is on the voyage; Winstay insists that he needs a vacation, too. Alva tells Emma that she is going to use the five-day voyage to try to patch things up with Holt, but Emma is skeptical. Even though Alva admits her methods are strictly show biz, she nonetheless believes in the supernatural.
>
> Parsons, a steward, recognizes Alva as his former wife and immediately wants to be cut in on whatever scheme she is concocting. Alva promises him a piece of the action, but insists he remain quiet about their relationship.
>
> On deck despite the unrelenting fog, Mary has a surprisingly pleasant encounter with Holt until she casually mentions that Madame Alva is a passenger, too. Holt flies into such a rage that the ship's physician, Dr. Alloway, is alarmed and must help the old man back to his cabin. Winstay insists that Holt take his daily medication, but the millionaire can't control his fury at the thought of Madame Alva and accuses Dickens of concealing the fact that the crystal gazer is on board.
>
> Mary finds herself receiving attentions from both Brown and Dr. Winstay, but the two men's

**The book combines bridge and murder.**

antipathy for each other seems to stem from more than romantic rivalry. Alva bribes Mullaney to admit her to Holt's cabin, but the old man won't be placated and orders her out, telling her that she'll never get a penny of his fortune. He also fires Mullaney.

Mrs. Jackson, a bridge fanatic, organizes a game in the main clubroom and insists that Brown and Winstay participate. In the middle of the game, Madame Alva collapses, and Winstay helps her to her cabin. Brown also finds an excuse to leave. Mary is strolling around on deck when she comes upon the body of Holt hanging from the rigging. Her terrified screams bring guests and crew to the grisly scene.

Brown offers his services to the captain in solving the crime. Harris, the ship's bumbling detective, objects, but the captain puts Brown in charge of the investigation. Dr. Alloway insists on doing an autopsy on Holt for the coroner's report. Winstay initially balks at this, but then relents and the millionaire's body is removed to his own cabin.

**Madame Alva (Helen Freeman) goes into an impromptu trance just before she and other passengers board. The scene ended up on the cutting room floor.**

Brown questions Mary, Dickens, and Mullaney. Mary is resentful of Brown treating her like a suspect, and Dickens and Mullaney end up accusing each other. Dickens tells Brown and the captain about the new will and the fact that that Madame Alva was totally cut off. Brown questions Alva, who claims to know nothing about the will, and who insists that she was ill in her cabin being tended to by Dr. Winstay when Holt was murdered.

Brown and the captain go to Holt's cabin where they find that his body has disappeared and that Dr. Alloway has been strangled to death. The captain insists on a search of all the crew's lockers. Alloway's wallet is found in Parsons's locker, and the captain orders the steward locked in the brig in spite of his protestations of innocence.

Brown convinces the captain to put an article in the ship's newspaper about Alva being disinherited in order to see her reaction; however, she responds unemotionally to the news. One of the guests suggests that Alva conduct a séance to find the killer, and Alva consents. Though he is a skeptic, the captain agrees to have the séance held in the clubroom that night. Numerous guests attend, and the captain insists on posting a guard at the door. While the spellbound guests watch, Alva goes into a trance and begins describing Holt's murder. She is about to name the killer when she sees a shadowy figure—dressed in a long coat and with a hat masking its face—through the porthole. As this was Holt's standard garb, Alva screams that it's Holt's ghost. "I'll tell the truth," she cries. "The man who killed Holt is in this room. His name is ..." Before she can continue, the room is thrown into darkness and panic ensues. When the lights are turned back on, she is found, strangled, and the man guarding the door says he was struck on the head as someone fled the room. Both Winstay and Brown are absent, and news comes that Parsons has escaped the brig.

Winstay finds Brown in Madame Alva's room. When the captain questions Brown's motives, he responds that he is Alonzo Holt's son and heir, and that he is determined to find his father's killer. Harris jumps on this new information and accuses Brown of the murders, but the captain is not convinced. Mary, however, finds herself uneasy in Brown's presence.

The mysterious figure in the coat and hat is spotted again by Brown and Dickens. Dickens takes Brown to Holt's cabin to explain matters. Brown subsequently gives the captain a list of guests he wants to gather in the captain's quarters. There, Brown announces, at exactly nine o'clock, the ghost of Holt will reveal the real murderer.

At nine precisely the man in the coat enters, looks the assembled guests over and points to Winstay. The "ghost" is revealed as Henry Stevens, a stowaway who stole some of Holt's clothes after the millionaire's death. Stevens was hiding in a lifeboat when Holt was killed and witnessed Dr. Winstay doing the deed. Brown explains the whole conspiracy: Alva and Winstay were in cahoots and were going to split the million dollars left to Alva in Holt's will. Winstay was also slowly poisoning the millionaire. When it looked as though Holt was going to change his will, Winstay decided on quicker action, not knowing that there was already a new will. He realized that if Alloway—already a bit suspicious of the medication Holt was taking—did an autopsy, he would find evidence of poison so the physician had to die, too. The old man's body was then thrown into the ocean, and Alloway's wallet was planted in Parson's locker to throw suspicion on him. At the séance Alva was going to name some random innocent as the killer, but panicked when she saw the "ghost." Realizing that the hysterical medium was now going to tell the truth, Winstay had to kill her as well. Threatened with being named as an accomplice, Minna confirms that Alva and Winstay knew each other and that Winstay was not in the cabin tending to Alva's phony illness when Holt was killed. Faced with all this, Winstay bolts from the cabin and then commits suicide by jumping into the ocean. Brown expresses satisfaction that his father's murderer will share the old man's watery grave. Brown and Mary are now free to resume their romance.

*Terror Aboard.* Neil Hamilton and Shirley Gray, in roles originally intended for Cary Grant and Carole Lombard, are the worse for wear but have been rescued by Stanley Fields and company. Fields, who bore a resemblance to Al Capone, usually played thugs and gangsters but sometimes with a comic, Wally Beery type edge.

As was customary, scenarists Ethel Hill and Dore Shary did make some changes in adapting the novel to the screen. Williams and Sims's Winstay attempts to poison himself when the jig is up—not hurl himself into the foam—and the novel features a longer list of suspects, including a crazy second wife for Holt. In print, Brown is a scientist and not a criminologist, and while Madame Alva does get strangled, the reader is spared the film's highly improbable depiction of her death during a séance. (Winstay's ability to throttle Alva in the dark and then flee in the space of less than a minute stretches credulity even for a thriller.) Holt's "ghost" is also built up a bit more believably in the book, which also does a much better job capturing the increasing panic of the passengers than does the movie, wherein the level of concern is akin to that of travelers on *The Love Boat* worrying that lunch will be late. Then, too, Sims weaves quite a mention of bridge into the story, even to the point of having Brown initially suspect Winstay because of the latter's underhanded maneuver during a game.

The book also has an episode early on wherein Alva goes into a trance as she boards the ship; this is meant to establish that Alva really believes in her own shtick, whatever her theatrics. The film omits the scene, but has Alva and Minnie refer to it in conversation later on; it seems the sequence was filmed and then later cut. The grim silhouette shot of Holt hanging from the rigging was apparently meant to be shown three times as the different characters come upon the scene, but, in the print we viewed at the Library of Congress, there's only a black screen the first two times; possibly, the shots were deleted by local censors and never restored. There *is* a surprisingly gruesome close-up of the murdered Alloway, his eyes open and staring, and we can only hypothesize that such moments were compensation for the fact that the actual killings aren't depicted onscreen.

Few of the reviews we consulted rated the film as little better than fair, and most found it to be flawed somehow. The anonymous critic for *The Oakland Tribune* (April 16, 1934), for example, was decidedly unimpressed, writing that the feature was "peopled with good actors who seem to be walking through their roles. Nobody but the audience seems to sense who the villain is." *Motion Picture Daily*, dated January 6, 1934, found the picture's details to be, well … *foggy*:

> A fairly good mystery drama which succeeds in holding the interest to the end despite some confusion and delay at the outset in establishing motives for the murders that follow. This delay, leaving most of the suspects without a motive for associating them with the crime delays establishment of proper "menace" as well as the result that the picture is without a great deal of suspense at the time the crimes are committed.

*Variety*, with a print date of three days later, found *Fog* to be

> a commendably directed film but Reginald Denny makes a poor menace. Thus, because most of the action centers around Denny's supposed villainy, the dramatic tenor of the story screens unconvincing. Making the dialogue the instrument of arriving at the mystery solution is where the script takes its biggest spill…. Helen Freeman played in unusually panting fashion.

*Harrison's Reports*—three days later still—had more of the same.

> A fairly good program murder mystery. There is no human interest. Suspense is sustained because the identity of the murderer is not known until the very end. The first part is draggy but once the different characters are established the action is faster. The usual tricks are employed to create an eerie atmosphere.

Ward Marsh of the *Cleveland Plain Dealer* (February 16, 1934) found the film to be "a diverting mystery if you take it with a bag of salt," and felt that, at the very least, it got off to a good start:

> *Fog* becomes as mysterious and exciting as an Edgar Wallace chiller—for a few moments. Its eerie atmosphere however is more convincing than some of the following melodrama. Director Albert Rogell is a clever fellow with the camera but he makes the arm of coincidence stretch itself all the way down to 9th Street in this yarn. He also uses too much dialogue in a climax that's a bit weak but heavy in thrills.

(Marsh thought that it was time that old millionaires be given a break as murder victims. "Why don't they pick on a young crooner for a change?" he asked. The critic also opined that Reginald Denny [Winstay] should stick to comedy and that "Helen Freeman portrays the medium in the chest-heaving style of the old school.")

One person who did *not* think Albert Rogell to be clever was the film's sound man,

**Jack La Rue, Vera Teasdale and Morgan Wallace don't suspect that their genial host John Halliday plans to dispose of all them. Alas, ship steward Charlie Ruggles is not at the top of his death list (*Terror Aboard*).**

Frank Bernds, who described him as "my least favorite director." Nor did Bernds think much of Dore Schary's script:

> It should have created suspense and menace, but because of clumsy plotting it did not and Albert Rogell's sometimes hysterical method of directing did little to help.... We finished *Fog* on schedule, fifteen days of filming, some of them ten and twelve hour days, generally caused by Rogell's tendency to shout at actors, causing them to blow their lines.[1]

Schary, of course, having labored in the humble vineyards of Columbia as a staff writer, went on to become a major producer at RKO and M-G-M.

The performances in *Fog* do seem off. Donald Cook, hardly the most charismatic of heroes, is particularly glum here and has no chemistry with leading lady, Mary Brian. As a couple of reviewers noted, the final scene between them seems to have been added just to remind the audience that they are the "romantic interests." Helen Freeman's Madame Alva is certainly a bit too wide-eyed, and Robert McQuade as Holt seems to be doing a parody of Ebenezer Scrooge. The only treat in the supporting cast is genre-favorite Samuel S. Hinds, who, while hiding behind bushy eyebrows, librarian glasses, and some kind of accent, is not playing his typical judge, lawyer, or doctor, but rather Holt's loyal minion.

Nor is Reginald Denny happily cast as Winstay. One easily recognizable problem with the film is that suspicion is continually being shifted between him and Cook, but would any viewer—possessed of '30s sensibilities—really buy the notion that Cook, conducting the investigation, is going to turn out to be the killer? That pretty much leaves Denny as the only viable suspect, given that characters like Mullaney, Dickens and Parsons are obvious red herrings. The book, of course, can take the blame for the talky climax, but gathering all the suspects in one room for the big revelation—a device so beloved in Charlie Chan movies—seems particularly dull here, and the script should have found a way around it. Nor does Rogell bring any serious tension to the arrival of the "ghost"; one is instead left wondering whether the benighted captain has been at sea too long, allowing as he does first a medium and then a spook to try to solve the mystery.

Rogell's direction *does* have its bright spots: the never-ending fog and the mournful sound of the ship's horn certainly set the stage for the early scenes and Holt's subsequent death. Rogell has fun with sinister close-ups of hands. The first instance involves Mullaney's mitts in Holt's cabin: the aide looks like he's going to throttle his boss, but he's actually only adjusting a light. And later, when Mary and Brown are alone, she stares at his hands with fear as she begins to wonder whether he could be the strangler. Spook-wise, the supposed "ghost" isn't the only figure to smack of otherworldliness: Madame Alva's entrance to the hall for the séance is flamboyantly weird, for the woman positively *glides* toward the camera in flowing robes as her captivated audience watches. The séance that follows is well handled, too, although hopelessly cliché.

While *Fog* seems to have had a relatively uncomplicated production history, the same can't be said for *Terror Aboard*, which had casting and writing problems right up until the shoot. Initially called *Dead Reckoning*, the film was to have starred Carole Lombard and been directed by Earle (*Island of Lost Souls*) Kenton. The January 11, 1932, issue of *Film Daily* announced that the picture would be shot four weeks subsequently. In late January, *The Hollywood Reporter* mentioned that the film would star Lombard, Cary Grant, Charlie Ruggles, John Halliday, Henry Stephenson, and (possibly) Lowell Sherman, and that Paul Sloane had replaced Kenton as director. Early in February, Lombard and Henry Stephenson—who did not feel their roles were worthy of their abilities—got permission from Paramount to withdraw from the film. Stephenson was replaced by Morgan Wallace, and Lombard, much to her chagrin, found herself cast in *Supernatural*, which she loathed.[2]

The February 2 edition of *Motion Picture Herald* announced that *Dead Reckoning* would star Wynne Gibson and Cary Grant. Gibson absolutely refused to be in the picture and suffered a four-week suspension without pay from Paramount as a result; she was replaced by Shirley Gray. The studio publicity department trumpeted Gray's resemblance to Lombard, and, perhaps relieved to finally have found a blonde willing to play in the film, Paramount gave Gray a contract as a reward. At around the same time, Cary Grant bowed out of the production, citing his need of minor surgery; we can only presume that it was Grant's role that ultimately went to Neil Hamilton.

Assisted by Manuel Siff and Robert Presenell, veteran scenarist Harvey Thew did the script, but there appears to have been a great deal of back-and-forth on how to make the grim story a bit lighter. On February 4, it was announced that writer Barry Travers would work on dialogue and comedy situations for the film, and a week later, Bobby Vernon, a former Mack Sennett comic, was brought in to do "comedy construction." Shortly after *that*, Frank Butler and Claude Binyon were diverted from *College Humor*, the picture they were then working on, to do rewrites for *Dead Reckoning*. In the end, none of these gentlemen received screen credit, but a few critics thought the movie's saving grace was to be found in its comedy elements. (Modern fans of vintage horror might have a different opinion.)

On February 20, the title was officially changed to *Terror Aboard* (*Killer Aboard* had also been considered), but the trade press didn't get the memo right away. As late as in its February 28 number, *Variety* reported that, for budgetary reasons, "the shooting schedule for *Dead Reckoning* has been set at 16 days, shortest yet for a feature at Paramount." Late January and February was a particularly busy time at Paramount, with no fewer than 12 pictures going before the cameras, so it's hardly surprising corners were cut for a programmer like *Terror Aboard*. While *Fog* is basically just a whodunit set at sea, *Terror Aboard* is a watchhimdoit. Universal may have had its monsters, but Paramount horrors (*Island of Lost Souls*, *Murders in the Zoo*) one-upped Uncle Carl's studio in the gore department, and *Terror Aboard* continued the gruesome tradition.

Synopsis based on our viewing the film via VHS:

> In the Pacific Ocean not far from the Samoan Islands, the ship *City of Hope* nearly collides with a luxury yacht that has no one on deck and that displays no other signs of life. Captain Williams and a few of his crew row over to the yacht, and their engineer, Larson, boards it while the others wait. When Larson does not return, the captain and his search party go on board. They find the man dead, his skull crushed. They also discover another man hanging in a stateroom and the corpse of a woman who has died of hypothermia even though it's the middle of July.
>
> They also find a discarded radiogram, and, at this point, the story flashes back to when Maximilian Kreig, the yacht's owner, first gets said message. Accompanied by some guests, Kreig and his fiancée, Lili, are going to Australia to be married, but the telegram informs Kreig that he is financially ruined and will be arrested for fraud and various other crimes as soon as he lands.
>
> Kreig reasons that if the yacht never makes it to Sydney, people will assume that it has been lost with all hands, so he embarks upon a violent scheme to kill off guests and crew and escape to one of the nearby habitable and sparsely-populated island paradises with Lili. He first shoots the radio operator and destroys the radio. On the pretext of investigating the operator's death, he discloses to one of his guests, Morton Hazlitt, that Morton's wife Millicent is being unfaithful to him with musician, Gregory Cordoff. Kreig then tells Cordoff that Morton has a violent temper and may harm Millicent. Cordoff ends up stabbing Morton and is imprisoned in his room. When later confronted by Millicent, Kreig locks her in the freezer and turns down the temperature until she freezes to death. He subsequently informs the weak and unstable Cordoff that Millicent has committed suicide; not long afterward, Cordoff hangs himself. Kreig also poisons the cook.
>
> Kreig's plans are somewhat complicated by the arrival of Lili's former fiancé, the aviator James Cowles, who, after following the ship via the air, crashed his plane in the ocean. Rescued and now a passenger, Cowles rekindles his romance with

Lili—who is having doubts about her engagement to Krieg. When a maid becomes suspicious of Kreig's behavior, he throws her overboard. The captain witnesses this and confronts Kreig, who impales him on a spike on his desk. The superstitious crew is already in a state of panic that is exacerbated when Kreig moves Millicent's body to the fog-shrouded deck. The millionaire encourages the crew to escape via the one remaining lifeboat, but the line has been cut and they plunge into the ocean to their deaths as the lifeboat hangs from the side of the ship.

Having witnessed Kreig's treachery, Lili runs to Cowles for help. Together, they go into the engine room and Cowles exchanges gunfire with Kreig. Meanwhile Blackie, the steward, hides in a closet with his cat and a supply of liquor.

The story then resumes in the present. Kreig kills Larson when he boards the ship and then shoots into the fuel tank in the engine room. A huge fire erupts and Kreig leaps overboard. Captain Williams and crew rescue Lili and Cowles from the inferno, and, with a drunken Blackie in tow, escape back to their ship just as the yacht explodes. Kreig swims for one of the islands, but a hungry shark pulls him under.

The pressbook for *Terror Aboard* has a different account of the villain's death:

> Off the rocky shores of the little island, Kreig is battling the breakers desperately. He clutches at a rock but a wave throws him off. He tries again … and fails, disappearing below the surface.

Perhaps the producers felt Kreig deserved a grislier end, or wanted to avoid repetition as a number of characters had already met death by drowning. In one passage, the pressbook identifies the death yacht as the *Celeste*, but in the film it's called the *Dulcina*. Possibly someone at Paramount had heard the famous story of the *Mary Celeste*, the ship that was found in good shape, but deserted, on the Atlantic Ocean in 1872. No one knows what became of the crew, and—despite numerous theories—it remains an unsolved mystery. A fictional version of the tale was told by Arthur Conan Doyle who called the ship the *Marie Celeste*. In 1935, the legend was turned into the British film *Mystery of the Marie Celeste* (*Phantom Ship* in the U.S.), starring Bela Lugosi and—in her last film role—Shirley Gray. Surprisingly, publicity for *Terror Aboard* didn't capitalize on the *Mary Celeste* angle, although the campaign did include the occasional article on unmanned "mystery ships" seen at sea. Naturally, the pressbook churned out a good number of gimmicks to promote the film. One idea was to have a radio receiver in the lobby with a message received in Morse Code (suggestion: "What made Max Kreig kill eleven people aboard his luxury yacht?") Patrons correctly identifying the message would get free admission, and for all its relevance to the picture, this bit of hoopla had already been used for the studio's *Island of Lost Souls*. Ads and publicity also made much of Millicent's demise and the mystery of her freezing to death in tropical weather. The pressbook suggested the following:

> Borrow a life-sized dummy from a local store and have the local ice plant freeze it into a cake of ice. Place the ice-frozen dummy in the outer lobby so the water can run off. If you can't get a life size dummy, a large doll will do. When the ice melts replace it. And keep the question "How was it done?" alive.

We don't know if exhibitors actually tried any of these stunts, but it probably wouldn't have mattered much as the public stayed away, and the film took a terrible drubbing from the critics. These comments from the March 22, 1933, number of *The Hollywood Reporter* were typical: "This picture, for all its faults, should have a beneficial effect upon the industry. It should be the final period to the gory series of blood-letting operas simply because there's no place for anybody to go after this one." The reviewer went on to say that audiences gasped at the first few murders, but eventually found the continual mayhem comical:

> Even though the film showed the slaughters taking place, the spectators refused to take most of them seriously. Halliday, the arch killer, split the sum total of the evening's laughs almost evenly with Charlie Ruggles, the official comedy relief.

The reviewer in the 23 June issue of *Photoplay* agreed.

> Inexcusably improbable and wooden direction. As a *Grand Hotel* of murder in every form possible, *Terror Aboard* ought to cause every exhibitor in

the country to scream for fewer and better blood and thunder mellers. If this one pleases it will be largely due to Ruggles and his bag of tricks.

The *Motion Picture Herald* (June 5, 1933) saw little hope for good box-office:

> This will be a difficult picture to sell as there is so little of what people consider entertainment in it. If it plays as a single it should be publicized as a straight terror picture, one wherein gasps override everything else. As a saga of death in wholesale and retail lots and a graphic exposition of unique methods of bringing death, *Terror Aboard* may have some things that appeal to certain classes of audiences. It can hardly be called a drama; there is a bit of romance in it but it only plays a distant second to the terror premise; only occasionally is the comedy relief of sufficient strength to offset the gruesomeness of the underlying theme.

A quick survey of other contemporary reviews shows that this sort of thought was the rule, and not the exception. *Film Daily* (July 3, 1933) was a bit less negative than the other trades.

> Evidently they intended to make this a sensational shocker but the long list of murders grows unconvincing and gives a distinct impression of being vastly overdone.... It is a wild tale and the fact that it is done with class and a good cast doesn't alleviate the morbid theme and overdone melodramatics.

The reaction in *Harrison's Reports* (April 15, 1933)—not exactly *Fangoria* when it came to horror—was hardly surprising:

> Terrible! It should sicken even the most morbid followers of horror melodrama for there is one killing after another. And the audience is not made aware of these killings by suggestion, it is shown clearly how the sadistic villain commits each one. As a lesson in fancy and varied types of murder it is in a class by itself. It is almost with relief that one sees the death of the villain.

The exhibitors themselves were scarcely more encouraging. A showman in Garber, Oklahoma, groused: "A very mixed bunch of nothing that leaves the people wondering how they were fooled to sit through it. Very poor job of recording and amateur photography. Lay off it. No sense turning out a picture like this." A movie-palace mogul from Blackstone, Virginia, chimed in, "Our people fed up on this type of picture long ago."

And box-office receipts proved to be so alarmingly poor that Paramount changed the publicity and ads to refer to the film as *Love and Terror Aboard*. Late in the summer, *Variety*—which seemed to be smirking at the failure of this latest gimmick—commented that the picture (no matter *how* it was entitled) "was not going anywhere" and was "not helping anybody."

At least the picture's structure—presenting a mystery, solving it via flashback, and then returning to let the action play out in the present—works quite well. Borrowed from *Beau Geste*, the format is helped immeasurably by Eda Warren's quick and imaginative editing. Harry Fischbeck, the cameraman whose images lent macabre power to the studio's silent *Sorrows of Satan*, also helps infuse the atmosphere with a nice dose of night, shadows, and fog.

Even though most of the film's humor lay in Charlie Ruggles's running away from black cats and cross-eyed sailors and accidentally incriminating himself while suggesting solutions to the mystery, there *are* a few mildly off-color moments, pre–Code or no. For example, at one point, Neil Hamilton gives Charlie Ruggles his cat and suggests giving the animal some milk. Ruggles responds, "I'll be like a mother to her," and then does a double take when he realizes he's holding the cat to his chest. When the captain asks Ruggles about his romantic interest in Lena the maid, Charlie responds, "I think she's in trouble," only to quickly add that he didn't mean it *that* way. Not at all helpful in that situation is the fact that Lena is played by Leila Bennett, whose equally unfunny antics (as yet another maid) in *Mark of the Vampire* helped slow that picture down, too. At least here, the viewer has the satisfaction of seeing her tossed into the drink.

The film is pretty much John Halliday's show, and he makes the crooked financier-turned-mass murderer a chilling figure indeed. Some might wish for a Bela Lugosi or Lionel Atwill—gleefully relishing each killing—in the role, but Halliday's cold-blooded, relentless sociopath is a portrait of a ruthless man utterly without remorse. "A determined man in desperate circumstances could do it," muses Halliday to the radio operator about the possibility of disposing of all the ship's company. Ever efficient and business-like in enacting his plans, Halliday keeps a list of guests and crew and, as they are eliminated, crosses them off one by one with no more emotion than a stockbroker looking over his portfolio.

There's not much for the supporting cast to do except die. It's a little odd to see Jack LaRue—a born hoodlum, if ever there was one—sporting curly hair, speaking with a Russian accent, and playing a musician. He's supposed to be sensitive and romantic, but looks more like a lounge lizard (LaRue would soon revert to type while playing the sadistic thug, Trigger, in *The Story of Temple Drake*). It's also disconcerting to see perennial detective, Thomas B. Jackson, in a captain's uniform; usually, he's grilling suspects in that tough-guy rasp that had served him well since *Broadway*. At least Stanley Fields stays true to form, playing a more sober version of the rough sea-dog he enacted in *Island of Lost Souls*.

All in all, *Terror Aboard* is indeed pretty gruesome fare by 1930s' standards: The radio operator (played by the likeable William Janney) expires in a pool of blood; there are vivid shots of Cordoff (Jack LaRue) dangling from a cord; the captain, after being impaled, writhes in agony as he dies. These vignettes provide quite a contrast to the murders in *Fog*, which all take place off-screen. No doubt chastened by the failure of *Terror Aboard*, Paramount subsequently left hard core horror to Universal, and instead offered borderline and comparatively sedate fare like *Double Door* and *The Witching Hour*, or romantic fantasies like *Peter Ibbetson* and *Death Takes a Holiday* (vid.).

*Fog*'s melodramatics may seem quaint to today's viewer, but are modern variations like *Flight Plan* and *Non-Stop*—both set in the air instead of on the sea—any less unbelievable? Audiences may have rejected *Terror Aboard*, but basically the picture was just ahead of its time in prefiguring the slasher movies of the 1970s and 1980s, when the whole *raison d'être* of such films was the presentation of an unlimited variety of grisly deaths. Max Kreig, however, may have had more logical motivation for his crimes than had Jason or Michael Myers.

And as for his portrayer: John Halliday was certainly the best actor of the lot.

# *The Horror:*
# The Patchwork Cinema of Bud Pollard

F.P. Productions—September 8–mid–September 1932; added scenes in October 1932—7 reels; Released as *Jumen* in Japan—1934; reedited as *John the Drunkard*—1944 **Cast**: Leslie King as John Massey; Nyrida (Nyreda) Montez as Mrs. Massey; Rajah Reboid as the Hindu priest; with Ilene Myers; Reed Brown, Jr.; Jimmie Kelo; Gus Alexander; John Gray. Narrator for *John the Drunkard*—Bud Pollard

**Credits**: *Director*: Bud Pollard; *Script and Dialogue*: Basil Smith; *Cinematography*: Dal Clawson; *Music*: J.L. Merkur; *Make-up*: Bert Tuey; *Editor*: John E. Gordon; Photographed at Atlas Soundfilm Recording Studio, New York

On December 16, 1952, Bud Pollard, with his friends Will Morrissey and Edward Tierney, went to the Knickerbocker Grill, a Culver City nightclub whose featured comic was the notoriously vulgar Joe E. Ross (best known for playing Officer Toody in TV's *Car 54, Where Are You?*). Pollard, who had done club and vaudeville comedy himself, exchanged good-natured insults with Ross. At some point, Ross uttered his signature crack, "This one'll kill you." Almost immediately, Pollard keeled over on the floor. It wasn't a gag though; he had suffered a fatal heart attack. Paramedics carried Pollard—all 250 pounds of him—to the ambulance, but he was already gone. Order was restored, the lights dimmed, and the show went on. Pollard died broke and had to be buried by the Motion Picture Relief Fund.

Obituaries for Pollard were both brief *and* inaccurate. The December 17 issue of *The Bakersfield Californian* described Pollard as an actor and stuntman, and maintained he was the brother of silent-movie comic "Snub" Pollard. In another obit, he was said to be the brother of Ben Pollard. This probable muddling of "Snub" Pollard and Ben Turpin shows that, by the 1950s, the Silent Era might as well have come to pass in antediluvian times as far as Hollywood was concerned.

John Bud Pollard—he never used John, and sometimes put Bud in quotes—was not related to "Snub" Pollard[1] though he apparently claimed he was when the occasion was to his advantage. Even in his younger days Bud was built more like Lou Costello than Yakima Canutt, and it is not likely that he ever was a stuntman, although he certainly pulled his share of stunts.

*Variety* called Pollard a "pioneer filmite," provided a somewhat inaccurate list of his credits (the publication attributed *Drums O' Voodoo* to him), and stated that he had been the first president of the Screen Director's Guild. Actually, the first president of the Screen Director's Guild—founded in 1936—was King Vidor, and it's never even been made certain whether Pollard was a member. He was, however, occasional president of the Screen Director's Guild of New York, a much smaller organization that was founded somewhat later. These inaccuracies are not surprising, given that Pollard was a pretty obscure figure who worked largely outside Hollywood and was prone to telling self-aggrandizing fibs. His career evolved primarily in the East, where he made—or perhaps it should be said, he *concocted*—a variety of films that could never be considered "mainstream" and that were on budgets that made Monogram seem like M-G-M. His toehold on horror-genre history is his direction of *The Horror*, a film so hard to track down that, for many years, people were unsure as to whether it had actually been made.

Will Morrissey, one of Pollard's friends who was with him when he died, wrote about the director in his rambling and sometimes incoherent autobiography, *On a Shoestring*. Morrissey, a character right out of *Broadway Danny Rose*, was a comic, tunesmith, and director who had had many a Broadway flop and was often just one step ahead of creditors and the sheriff. Possessed of a temper, he once got into a drunken fistfight with Tom Mix over whether Westerns had a future in the Sound Era. Morrissey had worked with Pollard on the latter's *Look-Out Sister* (1947) and thought very highly of the director, claiming, "He'd do more work with less money than any man in the picture business." On his own, Morrissey played a pretty big part in muddling Bud's film history. Not only did he repeat the fiction that Bud was part of the famous Pollard family that included Snub and Daphne, but also that he was

> one of the original Keystone cops with Mack Senet [sic], then a comedian in the team "Ham and Bud" and then as a director went to Europe. It was Bud's great heartbreak that it's hard to make the fellows think you're a director once you've been a comedian…. They would never give him the big budget to make the picture because they'd laugh and say he was a comedian.[2]

There's no proof—via film credits—that Bud Pollard was ever a Keystone cop, or even worked for Mack Sennett. In conjunction with the release of 1949's *Down Memory Lane*—Steve Allen was the star, but much of the film consisted of clips from silent comedy—the producers put ads in *The York Times* and *Herald-Tribune* looking for Mack Sennett alumni to promote the picture. Subsequently, the *Showman's Trade Review* (August 27, 1949) reported the following:

> The ad has already paid off in a two column spread as the *World Telegram*'s Ed Wallace interviewed Bud Pollard, the guy with the twisted walk in the old days of the team of Ham and Bud, who is a producer in New York. Pollard was very helpful. He cited slapstick as the sure way to tickle funnybones and pointed to the history of the chase in comedy and told of some of the Sennatorial gags.

In actuality, Bud—the lesser half of the team of Ham (Lloyd Hamilton) and Bud—was Bud Duncan, who had retired, was likely living in California, and doubtless did *not* see the ad. Pollard was able to pull off this impersonation because there was no scholarly interest in silent slapstick at the time, and obviously few were likely to remember an obscure comic whose heyday had been some

Bud Pollard didn't have much talent as a director but he was an expert at self-promotion. Here he advertises "Bud Pollard comedies" featuring his "famous characterization" but films featuring said characterization have yet to surface.

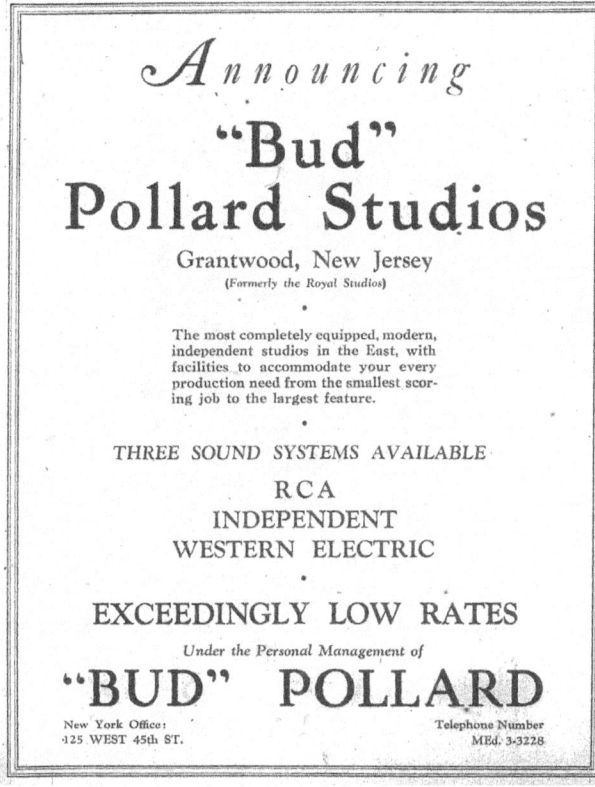

Bud's attempt at running his own studio proved short lived.

30 years earlier, despite the fact that Pollard resembled Roscoe "Fatty" Arbuckle more than he did the pint-sized Duncan.

Did Pollard have *any* connection with Mack Sennett? In *The Road to Hollywood*—his "documentary" on Bing Crosby—Pollard claimed that he, like Crosby, had gotten his start with Sennett. In 1929, Pollard had toured in a vaudeville act called "Goofy Tone Films" with Frank B. "Jack" Cooper, who had indeed been a Sennett player, albeit a fairly minor one. The act was described as a satire of talking pictures and apparently consisted of the two comics offering live commentary on a film that was being screened. Cooper left the act, but Pollard continued the tour with ads saying that he "was late of the Mack Sennett Studio." The November 10, 1937, edition of *Variety* reported that Pollard was "to direct a scene from a Keystone comedy for 'A Night of Stars's [presumably a vaudeville skit]. Will use some of the old timers. Mack Sennett and Al Christie expected to attend." We have no further information on whether the skit was actually performed or who may have been in attendance, and we've yet to run across the credits for any Mack Sennett film that featured Bud Pollard.

So who *was* Bud Pollard? One of his obituaries stated that he had started acting when he was 15 years old (c. 1901). Of course actors didn't receive screen credit in those early years, so it's not *impossible* that he might have done some performing before the 1910s. *On a Shoestring* contains a series of badly reproduced photographs of Pollard—dressed in cane, derby hat, and striped baggy pants—cavorting in a field with a young woman. He does look like he might be in his 30s, but it's hard to tell. Unfortunately there's no date on any of the stills, so we don't know if they're from the 1910s or the 1920s, but they do bear the printed inscriptions, "Bud Pollard Comedies" and "Produced by Fred J. Balshofer." Balshofer was a genuine film pioneer whose work started at the very dawn of cinema and included many Westerns and comedies. By the 1920s, though, he did more producing than directing, and his career was on the decline.

On the cover of the November 1930 issue of *Talking Picture Magazine*, a picture of Pollard in the same comic garb bears the caption, "Bud Pollard in his famous characterization as he appears in Bud Pollard Comedies." It should be noted that this magazine was not a trade publication, but rather was aimed primarily at budding scenario writers who would pay to have samples of their work printed therein. Thus, there is no doubt that Pollard's picture was

*Rio's Road to Hell.* The New York censors denied Bud's attempt to title the film *Girls for Sale* but that didn't stop him from using it as a tag line in even bigger lettering than the actual title.

Notice that the showings were segregated by gender. Did someone really think that there would be orgies in the balcony if men and women were allowed to attend this "risqué" film together?

a paid ad, used for publicity purposes, and a copy of the magazine—with information added that he was the producer of "Bud Pollard Comedies"—was even sent to the New York State Censor Board. Nonetheless, while Pollard would dutifully submit all of his films to the State Board, there is no record of his having done so for any "Bud Pollard Comedies," nor have we found any mention of them in the trade papers. One might therefore doubt whether they were actually ever released or even if they were finished. Then again, the same was said of *The Horror*.

Our first solid sighting of Pollard on the public record is in May 1922, when he was headquartered in Oakland, California, and placed several ads in the *Oakland Tribune* stating that he was head of a film production company, was looking for actors of all types, and would consider talented amateurs. Notices of this sort suggest he had *some* kind of prior film experience, even though we have no specifics. Other ads offered instruction in musical comedy and drama, while still another boosted his services as a music publisher and promoter for vaudeville. The July 13 issue of the *Tribune* announced that, with the exception of the two leads, Bud Pollard Productions would draw on local talent for his first film which, though a comedy, would be "educational in nature." The male lead was little-known comic, Harry Layton, and Pollard conducted a beauty contest to lure the Mary Pickford wannabes of Oakland to his film. Seven-year-old Joey Otis was also enlisted, and the *Tribune* speculated that he could be the next Jackie Coogan. He wasn't. The whole thing sounds like something out of *The Music Man*, but in the end, a two-reeler, *Cow Pasture Pool* (the title is slang for golf), debuted on August 26 at the Franklin Theater. Appropriately enough, the main feature was *If You Believe It, It's So*.

The *Tribune*, apparently hoping *Cow Pasture Pool* might mark the beginning of Oakland's rivaling Hollywood, published more of Pollard's plans, including a series of ten two-reel comedies (scripts by Jack Blackwood, starring Marjorie Daw, and to be filmed in Oakland in October) and a collaboration with director Finis Fox on a tale based on Indian folklore. In September it was reported that Pollard was also looking into buying property to start his own movie studio. Said property was in Moraga in Contra Costa which, Pollard said, would be perfect for filming because "the clear atmosphere on the other side of the hills will act as a 'backstop' from the fog from San Francisco Bay." Pollard said that the studio, to be named—Look out, Uncle Carl!—Pollard City, would be opened in October, following a pageant and ball.

Not surprisingly, none of these projects came to fruition, but they did leave Pollard a fistful of newspaper clippings he could use to his advantage, provided that he didn't mention the end results of his efforts. In August 1924, *Variety* announced that the Selznick Film Corporation of New York had a struck a deal with Trianon Film of Berlin to distribute Trianon's product in the U.S.

and, in return, to make four films at Trianon with American stars. The announcement also mentioned that Trianon had hired Bud Pollard to direct a series of two-reel comedies. Granted, Trianon *was* a new company, but it's still puzzling that they would hire someone as unproven as Bud Pollard. Trianon's president, David Schratter, had an ambitious program for Trianon, but apparently little knowledge of American film. Had he confused Bud with the well respected director, Harry Pollard? Or did he think he was getting "Snub" Pollard, as one German trade magazine mistakenly reported he did?

In any event, Pollard arrived in Berlin

**Leslie King did his own bit of self-advertising in the June 12, 1920, issue of *Motion Picture News*.**

to oversee a contest run by Trianon to choose the "new Harold Lloyd." Pollard filmed the competition (*Ein Filmstar wird gesucht*; *A Film Star Is Wanted*) in which reputedly 700 contestants took part; however, the whole thing was bogus, as the winner was Curt Bois, who had been onstage and onscreen since childhood, and who, according to the aforementioned *Variety* piece, had *already* been signed by Trianon. Pollard went on to direct three two-reelers with Bois, and the filming of one of them drew some attention in an article in the September 24 number of *Berliner Tageblatt*:

> There was a tumult in Berlin in the early afternoon. Masses of people saw a woman dressed in black with about 50 balloons in her hand. A sudden gust of wind blew her into the air. People screamed and then one man ran out of the crowd and ran after her. He climbed the front of the Mosse house right up to the roof. Amazement turned to surprise when it turned out that it was Curt Bois, the German Harold Lloyd, and Uschi Elliot who acted on the command of the American comedy director Bud Pollard for the main sensation of his next film.

This sounds more like public relations than journalism, so perhaps it's not coincidental that the Mosse House (a building famous for its futuristic look) was also the headquarters of the *Berliner Tageblatt*.

Not only were the three shorts done by Pollard—12 were originally planned—never released, we don't even know their titles. Schratter had borrowed heavily to keep Trianon's program afloat, but, in the end, his company went under, and there was a certain amount of scandal in that the agency that lent him the funds was supposed to be financing housing for workers.

According to *Film Daily*, Pollard returned to New York in September 1925, but the possibility of his first having stopped over in England is raised in the May/June 1944 issue of *Cine-Technician*. The piece is about a certain Charlie Wheeler, who, in the 1920s, alternated working as a film technician with doing manual labor:

> So the odd jobs were followed by going with his old cameraman Phil East and a still man called Jonas into the photography and shorts business. They did all right for a time but were finally wrecked by a sharper who called himself Bud Pollard. Claimed to be Snub Pollard's brother. He arrived from Vienna, set up at the Savoy with trunks full of bricks and contracted with them to do film tests. Needless to say they didn't get a penny and only just escaped being jailed.

After his less than triumphant return to the States, Pollard seems to have focused on vaudeville tours and personal appearances (as "a real live movie star," which probably sounded better than "that guy who brought you *Cow Pasture Pool*") until around 1930, when he settled into the New York filmmaking scene. As Richard Koszarski explains in his excellent *Hollywood on the Hudson*, the East was once a thriving center for moviemaking, but, by the 1930s, the big studios pretty much gave up on it as far as major production was concerned. Studio politics, the mild California weather, and weak unions in the Golden State gave Hollywood the decided edge. Nevertheless, the studios in New York and New Jersey didn't disappear from the face of the earth, and there were labs, sound facilities, and a bevy of theater actors and (underemployed) tech-

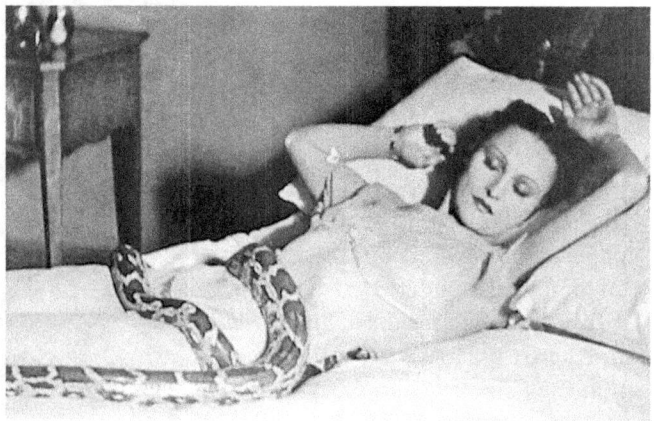

The only screen appearance of Nyrida Montez and her snake.

Leslie King mid-way through his transformation into *The Horror*.

The final result is a little too grotesque to be taken seriously.

nicians to draw from. East Coast studios produced shorts, independent productions, cartoons, documentaries, and ethnic films (aimed at Jewish, Italian, and African American viewers). They could hardly rival the big budgets of Hollywood, but they never expected to make large profits; the niche-market status filled the bill. In addition to the ready-made large audiences in New York and New Jersey, producers could use the states rights system to get broader distribution for their work, and there were foreign sales as well. For good or ill, Pollard's work in the East in the 1930s included just about every type of film that was being made there.

Pollard took out ads in the trades announcing he was available for "directing, producing, financing, lab work, recording, editing, writing and cutting." Initially, though, he focused on reissuing films from the Silent Era and adding synchronized sound. By the early 1930s, talkies were becoming the norm; each theater that was being wired for sound inflicted one more wound in the death of a thousand cuts for the silent cinema. Pollard (and others) saw there was no longer a big market for silents, but realized that, with the addition of sound, these oldies could be passed off as new movies (at least in the ads). In 1930, Pollard took the 1926 Charles Hutchison serial, *Lightning Hutch*, edited it down to feature length,

added sound, and changed the title to *Danger Man*. Ads for the film promised the following: "Mr. States Righter, now is your opportunity to clean up with the talking screen's first stunt picture. Talking! Singing! Sound!"

The reviewer for in the May 24, 1930, edition of *Motion Picture News* wasn't buying it:

> It's nice to know that only occasionally do we have to witness pictures as utterly hopeless as the *Danger Man*, an unbearable piece of screen fare. Immediately after they flash the main title a sub caption informs us of the existence of a prologue, necessitated, it is said, because the producers had reversed the usual order and tacked on "the happy ending" at the beginning of the picture rather than in the last reel. The truth of the matter, however, rests in what follows the prologue: A CHOPPED UP SERIAL, amateurishly dubbed with musical and effects in sound and, gawd, how they sounded. It's a mess.... The sound was deafening, to say the least, though we appreciate the toughness of the synchronizer's job in adapting a fast action serial negative to music and sound.

The critic went on to say that the audience was more amused than thrilled, but at least the film provided a look at moviemaking in a bygone age (that age being only four years prior!).

Undeterred, Pollard gave the synch-sound treatment to two 1921 Westerns, *Jesse James Under the Black Flag* and *The Jack Rider*.[3] For the latter, he added narration for the first scenes, but let titles tell the rest of the story. Perhaps feeling nostalgic about his time in Deutschland, he added sound and music to both the 1929 German film, *Richthofen the Red Knight of the Air* (rechristening it *Richthofen the Red Ace of Germany*), and the 1928 *Rasputins Liebesabenteuer*, released in time to capitalize on M-G-M's *Rasputin and the Empress*.

Pollard also discovered that, in addition to being fitted for sound, certain risqué silents could be repackaged as "adult films." His first attempt at this did not go well. Taking the 1928 *Trial Marriage* (also known as *About Trial Marriage*; no connection to the 1929 Columbia film also entitled *Trial Marriage*), he added sound and very unwisely retitled it *Sex Madness*—a title Dwight Esper used for his 1938 film. The silent film—which included instances of incest and prostitution in its lurid story line—had previously run into serious censor trouble, and the New York Board did not find Pollard's sound version an improvement; the picture was banned outright. When an attempt to show the film in Chicago was nixed by the censors, the distributors appealed and actually got a jury trial which found the film was fit to be shown. The prosecutors then took the matter to the appellate court which upheld them in a rather significant ruling that stated that the opinions of jurors and judges were beside the point on this issue, and that it was up to the duly appointed censors to decide whether a film should be exhibited or not, as long as they were acting in good faith.

Pollard's next choice was more conservative: 1924's *Missing Daughters*[4] which concerned racketeers who run a night club called the Golden Calf. They try to lure young girls into their clutches, but the Secret Service infiltrates the gang and brings them to justice. The story remains circumspect as to what exactly the bad guys are up to, so the New York censors passed the film although they asked for a few cuts (like the title card: "They were wild about that last shipment. The blondes light up the place").

Pollard also added talkie opening and closing scenes depicting reporters interviewing the head of the Bureau of Missing Persons. Perhaps as a concession to culture—and because he didn't have to pay for it—he used Richard Wagner's "Ride of the Valkyries" for the music.

Without a doubt, Pollard's most profitable sexy soundie was provided by 1927's *Das Frauenhaus von Rio* (*The Women's House of Rio*), which was based on a book by Norbert Jacques, the creator of Dr. Mabuse. The story concerns a German businessman who is outwardly a respectable citizen, but who is really a criminal who runs a bordello in Rio. A disgruntled confederate, learning that the businessman's beloved daughter aspires to be a dancer, lures her onto the boat heading for the whorehouse by promising her a nightclub contract; murder and suicide are the result. Although German censors were much more lenient than their American counterparts when it came to depicting prostitution on the screen, they banned *Das Frauenhaus*, claiming it made the oldest profession seem glamorous and exciting. Making a few cuts, the producers enlisted the aid of an organization called The International Commission to Fight the

The ape. We don't know who played him or designed the costume. It's not likely Charles Gemora was jealous.

White Slave Trade, who then endorsed the film as a cautionary tale. The censors were mollified and the film was a big hit (and it was recently screened at the Cinema Muto at Pordenone).

Pollard took *Das Frauenhaus von Rio*, cut it down, and threw out most of the title cards. substituting a "dramator"—one A. Homer Dary—to describe what's being shown on the screen. In the Pollard version of the tale, the hapless maidens are being lured to Rio to work, not in a bordello, but rather, in a "common cabaret" where they participate in "dizzy night life." The pious, moralizing narration warns about stern fathers who keep their daughters in a gilded cage, thus causing them to rebel and fall under the influence of evil parasites who lure them astray and who will surely burn in hellfire for their crimes. Scenes of girls prancing about in scanty attire had to go, of course, as did any suggestion of prostitution, and Pollard changed the title card "Rio de Janeiro, cesspool of vice and port of missing girls" to "Rio, port of twinkling bright lights." Perhaps to make up for the missing footage, Pollard took reel five of the film and interspersed a travelogue on Rio.

After much back and forth with the New York Censor Board, Pollard finally got the film passed, but the board rejected all the titles he had suggested: *Girls for Sale* (which was the title he had used the first time he submitted the movie), *Her Soul for Sale*, and *Traffic in Souls*. Agreement was finally reached with *Rio's Road to Hell*, and the film was released in February 1931; still, that didn't stop Pollard from using "Girls for Sale" as a tagline.[5] However, the Brazilian ambassador took exception to the slur on Rio and complained to the State Department in New York. The Board of Censors replied there was nothing they could do, but Pollard agreed to shorten the title to *The Road to Hell* (though in some venues, Rio stayed in the ads).

The advertising campaign was very sleazy ("Sex-Sational!")—in some instances, "Live Models on the Stage" were promised—and the picture was sometimes accompanied by a sex lecture—replete with films or slides—by people who were supposed to be doctors. More complaints were made to the Censor Board who responded that curbing tasteless ads was not in their jurisdiction. Suspicion arose as to whether Pollard had indeed made the cuts he had promised; further investigation confirmed that he had, indeed. There was also some question as to whether the lecturing "doctors" had a license to practice in New York State, but the gentlemen in question insisted they had not shown their sex-education reels in New York since they had not been submitted to the censors, so the matter was dropped. And how did audiences ("For Men Only" according to some ads), expecting to be titillated, respond to the film? According to the July 4, 1931, edition of *Motion Picture Herald*:

> The film, its music, the voice and acting of the cast in general was described by members of the audience as one of the worst examples of motion picture producing and reproduction they had even seen. They termed it propaganda and several present voiced their disappointment at having gone into the theater.

Too late, suckers; you've already paid your 50 cents.

Documentaries about the Great War were enjoying a vogue in the early 1930s, what with the bonus marchers's action in Washington and the increasingly unstable situation in Europe. Pollard did his bit by directing *Forgotten Men*, which consisted mostly of newsreel combat footage (gotten from government sources, presumably at little or no cost), but which contained interviews with veterans, as well. Whatever his exact role was in putting the footage together, Pollard was pretty much the forgotten man in critiques of the film. Some found the picture quite gruesome, and the *Variety* reviewer—who gave the film a favorable write-up in the May 16, 1933, number—was a little skeptical about the authenticity of some scenes:

> There is also a generous sprinkling of close-ups and semi close-ups which, from every point of view of logic, could only have been made in a studio. *What Price Glory, Lilac Time* and *Q Ships* are all suggested in certain[?] of the assemblage. If this is true then the compilers are to be congratulated. There is nothing so boring as 86 minutes of rainy government matter.

The film seems to have done very well, and the producers cannily promoted it in conjunction with different veterans's events and gatherings.

Jungle documentaries—real or faked—were also popular at that time, so Pollard put together *Voice of the Jungle* (released as *Jungle Killer*) in November of 1932. Surprisingly, the title does not refer to lions or tigers, but rather to Great White Hunters who, the film maintains, are by far the more dangerous predators. Reviewers thought the movie's theme—unusual for the time—was somewhat weakened by gratuitous shots of native bearers being eaten by alligators or trampled by elephants. The ever vigilant New York censor, who perhaps had never seen a copy of *National Geographic*, objected to nudity on the part of some natives, but the picture faced a more serious problem, as filmmaker Frederick Patterson claimed that some 1,000 feet of film from his 1928 documentary, *Shooting Big Game with a Camera*, had been inserted into *Jungle Killer* without his permission. The courts ordered the footage removed, the producers complied, and all seemed well until explorer Caveth Wells, who narrated *Jungle Killer*, insisted that his vocal track be excised, saying the gaps left by the missing footage made him look "undignified." In addition, the court allowed Patterson to sue Century Productions, the owners of the rights to *Jungle Killer*, for $15,000 in damages. Century argued that not only had Patterson not properly copyrighted his film, but he had also allowed it to be shown in schools and clubs without charge. How, then, were "damages" incurred? Century kept appealing and the case dragged on for years, finally ending up at the Supreme Court in 1938. The big issue was whether pictures classified as "M" films (documentaries, travelogues, science movies) were entitled to the same copyright protections as "L" films (photoplays). The Court decided they were, and Century ultimately had to pay Patterson $2,000 in damages. Once again Bud Pollard had contributed (inadvertently) to the writing of entertainment law. (It should be noted that only a legal technicality kept the makers of the 1927 documentary *Jengo* from also filing suit, claiming that part of their film, too, had been lifted by *Jungle Killer*.) In the end, *Jungle Killer* was actually something of a hit and was sold to Japan, Austria, and India.

Pollard also directed at least two shorts in 1931: *Vida de Noche*, a musical featuring Cuban baritone, Juan Pulido, and dancer Nina de Silva, and *Goofytone News*, with the latter likely a variation on Pollard's earlier vaudeville act, *Goofytone Films*, with Frank B. "Jack" Cooper. Presumably, the *News* showed clips from either newsreels or silents, and added humorous commentary ("He took the opportunity to direct that great moaning picture star, Miss Dill Pickleford, in her latest squawky entitled SHE WAS ONLY A FIREMAN'S DAUGHTER, but found that she never gets alarmed"). A little later, Universal did something similar with its series spoofing newsreels, *Goofytone Newsreel*, and M-G-M offered *Goofy Movies*, which featured snippets of silent movies with "comic" narration by Pete Smith. We might view these as antecedents of *MSKT* or, at least, as proof that bad ideas never die. In any event, the New York State censors insisted that Pollard eliminate "an immersion scene" from *Goofytone News* because it was "sacrilegious."

Nineteen thirty-one was also the year of Pollard's first feature film, *Alice in Wonderland*, with Ruth Gilbert as Alice and Leslie King—who would later star in Pollard's *The*

*Horror*—as the Mad Hatter. The costumes and sets suggest a high-school play, but while critics at the *New York Times* and the *Wall Street Journal* may have snickered at the threadbare production values, was the film really any further off the mark than the big-budgeted, star-studded Paramount version that followed two years later? Rita McGoldrick's comments (in the October 17, 1931, *Motion Picture Herald*) seem right on the money:

> This is an ingenious production, far from the Hollywood manner. Its settings are simple, its costumes modest and its lack of extravagance notable. But Alice herself acts convincingly, there is an exceptional musical score and the little picture has caught something of the illusion of the childhood classic. Little children will love it; older ones will scoff at it and the mothers and fathers who take the small persons to the show will be bored to death.

Unique-Cosmos Pictures, the producers of *Alice*, took the rather unusual step of issuing the film on 16mm for the home movie/school/church market during its first theatrical run. Unique then announced a follow-up, a version of *Rip van Winkle*, also to be directed by Pollard. What's more, the company hoped to use Pollard to direct a series of short films starring "Uncle Don" (Carney), the host of a children's radio program. Both projects fizzled.

While Pollard was firmly ensconced in the East, he hadn't given up on Hollywood, and the trades duly reported his trips to the West Coast. In July 1932, for example, Pollard and Lew Maisell formed a production company to make movies for Monogram, but the deal fell through. Pollard came back from another of his West Coast trips to reveal that he had made a discovery in Hollywood High: a 17-year-old girl named Doris Daniels, who was a "combination of Joan Crawford, Greta Garbo, and Marlene Dietrich." Pollard put her under contract. She was never heard from again.

Pollard also tackled the ethnic films that were so popular in New York. Again, in July 1932, producer Clemente Giglio signed singer, Oreste Sandrino, to star in a series of films aimed at Italian American audiences. The first, *Thou Shalt Not Kill* (aka *O Festino o la Legge*), was apparently concerned with the conflicting claims of love, religion and the family. If that doesn't sound like a viable premise for a musical, it should be remembered that Giglio mounted a musical version of *The White Sister* on Broadway in 1927. The play had flopped, but, nevertheless, Giglio announced that Pollard would be doing a film version of it following *Thou Shalt Not Kill*. Not surprisingly, it didn't happen.

Next up was *The Black King*, planned as the first of a series of pictures—the second was to be titled *Bondage*—that were to be made by Southland Pictures Corporation at the Metropolitan Studio at Fort Lee and aimed at black audiences. Donald Heywood, Southland's president, hailed from Trinidad. A composer and producer by trade, he had mounted a number of Broadway shows, none of them very successful even though musicals with African American casts were then enjoying a certain vogue on the Great White Way. When Broadway passed on *The Black King*, Heywood settled for a film version with Bud Pollard as director. The story is a take-off on Marcus Garvey's "Back to Africa" movement, and there's even some footage of an actual parade staged by Garvey's group. The awkward aspect is that it's difficult to determine whether the film is meant as a comedy or a drama. A.B. Comathiere plays the Garvey counterpart, Deacon Charcoal Johnson, in a broadly comic-villain style, but the script often seems to be taking things more seriously. Interestingly enough, Johnson—though he's venal and corrupt—really does intend to take his followers to Africa, but the State Department refuses to issue passports, and their intended destination, Liberia, won't accept them. The picture also features the lovely Vivianne Baber looking particularly fetching at a fancy dress ball, a hero who says, "I don't give a damn," and Bud Pollard himself—the only white member of the cast—playing a judge. Reviewers called the film amateurish with weak direction, but, in its July 15, 1932, issue, *Film Daily* noted that a Harlem audience howled with laughter at the ball sequence where Johnson's followers assume fancy dress and fancier titles. *Variety* (July 19, 1932) made the snide, racist comment, "As is the average colored fan will probably have few complaints but whites would." The Bible of Show Business may have been mistaken there; the film tanked and took Southland Pictures with it.

Having done what he could for Italians and African Americans, Pollard then decided it was time to share his talents with Jewish moviegoers. Producer William Goldberg hired Pollard to direct *Victims of Persecution*, a plea for Gentile and Jew to work together for social justice. Unlike some other films aimed at Jewish viewers, the film was in English rather than Yiddish. Goldberg was certainly the appropriate producer for Pollard, as the following *Variety* article (June 27, 1933) indicates:

> Era of shoestringing so common in legit looks to have finally hit pictures. Outstanding instance is "Victims of Persecution," full length at total cost of $2,400. It got a full week's booking at the Cameo, New York, for its first run.
> 
> Producer of the picture is William Goldburg [sp]. All the actual shooting was done in a single day, studio space engaged for just for that one day.
> 
> Betty Hamilton, featured, is understood to have been paid $35 for the job. And Judah Bleich, supporting was satisfied with $25. All other actors pro rata.
> 
> Script was written on pads as it was being taken. For a musical background the producer borrowed a handful of phonograph records.

The article doesn't mention that considerable padding was added later to bring the film up to sixty minutes, including two reels of a silent film (Goldberg had done something similar for his movie, *Yiskor*) and some documentary footage on Palestine. No doubt as a further cost-saving measure, Pollard himself appeared in a small role as a politician.

And what did *Variety* think of the finished results? "Crude acting throughout. Three scenes and they bore. Photography nil" (June 20, 1933). *Motion Picture Herald* (June 24, 1933) concurred, calling the film "drab, without wide appeal" with players who were "completely inadequate." The June 17, 1933, issue of *Film Daily* was much more positive: "A natural for Jewish neighborhoods because of its timely newspaper importance at this time with the Hitler situation although Hitler and his policy are never directly alluded to in the drama."

The plot is certainly one Hollywood would never have touched at that time: A Jewish judge who is thinking of running for governor is faced with the case of a black man being railroaded to the gallows. If the judge insists on getting the man a new trial, he might well lose his shot at the nomination. He receives a threatening letter ("Take warning—Don't play God to the niggers—If he don't hang, you will"). The judge's family and friends urge him to drop the case, but his elderly father-in-law, newly arrived from Palestine, tells him to do the right thing and relates the story of Leah, a Jewish maiden, who tried to save her people from an anti–Semitic pogrom (this is where the silent film, whose title is not known, plays a part). The judge is nearly killed by a bomb, but he perseveres and, ultimately, his family sides with him.

The reviewer in the June 17, 1933, number of the *New York Times* found the film's theme "lofty and courageous" but "its technical deficiencies are too numerous to be hurdled by the average audience…. A stage play could not be no more static or land-locked and the story is told in dialogue by characters who are frequently bunched stolidly before the camera." Goldberg had planned a series of films on Jewish life in America, but *Victims* turned out to be the only one.

By 1932 it was clear that the horror genre was very profitable and there to stay. Bud Pollard couldn't hope to compete with

Universal or Warner Bros. in the monster sweepstakes, but he could certainly aspire to the likes of *The Monster Walks* or *Sinister Hands*. He had no Karloff or Lugosi, but he did have the services of Leslie King, who had often played grotesque roles in the Silent Era. In the 1920 serial, *The Evil Eye* (meant to showcase the talents of Lightweight World Boxing champ, Benny Leonard), King played a monstrous villain, complete with Nosferatu-like claws and a cyclopean eye. Perhaps a bit put-off that the trades rarely mentioned him in the publicity for the serial, King placed his own ad—showing him in a variety of Lon Chaney–like make-ups—in an issue of *Motion Picture News*. Some say King resembled The Man of 1,000 Faces, but we don't see it. (Actually, in some stills from *The Horror*, he looks a bit like Karloff in *The Ghoul*.) King also appeared in the bizarre *Shielding Shadow* serial; the 1921 allegorical drama, *Experience* (in which he played either "Temperance" or "Gloom"— we suppose the two could be related); and D.W. Griffith's *Orphans of the Storm*, wherein he had the role of "Jacques Forget-Not," who witnesses the barbaric torture of his father and later becomes a merciless judge for the Reign of Terror. King also had a great deal of stage experience, both in stock and on Broadway. In 1936 he would play a role in a production of *Dorian Gray* written by Jeron Criswell (Yes, *that* Criswell). Except for his dealings with Bud Pollard, King seems to have abandoned films in the 1930s; no doubt he stayed in New York for the stage work.

Also featured in *The Horror* was Rajah Raboid,[6] a stage magician, mentalist, and fortune teller who had done quite well in the 1920s. Later, his most famous act involved Johnny Eck, the legless man in Tod Browning's *Freaks*: Eck had a normal twin, and Raboid would "saw him in half" on stage. Johnny would then emerge from the box and run around on stage on his hands— screaming, "Where are my legs?"—a sight that no doubt inspired a few nightmares. In the early 1930s, Raboid got into trouble for fortunetelling: the FCC canceled his radio show, the Society of American Magicians expelled him, and he was even arrested. These setbacks doubtless resulted in his sticking to stage magic and, in September 1932, he formulated an act called "Spookeasy." This would play in theaters to accompany whatever film happened to be showing, and Raboid, perhaps thinking musicals and comedies didn't jibe well with his act, hit on a new approach. Per Mark Walker's *Ghostmasters*:

> Raboid decided he wanted to make his own starring film to rent to movie theaters that booked his attraction. *The Horror*, an independent film, was shot in a studio on Long Island and starred the Rajah, a chimp and a dwarf. The backers who financed it arranged for a private showing on a movieola machine but the feature was never released. Several years later Raboid tried to obtain the print but it already been destroyed.[7]

This version of the film's status is problematic. Raboid's role in *The Horror* is quite brief, and, even allowing for the fact that we only have a truncated copy of the film, he certainly was not the star, nor was he even mentioned in any of the publicity. Knowing what we do of Bud Pollard, it's not hard to imagine him talking Raboid into doing the film gratis since it would advertise his stage shtick. Still, in any case, we know the film wasn't destroyed. The first press mention of *The Horror* that we have is from the September 3, 1932, issue of *The Daily Star* (Long Island City): "Shooting of *The Horror*, a six-reel feature, began today." The brief article went on to say that director Bud Pollard was going to do several more films at the studio before signing up with Monogram. A longer, somewhat contradictory piece appeared in the same paper on the September 12:

> Shooting of the 7 reel picture started yesterday. Six exploitation features are being planned the second of which will be *Dance Hall Dames*. *The Horror* seems to be a combination of *White Zombie*, *Hairy Ape* and *Dracula* [We're not sure what the Eugene O'Neill play is doing there; maybe someone mixed it up with *The Gorilla*]. Nyrida Montez will do a spine tingling act when she

struts around with a 14 foot live snake wrapped around her body.[8] Leslie King "the horror" himself has an extraordinary make-up. So intricate is the make-up that it takes 5 hours of expert manipulation by Bert Tuey, chief make-up artist to get the correct illusion.

*The Horror* was the first film shot at Atlas Sound Recording at their new headquarters in Long Island City; two years later the studio was shut down for fire code violations. A September 9, 1932, piece in *Film Daily* sang the praises of East Coast production and interviewed Pollard about shooting outside of La La Land:

> I was all set to go to Hollywood for this series of six features when I discovered a studio right here in Long Island that had every facility. As all my features are exploitation specials [...] that is novelties planned for exploitation angles in which I will use a lot of theatrical talent that I cannot get on the West Coast. For instance, in "The Horror" I am using five different people who are in New York Stage productions. They double up with me in their stage work. They get a break and I get talent I could not get in Hollywood.

The *Film Daily* scribe went on to briefly describe the shooting of *The Horror*:

> We witnessed shooting start yesterday on Bud's feature. With 5 complete set ups in two days [...] and we never see a studio crew move as efficiently as those boys for all the union lads realize that here is their chance to prove that an indie producer can get service in the East.

The September 18 edition of *Film Daily* announced that *The Horror* had been completed, a record schedule for a seven-reel feature. The September 22 issue reported that Pollard's F.P. production company was moving on to do *Dance Hall Dames* next, which then was to be followed by *Lunatic at Large*, *Metropolitan Murders*, *Framed*, and *The Green Jade*. On October 25, though, *Film Daily* noted that "additional shots for *The Horror* have been completed."

In any event, Pollard had a distribution deal with Stanley Distributing Corporation to release *The Horror*. Stanley took out an ad in the October 1 issue of *Film Daily* to announce the following: "Now ready for the state right market: *The Horror*, an original mystery drama." The ad was repeated in *Film Daily* throughout October, November, and December, ending with the January 13 issue. But was the film really ready? The "additional shots" notation for the October 25 and the November 23 numbers mention that "F.P. Productions have finished their cutting and editing of their feature production *The Horror*" leaves room for doubt that the film was really in shape to be shown by the first of October.

It mattered little. Complete or not, *The Horror* was not released. In February 1933, Ira Simmons, the head of Stanley Distributing, quit. Though there was talk of the company forging on, Stanley Distributing quickly folded with the departure of its boss. That left *The Horror* without a distributor and put *Dance Hall Dames* and Pollard's other film projects in limbo. It's curious that Pollard, who was resourceful enough when it came to getting his movies shown, didn't try to find another distributor or even submit *The Horror* to the New York Board of Censors as he did with virtually all of his other films. One suspects there was a debt of some sort—from a lab or film storage facility or some part of the now soured deal with Stanley—that prevented Pollard from making a serious effort to get his movie out there.

Pollard didn't remain idle, though. In October of 1933 he took over the old Royal Studio in Greenwood, New Jersey, and renamed it—what else?—Bud Pollard Studios. Ads for his new project promised "The most completely equipped modern, independent studio in the East with facilities to accommodate your every production need from the smallest scoring job to the largest feature." In addition to being available for rental "at exceedingly low rates," the studio was going to be the setting for ten more exploitation features to be directed by Pollard, one of which, *The Horror*, was already completed. Other titles announced were *Strange Women of the World*, *Kings of Laughter*, *Manhattan Madness*, *Chinatown Nights*, and, of course, the inescapable *Dance Hall Dames*. This line-up for the 1933–1934 season was published in the trades several times. It was also reported that Pollard would shoot eight commercial shorts for General Business Films as well as some musicals using child talent from the Jules Stone Studio.

At this point *The Horror* disappears from the record, and for years it remained a mystery with only a handful of stills left behind testifying to the *possibility* that it had actually been made. Eventually detective work by George Turner, Michael Price, Scott MacQueen, and others revealed that *The Horror* had played in Japan in 1934 under the title *Jumen* (*The Human Beast*), and had been reviewed in the Japanese film magazine, *Kinema Junpo*.[9] The critic took the film seriously, perhaps thinking it was meant to be like the classic Expressionist Japanese study of mental illness, *A Page of Madness* (1926).

In 1944 Pollard cut the film down to four reels, retitled it *John the Drunkard*, added some narration, and passed it off as a temperance film to the church/club home movie market. The Library of Congress acquired a copy (possibly in 1974); we've watched it there and we have to say what they actually have is something of a puzzle.

The first reel has no visual element, just sound. Bud Pollard tells us, "If you have a weak heart leave this theater now. This is not for the timid. Since I'm the only living soul who knows the actual facts of this strange tale, I'll return to ease your mental strain whenever the story gets complicated." Pollard also notes that he started production on the film many years ago, and our honest opinion is that he probably thought the clothes the actors were wearing was something of a giveaway. The scene shifts to New York City. It is Prohibition, Pollard tells us, and people in need of a drink have to rely on bootleg liquor that is not always the best quality. John Massey, an antiques dealer lingering at a newsstand, feels he's being watched. He ducks into the office of his friend and physician, Dr. Babcock, and tells him a strange story. John claims that he was hired by a collector to go to India and acquire an idol the collector desperately wanted. He found it in the Temple of the Inya, and, when the priest refused to sell it to him, John stole it and returned to America where he discovered that his client was dead, a Hindu dagger in his heart. Since then, John is convinced he's being watched. The doctor dismisses his fears and tells him his obsession could result in a nervous breakdown. Leaving the office and still frightened that he is being followed, John flees to his Long Island mansion.

The next reel lists credits and cast and is titled *The Horror*. We see the words "Copyright 1933 by F.P. Productions" even though the film was never actually copyrighted at Library of Congress. Possibly Pollard added the words hoping they would give him some kind of legal protection on the cheap. Pollard's narration over the credits tell us that he has "pieced together this story from the lips of John the Drunkard, himself." The film seems to take up where the earlier reel left off with John at his Long Island home; however, in spite of the incoherence of much that follows, there is no more narration. There is also no mention of drink or alcoholism in the picture itself, so it's hard to see how Pollard could have presented this as a temperance film. Does the Library of Congress actually have a combination of *John the Drunkard* and the original *The Horror*?

In any case, the subsequent action seems to unfold in one night, and, while there is a kind of progression to the story, shots seem jumbled together and in desperate need of editing. This suggests that we're dealing with a work print, but perhaps that might be giving Pollard too much credit. The following is as close to a synopsis as we can get.

Jimmy the chauffeur and Marie the maid are engaging in a mutual flirtation in the garage. A storm threatens, and they run to the house. We learn that John's household staff is perturbed by his increasingly bizarre behavior; he's not eating and he's given to fits of anger and fear. John screams, "Get out!" to the butler. There's a close-up of a squawking parrot. Jimmy and Marie continue to play around in the kitchen as the storm rises, and their smooching is intercut with shots of John's pacing feet. We see John's wife and the butler ascend the stairs, but the shot is so oddly framed that the top of the stairs and hallway are cut off. This happens again and again. [It's hard to believe this is the work of cinematographer Dal Clawson, an exceptional cameraman and documentary maker from the 1920s.]

John's wife undresses for bed while the black nanny cares for her baby. Jimmy and Marie are still hanging out in the kitchen. A dog barks. The service bell is rung for Marie. As Marie answers, the lights go out, and we see two turbaned visitors suddenly appear in the living room. Marie faints. We see the mysterious statue John has brought from India. "Do not be alarmed!" Rajah Raboid intones in his corniest stage voice. "We need shelter for the night." His companion is played by Gus Alexander, who portrayed the Mock Turtle in Pollard's *Alice in Wonderland*. [Alexander, who was about four feet tall, played in many silent comedies, notably a series of shorts—no pun intended—based on the popular "Mutt and Jeff" comic strip.] Jimmie enters and tells John that they've blown a fuse [he pronounces it foo-ss] and asks. "Do you want me to fix it?" "Yes," John replies portentously, "I want you to fix it." Rajah then announces, "I am the one who reads the future." His companion produces a basket with a snake in it. Close-ups of the swami's eyes alternate with close-ups of John's eyes. John offers his visitors food. "No need for food" is the response. "We go now." John gives him a coin, and Jimmie goes to prepare a room for them for the night. Marie, having recovered, goes back to the kitchen. John seems agitated to the point of frenzy. He begins writing his last will and testament in which he states, "They want revenge for stealing the idol. The fear is driving me mad. My doctor said I could have a nervous breakdown." John puts the will away in a safe and is then haunted by disembodied eyes.

Meanwhile Jimmy joins Marie in the kitchen and complains about the hygiene of their Hindu guests. Jimmy sends Marie to bed and vows to keep watch. We see Marie undressing. Jimmy dozes off in the kitchen. John, fleeing the floating eyes, locks Jimmy in and utters a diabolical cackle [the sort of exaggerated creepy laugh you might hear from a horror-movie TV host like Zacherley]. As the eyes continue to haunt John, he goes upstairs to the bedroom, where—seeing his wife in bed—he forgets his fear and leers at her sleeping form; however, when he pulls back the sheet, he discovers the snake is wrapped around her.

John screams and—in the one effective scene in the film—is transformed into a monster. The monster is a mass of latex and hair and reminded us a bit of the creature in *The Brainiac* [except for the tongue]. John's wife rises as if in a trance. An ape [a laughably cheesy costume] enters the room.

Alerted by all the racket, Marie wakes up and lets Jimmy out of the kitchen. They hear noises in the living room, and Jimmy tackles a shadowy figure that turns out to be the butler. Upstairs, monster and ape are squaring off. The ape carries off the wife. There's a shot of the housekeeper in bed reading an issue of *Weird Tales*. Jimmy phones Dr. Babcock and tells him to come at once. Meanwhile, monster-John and the ape do battle. The ape strangles John as the short Hindu watches and applauds with delight.

Next we find John recuperating in bed. The gorilla turns into the smiling nanny[!] John sees his wife with the snake still wrapped around her, but then the image is replaced by the wife with their child. Dr. Babcock tells John the idol has been stolen, but that that has no connection to his illness. "I wonder" is John's response.

And of course we do too. Were there really three more reels of this? and, if so, what could be happening on them? It would not be a surprise if *The Horror* were originally closer to five reels than seven. Had the film been released in the U.S., Pollard could have done his usual thing and increased the running time by adding documentary footage on India or by dredging up part of some forgotten silent to pad things out. Unfortunately, the review of the film in the Japanese magazine does not give a footage or time length.

According to Richard Koszarski, "The film is an uncredited adaptation of Arthur Conan Doyle's *The Sign of Four* with lengthy hallucinatory sequences making up for the absence of Sherlock Holmes."[10] It has far more in common, though, with *The Moonstone* and its endless variations wherein avenging Eastern priests go in search of sacred objects stolen by Western unbelievers. The dialogue and continuity are attributed to Basil Smith. Presumably this is the same Basil Smith who directed short comedies and musicals and at one point was the manager of the famous Roxy theater in New York. If so, he was quite out of his element with *The Horror*. The one good gag is the housekeeper absorbed in *Weird Tales* while all these ghastly things are happening right around her. We were hoping that the whole story would turn out to be a projection of what she was reading, but we're pretty much stuck interpreting the film as a series of John's hallucinations arising from guilt at stealing the idol.

The remainder of the 1930s were not the best of times for Bud Pollard. In addition to financial setbacks with his studio, he had to deal with the tragic death of his protégé, Betty Hamilton. Hamilton had had a role *Victims of Persecution* and was slated to star in the never made *Dance Hall Dames*. In 1933, Pollard arranged for her to go on a musical comedy tour in England, and while some reports have her appearing in five films there, the reality is she landed only one part, a small role in *The Private Life of Don Juan*. Back in the U.S. after two years abroad, she became engaged to radio station owner, Fred Levy. When they broke up, Hamilton became suicidal. Even though Pollard had a nurse watching her, the 21-year-old starlet was able to jump out of her hotel window and land on the roof of an adjoining building, several floors below. Still alive when they carried her to the ambulance, she made an attempt to throw herself from the stretcher to finish things off; she died en route to the hospital. Betty Hamilton received far more publicity in death than she ever had in life, with articles making it sound like she was on the brink of stardom rather than just a minor player with a brief and unimportant career. Pollard was the only "Hollywood figure" to attend her funeral in her small Pennsylvania home town, and while he muttered darkly about filing a lawsuit, nothing came of it.

Switching media, Pollard turned to staging risqué live performances. In April 1935, he announced he was going to put on the first all-nude play, claiming that he and all the cast were nudists who wanted to promote the cause. The play was entitled *The Girl from Child's in 1950* (the 1950 part was meant to suggest that nudism would be completely acceptable by that future year), and the publicity stirred both amusement and indignation. As local nudist colonies disavowed any knowledge of the play—which was set to be staged in Vernon, New York—Bud stuck to his claim of being a nudist, but denied ever having gone to a nudist colony ("I have my reputation to consider"). Annoyed at some of the negative comments about his plans, Bud insisted that pioneers were always subject to derision: "As was the case when Columbus first spoke of a new route to India and a round globe. Also when Margaret Sanger[11] made her courageous fight for birth control so have tremendous obstacles been placed in our path" (*Oakland Tribune*, March 22, 1935). The obstacles were apparently overcome and the play had a week's run; however, this turned out not to be a predecessor of *Oh! Calcutta!,* and the players, though scantily attired, were not actually nude, much to the disappointment of patrons who had paid $3 a pop to get a look. A Broadway run was announced, but, to the surprise of no one, this never materialized. Pollard then attempted to do the first nudist floor show at a place called the Sea Grit Inn, but the authorities put the kibosh on that by threatening to take away the Inn's liquor license. In December 1936, Pollard declared bankruptcy, listing no assets and $15,850 in debts. It's not clear from the record at precisely what point Pollard Studios went under.

Bloodied, but unbowed, Pollard then began promoting a three-tint color process called Brewster Color, which he claimed was excellent for night photography, and, working out of the old Biograph Studio in The Bronx, Pollard planned a series of short subjects using the process. Showgirls from the Hollywood Restaurant were to be the subjects of one of the films. Nothing further was heard of this, either.

Surprisingly, Pollard *did* have one solid

success in this period: the anti-war documentary, *The Dead March* (1937), which, in its climax, anticipates to some extent the parade of the fallen soldiers in Abel Gance's *J'Accuse*. In addition to utilizing newsreels from the Great War, Pollard had access to footage from more recent conflicts, such as the Italian invasion of Ethiopia and the Spanish Civil War. *Film Daily* (August 19, 1937) gave a good description of the film:

> The footage is well chosen and efficiently assembled.... Producer Bud Pollard has organized the picture into three main divisions, namely the recent recourse to war by nations bent on exploiting weaker nations as well as countries resorting to arms to settle their "difficulties"; the current prodigious preparation for war by the great powers and finally the World War which is called up to testify to the fact that it was a terrible human catastrophe and the next big war will be infinitely more horrible ... the fine finale finds the Unknown Soldiers of Germany, France, Britain, Italy and the United State individually recounting, as their armies are revealed in action, the reasons why each fought in the World War.

The critic for the *New York Times* (September 20, 1937) had mixed feelings about the film's message, but thought the picture as a whole achieved

> impartiality, especially in conclusion, when the Unknown Soldiers of five nations are allowed to present their own, narrow national views of the things they died for. The most impressive horrors are saved for these sequences, including the sinking of an Austrian superdreadnought and Italian motor boat; the most astounding factual shot this reviewer has ever witnessed.

Not everyone thought the ending worked: The reviewer in the September 11, 1937, number of the *Motion Picture Herald* found the finale with the risen soldiers "confusing and illogical to the picture's original purpose," and *Motion Picture Daily* (August 20, 1937) concurred: "The idea introduced in the outset is logical but the concluding sequences seem to contradict the original thought." The reviewer also opined that the war footage had been seen many times before. No doubt remembering how *Forgotten Men* was promoted, Pollard had *The Dead March* debut in the Big Apple during the American Legion convention.

In the 1940s, Pollard alternated film work with touring with a comedy act. He and his wife, Helene Francis (a stripper who once billed herself as Sylvia Sydney's stand-in), called themselves the "Aristocrats of Comedy." The act was apparently a hit and played in clubs in San Francisco, Hollywood, and Las Vegas. Pollard also went back to the African American market, directing *It Happened in Harlem* and *Big Timers* (both 1945), *Tall, Tan and Terrific* and *Beware* (both 1946), and *Look-Out Sister* (1947). Cinematically, these were negligible; at their best they could pass as something out of Monogram. On the plus side, they preserved on film the performances of black entertainers like Louis Jordan, Francine Everett, and Chris Columbus.

In 1941, Pollard announced a new war documentary (no one was making *anti*-war documentaries in 1941), *America Speaks*, with "8000 feet of action"; this eventually became *Invasion* (when released in 1942). *Invasion* brought world events up to date since *The Dead March* and used much footage from that previous film. If nothing else, Bud Pollard had gotten to the point of stealing from himself.

Much more notable was Pollard's contribution to another documentary: *Kukan; The Battle Cry of China* (1941). The footage, detailing the resistance of the Chinese to the Japanese invasion, was taken by Rey Scott, a foreign correspondent for London's *Daily Telegraph*, who filmed some extraordinary scenes of the conflict at great risk to himself. Franklin D. Roosevelt screened it at the White House, and Scott was given a special Academy Award. While "White House" and "Academy Award" are not words usually associated with Bud Pollard, he did in fact work on the film, probably supervising sound effects and the like. In spite of all the praise, *Kukan* disappeared after the war, and for many years was thought to be a lost film. A worn 16mm print was finally located and, in 2012, it was sent to the Academy of Motion Picture Arts and Sciences for restoration.

Perhaps most typical of Pollard's work in the 1940s were the pictures *Birth of a Star* (Danny Kaye) and *The Road to Hollywood* (Bing Crosby). In the early days of their careers in the 1930s, Kaye and Crosby had both made shorts for Educational Pictures, and these—and others—were snapped up at auction by Astor Pictures in 1940 after Educational went belly up. Pollard strung the shorts together, added a narration, and Astor then passed them off as new movies featuring the now-popular stars.

Pollard's final film (before his fatal encounter with the comedy of Joe R. Ross) was *Love Island* (1952). The film was originally released in Cinecolor, but the copies floating around on the Internet are in black and white and are missing some scenes. (It remains unlikely that anyone is going to undertake a restoration.) The story concerns an Air Force flyer who parachutes onto a tropical island where he meets Eva Gabor (in a black wig). When the two aren't talking cute, the flyer sings a song or two, and the lovebirds look out the window of their hut and watch stock footage of wedding customs in Bali. There's a fat bad guy and some other equally terrible actors playing islanders, and, after a while, you wish the Tabonga would show up to throw a couple of them into quicksand. *Love Island* was reissued in 1960 and, passed off as an adult movie, was often paired with Russ Meyer's *The Immoral Mr. Teas*. Somewhere in purgatory—a purgatory no doubt made up of footage from *Maciste in Hell* and *Häxan*—Bud Pollard is probably smiling.

# Return of the Terror

First National Pictures, Inc. (Warner Bros.)—July 7, 1934—65 minutes **Cast:** Mary Astor as Olga Morgan; Lyle Talbot as Dr. Goodman; John Halliday as Dr. John Redmayne; Frank McHugh as Joe Hastings; Robert Barrat as Pudge Walker; Irving Pichel as Daniel Burke; George E. Stone as Soapy McCoy; J. Carroll Naish as Steve Scola; Frank Reicher as Dr. Franz Reinhardt; Robert Emmett O'Connor as Inspector Bradley; Renee Whitney as Virginia Mayo; Etienne Girardot as Mr. Tuttle; Maude Eburn as Mrs. Elvey; Charles Grapewin as Mr. Jessop; George Humbert as Tony; Edmund Breese as the Editor; George Cooper as Cotton; Cecil Cunningham as Miss Doolittle; Frank Conway as the Prosecuting attorney; Howard Hickman as the Judge; Harry Seymour as the City reporter; Lorena Layson as the Maid; Philip Morris as the Guard; Bert Moorehouse as the First trooper; Eddie Schubert as the Second trooper; Al Stewart as the Skeleton

**Credits**: *Director*: Howard Bretherton; *Dialogue Director*: Arthur Greville Collins; *Supervisor*: Sam Bischoff; *Screenplay*: Eugene Solow, Peter Milne; *Cinematography*: Arthur L. Todd; *Art Direction*: John Hughes; *Editor*: Owen Marks; *Costumes*: Orry-Kelly; *Music*: Leo F. Forbstein; *Vitaphone Orchestra Conductor*: Leo. F. Forbstein. *Based on the 1927 play* **The Terror** *by* Edgar Wallace

> It'll grow icicles on your heart!
> —Tag line from *Return of the Terror*

Nineteen thirty-four was not a banner year for the horror film.

Admittedly, there *was* Universal's *The Black Cat*, and chillers released late in 1933—*The Ghoul, Son of Kong, The Invisible Man*—continued to do well at the boxoffice throughout much of the following year. Still, for most of '34, Hollywood seemed to take a breather and step back a bit from trying to terrify audiences. In place of the ghoulies and ghosties and long-legged beasties, there was a return to thrillers of a tamer, more sedate sort: no monsters need apply. Thus, *Black Moon*: a voodoo film with no zombies; and *Double Door*: an atmospheric study wherein the grotesques found in *The Old Dark House* were replaced by one *very* mean old lady. Producers turned back to the Silent Era for inspiration, and there were remakes of borderline horror pictures like *The Witching Hour* (filmed in 1916 and 1921) and 1923's *Red Lights* (revivified as *Murder in the Private Car*). In 1933, Warner Bros. did its part to keep the horror genre profitable with *Mystery of the Wax Museum*. Six months earlier, the studio had unleashed *Doctor X* onto a host of wide-eyed viewers, and, in 1928, the brothers Warner had been responsible for *The Terror*, the screen's very first horror talkie (and only the second all-talkie movie ever). And even though *Death* took a *Holiday*, the outcome was pretty tame.

*The Terror*—based on Edgar Wallace's eponymous play—had as its titular villain a maniacal arch-criminal/master of disguise, and not some fiend of supernatural origin. Betrayed by The Terror, two former confederates are bent on revenge and plot to recover a big haul of stolen loot. Their quest takes them to the English countryside and a former monastery that has been converted into a rest home peopled by eccentric characters; among them is a ghastly, hooded figure, seen prowling the corridors at night. There's also spooky organ music emanating from God knows where, hidden passages galore, a séance, and, of course, several murders. Edgar Wallace pronounced the film to be "good," although he also grumbled that his play had been burlesqued a bit. (On another occasion he was less complimentary.) Some critics found the picture static, while others thought the sound effects—screams, howling winds, crazed laughter—made it far more terrifying than had it been released as a silent. In any case, whether due to the novelty of sound or the plot's own merits (or both), the film was a huge hit.

Some five years later, the fact that the studio was considering a remake of *The Terror* was mentioned, en passant, in one of Harriet Pearson's movie columns.

> When Leslie Howard returns from Europe, he'll find a new kind of picture waiting for him. Warners will star him in *The Return of the Terror* by the late Edgar Wallace but don't worry—Leslie isn't going to do a Boris Karloff. He'll play a Scotland Yard man. Margaret Lindsay will have the feminine lead opposite him. *Return of the Terror* is a typical Wallace thriller about a monster who haunts an English castle. Leslie, who hasn't gone in for gumshoeing will be one of those restrained gentleman detectives who always get their monster.[1]

There is, after all, no Scotland Yard detective in *Return of the Terror*, but in the original film there is one, and his strategy of initially presenting himself as a silly ass disguises his sleuthing skills and enables him to save the heroine and solve the mystery in the usual fashion. One could certainly see Leslie Howard in such a role.

In any event, when *Return of the Terror* went before the cameras in February 1934, it was without the services of either Leslie Howard or Margaret Lindsay, and—as the following synopsis shows—it was certainly neither a remake of nor any kind of sequel to 1928's *The Terror*.

> Dr. John Redmayne, director of the Morgan Rest Home, is on trial for his life, having been accused of poisoning four patients with arsenic. The papers have dubbed him "The Terror," and public opinion is very much against him. Nonetheless, he receives support from his fiancée Olga—whose late father owned the sanatorium—and his colleague, Dr. Goodman. On the witness stand, Redmayne vigorously denies the charges, but admits he believes that incurably ill mental patients should be euthanized ["It is a radical theory but it is sound and not brutal," the doctor insists]. Redmayne also does not deny that he aided in the suicide of an old man who was in excruciating pain. While the testimony of Virginia, a young nurse at the sanatorium, proves inconclusive, attendant Steve Scola claims that he witnessed Redmayne several times preparing a particularly potent arsenic mixture. Redmayne's case looks so hopeless that Burke, his lawyer, urges him to enter an insanity plea. Redmayne is reluctant, but Burke tells him that it's his only hope and that at least it leaves open the possibility of an appeal. The plea is accepted, and Redmayne is remanded to the State Asylum for the Insane.
> 
> Reporter Joe Hastings has known Redmayne for years and doesn't believe he's guilty, but he is unable to convince his editor to publish an article sympathetic to the doctor. Joe is very suspicious of Scola, given that the latter is able to afford a fancy car on a low-wage job. Joe is also smitten with Virginia and finds that Scola is his rival.
> 
> Six months pass. At the Morgan Rest Home, Dr. Goodman, with the help of his assistant Dr. Reinhardt, is close to perfecting the Flurexray, a machine that "reveals every bone in the body with no trace of organs or flesh." [It also doesn't require a screen and merely needs to be pointed at the patient who then appears as a skeleton.] Reinhardt urges Goodman to present the machine to the scientific world, but Goodman insists it was Redmayne's discovery and he must give him full credit for it. Goodman receives a telegram telling him that Redmayne's appeal has been denied. Olga is disappointed, but Goodman tells her not to lose hope.
> 
> At the asylum, Redmayne is distraught when Burke tells him that it may take as long as a year for his case to be reversed. Redmayne screams that the place is driving him mad and that he can't stand it any longer. Feigning illness, Redmayne later overpowers a guard and escapes. As a terrible storm pours down drenching rain, Redmayne hops a freight train.
> 
> Not far from the Morgan Rest Home, Joe is out on a date with Virginia. Joe's car stalls and, just as they are about to walk in the rain, Scola pulls up. He gives Virginia a lift but leaves Joe stranded.
> 
> At the sanatorium, Goodman is interviewing two new potential patients who identify themselves as Walker and McCoy, and who claim it was Burke who sent them there. Goodman is skeptical of their motives but admits them. We soon learn that the men are crooks who have recently pulled a jewel robbery. In addition to being their lawyer, Burke is also acting as their fence and has advised them that the sanatorium would make a good temporary hideout.

Virginia and Scola arrive at the sanatorium, and Joe arrives a few minutes later. Goodman reluctantly allows Scola—who was fired earlier—and Joe to spend the night because of the storm. Walker and McCoy know Scola and obviously don't like him.

At dinner that night, Walker and McCoy find the other patients a rather irritating lot. One of them, a Miss Doolittle, insists on giving McCoy a pill, and Walker grows increasingly impatient with the talkative Mr. Jessop. Meanwhile, Redmayne, who is lurking around the sanatorium grounds, enters Olga's room through her window; she is so startled by his appearance that she screams. Redmayne flees and Goodman calls the asylum where it is confirmed that the doctor has escaped and that "he's violent beyond control." Goodman doesn't want to call the police, but instead organizes a search of the grounds.

Redmayne steals a raincoat, opens a kitchen window, and grabs a butcher knife. The cook—who's as crazy as the patients—blames Cotton, an attendant, for the open window. Mr. Jessop has also managed to procure a carving knife.

The search party has little luck finding Redmayne; however, Olga spots him in the bushes. Something startles him, and he runs before he can talk to her. Meanwhile, Joe ends up scuffling with Scola, McCoy discovers that the telephone wires have been cut, and a figure in a raincoat attempts to stab Goodman. His would-be assailant turns out to be Mr. Jessop, who was actually hoping to stab Walker for having insulted him at dinner. Back inside, Goodman decides to call the police, but finds that the phone is dead. He blames it on the storm.

Joe discovers the phone line has been cut, but manages to splice it together and call his friend, Inspector Bradley. Joe tells him what's going on and advises him to take the back roads to the sanatorium, since the main highway is impassable because of the storm. Upstairs, a mysterious figure whose face cannot be seen comes into Virginia's room via her window; her screams drive him off. Joe, Goodman, and Scola answer her cries, and Joe decides he will search the grounds again himself.

Redmayne sneaks into the cellar, but the mystery man knocks him out, drags him to the vegetable pit, and closes the trapdoor over him. He then turns an outdoor drain pipe into the open window, flooding the basement. Joe comes into the cellar and sees that the trap door is starting to move. Before he can investigate further, he is knocked cold by the mystery man.

The next morning Inspector Bradley arrives with a contingent of state troopers. Joe, having recovered from his injury, brings them to the basement which is completely flooded, although the drain pipe is back in place. Bradley is skeptical, but agrees to have the troopers drain the basement so they can see what's in the vegetable pit.

The troopers discover Scola shot dead in his car. A note by his side reads: "I am still with you and will remain until I accomplish my purpose. To you who made me—The Terror." Inspector Bradley and Joe are both suspicious of Reinhardt, a drug addict who is constantly prowling around the house and grounds. Joe suggests taking away Reinhardt's drug supply to see if he'll crack. Bradley questions Goodman, who tells him he knows of his assistant's addiction and is trying to cure him. Nonetheless, Bradley confiscates Goodman's supply of narcotics.

Burke arrives at the sanatorium and is berated by Walker and McCoy for his choice of hideouts. Burke assures them that all will be well since the troopers are searching for Redmayne, and not for them. The crooks are angered that Burke has given them a paltry $500 for the stolen jewels, but the lawyer promises them a better deal when the heat over the robbery is off.

The cellar is finally drained, but the vegetable pit reveals only carrots, beets and potatoes ["Irish stew" snickers the Inspector]. Bradley decides to question everyone in the house. A note is found on a closet door, and when the door is opened, the body of Burke falls out. The lawyer has been strangled, and the note is the same as the previous one ["He must have 'em mimeographed" cracks Joe]. McCoy and Walker attempt to escape, but the state troopers shoot up their getaway car. Bradley recognizes the fugitives and has them arrested, but they deny killing Burke and Scola.

Bradley and Joe search Goodman's laboratory. Upstairs, Reinhardt demands that Goodman give him drugs or he'll tell the world that Goodman is a fake and had little to do with the invention of the X-Ray machine. In the lab, Joe and Bradley see a skeleton in front of the machine start to move. Joe turns the machine off, and the skeleton image fades into Redmayne, who proclaims his innocence. Shots and screams are heard from upstairs. Bradley and Joe investigate and find that Reinhardt has been shot dead and that Goodman has a flesh wound. Goodman claims that Redmayne killed Reinhardt, but Bradley and Joe know better.

Now exonerated, Redmayne enters and explains: with Scola and Burke's help, Goodman framed Redmayne for the arsenic murders [with the intention of claiming the credit for the invention of the X-Ray machine for himself]. Redmayne's escape from the asylum gave Goodman the opportunity to murder his blackmailing associates and put the blame on the doctor. It was Goodman who knocked Redmayne out and put him in the vegetable pit, but the water he let into the basement in the hopes of drowning the physician revived him instead. Goodman does not deny any of this and is led off in handcuffs as Olga and Redmayne are reunited.

While the plots of *The Terror* and *Return of the Terror* are entirely different, they do have a couple of minor points in common: the guests in the inn/rest home of *The Terror* are similar to the sanatorium patients in *Return* (including a writer of murder mysteries), and a number of the characters—Redmayne, Olga, Walker, Mrs. Elvey—share the same names (Goodman turns out to be the Bad Man in both films). Although Edgar Wallace had died in 1932, his international reputation as a master mystery writer made his name a major selling point for *Return*, even if the connection between author and film jumped all over the place: depending on the publicity puff-piece, the film was "based on" or "inspired by the *play* by Edgar Wallace"; "taken from the *story* by Edgar Wallace"; "said to be based on the Edgar Wallace *novel*," etc. Reviewers bought into it without a murmur of dissent: "The late Edgar Wallace," wrote the *Hollywood Filmograph*, "must have been very screen-minded when he wrote the book *The Terror*, for Warner Bros. have made it into very good screen fare." Apparently no one was familiar either with Wallace's play (which did *not* make it to Broadway) or with his 1929 novelization, while the original film—produced a mere six years earlier—had been totally forgotten after its initial release. In spite of occasionally being referred to in the press as "an Edgar Wallace horror movie," *Return of the Terror* was marketed primarily as a mystery:

> You'll get hot under the collar trying to solve it. Match your wits with the greatest mystery writer of all time—Edgar Wallace. One of the most unique and baffling mysteries even created.

Still, the horror angle was not completely neglected, and we read that the film is "one of the spookiest mysteries to leave Hollywood studios" and that "its thrills will chill you to the bone." One of the film's macabre undertones is highlighted in an article that appeared in a local newspaper:

> Actors often find themselves playing strange and unusual parts in motion pictures all the way from invisible men to off-stage shouts, but probably no actor has had a more fantastic assignment this season than Al Stewart. Al portrays the man behind the skeleton in *Return of the Terror*.... To be exact he plays two skeletons, doubling "in bones." During a number of scenes in the laboratory of the sanatorium where revolutionary experiments with the "fleurxray" are carried out, he plays the skeleton of Frank Reicher.... Later in the picture he becomes the skeleton for John Halliday. It took Al two and a half hours each day to transform himself into a skeleton. When the process was com-

British reviewers were not impressed with *The Terror* and the critic for *Picture Show* was no exception. U.S. critiques were generally more favorable.

pleted and he walked out into the lot from his dressing room, the effect was startling even in broad daylight.[2]

What? No story about how passers-by were terrified by his appearance? Strange the Warners's press flacks missed that hoopla cliché. The skeleton's appearance is actually a very clever effect (done by luminous paint?), but director Howard Bretherton doesn't do much with it. Another publicity piece dealt with the set and special effects:

> One sound stage 280 feet long and 160 wide was cleared and turned over completely to the use of the Edgar Wallace picture. The front elevation of the mansion around which the action revolves was built complete to the roof line and side walls were added as far back as the camera could reach. The house itself occupied one end of the sound stage. In another the interior of the house was built. The rest of the space was turned over to the studio landscape department. In that stretch they built lawns and gardens, complete with ivy covered walls, grilled gateways, concrete drives, huge spreading trees and flower borders. Meanwhile the technicians piped and cross-piped with sprinklers the entire stage roof except that portion over the interior of the mansion, and connected them with an adjustable control. Thus rain could be made to fall everywhere or anywhere at the discretion of the director. It could be made to rain outside one window and not the others. Wind and lightning were also under similar control thus permitting the actors, in the words of director Howard Bretherton "to play around like the witches in 'Macbeth'—in thunder, lightning and in rain."[3]

The effects and set also impressed S.R. Mook, who visited Warner Bros. in preparation for his "Studio News" article in the May 1934 issue of *Silver Screen* magazine. In at least one scene, he was also quite taken with the camerawork:

> Lyle [Talbot] is at his desk when George Cooper enters, crosses the floor and gives him a note: "Two gentlemen to see you, sir," he announces. "All right," says Lyle after glancing at the letter. "Cut," calls the director. I've never seen a camera mounted like this one before. It is on a very low truck—so low that the camera is only six inches off the floor. It is also on a universal joint, so it can be tipped back and pointed at the door through which Cooper enters. It is pulled back as he comes toward the desk so it keeps him in full view all the time and, when he is standing at the desk opposite Lyle, it is tilted further back so it takes in both of them. Instead of shooting directly at them as most shots are made, it is shooting up [at] them which will give them a distorted mysterious look—unless I miss my guess.

Despite the reviewer's wide-eyed impression of the cinematography, there's actually nothing at all distorted or mysterious about the camerawork for that particular scene in the finished film, nor was Howard Bretherton an innovator. Mook was also wrong in his hope that *Return* would be Lyle Talbot's "breakthrough film"; it was not to be. In spite of good wishes from the critic and from a number of movie magazines at the time, Talbot remained on the B-list as a Warners contract player before going independent in 1935. *Return of the Terror* received mostly good reviews, though a few critics poked some good-natured fun at the melodramatic proceedings. Typical was Philip K. Scheuer's write-up, which appeared under the headline "Terror Makes a Big Come-Back":

> As for the "Terror" himself, I didn't, as the old story goes, even know that he was sick, but now that he has seen fit to come back, I am willing to concede that he kicks up, in this brief reincarna-

*Return of the Terror.* **Lyle Talbot, years away from his encounters with Ed Wood and Ozzie Nelson, tries to calm Frank Reicher who plays a dope addicted doctor suffering from withdrawal. While horror fans remember Reicher for his character roles in films like *King Kong* and *The Mummy's Ghost*, he had a notable career directing and acting on Broadway and also helmed a score of silent films.**

tion, enough jitters for anybody. I don't propose to tell the story because I am not too certain of it myself. The action of that time-honored preposterous kind will not bear analysis before the self-evident fact that it is, per se, shriek inducing so far as the ladies of the audience are concerned—involved two murders and more scares than that. The characters—required merely, according to sex, either to scream or "take it big"—do both with necessary responsiveness.[4]

While Scheuer reviewed *Terror* as a horror film, critic Ward Marsh was glad it *wasn't* one:

> We seem slowly and surely headed back to the good old days when the intentions of the melodrama was to excite rather than terrify you.... I thought it unusually good entertainment for all—small children excepted—because director Howard Bretherton had all the ingredients for a shocker but elected to mystify the spectator and keep up suspense rather than belt him down with abnormal characters. He has, for an example, a half-dozen insane creatures and he might easily have used them to scare what is called the living daylights out of you. Instead he has for the most part used them for comedy effect to relieve the tense moments of his respectably honest melodrama.[5]

The June 30, 1934, *Harrison's Report* critique found "somewhat unpleasant" the antics of the mental cases that so amused Marsh, but gave the film high marks as a thriller:

> It is exciting and eerie and holds the spectator in suspense throughout.... Some of the situations will hold the spectator breathless.... The closing scenes will hold [one] in tense suspense. The identity of the murderer does not come as a surprise, since he was one of the people suspected; yet it is logically worked out. And for this reason holds one's attention.

The reviewer from the *New York Times* enjoyed the film, but wrote (in the newspaper's July 11, 1934, issue) that he did not think logic was its strong point:

> It happens that during its manufacture several loopholes were left in the theoretically solid structure of *The Return of the Terror* thereby providing the amateur Hawkshaws with the material for a good post-mortem. Why, for instance, did the killer enter the bedroom of Olga, the heroine, and why didn't Olga, who screamed when she saw his face, expose him to the police? And by the way how did he manage the lightning change which made it possible for him to appear innocently in the doorway about four seconds later?

We might take this a step further by mentioning that he (Lyle Talbot) was completely dry though having just been out in a deluge that would have sent Noah running to the Ark. In fairness—and it is *Virginia's* room he enters the second time, not Olga's—the killer is sufficiently in the dark that his face cannot be seen, although there really is no logical reason for him to be there in the first place. "The Grey Lady" might also have pointed out a "cheat" in an earlier scene, wherein the dialogue between Goodman and Reinhardt—meant no doubt to throw the audience off and establish Goodman as innocent—really doesn't make any sense, given that both men know what's really going on. The reviewer for *Motion Picture Daily* used his May 25, 1934, column to join in the praise for the film as a crowd pleaser that delivered the goods:

> Murder mystery hokum again that succeeded in keeping the audience on the edge of its seat throughout the preview, extracting some spontaneous screams here and there. From the box office point of view the film is a well produced screen version of the Edgar Wallace yarn ... Eugene Solow and Peter Milne retained all the Wallace suspense in the screenplay, aided by the capable direction of Howard Bretheron.

Only *Variety*'s "Shan" was a naysayer, calling the film "lukewarm" and "commonplace," with the ending "leaving the dialog to explain things unsatisfactorily." Still, he did devote a few lines of his July 17, 1934, opinion to commending the picture's fast pace, John Halliday's performance, and the fact that "the dialog is at least easily understandable."

Howard Bretherton has been called everything from a journeyman director to being barely competent, but no one would ever tag him for having an affinity with the horror genre. He was a respected film editor in the '20s, but then—perhaps illustrating the Peter Principle—Warners made him a director. Bretherton's best known films—*The Match King* and *Ladies They Talk About*—were both co-directed by William Keighley.

Warners may have wanted something more from Bretherton than just speed and efficiency, and the man may just not have been able to deliver. He left the studio in 1935 and settled comfortably into making B-Westerns and working on Poverty Row. In any event, the decision to downplay the horror in *Return of the Terror* was hardly likely his to make.

The constant rain and storms make for some spooky atmosphere, but when the action moves indoors, the eerie effect is dissipated; no low key lighting or shadows or *Cat and the Canary*–style sets. There *is* a slight Expressionist look to the long hallway of the lunatic asylum when Redmayne escapes (followed by an odd shot of just his feet in the basement, as though the director is—illogically—trying to conceal the doctor's identity), but, for the most part, Arthur L. Todd's photography is serviceable but nondescript. "Is there a secret passage where Dr. Redmayne might be hiding?" asks Inspector Bradley at one point. "Not as far as I know," Olga responds, much to the disappointment of horror fans yearning for just one creaky-but-enjoyable touch to push the film a little further into Grand Guignol territory.

Perhaps the most curious conceit of the story is the depiction of Redmayne as an advocate of mercy killing: a '30s Jack Kevorkian. In Hollywood films of that era, what was at first glance possibly euthanasia usually turned out to be either murder (*As the Devil Commands*) or suicide (*The Crime of Dr. Forbes*). Here, though, Redmayne indisputably admits that he gave a patient "a boost into the Great Beyond," and also subscribes to the Nazi-like belief that killing incurable mental patients is "humane." Had the film been released on or after the July 1, 1934, when Joe Breen and the Production Code would bare their teeth, a person possessed of such opinions could not have been shown in an heroic light. Nor would Reinhardt's addiction or his being described as a "hophead" have escaped the censorial scissors.

Today, the main joy of *Return of the Terror* lies in watching its great character actors doing what they do best: Was there ever a more crooked crooked lawyer than Irving Pichel? Or a more Irish Irish cop than Robert Emmett O'Connor? Or a slimier bad guy than J. Carroll Naish? Or a more likeable thief than George E. Stone (highlight: his attempt at ballet to convince Dr. Goodman that he belongs in a mental hospital)? And we have the lovely Mary Astor, the affable Lyle Talbot (He? The bad guy? Surely not!), a not unfunny Frank McHugh, and the reliable Frank Reicher, always better than his material. Nor can we ignore Robert Barrat; the *Los Angeles Times*'s comment about his performance as Walker is worth repeating: "Mr. Barrat's delineation of this shifty underwordling is considerably enlivened by the facility with which he manages to consume a dinner, presumably from soup to nuts, without once removing an unlighted cigarette from the corner of his mouth."[6]

Main acting honors of course belong to John Halliday—that suavest of screen villains—who has the difficult task of appearing crazy enough to be menacing, but not *so* looney that he'll turn out to be the murderer. At one point, a close-up of Halliday with a maniacal expression on his face gives one hope that he may repeat his mass-killer antics of *Terror Aboard* and murder the men who framed him. Unfortunately these notions are dashed all too soon when he gets knocked out in the basement, and it becomes obvious that something else is up. Of course, it doesn't make much sense for Dr. Goodman to dispose of Redmayne *before* Goodman commits the murders he hopes to frame the doctor for, but such lapses don't detract from the fun.

Nineteen thirty-eight saw a British version of *The Terror* that was faithful to Wallace's play. The latter film is readily available on video, but *Return*, after playing on television right up until 1965, has vanished from sight. Fans of vintage horror are intrigued by a poster from the film, printed in Dennis Gifford's *A Pictorial History of Horror Movies*, that depicts a fanged fiend in a slouch hat, looking just a bit like the Maniac from *Night of Terror*; sadly, no such character actually appears in the movie. For reasons that aren't entirely clear, the film has stubbornly refused to turn up on Turner Classic Movies or be issued on DVD. The possibility that the problem is due to rights's issues with the Edgar Wallace estate would be particularly ironic, since the film is not based on anything Wallace wrote, in spite of what is listed in the credits. For all that, a print in very good shape can be found in the Library of Congress.

# Death Takes a Holiday

Paramount Productions, Inc.—March 30, 1934—9 reels/78 minutes

**Cast**: Fredric March as Prince Sirki/Death; Evelyn Venable as Grazia; Sir Guy Standing as Duke Lambert; Katharine Alexander as Alda, la Contessa di Parma; Gail Patrick as Rhoda Fenton; Helen Westley as Stephanie; Kathleen Howard as Princess Maria; Kent Taylor as Corrado; Henry Travers as Baron Cesarea; G.P. Huntley, Jr., as Eric Bagley; Otto Hoffman as Fedele; Edward Van Sloan as Doctor Valle; Hector Sarno as Pietro; Frank Yaconelli as the Vendor; Anna De Linsky as the Maid

**Credit**s: *Producer*: E. Lloyd Sheldon; *Associate Producer*: Emanuel Cohen; *Director*: Mitchell Leisen; *Screenplay*: Maxwell Anderson and Gladys Lehman; *Photography*: Charles Lang; *Technical Effects*: Gordon Jennings; *Art Directors*: Hans Dreier and Ernst Fegté; *Costumes*: Travis Banton and Edith Head; *Recording Engineer*: Harold Lewis; *Based on the play* **La Morte in vacanza** *by* Alberto Casella (1924), *and the English-language adaptation by* Walter Ferris (New York, February 26, 1929).

From the very beginning of recorded history—and we'd venture an educated guess that even *before* somebody started keeping notes on his cave wall—mankind has anthropomorphized every force in nature he knew hadn't stemmed from his own actions. Loud, scary noises emanating from the sky while one was soaked to the (animal) skin? Someone came up with the notion that there was a god of thunder, and—millennia later—her descendent exploited same for a lucrative movie franchise. While not every member of the human society bought into everything—odds are the earliest of farmers were not terribly devoted to the goddess of the hunt—there were innumerable experiences that our ancestors had, no matter from whence they came or where they settled, that were common to existence and so may be found in all mythologies.

"Common," of course, did not necessarily mean "popular," so the universality of the quest to understand death in human terms has never been attributed to the warm and fuzzy side of life's ledger. When one's friend (or foe) ceased talking, eating, and *moving*; when she (or he) began to smell worse than usual, to attract more vermin than was his custom, to change color and texture (and not for the better) … this was a condition that one deplored and that one earnestly hoped was not to be found in one's own future. Even Gilgamesh—who was two-thirds a god—was hardpressed to understand at first what had happened to Enkidu, and it remained for generations of college students to debate just how dense the king of Uruk actually was.

It's obvious that mankind fairly quickly came to realize that said experience and the experient's subsequent appalling condition were what some wag would come to call "a foregone conclusion," so the quest for immortality became relegated to the stuff of legend. Ancient religions offered supernatural explanations laced with promise, and some that have survived teach that death is a reintroduction into the sphere of the gods, with different levels of said sphere available to mortals who, during life, displayed the requisite virtue, skill, or luck. With death itself never making anyone's bucket list, many faith systems have thus sought to "take the edge off" both the act of dying and the question of the essence of the afterlife so as to make this most feared and least understood of transitions less appalling—if still not terribly palatable—to their believers.

Paramount's early sound adaptation of an Italian stage play was the first film to give Death a voice ... and a soapbox.

> The picture opens amid a wildly festive celebration of something or another in an unidentified region of Italy. Everyone is joyous, flowers are ubiquitous, and among the crowd—laughing and playfully lobbing the last blooms of the season at each other—are Duke Lambert and his wife, Stephanie; their son, Corrado; Baron Cesarea; Princess Maria and her daughter, Grazia; Alda, the Contessa di Parma; Eric Bagley; and Rhoda Fenton, a young American woman. The duke and the others pile into two convertibles and make off for his sumptuous home, the Villa Felicità [the villa of happiness]. En route, both cars veer wildly because of the presence of a mysterious black shadow, and a flower vendor and his horsecart are struck by one of the cars. Thankfully, no one is hurt. "I marvel I'm still alive," Stephanie exclaims, while her husband agrees. "We all ought to be dead." They arrive safely at the villa, where the two young men pair off with their female counterparts.
>
> Eric and Alda are somewhat/somehow involved, but the contessa is "too restless" for marriage; "Besides," she tells him, "I've already had that once." Corrado, who is deeply in love with Grazia, finds that his ardor is not returned. Grazia cannot put her feelings into words; she loves the duke's son, but she is looking for "something out there that I must find first. Something that I must understand." She walks, alone, into the garden, and—moments later—her scream is heard. When she's carried into the house, she explains, "There was something cold and terrible.... Something touched me, something cold."
>
> Everyone prepares for bed, save for the duke, who decides to have a drink before retiring. As he sits down, into the room walks a featureless black figure, apparently hooded and cloaked. Frightened, the duke fires his pistol, only to find that the gun does not work. Perplexed, he can only look at the figure, who goes on at length before identifying himself:
>> Strange as it may seem, this is my natural appearance. I am not of your world. How shall I describe it? Sort of a vagabond of space. I am the point of contact between eternity and time. Do I make myself clear? ... You see, I am ... or I was, until I crossed your threshhold, Death. Please be reassured. I am not on my usual mission.
>
> I am wanting to take a holiday. I shall take only three days. After that I must go back. Why? To discover why men fear me as they do.... Will you accept me for these few days as a guest?
>
> The duke is speechless, and can only agree to present his guest as Prince Sirki, a royal of the duke's—but of no one else's—acquaintance, who has recently passed away. Death then puts forward conditions under which his visit would be "not a menace, but a protection": "No one under this roof will show repulsion or fear under pain of my instant displeasure." When the duke agrees, the hooded presence self-apostrophizes: "I, Death, hereby do take on the World, the Flesh, and the Devil!" As Death exits through the French doors, Corrado appears; *his* pistol works, but to no apparent effect. The servant, Fedele, is ordered to prepare the room in the villa's west wing, as the duke maintains that the figure at which Corrado had fired was a messenger of Prince Sirki, who will soon arrive as the duke's honored houseguest. Still, the duke's advice to his family and friends is not terribly reassuring:
>> You mustn't be afraid and, no matter what happens, you mustn't shun him or protest or run.... You can't run from things like that. You must all remain if you value your lives, or mine.
>
> These are ominous words to be heard in the Villa Felicità.
>
> Prince Sirki, festooned in military medals, regal of bearing, and—like the duke—boasting a monocle, arrives shortly thereafter. He is introduced to the assembled family and friends, and then—in a sublimely comic moment—quaffs his first glass of wine. "I have never tasted wine," the prince says, only to quickly qualify "... ummm ... of your country." The prince and Grazia exchange somewhat meaningful glances, after which Sirki et al. retire for the night.
>
> The following day finds the villa gardener surprised that the flora has stayed in the fullness of bloom. At breakfast, Baron Cesarea notes how a man who had jumped from the top of the Eiffel Tower "picked himself up, unhurt," and how a fierce battle on the Algerian front had surprisingly produced no fatalities. Sirki—who himself gapes wondrously at how a rose, affixed to his lapel by Grazia, does not wilt—takes the opportunity not only to grumble at man's propensity to wage war ["Your sacred privilege of blowing each other to bits is quite safe"], but also to bridle a bit when the baron refers to death as "The Old Man." He is likewise visibly annoyed when Grazia and others leave the villa, and is calmed only when the duke informs him that they were not regular houseguests, but had come to spend the night only after that black shadow had terrified Grazia.
>
> A montage of activity follows Sirki, Rhoda and Alda, who are variously occupied as a number of usually catastrophic incidents occur: a steamship explodes, a school is gutted by fire, a racing car overturns, jockeys are involved in an horrific spill—yet, miraculously, everyone involved survives. At a casino, Sirki keeps doubling his winnings, as roulette wheel stops at the number six time and again. "You make it necessary to take a great deal of this metal away with me," he observes, before giving it all away to Alda,

Rhoda, and a couple of lucky bystanders. Seeing this, Baron Cesarea asks him "What in the world are you looking for?" The prince replies, "I came here looking for a game to play. A game worth playing. I have been among you for two days. What you do with yourselves still seems so futile and empty." "There are only three games," the baron responds. "Money, love and war … [but] one never grows tired of love." Sirki agrees, but closes by saying, "[Love] seems to be the strangest, the saddest, the emptiest of all."

Rhoda, alone with Sirki, is annoyed to find that the prince is more interested in analyzing her personality than in pursuing her romantically. "If I'm not your type, then I'm just not your type," the American says, before walking out on the amused prince. Later that evening, during a soirée at the villa, attended by local nobility and religious and political leaders, Sirki and the contessa find themselves alone in the garden. Alda tells Sirki that she would give up her own soul, if she were in love, to which the prince replies, "I have come, asking for that … a mate." When Alda presses the issue, Sirki drops all pretense:

> You will take one step toward me and know my secret … and lose courage. You can give me a soul only if you know me and can still love me. Look into my eyes—look into those shadows—I will you to know who I am!

Rhoda sees the truth in Sirki's eyes and cries out for Eric, who—along with Corrado and other men—comes running. "Stay back, all of you!" Alda cries out. "How do you know if he'll strike?" When Corrado is on the verge of physically attacking him, Sirki asks, "Would you threaten the stars because you dislike your destiny?" Stephanie informs Corrado that Grazia has arrived and is looking for him. The young man leaves, and Sirki snarls:

> To die alone without loving or being loved…. That I will not have! There should be one death among you. You have years to live! Years! And I have what remains of this day.

The clock strikes 10:30.

In the garden Sirki comes upon Grazia. The two begin to dance, only to have Corrado cut in. He warns her of "a terrible danger," but when he leaves to fetch Grazia's cloak ["I feel a little cold"], Sirki drapes the young woman with a long, black cape that trails behind her on the ground. Sir Guy notices the prince and Grazia walk through the garden and, when Corrado and the other guests come onto the scene, reveals the prince's true identity: "He's the one who all men dread. He is Death. His Majesty, Death, amusing himself on a holiday and filling himself with love."

In another part of the garden, Sirki and Grazia come to terms with their feelings. "[You are] something that draws and frightens me," she says. "I am Sirki, who loves you more than any man could love you! I am a great power," he continues, "and I am humbled before you, and tonight I must go back to my distant kingdom!" "Will you take me with you?" she asks. "You are the meaning of beauty that I must know."

Moments later, Sirki crosses the garden, alone, to confront Sir Guy and the others. Corrado demands that Sirki give Grazia back to them. "One lover must always lose," the prince responds. "You have ten minutes more of life," Corrado says. "After that, what more can you give her?" "Sleep, perhaps," Sirki answers. "And the release of dreams. And beyond that—there are no words by which to tell you."

The mortals ask that Grazia be given the chance to choose for herself. Sirki brings her back into the scene, and—perhaps moved by the pleading of the people standing before him—suddenly reverses his own plea: "Grazia, listen! You must stay here with those who love you!" Midnight strikes, and the dapper prince is once again the black shadow.

> Goodbye, my friends. Remember, there is only a moment of shadow between your life and mine and when I call, come bravely through that shadow. You will find your familiar friend. Goodbye, Grazia. Now you see me as I am.

"But I've always seen you like that," Grazia cries out. "You haven't changed!" Everyone is stunned, including Death, who answers, "Then there is a love that casts out fear and I have found it! Love is greater than illusion! And as strong as death!"

They depart together, and the film ends.

*Death Takes a Holiday* is, in 2016, a delicate and intelligent—if somewhat dated—fantasy that remains miles ahead of the sundry big- and small-screen remakes and reworkings that have followed in its wake. The picture, which had disappeared for quite a while as completely as did March and Venable at its denouement, resurfaced as a "bonus" when Universal released on DVD the "ultimate version" of *Meet Joe Black* (1998), the studio's updated Americanization of the story and the best of that gaggle of doppelgangers and imitators. *Holiday* premiered in the midst of that period we now refer to as the "first classic horror cycle," not because it was a logical addition to the current roll call of ghoulies and ghosties and long-leggedy beasties, but because it had been a hit on The Great White Way only a few years earlier. Although certainly not a formulaic horror film, *Holiday* sought—in giving it a name and a human face—to assuage Death's reality and inevitability just as Universal's treatment of its soon-to-be iconic monsters posited rules and boundaries in which one could safely navigate a

"Hilde Warren and Death." Mia May as Hilde Warren and Georg John as You-Know-Who...

world populated by werewolves and vampires and such.

*La Morte in vacanza* proved to be the jewel in Italian playwright Alberto Casella's crown, and his drama's premiere in Florence in 1924 led to any number of translations and performances throughout Europe. In the fall of 1929, the play—adapted by writer Walter Ferris and retitled—opened in Washington, D.C., where it "was greeted with considerable ill-suppressed [sic] excitement."[1] Thence to Broadway where, within the space of two years, the play not only enjoyed a successful first run at the Ethel Barrymore Theatre, but also a purposefully limited-run revival a couple of blocks further uptown, at the Ambassador Theatre. India-born Brit Philip Merivale played the title character in both productions, with Rose (*Dr. Jekyll and Mr. Hyde*) Hobart his Grazia first time around, and Helen (*Transatlantic Tunnel*) Vinson falling for him the second.

Only a few weeks before Death and Grazia exited the Ambassador stage for the last time, a film publicized as "the strangest passion the world has ever known" opened at New York City's Roxy Theatre. Like *Death Takes a Holiday*, Tod Browning's *Dracula* was also based on a stage play that was written abroad in 1924 and that was subsequently adapted before settling comfortably onto Broadway a few years later. Junior Laemmle—scion of Laupheim-born Carl Laemmle, head of Universal Studios—had gambled that the tale of the desire that a deathless horror felt for the flower of feminine youth and beauty would resound with the public, and he had won, big time. Even if Mina Seward hadn't sauntered off on the arm of her aristocratic vampire as the end credits rolled, *Dracula* was the de facto cinematic sire of the many grotesques that swanned or stumbled or stalked in his wake. The medallion-wearing count who wasn't into wine had started a fashion.

Yet it was Paramount, and not Universal, that brought that ages-old mulling over the ultimate fate of all love—and of all men—onto the screen. For Paramount, Fredric March had given what is still regarded by many as the definitive portrait of humanity's struggle with good and evil with Rouben Mamoulian's production of *Dr. Jekyll and Mr. Hyde*, which had opened in New York on New Year's Eve, 1931, scarcely six weeks after Junior had doubled down with the release of *Frankenstein*. Intriguingly, the Hays Office—Hollywood's newly instituted board of censorship—had earlier "cautioned Paramount studio chief B.P. Schulberg against the line in which Ivy tells Hyde 'Take me!'" and Hyde's line, "'I'm going to take you,'" and the film was cleared to for reissue in 1935 only after "Paramount agreed to delete the ... line in which Jekyll tells Ivy he 'wants her.'"[2] Yet no such problems with censorship arose in 1934 when Death—having dropped his Prince Sirki charade—exchanged passionate declarations of love and desire with the young daughter of the

Italian princess. Either the sights and sounds of Death pledging his troth had even weirded out Joe Breen, or the chief censor's job had been made easier by the fact that Evelyn Venable's father had insisted contractually that Fredric March's lips would not touch those of his young daughter, no matter how purple the prose that passed through their lips onscreen.[3]

Because March's dual portrayals quickly took their place among that pantheon of "classic monsters," some felt his being tapped to play Death—with the purchase of Casella's play, now under contract to Paramount—was another of those foregone conclusions. But Death, in any of its guises, has never been viewed as a "monster." While dreaded as the ultimate horror, Death has pretty much always been presented as being, among other things, the *end result* of confrontations with "monsters"; to avoid them was to avoid it—at least for the nonce—but no myth or book or film so structured had ever dared suggest that, in reality, death had merely been postponed until that particular, individual life had run its course.

When yclept the "Grim Reaper," Death has traditionally been depicted as being a hooded skeleton, the cloaked framework on which all of fleshly humanity hangs, and bits of pieces of same—like the skull and crossbones associated with pirates, or the skull printed on boxes or bottles of toxic substances—are warnings about death's proximity. Other than utilizing this type of skeletal imagery, the silent-cinema pioneers—apart from the Germans, of course[4]—steered pretty clear of personifying Death. The 1912 Oscar Messter production, *Der Schatten des Meeres* (*The Shadow of the Sea*), had a shadowy figure emerge from the deep to convince Henny Porten that suicide was the answer to all her problems. Joe May's *Hilde Warren und der Tod* (*Hilde Warren and*

**Prince Sirki has just arrived. Duke Lambert (Sir Guy Standing) is positively knickered over this, but faithful manservant, Fedele (Otto Hoffman), is unfazed.**

Grazia (Evelyn Venable) announces that she is in love with Prince Sirki, even though she is aware of his real identity.

Death, 1917) provided a rather mournful looking "gentleman"—veteran stage actor, Georg John, making his feature-film debut—to represent Himself in a film that has been described more than once as the "Ür-Rosemary's Baby." In 1919's *Die Pest in Florenz* (*The Plague of Florence*), Fritz Lang's screenplay (the picture was directed by Otto Rippert) was an adaptation of Poe's "The Masque of the Red Death," so we can only assume that the black and white film stock muted that particular color. And the title character in Lang's *Der müde Tod* (*The Weary Death*, 1921; Lang directed and co-wrote the screenplay with Thea [*Metropolis*] von Harbou) was, again, a rather nondescript older chap clad in black.

Death first appears to Duke Lambert in his "natural state"—semi-transparent, amorphous, and, of course—Poe, apart—black. Not being human, Death can have no human form; how he is represented to humankind differs according to countries and cultures. In the Western world, black—*not* a color, per physicists, but the absence of visible light—is the color of mourning, of fear, of blindness, of loss, of evil ... of death.[5] With the setting of the sun, our European ancestors could no longer discern what the world would set in their path; the blackness of the night hid a multitude of ills. Grazia only sees that "strangest shadow" that is following them—just before they collide with the flower vendor and his horsecart—because that darkness is in stark contrast to the light of day. Whereas in ancient times death's approach seemed more probable after the sun had set and darkness had overtaken the world, Grazia—and modern man—must come to realize that its presence is no less likely even when one is in the midst of a multitude in broad daylight.

*This* Death—Casella's, Anderson's, Lehman's, March's—seems to be *The* Death, a unique entity, for as he relaxes in and around the Villa Felicità, there is, apparently, none

From the artwork, one might think this was yet another tale of three beautiful women befuddling the juvenile lead.

other of his kind whose task it is to make humans aware of what mortality means. Considering the world's birth rate and ever-growing population, Death's messing about for several minutes as a black cloud on an Italian country road betokens a real falling down on the job. How *does* he manage to collect the victims of an auto accident in Brooklyn when, at the precise same millisecond, a couple of erstwhile mountain climbers have just discovered the base of Mount Everest the hard way, an infant has suffocated in Tokyo, food poisoning has done its worst in St. Petersburg, a matador has made a wrong move in the corrida on Mallorca, etc., etc.? The "hows" matter not; Death is ubiquitous.

What's more, *this* Death, the one looking for a few days off the job, is a different representation than the figure usually proffered by myth or religion; he seems totally unaffiliated with "whatever gods there may be." He gives no inkling that there might be eternal paradise or punishment; indeed, he speaks only of how there are no words to describe the realm in which he—and, presumably, those whom he encounters while working—exists. He also speaks of his loneliness and his inability to understand why men fear him so. Unlike the comforting words Brad Pitt shares with Anthony Hopkins during their last moments together in *Meet Joe Black*, Fredric March doesn't offer any hope for a benign verdict at an individual's Judgment Day; no such scene is ever mentioned. March's Death is an autonomous authority, and—per his opening speech to Sir Guy Standing—is bound by no rule, is constricted by no one and nothing, and may bring about the abrupt and unexpected end of anyone at anytime while in a fit of pique. Despite declaring that he *must* be back on task at the end of his three days off, the Death who takes a holiday apparently has no boss watching the clock or the calendar. Or, at least, no boss about whom he makes his "human friends" aware.

If this Death offers no view of an idyllic afterlife, thinks to mention no deities, is checked by no higher authority, can assume whatever form he chooses, and be everywhere at once, is *he* God? Or, because he has no role in the birth or creation of anything, is he *one* of the gods?

Naturally, addressing questions such as these is not the intention of this film—or the play, itself, or any of the other takes on this theme. The intent is that the audience enjoy the wry humor found in Death's discomfiture while posturing among humans, like the moment when Sirki smirks as Baron Cesarea reads of miraculous endings to what should be indubitable tragedies in Paris and on the Algerian front. The comment "If the 'Old Man' were so neglectful, there would be a serious overcrowding" touches on the ubiquity of death while giving one momentary pause for thought on death's *necessity*.

The setting for most of the film is Duke Lambert's Villa Felicità, a mansion up there in size and sprawl with the U.S. Capitol. Inasmuch as Death must come to all, it only makes sense that he would opt to vacation with Italy's "One Percent"—in the company of nobles and royals—rather than sit on his haunches in some peasant's hut, looking for an eternal soulmate while musing over the unfairness of life and the dreadful economy. And even within that upper echelon of Western society, those who opt to partner ceremoniously in love and knowledge and support make passionate vows with an expiration date: "until death do us part." The irony lies in that Death is looking for a depth of devotion from a species that cannot conceive of relationships that last beyond one's last breath, and this is why a good handful of the more perceptive critics felt that the picture had been targeted, not at your average audience, but rather at the "intelligentsia."

Moving from the message to the medium, we opine that Mitchell Leisen, in 1934 still fairly new to the megaphone and jodhpurs, did a wonderful job in incorporating humor, dread, philosophical argument, and dramatic resignation into the production. It may well be that the participation of many of the cast members from his first directorial effort, 1933's *Cradle Song*—Evelyn Vanable, Sir Guy Standing, Kent Taylor, Gail Patrick—established something of a comfort zone for him. Nonetheless, Leisen—a Michigander who would go on to demonstrate he could also function as a producer, art director, costume designer, and if, absolutely necessary, an actor—always viewed this, his second major motion picture, with joy and gratitude. One of the chief complaints about the film—the didactic nature of much of Sirki's dialogue—is traceable directly to Maxwell Anderson and Gladys Lehman's adaptation of Ferris's translation of Casella's original, which was obviously intended to be delivered in stagespeak, under the proscenium arch. Leisen did what he could with scenes wherein Sirki's every line was either meant to be a *bon mot* or a double entendre, and both lengthy expository passages—the most necessary of evils if one is to understand whence comes and whither goes this enshrouded phantom—*are* addressed directly to onscreen audiences whose lives may depend on their absorbing respectfully every word.

Anderson and Lehman's screenplay kept the venue and character names from *La Morte in vacanza*, thus affording the story a slightly exotic, "foreign" setting for audiences throughout the New World. The tack taken in establishing background for fables and fairy tales, "Once upon a time, far, far away..." allows the comfortable mingling of relatable events and experiences with unfamiliar climes. Albeit set in Italy, the picture mostly spares us the usual early-talkie custom of having the characters read their lines in a faux Italian accent; other than Frank Yaconelli as the vendor nearly killed on the

**Fredric March as Death at his handsomest, most menacing, and least enshrouded...**

country road, the cast members all speak with the natural tones of American or British thespians. March, of course, affects an unusual vocal lilt when onscreen as Sirki; we can only assume that, while becoming acclimated to the late prince's husk, Death is likewise utilizing whatever inflections came naturally to a royal native of Vitalba Alexandri speaking English as a second language.

While there is no art director credit onscreen, there is little doubt that German emigrés Ernst Fegté and Hans Dreier picked up on Leisen's vision. Dreier retired with well over 500 movies in which he *did* receive credit for his creative eye, and a good handful of those were silent Richard Oswaldfilme (*Nachtgestalten, Die Liebschaften des Hektor Dalmore, Kurfürstendamm*) that starred Conrad Veidt. The Hamburg-born Fegté had but a fraction of Dreier's credits, but this still saw him with nearly a hundred titles representing virtually every cinematic genre, including—for us folks—the lighthearted fantasy *I Married a Witch* (1942); the definitely *not* lighthearted supernatural thriller *The Uninvited* (1944); and *Superman and the Mole Men* (1951), which, if nothing else, showed that the Big Guy had his super heart in the right place.

With the Villa Felicità a breathtaking example of the money making it onto the screen, it did cause a bit of a dust-up at the studio:

> Friction developed on the Paramount lot between Josef von Sternberg and Mitchel Leisen over the site of their respective directorial efforts, *Catherine the Great*[6] and *Death Takes a Holiday*. Mr. von Sternberg, for whose picture the most unusual sets have been erected and which have been described as "the product of a mad mind—my mind," charged that Mr. Leisen had infringed upon his artwork in a Florentine palace and the Louvre in which much of the action of *Death Takes a Holiday* is laid.[7]

Actually, von Sternberg's grousing had nothing to do with either the palace which doubled for the Villa Felicità or the Louvre, itself; rather, the short-tempered director felt that the *Holiday* company had appropriated statuary on loan from the renowned Paris gallery that had been intended for the palace set of *Catherine the Great*. With neither Dreier nor Fegté receiving onscreen credit for *Holiday*, the wrath of von Sternberg went awry, and Leisen, taking the heat for his art directors, avoided further hostility by arranging for duplicates of *other* Louvre masterpieces to be sent to the Villa Felicità. Leisen's shrewd accommodation calmed the cranky von Sternberg, thus sparing Paramount further delays and budgetary concerns.

Charles Lang's camera work is quite good, if unremarkable, but the veteran cinematographer seamlessly incorporates the special effects required by the film into the mix without making them seem "special"—and therefore artificial. (No mean feat when you're dealing with Death in his non-human guise.) At the outset, when Death—in his "true" state—confronts Duke Lambert to deliver the necessary exposition, Lang was required to photograph March as the black, featureless figure we mentioned above. Piece of cake, except for a sudden bump in the road: Leisen wanted Death to be transparent, and wanted the effect done in the camera, rather than added in later by the effects department. Lang conferred with the crew and then

> duplicating certain pieces of the set in black velvet, they placed a mirror in front of March that was only 30 percent silvered so that the crew could shoot through it. Then they lit up certain portions of the black set, which reflected in the mirror superimposed over Fred, giving the appearance that he was transparent.[8]

The process was repeated on the garden steps at the picture's climax, and Lang—who would go on to photograph such genre gems as *Peter Ibbetson* (1935), *The Cat and the Canary* (1939), *The Ghost Breakers* (1940), and the aforementioned *The Uninvited* (as well as over a hundred other features) for Paramount—earned his genre stripes. (Several other effects in the picture—which, for a film with a supernatural theme, has surprisingly few—were not so well done. The exploding steamship is an obvious miniature, as are the cars in long-shot on the mountain road, and the rear projection with same—the scenes featuring the black shadow—is second rate.)

Cast-wise, Leisen and the studio made great use of the Paramount roster of contractual players. Purely from a genre point of view, Sir Guy Standing would add his formidable presence to the studio's *The Witching Hour* and *Double Door* before the year was out. Evelyn Venable, also in *Double Door*, went on to provide the voice of the Blue Fairy in Disney's 1939 masterpiece, *Pinocchio*. Late in '34, G.P. Huntley, Jr.—"Bruce" to his friends—signed up at Universal to appear with Claude Rains in *The Man Who Reclaimed His Head*, and, within a few years, the Boston-born actor would cross paths with both Charlie Chan (*at the Racetrack*, 1936), and Mr. Moto (who took a vacation of his own in 1939). Gail Patrick had done *Murders in the Zoo* the year before *Holiday* and would make an uncredited appearance in RKO's sound remake of *The Hunchback of Notre Dame* (1939), but her most enduring role was that of executive producer of TV's phenomenally successful dramatic series, *Perry Mason*, which lasted 271 episodes over the course of 10 seasons. Kent Taylor—TV's Boston Blackie, himself—was born Louis Weiss in Iowa in 1907 and did a hundred and a half turns before the camera before retiring in 1974. *Also* in Paramount's *Double Door*, Taylor was a fairly regular genre presence for a good part of his career, with *House of Horrors* (1946), *The Phantom from 10,000 Leagues* (1955), *The Day Mars Invaded Earth* (1962), and *The Crawling Hand* (1963) among his credits.

Tucked in the mix there is Edward Van Sloan as Dr. Valle. Surely we needn't remind you of Dr. Waldman, Professor Van Helsing, or Dr. Muller, do we?

Fredric March—like so many of his contemporaries—had quickly worked his way up from extra to secondary cast member to leading man, but had he acceded to playing even one more titular horror for Paramount, he might have morphed into that studio's Boris Karloff. As it was, he had already made the move from playing John Barrymore (or Tony Cavendish, as he was called in 1930's *The Royal Family of Broadway*) to playing one (two, actually) of Barrymore's more memorable screen roles when he donned the cloaks of *Dr. Jekyll and Mr. Hyde* in 1932. March would not visit the genre again, apart from the aforementioned 1942 fantasy-comedy, *I Married a Witch*; nor would he miss it, as he had a film (and stage) career that itself seemed as wildly unlikely as Death cracking wise as the breakfast table.

Such mega-titles as *The Barretts of*

**Grazia (Evelyn Venable) and Prince Sirki (Fredric March) about to have the chat to end all chats.**

*Wimpole Street, Les Misérables, Anna Karenina, The Dark Angel,* and *Anthony Adverse* starred the handsome Wisconsin-born actor, and all within two years of *Death Takes a Holiday*. Again, like so many of his contemporaries, March moved from leading man to character actor as he grew older, but among the "characters" he brought to the screen were Samuel Langhorne Clemens (in *The Adventures of Mark Twain*, 1944), Christopher Columbus (in the eponymous 1949 feature), Willy Loman (in *Death of a Salesman*, 1951), and Matthew Harrison Brady (in 1960's *Inherit the Wind*). March won his second best-actor Oscar for his role as Al Stephenson in *The Best Years of Our Lives* (1946), with his first having been presented to him *and* to Wallace Beery—the voting was a virtual tie—in 1932 for *Dr. Jekyll and Mr. Hyde*. March also won Tony Awards as Best Actor twice: in 1947, for his role as Clinton Jones in Ruth Gordon's *Years Ago*, and in 1957 for his James Tyrone in Eugene O'Neill's *Long Day's Journey into Night*. To date, he remains the only actor to have done Best-Actor double-dipping onstage and onscreen.

When expostulating to Duke Lambert early in the film, March as Death-in-his-true-form is saddled with what is, objectively, stilted and overly formal dialogue. Given that this is the Grim Reaper's first vacation ever, we assume this is also his first stab at sharing his thoughts with anybody, so the entity who at the denouement will address his frightened and befuddled listeners as "my friends" needs take quite a while to get to that point from his initial introduction and his setting of the rules. For most of his turn as Sirki, March is priceless, hitting the mark with just the right balance of awkwardness, amusement and impatience; his observations and give-and-take at the breakfast and roulette tables are especially amusing. Sirki's lack of interest in Rhoda is expressed in a lighthearted fashion, with the prince almost bewildered at the young American woman's reaction to his "analysis." He turns ominous and threatening when dealing with Alda's declarations, though, as if he knows the love he is seeking will not involve this particular woman. Inasmuch as the assemblage who view him as he really is does not react with the degree of horror that Alda displays when looking deeply into Sirki's eyes, we are left to decide whether the Contessa di Parma was treated to an especially appalling vision due to Death's disinterest in her, romantically, or whether the *idea* of death is in itself so much more terrible than its actual appearance.

*Death Takes a Holiday* was well received, although a good many of the critics felt, as did *Variety*'s, that it was "the kind of story and picture that beckons the thinker."[9] Mordaunt Hall, writing (following the film's abbreviated preview run) in the March 4, 1934, edition of the *New York Times*, agreed with his colleague:

> From the reception the picture received at two performances, it is a good one.... Cinema-goers are taking an interest in a really intelligent fantasy.... To say that it is one of the most engrossing pictures of any year is but giving the film its due, for it has been directed with the necessary imaginative touch by Mitchell Leisen.... Then, too, Maxwell Anderson's fine hand is perceptible in the adaptation.

In addition to its leading to deep discussions over coffee or strong spirits, the film also led to a plagiarism suit. In May 1931, Oscar B. Wiren filed suit against the Shubert Theatre Organization et al. (including Alberto Cassella), alleging that the play *Death Takes a Holiday* (then being performed at the Ethel Barrymore Theatre) had been plagiarized "in substance" from the play *Most* by Myra Page Wiren, who had seen to it that her work had been performed and copyrighted back in 1910. The suit worked its way up to the Supreme Court by 1954, at which point it was dismissed.

While the wheels of justice were slowly turning, Death took a number of holidays in various media. March himself reenacted the role—with his wife, Florence Eldridge as Grazia—on *Cecil B. DeMille's Lux Radio Theatre* on March 22, 1937, and then headed to the stage, black cloak and all, for a limited run at Baltimore City College in May of 1938.

In 1950, the Latin-flavored drama was reworked for Latin audiences, albeit for Mexicans, and not Italians. Under the direction of Ernesto Cortázar, *La muerte enamorada* (*Death in Love*), dealt with what might be called "essence" of *Death Takes a Holiday*. A quick précis:

> Fernando is confronted by the beautiful Tasia who says she is Death, come to claim him. The distraught man asks for a few days to straighten out his life so his wife and young daughter won't be left penniless. Tasia agrees, but stays on Earth with him, since she hasn't had a vacation for thousands of years. Tasia is introduced as Fernando's "cousin from Greece" to his jealous wife Minerva, her shiftless brother Jorge, and their daughter, Lulú. Jorge is immediately smitten with Tasia, who uses her magic powers to obtain money for him and enjoys an evening in a nightclub. Lulú is pronounced gravely ill, but Tasia grants her a "pardon" and the girl recovers. The sight of Minerva embracing her child is too much for Tasia, who has fallen in love with Fernando—she tells him he is also pardoned. As Tasia prepares to leave, Jorge insists he wants to go with her. Tasia agrees, they kiss, and Jorge drops dead! As the film ends, Tasia enters heaven with an angelic Jorge.[10]

Any number of adaptations and variations followed, with perhaps the most intriguing being the "Kraft Television Theatre" abridgement that starred Joseph (*Dr. No*) Wiseman as Death/Sirki; the hour-long presentation aired on December 30, 1954. In 1971, Universal television produced its own take on the tale, with Monte Markham and Yvette Mimieux as the ... errrr ... star-crossed lovers. In addition to these (and other small-screen efforts), *Death Takes a Holiday* ventured onto the off–Broadway stage—as a musical!—in late July 2011. Despite nearly a dozen nominations for Drama Desk Awards, the play came away empty-handed; Prince Sirki, of course, left the stage with Grazia on his arm.

With its working title being *Strange Holiday*, the picture actually premiered in the Fresno and Sacramento (California) markets under that name. It was quickly discovered that if "Death" took the holiday, more folks would pay to see what was up, so *Strange Holiday* was mothballed, only to be used again for a quite peculiar film Claude Rains made with Arch Oboler in 1946.

Given its subject matter, *Death Takes a Holiday* might very well have been much more *in your face*—one can only imagine what a Millennium-Era remake would end up looking like—than in your thoughts, especially with the sundry monsters then onscreen at neighboring theaters everywhere. Logical points are scored with respect to overcrowding should the "Old Man" be negligent, and even if it would take the rare viewer to admit to feeling sympathy for Death's plight, rarer still would be the person who would not admit to having his/her mind opened a bit further.

Five years after March and company put a human face to humanity's greatest fear, Sir Cedric Hardwicke and Lionel Barrymore worked along the same lines in M-G-M's *On Borrowed Time*. On the eve of the Second World War, it seemed only natural that Death should once again be shown to have a human dimension.

# Hispanic Horrors

*El misterio del rostro pálido* (*The Mystery of the Ghastly Face*)—Producciones Alcayde—October 5, 1935 (Mexico); January 3, 1937 (U.S.)—90 minutes
**Cast**: Beatriz Ramos as Angélica; Joaquín Busquets as Pablo; Carlos Villarías as Dr. Galdino Forti; Miguel Arenas as Julio Montes; René Cardona as Luis; Natalia Ortiz as Engracia; Abraham Galán as Crescencio; Manuel Noriega as Justo; José Cortés as the Old Indian; Carlos Aganza as the Young Indian
**Credits**: *Director*: Juan Bustillo Oro; *Producers*: José Alcayde and Alberto Monroy; *Story and adaptation*: Juan Bustillo Oro; *Photography*: Agustín Jiménez; *Camera Operator*: José Gutiérrez Zamora; *Art Director*: Carlos Toussaint; *Editor*: Juan Bustillo Oro; *Sound*: Carlos Flores Gómez and Rafael Ruiz Esparza; *Costumes*: Germán Cueto; *Make-up*: Dolores Camarillo; *Music*: Federico Ruiz; *Assistant Director*: Antonio Guerrero Tello

*El baúl macabro* (*The Macabre Trunk*)—Producciones Pezet—February 26, 1936—(Mexico); November 29, 1937 (U.S.)—79 minutes
**Cast**: Ramón Pereda as Dr. Maximiliano Renán; René Cardona as Dr. Armando del Valle; Manuel Noriega as Dr. Monroy; Esther Fernández as Alicia Monroy; Ruperto Bátiz as Police Chief González; Carlos López "Chaflán" as Agent Méndez; Juanita Castro as Virginia; Juan García as Agent Gabilondo; Enrique Gonce as Mozabú; Victorio Blanco as the Beggar; Alejandro Galindo as the Journalist; with Luis Ladrón de Guevara
**Credits**: *Director*: Miguel Zacarías; *Producer*: Juan Pezet; *Story*: Jorge M. Dada; *Adaptation*: Alejandro Galindo; *Photography*: Alex Phillips; *Editors*: Miguel Zacarías and José Marino; *Art Director*: Jorge Fernández; *Sound*: B.J. Kroger; *Music and Songs*: Jorge M. Dada; *Arrangements*: Armando Rosales

*Una luz en la ventana* (*A Light in the Window*)—Producciones Lumiton—12—May 1942 (Argentina)—72 minutes
**Cast**: Narciso Ibáñez Menta as Dr. Hermán; Irma Córdoba as Angélica; Juan Carlos Thorry as Mario; Severo Fernández as Juan; Nicolás Fregues as Dr. Roberts; María Esther Buschiazzo as Mrs. Hermán; Pedro Pompillo as the Mute; Aníbal Segovia as the Watchman; Gerardo Rodríguez as the Police Official; Fernando Campos as the Police Sergeant
**Credits**: *Director*: Manuel Romero; *Story and Screenplay*: Manuel Romero; *Photography*: Alfredo Traverso; *Camera Operator*: Pedro Marzialetti; *Editor*: Antonio Rampoldi; *Production Design*: Ricardo J. Conord, Francisco Guglielmino; *Set Construction*: F. Guglielmino; *Sound*: Juan M. Sanchez, Ángel Zavalia; *Make-up*: Berta Gilbert, César De Combi (uncredited), Narciso Ibáñez Menta; *Hair Stylist*: Juan Magarola; *Music*: George Andreani

Back to the sixties, the decade that hosted a veritable cornucopia of violence, fury, and hatred. Few people look back on those years with anything other than disbelief and/or regret; however, to some, being a "child of the '60s" may trigger fewer true recollections than vague feelings of *sort of* remembering. *Very* intriguing decade, that one…

For genre fans of our vintage, the decade provided an inordinate amount of movie escapism: leading the pack were the last few years of Hammer exceptionalism, the majority of William Castle's epics, and AIP's Price/

Poe classics. In evidence, too, were non–British foreign imports that ranged from the sublime (Roger Vadim's *Et mourir de plaisir* [*Blood and Roses*] from France and Mario Bava's *La maschera del demonio* [*Black Sunday*] from Italy) to the ridiculous (Jesús Franco's *Gritos en la noche* [*The Awful Dr. Orloff*] from Spain and *The Mask* [aka *The Eyes of Hell*] from our neighbor to the North).

Also on display during the '60s, both in theaters and on television, was a fascinating array of Spanish-language knock-offs of Universal's stable of classic monsters from Mexico. Titles like *El mundo de los vampiros* (*World of the Vampires*), *Frankenstein, el vampiro, y cía.* (an unofficial remake of *Abbott and Costello Meet Frankenstein*, "cía" being an abbreviation for "company" and not, per early FJA, the name of a thitherto unknown grotesque), and *La invasión de los vampiros*—the Mexican market was big on vampires back then—were in select theaters at the beginning of the decade, and Azteca Films distributed similar horrors from South of the Border to local TV stations a couple of years later. Mixed among the vampire flicks were intriguing curiosities like Abel Salazar's *El barón del terror* (*The Brainiac*—a brains-eating monstrosity the likes of which had not been seen to that point), the sundry bouts of *Las Luchadoras*—the "Wrestling Woman"—with robot assassins, mummies, and the like, and the more traditional, classic-horror "tributes" from Spain—like 1967's *La marca del hombre lobo* (*The Mark of the Wolfman*, released in the U.S. as *Frankenstein's Bloody Terror!*)—usually starring former boxer/weightlifter, Jacinto Molina, aka Paul Naschy.

It would be a mistake, though, to think that the Spanish and Hispanic genre productions of the late '50s—early '70s owed their debt only to Uncle Carl's bailiwick. The spirit—if not the embodiment—of many of these later horrors could also be found in pictures produced in Mexico, Argentina, and elsewhere in the Spanish-speaking world during the '30s and early '40s. We've chosen several of that period's representative thrillers—all oriented toward nefarious scientific experimentation—to illustrate our argument.

• Juan Bustillo Oro's ***El misterio del rostro pálido*** (***The Mystery of the Ghastly Face***) is an intriguing (and fairly engaging) blend of essence of *The Phantom of the Opera* and Bela Lugosi's DNA from his '40s Gower Gulch features.

**Part One: *Dr. Forti's Expedition***—Dr. Forti and his son Pablo perform bizarre and mysterious experiments in their wildly Art Deco mansion-cum-laboratory, and the film opens with the burial of one of the subjects of their perennially less than successful endeavors to cure leprosy. Although a young man, Pablo appears to have prematurely aged, and we learn that his passions include the violin and Angélica, his fiancée, who lives in the Forti mansion along with her aunt, Engracia. In their midst appear Julio Montes, an old acquaintance of Dr. Forti's, and his son Luis, a friend of Pablo and Angélica's. Dr. Forti hands over his last will and testament to Montes, and instructs him to act on them if he and his son do not return within five years and if nothing further is heard from them. The doctor and Pablo are then off to *El lago negro* [The Black Lake], a remote area of the jungle to further their research. Before he departs, Pablo and his lady share a last musical moment together—he on the violin, she at the piano—as they play their favorite ballad.

In the next scene, Forti and Pablo seek an Indian guide to take them to *La tierra de los rostros pálidos*—The Land of the Pallid Faces. One young fellow agrees to ride off with them, but he

The Ghastly Face—El Rostro Pálido, himself. Pablo (Joaquín Busquets) glares balefully at Engracia (and the audience).

bails a bit later after seeing a skeleton hanging from a tree. Soon we watch natives—some of whom are wearing *very* oversized masks and/or headdresses—dance about a fire to the accompaniment of the beat gotten by drumming on human skulls.

**Part Two: *The Ghost of the Forti Villa*—**Back at the Fortis's ultramodernistic digs—eight years later—the glass walls are pocked with holes, the furniture is covered with sheets, and there is debris lying about. Angélica has become engaged to Luis, and she and her Aunt Engracia prepare for the wedding. While abed, Angélica hears Pablo's ballad being played on a violin, and the following morning, she makes her way to the Forti manse where she is told, by Crescencio, a new [and menacing] servant, that Dr. Forti has returned, alone.

Soon thereafter Forti informs the women that Pablo has died and that he—Dr. Forti—views Angélica as if she were his daughter. He invites Angélica and her aunt to return to live at his house; the young woman agrees, but her aunt is not thrilled with the idea. Troubled by the recent violin music, Angélica is persuaded by Forti to drink something that will calm her; in reality, it is a mixture that the doctor hopes will sap her of her will. When asked to play the familiar ballad on the piano, Angélica complies, only to almost immediately hear the violin part, played, presumably, from beyond the grave. We see the silhouette of the violinist, while Forti commands the young woman to "be strong." Later, while in bed, Angélica sees a masked and hooded figure peer in at her from a window mounted high in her room. In the words of director/scenarist Juan Bustillo Oro:

> Un rostro extraño se asoma à la ventana por fuera. Es visión de unos segundos, más reafirma los remordimientos de Angélica. Tiene las facciones de Pablo. O más bien las del cadaver de Pablo. En ese rostro, que muestra fugazmente lo inexpresivo y la palidez de la muerte, nada más los ojos parecen vivir.[1]

[A strange face peers in from outside the window. The grotesque sight, in a few seconds, deepens Angelica's remorse. It has Pablo's facial features. Or, rather, those of Pablo's corpse. On that face, which fleetingly displays the stillness and palor of death, nothing but the eyes appear alive.]

Forti's manservant, Justo, hearing violin music, wanders into the forbidden area of the house and opens the door to a room wherein a masked and caped man is moaning to himself while standing forlornly before a mirror. Justo tells all this to Engracia, who tells this to Mr. Montes, who, later that night, flashlight in hand, searches Forti's office. He finds a book containing Forti's observations on the people of the Black Lake. In the interim, Engracia has been ambushed by Crescencio and the woman, lying in the hallway [*Yo muero*—I'm dying], expires in Montes's arms. Returning to Forti's office, Montes finds the book on the Black Lake people missing. Hearing violin music, he takes a revolver from his back pocket, espies the caped violinist, follows him through yet another door, and ... we hear groans, not shots. Moments later, Montes stumbles into Justo's room, mumbles *El rostro pálido*, and then dies in the servant's arms.[2]

Justo is tied up and locked in *his* room. Onto his bed. Forti offers Angélica yet another quaff of his potion, but she empties her snifter into a nearby vase when the doctor's back is turned. At midnight, he tells her, she will marry Pablo! She dons a wedding dress laid out by Crescencio and, at midnight, the caped and masked figure enters her room. Angélica screams, faints, and is hefted up and out by the phantom figure, who takes her deeper into the warren-like house. Meanwhile, Luis has let himself in, having earlier been given a key by Justo. He unties Justo, but the men are surprised by Crescencio and Forti. Luis decks the gun-wielding Crescencio and then—spurred on by Justo—runs out to find Angélica.

Angélica, having regained consciousness, rips the mask from the hooded figure, exposing a pale and somewhat bloodied Pablo, a victim of leprosy

**A study in black and white: Pablo (Joaquín Busquets) confronts Angélica (Beatriz Ramos), who was forced into donning that wedding dress.** *El misterio del rostro pálido.*

made worse while helping his father near El Lago Negro. After they talk a bit, Pablo gets physical and demands to be kissed. As they struggle, in another room Forti and Justo shoot each other. Mortally wounded, the doctor walks some distance into the room where Luis now holds his fiancée protectively. Forti, before dying in Pablo's arms, apologizes for his sundry experiments, murders, and acts of madness. Pablo, retrieving his mask and cape, also apologizes and then rushes out. Luis asks him ¿Adónde va? [Where are you going?] and the tragic figure answers "To the Land of the Dead." Luis and Angélica following the remasked and once again caped figure to the top of a hill and watch as he hurls himself to his death.

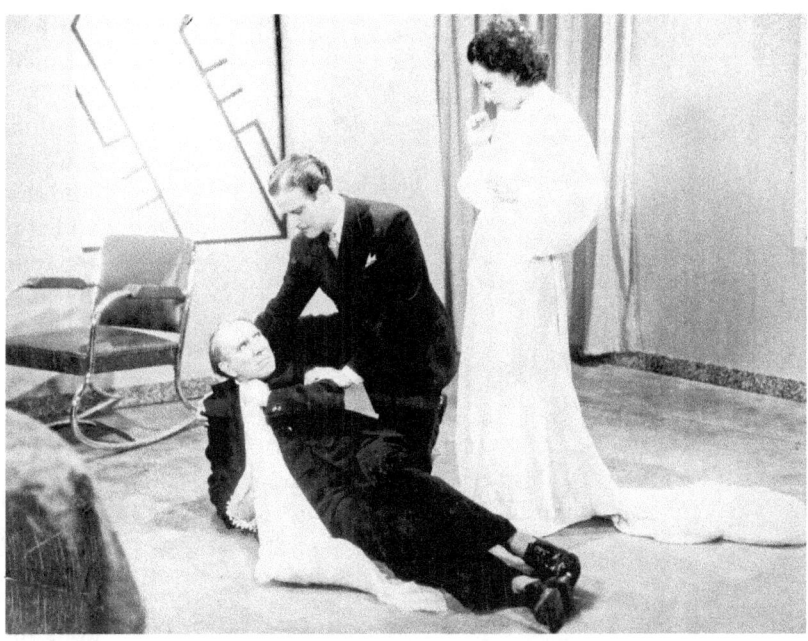

**Dr. Forti (Carlos Villarías) glares daggers at Luis (René Cardona), as Angélica (Beatriz Ramos) wonders where she's seen that veil before.**

The picture ends on a stark close-up of Pablo's masked face.

The very few English-language critical commentaries that we could find on this film translate *pálido* as "ghastly," and we'll go with that; as the Spanish word's first meaning is "pale," rendering the title literally leads to some political incorrectness. The unmasking scene—done as a given, almost in a heartbeat—reveals Pablo to be quite wan indeed, with some mottled blood on his jaw and his nose somewhat wider than before and quite flat. Unsettling, perhaps, but hardly ghastly. The question as to why he is traipsing about in hooded tights and a floor-length cloak is never asked or answered, but how else is a phantom to dress, anyhow? (In the picture's opening moments, both Pablo and his dad sport black capes. Let's not forget, though, that *su padre* is played by Carlos Villarías, aka Carlos Villar, aka Universal's Spanish Drácula. El Señor Villarías's name is above the title.)

The exterior of the Forti redoubt—from a distance, a fairly well-done miniature—is all translucent glass and metal framing; the effect is quite Flash Gordon–ish. The interiors vary, though, ranging from Art Deco flamboyance to frumpy austerity, depending upon who's occupying what, where and when. In virtually no interior scenes is a ceiling visible. With the exception of some picturesque scenery—against which the Fortis squabble with the *indios*—and the nondescript hill over which Pablo scampers and from which he takes a dive, the only exteriors seen are in brief shots of people climbing in/out of cars against a backdrop of generic vegetation.

Acting honors, such as they are, go to don Carlos and Joaquín Busquets (Pablo), both of whom wear their acting chops on their sleeves; their respective portrayals are—at least when viewed through the eyes of a pair of Americans of our vintage—the most theatrical and least realistic of the lot. As intimated above, Villarías's Dr. Forti gives an eerily spot-on ür-rendition of Bela's Dr.

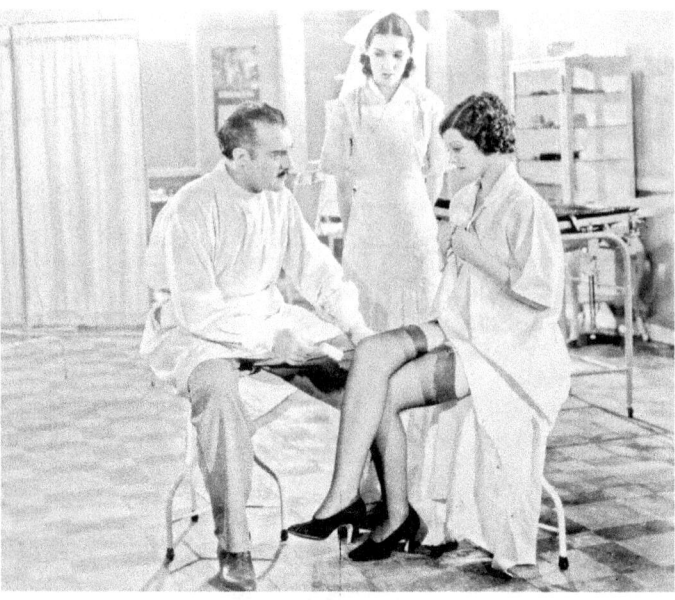

Dr. Renán (Ramón Pereda) checks for runs in Alicia Monroy's stockings. Unbeknownst to Alicia (Esther Fernández), she is being readied for a good, old-fashioned bloodletting. *El baúl macabro*.

Carruthers in 1941's *The Devil Bat*, while Busquets's Pablo—laboring under a half-inch of Max Factor from the get-go—strives for a sympathetic note by playing the obedient-but-doomed-son card as frequently as he does the violin. Per film historian David Wilt,[3] Busquets "lost his sight during the filming of this movie but continued to act in films until his death a few years later." *Rostro* auteur Juan Bustillo Oro elaborated on the actor's degenerating condition in his own reminiscences of the picture[4]:

> He would unexpectedly bump into the furniture on set and he displayed a growing clumsiness in his movements.... One way or another we were able to finish the film. Joaquín Busquets finished it completely blind. Nevertheless, he refused to be "doubled," not even in the scenes in which he was wearing the mask.

Nineteen thirty-five saw Carlos Villarías double down on his mad doctor role, albeit his character—Dr. Nutts, in John Boland's *Te quiero con locura* (*I'm Crazy About You*)—was obviously more of a spoof of Forti-like whackos than a replica. The Córdoba-born actor would go off the medical deep-end once again in 1937's *El superloco* (*The Super Madman*) as a physician who, among other things, has discovered that sexual abstinence fends off Father Time (this, never more apparent than when he finds that his lust for the heroine causes him to age at a rate that would impress Dorian Gray). Oh, and in the words of David Wilt, he keeps a "pet monster."

Everyone else in the cast is serviceable, although René Cardona enacts Luis—the male love interest by default—as the least excitable of heroes, his most strenuous moment requiring him to drape his arm over Angélica's shoulder a few moments before Pablo takes a brody off the cliff. Never moving much beyond glacial speed, Cardona's Luis makes any and all of David Manners's romantic leads seem like a combination of Mike Hammer and the Flash.

Bustillo Oro was as renowned as a writer as he was a director, and he made his cinematic mark early on, with 1934's *Dos Monjes* (*Two Monks*)—a tale of romantic rivalry, deception, and hallucination—acclaimed as one of Mexico's finest early sound features. The picture was included on *Somos* magazine's 1994 list of the "100 Best Films of Mexican Cinema"; two more of his films—1940's *Ahí está el detalle* (*There's the Detail*) and 1943's *México de mis recuerdos* (*Mexico of My Memories*) also made the list. The director, a man of many cinematic talents, won international acclaim during the '40s, a period referred to as Mexico's "Época de oro," or Golden Age. Besides *Rostro*, other of Bustillo Oro's contributions to the genre included *El fantasma del convento* (*The Phantom of the Convent*, 1934), 1937's *Nostradamus* (with the Messrs. Villarías, Cardona, and Noriega), and 1945's comedy/fantasy, *Lo que va de ayer a hoy* (*So Far from Yesterday to Today*), which—in essence—bears more than a passing resemblance to 1930's *Just Imagine* (vid).

Between the phantom fiddler swanning all over the place and characters dispatched and then, presumably, left lying on the floor hither, thither, and yon, the preposterousness level of *El misterio del rostro pálido* is up there. H.T.S., who reviewed the picture in the January 4, 1937, issue of the *New York Times*, found more to like than did we.

> It contains nothing essentially impossible and the dénouement involves no juggling of the laws of nature. Furthermore, the acting is generally good and the photography clear.

There was very little commentary on the film in the English-language press. In fact, the picture wasn't critiqued much or distributed widely *in Mexico* upon its release. Bustillo Oro reports that not only was there a labor strike that left movie houses without enough product to screen, but also that producer Monroy

> opened my *Misterio* without any prior publicity and without a premiere, in eleven neighborhood theaters, simultaneously.... It was October 5, 1935. This treatment was given only to third-rate pictures, and everyone took mine for one of those.[5]

Regardless of the attention it deserved but did not get 80 years ago, *El misterio del rostro pálido* is well worth a look nowadays. And for any and all Lugosi fans who have tired of mulling over the Bela/Carlos comparison-and-contrast from 1931, this picture gives them the opportunity to marvel at how el Sr. Villarías—only four years later—almost preternaturally presaged the look and feel of the '40s Lugosi.

- *El baúl macabro* (*The Macabre Trunk*) features a number of elements found in *Rostro*— cape-wearing villains, the nobility of mad doctors, violin music, René Cardona—but the pacing is faster and no one argues with indigenous peoples.

A mysterious, black-clad figure enters a women's ward at the hospital and chloroforms a patient, carrying her off to a waiting car. [Of the dozen or so patients in the room, only one becomes aware of what's happening; she awakens, only to almost immediately fall back asleep/pass out.] Once it has pulled through the gate of an elaborate mansion, the car stops and the unconscious woman is handed over to a servant, who brings her into an operating room. The figure—Dr. Renán—looks in on his ailing wife, Virginia, and then descends a circular staircase where he joins his servant, Mozabú, and the two prepare to drain the woman of her blood so as to help Virginia Renán be cured of her paralysis. Unfortunately, the patient dies on the operating table before the process can begin, and the "good" doctor announces *buscaremos otra* [We'll look for another].

The night nurse who had been on duty is questioned first by the police and then by a passel of newspaper reporters. Leading the Q&A is police chief González, assisted by detectives Gabilondo and Méndez, the latter being a comic-relief cop who parks his chewing gum behind his ear. Since everything happened while Dr. del Valle was on duty—and the doctor is intelligent, wry, and not a little condescending to the constabulary—the police have their eye on him as a suspect. Dr. Renán, present while the police make inquiries about his colleague, furtively makes off with a scalpel with which del Valle had been whittling.

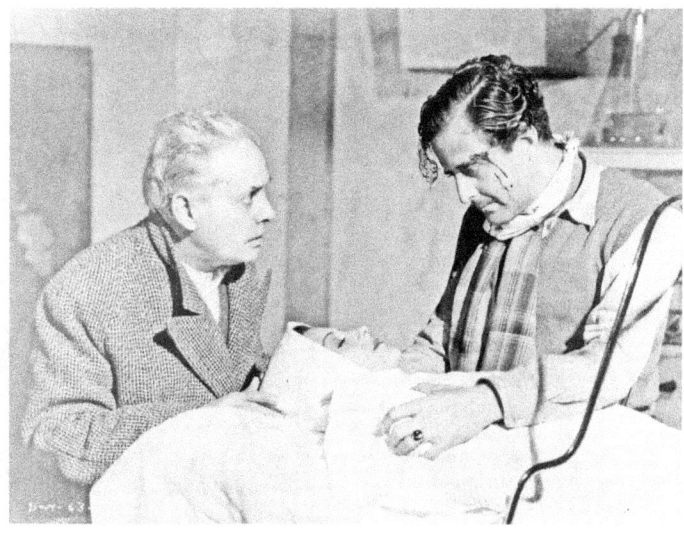

A tense moment: just before Armando (René Cardona) and Dr. Monroy (Manuel Noriega) discover that Alicia (Esther Fernández) will be just fine.

Armando [Doctor del Valle to us] sits at the piano next to his girlfriend, Alicia, daughter of Dr. Monroy. Armando plays and sings poorly, but when Dr. Renán comes to discuss an antique with Dr. Monroy, Alicia takes over, only to slip a record on the phonograph that picks up exactly where she stops singing; as the camera focuses on their legs, Armando and Alicia lock lips for the duration. This kiss-on-the-sneak is something of a recurring conceit. Renán meets Alicia—intriguingly, she responds to him coolly—and thus is set up a later scene.

Cut to the nighttime. A cane-wielding, eye-patch-wearing beggar limps down the street as a car pulls up, and Renán, carrying a small suitcase, steps out. After a brief altercation with the doctor, the beggar heads for a trash can into which Renán has emptied the contents of a small suitcase. Hoping for a good score, the beggar reaches into the refuse only to let out a scream as he comes up with a severed arm.

The next few minutes witness Méndez chew gum, Armando and Alicia smooch some more, and Mozabú read some suggestions to his *maestro* [master] from a notepad he carries. Cut to a newspaper headline: *Otra víctima del descuartizador. ¿Qué hace la policia?* [Another Victim of the Butcher (literally, the "one who quarters"). What are the Police Doing?] ... Cut to the police station, where Chief González and his crackerjack staff talk up a storm...

Cut to that newspaper again, albeit this time it's on a table in the operating room. Mozabú suggests a kidnapping and the doctor's all for it, that very night. We watch the two attack a woman and her daughter, knocking the young girl unconscious and carrying off the mother...

As she descends the grand staircase in her very grand home, Alicia admits to feeling queasy, and it is felt that that the young woman is suffering from appendicitis. Neither boyfriend nor father will operate on her, and the decision is made to have Dr. Renán remove the diseased organ. Alicia visits Renán at the hospital where, in the course of a minute or so, she disrobes, has her reflexes tested—she wears black silk stockings on her lovely legs—and some blood work done, before ending up in a bed in a private room. [The sequence in which Alicia is helped in and out of her clothing—actions bracketing a physical in which, it is assumed, she is nude under a sheet—is more than casually erotic.]

Alicia is in her hospital bed, chatting with Armando and listening to the radio as outside two beggars [one of whom is the one-eyed man] are

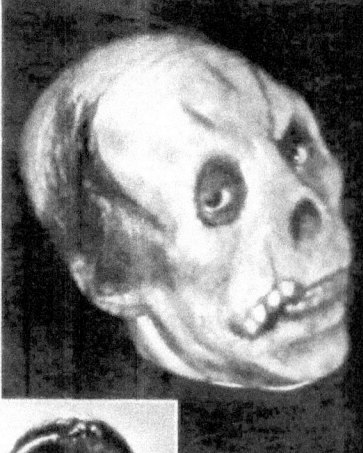

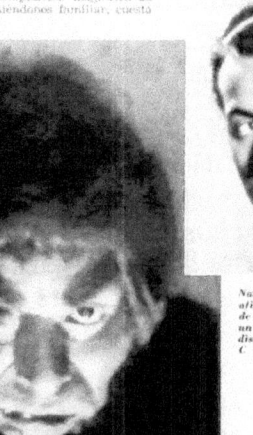

**Narciso Ibáñez Menta—"a disciple of Lon Chaney"—is celebrated in this trade journal article "A Weak Link in the Argentine Cinema: Make-Up."**

Mario (Juan Carlos Thorry) and Juan (Severo Fernández), between a rock and a hard place. Actually, they're between the menacing Mute (Pedro Pompillo) and the irritated Dr. Roberts (Nicolás Fregues). *Una luz en la ventana.*

chased off by the cops. The pair sit and scan the newspaper; its headline reads: "Up to this point, suspicion falls on Doctor del Valle!" and there's a photo of Armando standing between Gabilondo and Méndez. A bit later, the beggar with the eye patch comes up to Armando as he leaves the hospital: I know who the *descuartizador* is, he informs the doctor; I just don't know his name. Armando humors him and hustles the man into his car as Méndez notes the meeting and calls González. A quick follow-up sees the cops grabbing every one-eyed beggar on the street—and there are quite a few—in their futile effort at reaching the right one.

When Renán scans the results of Alicia's blood tests, he smiles; we operate tomorrow, he tells her. As Mozabú and Renán anticipate the operation [¿*Y yo, maestro?*—And me, Master?], Armando checks Alicia's lab reports. He finds nothing out of the ordinary and he—and Alicia's father—decide to call off the appendectomy. Armando informs Renán of this just as Mozabú is readying a trunk containing the remains of the latest unfortunate. Renán has him reopen the trunk and he places within it the scalpel he had appropriated earlier from del Valle. The trunk is later opened in the street by González and his men. They find the scalpel, identify it not long after, and prepare to arrest Doctor del Valle.

In the interim, though, the one-eyed beggar, having watched the *descuartizador* exit the hospital, asks the guard for his name. "Dr. Maximiliano Renán" he is told, and he repeats it to himself as he heads to inform Armando of what he has discovered. Through a phone ruse, Mozabú orders an ambulance sent to a bogus address, and Renán, who has slugged the ambulance driver, binds and gags Alicia and drives her off hospital grounds in the vehicle; he later moves her into his car and heads back to his operating room. Dr. Monroy is called and told that his daughter is missing. He, in turn, calls Armando, who puts two and two together. As they drive off, however, the police stop them and haul them from the car. Armando and the beggar fight back and Armando speeds off, leading the squad car on a merry chase.

As preparations for the operation are made—Virginia is carried down the circular staircase by her husband—the police mistakenly follow the wrong car, allowing Armando to reach Renán's. Climbing the wall, Armando gets into the house and heads for the cellar lab, where he and Renán fight wildly. Mozabú, whom del Valle had slugged earlier, recovers and, heading to the operating room, knocks Armando out with a stool. The police, having discovered their error, rush over to Renán's as the doctor begins to operate and Armando, bound and gagged, watches helplessly.

The police sirens unsettle Mozabú, however,

and, having been told that he'll have to wait until Virginia has been cured before he gets any of that help Renán had promised, fires three bullets into his master. The police burst downstairs and seize Mozabú. They discover Virginia has died and Renán *falta poco* ... will last only a short while. The misguided doctor dies with his head near his wife's face.

All is well the next day for Alicia and her dad. When Armando turns to face the camera, though, we see he has two beautiful black eyes, the result of the melee in the operating room.

Viewers of *El baúl macabro*, rapt as they may be, might nonetheless spend a few moments *en passant* during the screening wondering what in blazes the title refers to. The truth comes out somewhat late in the proceedings, and while the title appurtenance isn't a MacGuffin, it's not all that crucial to the goings-on. Perhaps a more accurate title for the picture might have been *Los contenidos repugnantes del baúl* (*The Repulsive Contents of the Trunk*), but that doesn't trip comfortably across the tongue.

The elements *Baúl* have in common with its predecessor, *Rostro*, are enumerated in our mini-intro above, but there's a minor adjustment made to the "boyfriends vs. beasts" conceit with respect to the heroine. Just as Angélica is the bone of contention for both Pablo and Luis, so also is Alicia considered the grand prize by Renán and Armando. Nevertheless, we're talking *les affaires de coeur* in one film and (basically) organic material in the other. With most traditional dramatic plots always having revolved about the damsel in distress, this is not terribly newsworthy, but the fact that it took the heroine's heart*beat*— and not the erotic beating of her heart—to get René Cardona's character to respond in extremis in *Baúl* must be noted. (Let's not quibble over the difference in scenarist and director vis-à-vis the two pictures, okay? Nor should we pick on el Sr. Cardona, who variously filled every major technical job in well over 150 films in the course of his career, and who began "a filmmaking dynasty as his son and grandson of the same name also became prolific directors."[6] Among the authors's favorite Cardona pictures is 1964's *Las luchadoras contra la momia* (*The Wrestling Women vs. the Aztec Mummy*). The man was a juggernaut. And while both movies's mad *médicos* are alarmingly casual about the ever-increasing body count due to their respective projects, only Maximiliano Renán opts to dispose of the evidence by dropping it, literally in pieces, across the environs. Miguel Zacarías's biographer, Rogelio Agrasánchez, Jr., writes that this aspect of the plot could be traced to

Original one-sheet for the film. Narciso Ibáñez Menta was photographed from behind or as he remained in the shadows for most of the film.

an article published by [the newspaper] *Jueves de Excélsior* [July 26, 1934] in which an unusual deed was described. It dealt with the case of a mysterious killer in London who had the habit of dissecting his victims [and] packing them in suitcases that he would send to different parts of the city. The article in question bore the suggestive title, "The Trunk Crime."[7]

Thus, the "novelty" of the theme. Try as we might, we can't think of a English-language Hollywood horror (of this vintage) in which the purposeful butchering of human corpses figures in the narrative. Much of the film is set in and around a hospital, as hospitals must have been envisioned (and only slightly romanticized) by Mexican storytellers like Jorge Dada[8] 80 years back: save for that one witness to the carrying-off, all ward patients enjoy the sleep of the just; all nurses are achingly beautiful and sashay rather than walk; security is left to old men who are easily overcome or are a tad too late to respond to a call. Medical staff are easily identifiable, sartorially, so Renán must don mufti while spiriting away some woman from her bed; why, though, does he need to dress with such operatic flair? Nobody sees him in the first place. In the opening scene, the black-enshrouded kidnapper could easily pass for Victor Jory in *The Shadow*. And it speaks volumes about the decade's societal perceptions that, when not on duty, Renán, Monroy, del Valle, and (presumably) *all* Mexican doctors live in a style in which only today's millionaires—or yesteryear's art directors, either with access to amazing locations or with astounding budgets—could relate to.[9] Zacarías's vision of Mexican society offered a much needed contrast to the common American take on its neighbor that lies south of the border.

*Baúl*, photographically, is marked less by fades and dissolves than it is by quick and inventive cuts and short scenes. As quoted by film historian Emilio García Riera,[10] director Miguel Zacarías explained, "We're using a dynamic technique—that's new right now—that of fast cuts, because it used to cost us a great deal to employ dissolves." Zacarías anticipated the bold cutting technique of Jean-Luc Godard by some twenty years, and García Riera is effusive in his enthusiasm for the director's use of "top shots" and "the frequent use of objects between the camera and the characters, in the baroque style."[11]

The Smart Car, 1942 version. Juan (Severo Fernández) in the rumble seat; his boss Mario (Juan Carlos Thorry) and Angélica (Irma Córdoba) as snug as two bugs in a Bug.

There are several instances of creative visual and audio cutting—for example, the transfer of scene via that newspaper headline and the switch of locations via a scream meshing seamlessly with a police siren—that still cause the viewer to nod appreciatively.

If *Rostro* owed big time to Gaston Leroux, *Baúl* must acknowledge its debt to Mary Shelley and Edgar Allan Poe, along with a nod to the brothers Warner for cops on running boards, gaggles of detectives, and scrums of reporters. The antics of Carlos López "Chaflán" as gum-chewing Detective Méndez bring to mind similar silliness perpetrated by comic-relief figures like his contemporaries, Warren Hymer and Ned Sparks. This is not necessarily a good thing, but all the aforementioned gentlemen *do* have their following, and el Sr. López had wowed *his* both onstage and onscreen until his untimely death in 1942. Agrasánchez informed us that the gorgeous Esther Fernández, pretty much an extra and bit-part player until *Baúl*, was using the picture to prepare herself (with Zacarías's mentoring) for the leading female role in *Allá en el rancho grande*, a prestige film to be shot next. A shy girl, the actress would not allow herself to be kissed onscreen, thus precipitating the need for the insert of her and René Cardona's feet on the piano pedals. Alicia was the first major role for the celebrated beauty, who would go on to pose for advertisements for … yes … silk stockings.

Four months after the picture had its domestic debut, it was reviewed for the El Paso, Texas, newspaper *El Continental*, which praised the film for being "nothing less than an undeniable advance in the national cinema." The review—dated June 26, 1936—went on to praise Zacarias's achievement:

> We watch flesh and blood characters, we admire the facile technique, the correct cutting of scenes, and we have to look at the program to remind ourselves that it's not an American film that is being shown on the screen.

*Baúl* finally made it to The Big Apple's Teatro Hispano in late November of 1937, and *New York Times*'s critic H.T.S.—who had sat through *Rostro* some ten months earlier—paused only to sniff, "This 'Macabre Trunk' really holds only an old bag of tricks."[12] As we noted above, although some of those tricks had been around for a while, the human-remains packaging proclivities of homicidal maniacs was a new riff.

• **Una luz en la ventana (*A Light in the Window*)** features more of the same with respect to unwilling victims of unprincipled doctors prone to clandestine surgical procedures, but this argument turns on deformity—acromegaly, actually, along the lines of what Rondo Hatton suffered through in real life and not anything concocted via the mortician's wax and collodion of screen phantoms Lon Chaney or Claude Rains (or Joaquín Busquets). Still, there are moments that recall Maureen O'Hara's Esmeralda interacting with Charles Laughton's Quasimodo.

> The night train pulls in and off hops Angélica, a nurse hired to care for an elderly, paralyzed lady at Las Tunas, a mansion set off in the hills. As she has arrived a bit early and it is raining buckets, the young lady accepts a ride from Mario—a handsome *bon vivant*—and his manservant/chauffeur/penance, Juan, the picture's comic relief. After some business involving Mario's car skidding off the road and the drenched trio's finally arriving at Las Tunas, the door is opened by an enormous servant who is implacable and seemingly mute. Although both the elderly, paralyzed lady—Mrs. Hermán—and someone identi-

Consuelo Frank, looking much the worse for wear, in *La herencia macabra*.

fied as Dr. Roberts insist that Mario and Juan be on their way, it is agreed that the men can stay until dawn. Angélica—who has noticed that the house is apparently mirrorless—is led to her room and the men are taken to theirs.

As she sleeps, the young nurse is viewed by a pair of eyes peering through a secret panel. Mario and Juan, hearing footsteps, head downstairs where they pause to read a few lengthy passages in a book on medical disorders. Dr. Roberts orders them back to their room and then heads through a trapdoor to an operating room in the cellar of the house. There he confers with two men dressed in surgical gowns and Dr. Hermán, son of *la dueña de la casa* and a victim of acromegaly, who remains in the shadows.

A bit later, the mute servant, Dr. Roberts, and Dr. Hermán, creep in, chloroform Angélica, and spirit her downstairs. Mario and Juan follow the men downstairs and through the trapdoor. Juan, who is forever complaining to his *patrón* in a loud, whiney voice, makes enough noise for the men in the operating room to realize that they have visitors. Mario is knocked out from behind by the mute, and Juan faints at the sight of Dr. Hermán's face. Mario is brought into the operating room, but as Juan is being carried through the trapdoor and up to the bedroom on the second floor, he makes a break for it and escapes down the road.

Angélica comes to in the O.R., but—after seeing Mario on the operating table—becomes frantic and is rechloroformed. Dr. Hermán speaks gently to her unconscious form.

Juan, behind the wheel of his *patrón*'s roadster, pulls up to a police station and convinces two cops to drive thirty miles with him to Las Tunas to rescue his master from the "*fantasma*." Dr. Roberts and the others have anticipated his return, though, and have rearranged the house so that the rooms in which the men and Angélica had been sequestered are no longer furnished as bedrooms. Although Juan and the police are standing but a few feet above the cellar chamber in which Mario is imprisoned—and from which he is yelling—nothing is heard, and once again Mario is overpowered by the enormous servant. When neither Mrs. Hermán nor Angélica—who has been promised her and Mario's freedom if she goes along with the charade—maintain that anything untoward had transpired there the previous night, the cops whack Juan over the head and drag him back to the police station, where we later see him being hosed down and locked up.

Back at the house, Dr. Hermán and Angélica have another talk and she is told *No pasará nada*—nothing will happen—to her. She is unaware that the men will operate on Mario's pituitary gland instead of hers. After a cut to Juan being let out of his cell by the police, the young nurse appeals to Mrs. Hermán, who gives her the key that allows her out of the house and within inches of the operating room, wherein she and Dr. Hermán arrive at an understanding. He gives her some paper and orders her to write...

Another cut to Juan at the gas station. He is thrilled to see Mario amble up to him. Mario shows Juan a note—penned by Angélica—and the second page of the note is shown to the audience: *Por la familia es mejor que se vaya y me deja aquí.... Gracias por todo y olvídeme.* [For the sake of the family it's best that you go and leave me here.... Thanks for everything, and forget about me.] Mario uses the gas station phone and we soon see him, Juan, and the two policeman who had junketed earlier out to Las Tunas in the roadster and on their way back there.

As our heroes and the cops hold everyone in Las Tunas at bay in the foyer, Mario and one of the police make for the cellar, where Angélica is preparing to leave together with Dr. Hermán. It is only now that the deformed physician steps from the shadows to reveal himself to the young woman. She gasps, but touches him gently. *Abre la puerta* — [Open the door] —Dr. Hermán says, and Angélica kisses him on his forehead. Mario and the policeman enter to find Angélica safe and Dr. Hermán dead, of fast-acting poison, on a sofa. Weeping, the young nurse covers the doctor's face with a sweater. After a silly scene in which Mario espies another old house and wants to check it out—Juan flees, promising to see the couple again in Buenos Aires—the picture ends.

The problem with *Ventana*—hailed widely as Argentina's first *película de terror*—horror picture—is that there's not much in it that's horrifying. Dr. Hermán *is* quite a sight, afflicted with acromegaly as he is, but his misshapen face is hardly enough to render the vigor and thrust of the film into the *terror* genre. Unlike the two other movies we have considered, *Ventana* gives no indication that bodies have been lugged in and snuck out in anyone's attempt at dealing with the medical matter at hand. Sure, there are those two surgical-gown-wearing guys in the basement, but—for all we know—they're just on alert, on standby, waiting for a pituitary-gland volunteer to show up like a Jehovah's Witness at the doorstep. Sure, Angélica's been hired to care for an elderly paralytic who—when push comes to shove—could probably run the mile in under five minutes, but the fact of the young nurse's being targeted, glandularly, is established in the realm of talk. And as for talk (talk ... talk...), all it takes is a couple of heart-to-hearts between our young heroine and the Man Who Dwells in the Shadows, and all those anticipated mad-doctor sequences go away. Ditto with the giant mute servant (Karloff as Morgan in *The Old Dark House*, everyone?), who, while undeniably tall, is mutely-challenged, as he's perfectly capable of chewing the fat with the idiot policemen when the time is ripe.

Even the scenes involving Mario (the most useless hero since René Cardona as Luis) are unexciting and, well ... frustrating. The flaccid romantic lead is repeatedly overpowered by the Morgan and is incapable of yelling loudly enough to be heard from five feet away. Then, moments before the action-free denouement, he saunters into the gas station, matter-of-factly hands over Angélica's passionate letter of self-sacrifice, and—only after his imbecilic factotum mentions the cops—does he summon the energy (and, perhaps, pay for the gasoline) to get the roadster headed back to Las Tunas and dramatic resolution. Since the Manuel Romero who wrote the story and screenplay was the same Manuel Romero who directed the onscreen interpretation and choreography, we hesitate to blame Juan Carlos Thorry—who would go on to become one of the most celebrated of Argentina's actors—for what transpired.

*Una luz en la ventana* marked the cinematic debut of Narciso Ibáñez Menta, a Spaniard who expatriated to Argentina to find fame and fortune in the movies, with most of said movies being thrillers. If genre fans were challenged to toast the Spanish actor who, during the past 50 or so years, reinterpreted many of the cinema's classic horror roles in color and with a distinct European flair, odds are the glasses would be raised to Paul Naschy. Creator of genre favorite, Waldemar Daninsky—the Polish werewolf[13]—and portrayer of sundry vampires, mummies, evil geniuses, prehistoric Cantabrians, and virtually every sort of offbeat grotesque devisable by the meanderings of the human mind, the madrileño—born Jacinto Molina—would be the logical choice.

Had we somehow had pushed the "start date" *back* a quarter century, though, the recipient of our good cheer would have been el Sr. Ibáñez Menta, the most prolific horror film star you never heard of. Asturias-born, Ibáñez Menta was onstage at age five (as Narcisín; his dad was Narcisón), had a tango (and a movie house and a street) named for him, and had successful—and mutually exclusive—careers in theater, the cinema, and television. In an Argentine documentary on his life,[14] it was stated that his greatest fear was that "no one would remember him." Feeling that there was an artistic bond between himself and Lon Chaney, Sr.—the actor claimed to have met The Man of a Thousand Faces in New York at some indeterminate point—Ibáñez Menta went on to appear onstage as Quasimodo, El jorobado de Notre Dame, and onstage and on television as Erik, El fantasma de la ópera. In both theater and on the screen, he became noted for his use of grotesque makeup. (In 1981, he left the make-up duties to his fellow Spaniard, when Ibáñez Menta—as "el profesor"—met up with Naschy's Waldemar Daninsky in *El retorno del hombre lobo* [*The Return of the Wolfman*].)

In a telephone interview with the staff of Argentina's *La Cosa* magazine,[15] the actor spoke of his role as the acromegalic Dr. Hermán in *Una vez en la ventana*: "It was a characterization on which I spent almost six hours. I have never had assistants, except to help me manage things, but no one has ever made me up but me." (Earlier in the interview, Ibáñez Menta spoke of his having corresponded with Boris Karloff about the make-up necessary for the role of Jonathan Brewster in Joseph Kesselring's *Arsenic and Old Lace*, a role Karloff that had created on the Broadway stage and that the Spaniard had recreated in Buenos Aires. Given that the role required Karloff to ... well, *look like* Boris Karloff, the discussion about the pertinent make-up must have been quite brief.) Although the make-up treatment created by Ibáñez Menta for the role of Dr. Hermán was effective—especially for the time; Universal had not yet produced a film turning on Rondo Hatton's physiognomy—the application left the actor's lower jaw seemingly immobile.

While his motion picture career displayed his versatility—he enacted poets and philosophers as well as madmen—it was on television that Ibáñez Menta made his greatest impact, genre-wise. His interpretations ran the gamut, from Dr. Jekyll and Mr. Hyde (*El hombre y la bestia*, 1959) to *El fantasma de la ópera* (1960) to Count Dracula (thrice: *Hay que matar a Drácula* [*Dracula Must Be Killed*] 1968; *Drácula otra vez* [*Dracula Again*] 1970; *La saga de los Drácula* [*The Dracula Saga*] 1973) to the protagonists in short stories by Poe (adapted by the actor's son, Narciso "Chicho" Ibáñez Serrador) to Adolf Hitler (*El monstruo no ha muerto* [*The Monster Hasn't Died*] 1970)! During the '50s and '60s, he hosted (and starred in) mini-series and anthologies that made his name—and his face, under the layers of putty and paint—synonymous with terror; *Historias para no dormir* (*Stories to Keep You from Sleeping*) ran sporadically and under more than one title from 1966 until 1982. In 1971, the actor hosted (and starred in) his own series—*Narciso Ibáñez Menta presenta*—and, three years later, son Chicho stepped up with the five-episode television series, *Narciso Ibáñez Serrador presenta a Narciso Ibáñez Menta*; Ibáñez films also directed his father in the production. (More than one commentary has suggested that the males in the Ibáñez line were all yclept "Narciso" for obvious reasons.) Narciso Ibáñez Menta, *el padre de terror español*, died—with his boots (and makeup) on—on May 15, 2004, at the age of 91.

Representative of the Hispanic take on our favorite genre in the '30s–'40s, *El misterio del rostro pálido*, *El baúl macabro*, and *Una luz en la ventana* are all slanted toward the science-fiction side, heavy on secret laboratories, unwilling patients, and bizarre surgeries motivated by compassion, but performed without mercy. Nineteen thirty-nine's *La herencia macabra* (*The Macabre Legacy*) took things a bit farther, with the surgeon mutilating his wife's lover and then burying a wax effigy of her although she has, in reality, been closeted in a "secret room." (They don't make 'em like *that* anymore...) Ramón Armengod—the unfortunate lover—had appeared a couple of years earlier with Carlos (Drácula) Villarías in *El superloco*, and unfaithful wife, Consuelo Frank, had also shared screen time with the erstwhile Conde in the aforementioned *Nostradamus*. (On a slightly different note, *Herencia*'s Miguel Arenas was featured in 1960's *El fantasma de la opereta*—not the Ibáñez Menta title mentioned above—a comedy in which an abandoned opera house, in the process of being reopened, is discovered to be filled with characters wearing the accoutrements modeled by Claude Rains a decade and a half earlier. You can't make this stuff up.)

Hollywood—at least the Monogram end of Hollywood—would spend the early '40s doing its part to keep the formula going: both Boris (*The Ape*, 1940) and Bela (*The Corpse Vanishes*, 1942; *Voodoo Man*, 1944) were equally guilty of misusing scientific knowledge (or, as in this last film, occult savvy) in their quest to restore vim, vigor, and the vital juices themselves to the less fortunate of the screenplays's females. Experiments gone awry would also underlie much of what we've come to term "'50s sci-fi," but—as we've seen—the sublime-to-ridiculous efforts of that decade owe their essence to the actions of their predecessors. While a bandaged Jack Griffin might embody that image to genre aficionados who were born and/or grew up in the United States, the Doctors Forti, Renán, Hermán, and other of their misguided ilk remain the models of madness for the Spanish-speaking world.

# *Der Hund von Baskerville*

Ondra-Lamac-Film GmbH—January 12, 1937—77 minutes

**Cast: Prologue**: Arthur Malkowski as Hugo Baskerville; Hanna Waag as Lady Baskerville; Walter Kynast as Sir Bettam; Mady Grund, Herta Humm, Gerti Krauss as Noble Ladies; with Bob Bolander, Michael von Newlinksi, Curt Lauermann, and with Siegfried Schürenberg as the voice of Sherlock Holmes

**Main Drama**: Peter Voß (Voss) as Lord Henry Baskerville; Friedrich Kayßler (Kayssler) as Lord Charles Baskerville; Alice Brandt as Beryl Vendeleure; Bruno Güttner as Sherlock Holmes; Fritz Odemar as Dr. Watson; Fritz Rasp as Barrymore; Lilli Schoenborn as Barrymore's wife; Erich Ponto as Stapeleton; Ernst Rotmund as Dr. Mortimer; Gertrud Wolle as Mrs. Garden; Paul Rehkopf as the Convict; Klaus Pohl as the Notary; Ilka Thimm as the Telephone operator; Ernst Albert Schaach as the Hotel director; Horst Birr as Godright; Günter Brackmann as the Newsboy

**Credits**: *Director*: Carl Lamac; *Producers*: Anny Ondra, Carl Lamac; *Assistant Director*: Herbert Grünewald; *Screenplay*: Carla von Stackelberg; *Director of Photography*: Willy Winterstein; *Production Design*: Willi Depenau, Karl Vollbrecht; *Editing*: Ella Ensink; *Sound*: Carl-Erich Kroschke; *Music*: Paul Hühn; *Line Producer*: Robert Leistenschneider; *Location Manager*: Veit Massery; *Based on the eponymous novel by* Arthur Conan Doyle (1902)

> A hound it was, an enormous coal black hound but not such a hound as mortal eyes have ever seen. Fire burst from its open mouth, its eyes glowed with a smoldering glare, its muzzle and hackles and dewlap were outlined in flickering flame. Never in the delirious dream of a disordered brain could anything more savage, more appalling, more hellish be conceived than that dark form and savage face which broke upon us out of the wall of fog.

"The Hound of the Baskervilles," serialized in *The Strand Magazine* between 1901 and 1902, is no doubt the best known and perhaps also the best loved of all the adventures of Arthur Conan Doyle's peerless detective, Sherlock Holmes. With more than 20 movie and television adaptions, it certainly holds the record as the most filmed. Nevertheless, in many ways it's not a typical Holmes tale at all: unlike the polite mysteries that Doyle had given his readers since the series began in 1887, "Hound" has a heavy dose of Gothic horror. What's more, Holmes is absent for part of the story (though he's working behind the scenes). Perhaps the latter is not surprising when one remembers that the novel was not originally intended to be a Sherlock Holmes adventure; in spite of international enthusiasm, Conan Doyle had grown weary of the character and had him plunge to his apparent death in a struggle with his archenemy, Professor Moriarty, in "The Final Problem" in 1893. Conan Doyle based "Hound" on a mishmash of legends (some set in Devonshire) about a demonic dog, but, well into the penning of the story, found he could not come up with a compelling protagonist. Nor was he entirely immune to the devotion of his public or to the revenue such devotion would produce. The master detective's fame was further spread by a number of stage versions of his escapades, most notably one starring William Gillette, who would become identified with the role. Reviving the character was a relatively simple matter for Conan Doyle: he just set the story at a time before the detective's seeming demise. In later stories, the author revealed that Holmes actually faked his own death.

"The Hound of the Baskervilles" received an enthusiastic response in Germany when it was published there in 1903 and some 40,000 copies were sold over the next few years. William Gillette had his German counterpart in actor/producer Ferdinand Bonn, who staged an adaptation of "Hound" in 1906. The Berlin critics may have been scornful, but the play received a considerable boost when both Kaiser Wilhelm and the Crown Prince praised it. Richard Oswald and Julius Philipp did their own version which played in Hanover and later Vienna in 1906–07.[1]

Of course, the problem with any stage version of this story lies with the depiction the title creature. Given the elaborate special effects currently seen on Broadway, showcasing a demonic dog nowadays wouldn't be much of a challenge, but in 1907 there was simply no effective way to bring the beast before the footlights. Thus, the creature's presence was suggested by off-stage howls, by the cries of the escaped convict Selden as he was pursued by the hound, and—during its climactic confrontation with Holmes—gunshots and the devil dog's death cry. Perhaps to make up for this lack of onstage menace, Oswald and Philipp made some significant changes to the story: Stapleton is revealed as the villain (to the audience at least) almost from the first, and—before loosing the hound—he tries first to dispose of Sir Henry with a bomb and, later, poison. Both attempts are foiled by Holmes. Barrymore the butler—a red herring in the original story—here becomes Stapleton's accomplice and, while clad in armor (!), struggles with Holmes at the finale.

Nineteen fourteen saw the very first film version of "Hound"; appropriately enough, it was scripted by Richard Oswald, who would soon become one of the most prolific (albeit not one of the best) directors of the German silent screen. The film has other impressive credits: cinematography by the great Karl Freund, sets by Hermann (*Cabinet of Dr. Caligari*) Warm, and direction by Rudolf Meinert, who had also been the co-producer of *Caligari*. Unfortunately, the picture is a travesty of the original story. Supposedly based on Oswald's play, it is no more faithful to it than the 1931 *Dracula* was to its Broadway inspiration. The characters of Selden, Mrs. Barrymore, and Beryl Stapleton are nowhere to be found in the film, while Laura Lyons becomes Lord Henry's love interest. Dr. Watson has only a bit part, and a somewhat demeaning one at that: Holmes summons him like a servant. It is Barrymore the butler who assists Holmes in foiling Stapleton's plot, and while he's still dressed in armor at the climax, this time 'round, he's wrestling with the *villain*! Stapleton does not perish in the Grimpen Mire (his presumed fate in the story), but rather is dragged off by the police to the approbation of a crowd of kilt-wearing villagers. In fact, the dreaded Mire itself has been replaced by a rather pleasant and totally unthreatening pastoral setting. Our knowing that Stapleton is the culprit right from the start and the fact that he makes a series of attempts on Lord Henry's life are the most notable elements shared by the play and the film.

Perhaps Oswald should have just followed the path taken by his play and kept the hound offstage, as its appearance in the film makes for some unintentional humor. Showing the hound on the stage or screen has always been a bit problematic: what, after all, could live up to Conan Doyle's conception, which appears almost demonic while remaining a real, flesh-and-blood dog? In this, its movie "debut," the hound is played by a friendly Great Dane who, in the first scene, slobbers over Sir Charles as though he's trying to lick him to death, rather than tear him apart. Later, when seen in Stapleton's house (which is outfitted like a serial villain's lair, full of secret passageways, booby-trapped chairs, and busts with cut-out eyes), the hound seems more like a housebroken pet than a half-starved, dangerous brute.

When Stapleton releases the hound (the shot, in silhouette on a hill, is one of the few good moments of the film)—while Lord Henry is out riding and flirting with Laura Lyons (who's in a carriage)—the scene is so clumsily edited that it's hard to tell what's supposed to be happening. The hound doesn't seem to even be in the same shot as Henry, nor does his intended victim appear to be in any kind of danger. The viewer is left to conclude that it's the scent—and not the *sight*—of the beast that's enough to cause the horses of both parties to panic and run. And instead of the suspenseful chase through and climax on the moors as described in the book, Oswald's hound is shot by Holmes after the detective is trapped with it in a secret tunnel in Stapleton's house. (Actually, Holmes not only seems to fire over the dog's head, but also—in the next shot—appears to be holding the pooch down! Apparently none of the production team had taught the dog to "play dead.") The film's final indignity is the final confrontation between Stapleton (disguised as Holmes) and Holmes (disguised as Stapleton), a situation that would seem more appropriate for a parody than a thriller.

Alwin Neuß makes for a stalwart but somewhat impassive Holmes, while Friedrich Kühne's Stapleton is straight from the "Curses,

Left: (background) the unfortunate convict (Paul Rehkop) who becomes the Hound's victim; (foreground): a shaken Sir Henry (Peter Voss) is helped by Watson (Fritz Odemar) and Holmes (Bruno Güttner). Right: (upper) Holmes and Sir Henry discover Holmes's hideout on the Moors; (lower) the mysterious Beryl (Alice Brandt) attends to Sir Henry who has barely escaped a bullet.

foiled again!" school of villainy. Critics were aghast at the dumbing down of the story, but *Hound* was such a hit with the public that six sequels[2] followed, with the whole series revolving around the attempts of Stapleton, who has escaped from prison, to avenge himself on Lord Henry and Holmes. With these episodes lost, there's no telling whether they were improvements upon the original. Neuß played Holmes in the first four before being replaced by Erich Kaiser-Titz (the mad doctor of *Die Insel der Verschollenen*; see essay). Kühne, for better or worse, appeared in them all.

In passing we should mention that, just as the German series was winding down in the early '20s, a whole new set of the detective's adventures was being filmed in England with Eille Norwood playing Holmes. Norwood, who resembled Buster Keaton more than he did the "traditional" image of the great detective, was adequate in the role, although his demeanor and performance are often reminiscent of the efficient but plodding Inspector Lohmann in *M*. The 1921 *Hound* is pretty much like the rest of the Norwood series: competently made and fairly faithful, but rather uninspired. The hound's eerie glow—in the book, Stapleton covers him in liquid phosphorous—was achieved by scratching out the emulsion around it on the film stock, and while it remains a modest special effect, it works well enough. There is, though, one unintentionally funny scene wherein the hound is leaping about the grounds of the Baskerville estate while the principals watch from inside the hall. The butler's frenzied reaction to the sight is in stark contrast to the attitude of the rest of the actors who seem more annoyed than anything else. (You half expect a title card reading "Damned nuisance!")

Richard Oswald, who had directed two of the original *Hound* series, visited the moors yet again with a whole new version of the tale in 1929. American actor Carlyle Blackwell played Holmes, and the part of Stapleton was in the capable hands of veteran bad guy, Fritz Rasp. Although it featured a number of incidents not in the book, this adaptation was a good deal more faithful to the original story than the earlier series had been, and this time the heavy did indeed perish in quicksand at the finale. While stills from the film do exist, we've yet to see any featuring the eponymous beast. For years rumor had it that Gosfilmofond, the Russian film archive, had a print of this version, but it's the 1914 version that is nestled in its holdings. Thankfully, the film—or, at least a part of it—was found to be in the collection of a Polish priest after his death in 2004, and Filmoteka Narodowa has gained possession of that print.

The story was filmed again in Britain in 1932[3] and, in 1937, the hound bared its fangs once more in Deutschland for the Ondra-Lamac-Film production company. Director Carl Lamac—despite a prolific Silent Era career as cameraman, actor, producer, and director—remains best known for his association with the films of Anny Ondra, who, like Lamac, was born in what is now the Czech Republic. The two married in the '20s and formed Ondra-Lamac-Film in Germany in 1930. Albeit they subsequently divorced (and Ondra married boxer Max Schmeling), the actress and her former husband continued to work together. In part because of her thick accent (she had to be dubbed for the sound version of Alfred Hitchcock's *Blackmail*), Ondra's light musical comedies—popular in Europe—found no audiences in America. Besides participating in these, Lamac occasionally did more serious pictures, including a pair of fairly undistinguished Edgar Wallace adaptations that *may* have sparked his interest in doing a Sherlock Holmes film. Dr. Goebbels may have disliked detective stories personally, but the German public viewed the Sherlock Holmes character with a great deal of affection. Thus, 1937 saw the latest iteration of Der

Hund and also the comedy *The Man Who Was Sherlock Holmes* (*Der Mann, der Sherlock Holmes war*) with Hans Albers. Scarcely a couple of years later, any sympathetic portrayal of the British on screen would be strictly *verboten*.

Still, one advantage to making a Gothic thriller in Germany rather than in Hollywood in the '30s was the abundance of spooky old castles in Deutschland, a circumstance that eliminated the need for miniatures and plaster mock-ups. Lamac's Baskerville Hall was Schloss (Castle) Moyland, located in Bedburg-Hau near Kleve, which is not far from the Dutch border; its environs provided an appropriately atmospheric backdrop. (The castle, still extant, looks as sinister as ever.) Lamac started filming in mid–September of 1936 and wrapped in time to submit the finished work to the censors on the December 10, 1936. Some of the interiors were shot at the Ufa's Neubabelsberg Studios, and rear-projection clips from newsreel footage filled in for London in the very brief sequences set there. The setting was updated to the '30s, but this is barely noticeable, as most of the action takes place on the moors, with horses and carriages in lieu of automobiles. There *is* one rather clever concession to modern times, though, in that the letters that are important to solving the mystery are here replaced by phone conversations. Other changes and accommodations were made as well, perhaps in the hope of adding a little vigor and variation to what had certainly become a very familiar story.

Synopsis:

After some mood music based on classical themes, we are shown a large book—dated 1490—that chronicles the history of the Baskervilles. The book is opened [perhaps by one of those slow readers who perused volumes in the opening credits of many a film based on great literature] and we come to the tale of Lord Hugo Baskerville. One night at a feast in Baskerville Hall, Hugo discovers that his wife is being unfaithful to him with one of the guests, Sir Bettam, and has even given her lover a prized family medallion. Hugo confronts Bettam and the two of them draw swords. Bettam is killed and Hugo then turns on his wife, who, far from protesting her innocence, proclaims that death would be a mercy to spending any more time with him. Taking her at her word, Hugo strangles her before the horrified eyes of their guests. The family dog, a huge Great Dane, then leaps on Sir Hugo and tears out his throat. [The dog shows much more enthusiasm for the task than his cousin in the 1914 film, though he's helped by some undercranking.]

We move to the present and the gloomy Baskerville Hall on a stormy night. [Willy Winterstein's camerawork expertly captures the Gothic mood.] Lord Charles, the current lord of the manor, is an elderly bachelor and semi-invalid with both a heart condition and an obsession with the curse that has followed his family since the time of Sir Hugo. Since the curse involves a demonic dog, Charles will allow no canines on the property and has even booby-trapped the surrounding grounds. Charles's friend, Dr. Mortimer, chides him for believing in such fantastic tales and assures him the strange, howling-like noises that are occasionally heard must be related to morass holes in the nearby Grimpen Mire.

Mortimer advises that Charles go to London and perhaps seek out some female companionship. Oddly enough, just then a carriage pulls up outside, and a beautiful young woman emerges. Barrymore the butler announces the woman as Beryl Vendeleure from London. Charles is not pleased; although the Vendeleures are distantly related to the Baskervilles, the former have a bad reputation. Despite his unease ["Someone by that name was in prison"], he reluctantly agrees to see her. She quickly charms the old man, even though he has no interest in the purported reason for her visit [to sell him some nearby land that belongs to her family]. As the hour is late and the weather is turning bad, Charles insists on her staying the night. Beryl feigns reluctance, but the driver has already unpacked her bags and given them to Barrymore, who also clearly disapproves of the whole situation.

Stapleton, an eccentric neighbor and avowed misogynist, arrives and exchanges uneasy glances with Beryl. After amusing the guests with his cynical attitude, Stapleton departs with Dr. Mortimer. A siren indicates that someone has escaped from the nearby Princeton prison. We then switch to the convict running through the moors as guards shoot at him. [This is, of course, Selden, but the character is credited only as "convict."]

Shortly before 11:00, while Beryl is upstairs dressing for dinner, Charles receives a phone call. He becomes very agitated and looks angrily up at Beryl's room. Then the operator interrupts and the call ends with Charles insulting the operator. He heads outside while Beryl quickly comes downstairs. Mrs. Barrymore becomes frantic when she learns Sir Charles has gone out, and her husband promptly goes looking for him, only to be interrupted by the convict who begs for assistance. Barrymore, who obviously knows the man, reluctantly assents. Meanwhile a terrible howl is heard, followed by a scream. Barrymore goes looking for Sir Charles, but he is too late: the old man is dead, and the tracks of an enormous hound are by his body.

As a mason chisels away on Charles's sarcophagus, people gather for the reading of his will. Much to everyone's surprise, Sir Charles has a hitherto unknown nephew, Henry Rogers, an engineer living in Paris. He is the new Lord Baskerville. Dr. Mortimer goes to London to meet the heir—and to consult Sherlock Holmes.

At 23 Baker Street, Dr. Watson is conducting a little experiment involving different types of tobacco ash, much to the disapproval of his shrewish landlady, Mrs. Garden. Sherlock Holmes enters, having just returned from solving a case of jewels stolen from the Vatican. [Presumably, this refers to "The Case of the Second Slipper."] Dr. Mortimer had stopped by earlier, missing both men, but leaving his walking stick behind. Holmes and Watson both speculate on what the stick indicates about its owner.

Meanwhile, Mortimer has met Lord Henry at the station, and they decide on a hotel for his visit. Henry has heard of the Baskerville curse, but dismisses Mortimer's fears as nonsense even though Mortimer tells him his uncle died of fright. Nonetheless, when they get to the hotel, Lord Henry is given a note warning him to stay off the moors if he values his life. But how could anyone have known where he'd be staying?

Mortimer visits Holmes and Watson and tells them that, even though *he* does not believe in the legend, strange things have been happening on the moors and he fears Lord Henry is in danger. Holmes discovers that the warning note is cut from letters from *The Times*, and that it was sent to 10 different prominent hotels to make sure it would reach Lord Henry. Shortly after, Lord Henry calls complaining about the hotel: first one of his new boots disappeared and then, after that turned up, one of his old shoes vanished. Holmes is intrigued by these developments and agrees to take the case. Watson will accompany Mortimer and Henry to Baskerville Hall, and Holmes will join them later.

To the strains of Mussorgsky's "Night on Bald Mountain," Watson, Lord Henry, and Dr. Mortimer arrive on the moors. The danger of the locale is demonstrated when a policeman is caught in the bog and has to be pulled out by a horse. The police are still looking for the escaped

**Left foreground: The doomed Sir Charles (Friedrich Kayßler), Holmes, Watson, Sir Henry and Barrymore (Fritz Rasp) in the rear. Upper right: Watson, Stapleton (Erich Ponto) and Sir Henry. Lower right: Alice Brandt seems to be strangling Fritz Rasp, a scene not in the film.**

convict, though they doubt he could still be alive. Stapleton, traipsing around with a butterfly net, joins Watson and the others on their ride to Baskerville Hall. Beryl is still there, having used an injured foot as an excuse for remaining. She captivates Henry as swiftly as she did his uncle, and he urges her to stay on at the Hall to help him get settled. Stapleton and Barrymore are both skeptical of her motives and suspect she was bitterly disappointed to find that she inherited nothing from the estate. Watson is likewise suspicious ["She's nice but dangerous," he tells Lord Henry, who responds "She's dangerous but nice."]. Henry unpacks and discovers one of his suits has been ruined by an ink stain. With Henry's permission, Beryl gives the suit to Barrymore.

Back in London, Holmes is making plans to come to the moors and studies a map of the caves that honeycomb the Grimpen Mire. Late that night Watson catches Barrymore at a window where, with a lantern, he is clearly signaling to someone on the moors. He tells Henry, but they do not confront the butler.

Watson discovers that Beryl had ordered ten issues of *The Times* which makes it obvious that she wrote the warning letter to Henry. Beryl admits as much to Lord Henry while they are out riding, and immediately thereafter shots are fired in their direction. Beryl warns Henry of imminent peril, but refuses to explain herself further.

At Stapleton's house, Watson peers through a telescope and sees someone prowling about the moors. He is able to pinpoint the person's location with a map. Watson decides that he and Lord Henry, with Stapleton's help, will look for the mystery man that night. That evening Beryl rushes downstairs. [In a rather odd shot, she moves directly towards the camera in slow motion, her gowns flowing about her in a ghostly manner.] Outside, she has a brief encounter with an unseen person in the bushes who warns her not to interfere.

Watson and Lord Henry venture out onto the moors and see the lantern signal from the castle again, as well as a lighted response to it from somewhere in the mire. Beryl catches Barrymore sending the signal again and demands an explanation. Tearfully, Mrs. Barrymore tells her that the escaped convict is her brother.

Watson and Henry discover a cave with a ladder leading up to the surface. They descend and find someone has been living there quite com-

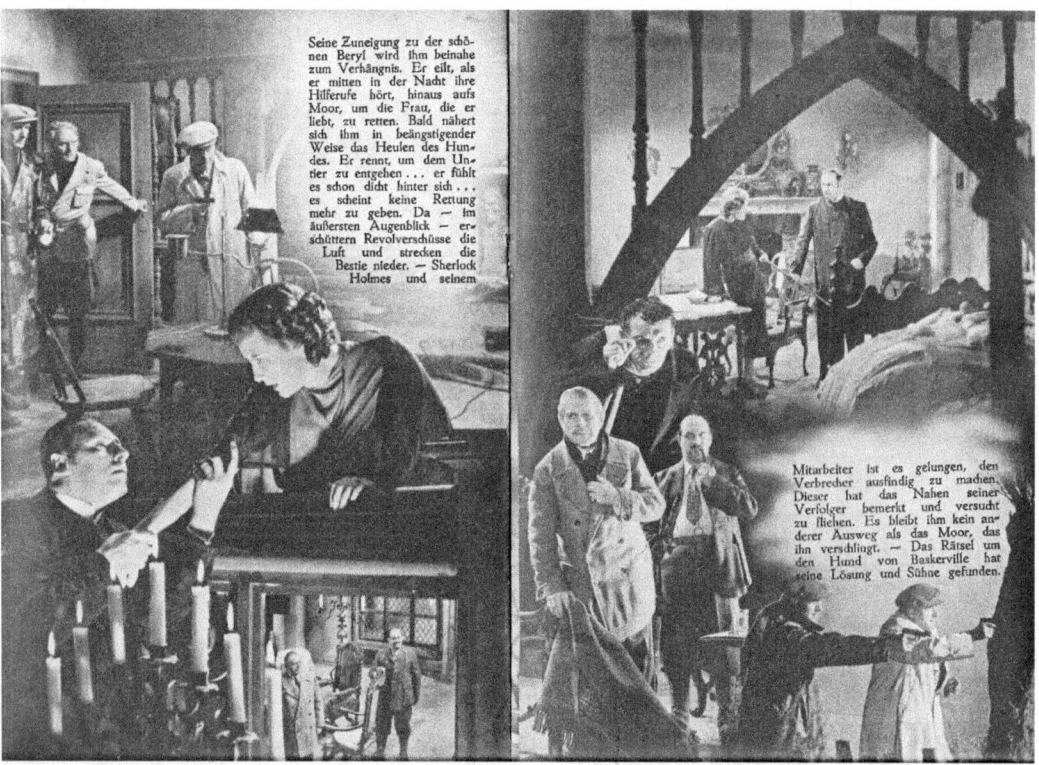

Left foreground: Now it's Fritz Rasp who is manhandling Alice Brandt, another shot not in the movie. The two characters are at odds but it never gets physical. Right (counterclockwise from top center): Rasp, Brandt, Ponto, Ernst Rotman (Dr. Mortimer) and Friedrich Kayßler; Holmes and Watson fire the shots that bring the Baskerville curse to its end.

fortably. It turns out to be none other than Sherlock Holmes, who has been residing on the moors and searching for clues. The terrible howling is heard again, and there are glimpses of a beast running through the mire and then a human scream. Stapleton, seeing only Holmes and Watson at first, tells them that a dog chased Lord Henry over a cliff to his death. However it is the convict, wearing Lord Henry's cast-off suit, who has been killed, much to Stapleton's surprise.

Puzzling over the mystery back at Baskerville Hall, Henry still refuses to believe that Beryl could be involved in a plot against him, though everything seems to point to her as she would be next in line to inherit [barring another male heir]. Looking at the portrait of Sir Hugo, Holmes and Watson realize simultaneously that he bears a striking resemblance to Stapleton, but they say nothing to Henry and instead insist on talking to Beryl. Beryl has disappeared, but they search her room. Holmes finds a photo of her taken with Stapleton and a complaint against Lord Charles from the local phone operator. The phone call in question was made just minutes before Sir Charles was killed and was doubtless what lured him out of the house. Holmes, Watson, and Barrymore head for the post office [which also doubles as phone service] to talk to the operator.

Nervous about Beryl's whereabouts, Henry phones Stapleton [much to the annoyance of the operator, who says calls made after 5:00 p.m. require double taxes and are not welcome]. He hears Beryl's muffled cry in the background and immediately sets out for the Stapleton cottage.

At the post office, the operator is once again indignant at being disturbed, but Watson's flattery works wonders and she tells them that it was Stapleton who called Lord Charles that night. They discover that Lord Henry has left Baskerville Hall, and they all rush to Stapleton's. Meanwhile the hound has been loosed and is chasing Henry. Henry makes it to the cottage, but the door is locked so he climbs a ladder to the second-floor window, only to be knocked backwards by Stapleton. Just as the hound is about to strike, Holmes and Watson shoot it. Stapleton, on a wagon, attempts to escape, but Barrymore follows. Beryl is found tied up but unharmed in the cottage. She tells them Stapleton is a Vendeleure and her brother. Knowing he was scheming to possess the Baskerville fortune, she came to the Hall in an attempt to thwart him. Meanwhile, Barrymore jumps on the wagon and struggles with Stapleton. Stapleton knocks him off, but then the horses come unhitched and Stapleton and wagon get stuck in the mire. Stapleton screams for help, but Barrymore watches impassively as the killer of his brother-in-law and Lord Charles sinks into the bog.

Back in London, Holmes and Watson receive a letter from Lord Henry. Holmes doesn't open it, but Beryl's perfume on the envelope tells them all they need to know.

What's immediately striking about this adaptation is that Sherlock Holmes is close to being no more than a supporting character; his presence herein is even briefer than the unusually abbreviated role he played in Conan Doyle's original novel. It's some 25 minutes into the film before he makes his first appearance—and then his back is to the camera and several of his lines are read over the reaction shots of other characters. Watson (played with energy and wit by Fritz Odemar) is not seen in his usual role as sounding board for the detective's brilliant ideas, but rather as pretty much his equal. The men even have a young assistant, named Godright (Holmes calls him "Corporal" at one point), who may have been meant to suggest the Baker Street Irregulars, but the character seems like he would be more at home in the Hitler Youth. At one point even the landlady, Mrs. Garden, gets in on the detective work when she insists the warning note for Lord Henry was cut from pages of "The Times." It's only toward the end of the film that Holmes does some serious sleuthing, and even then he doesn't have it completely right, assuming as he does that Beryl and Stapleton are partners in crime.

Perhaps there was a very practical reason for playing down Holmes's role. He's portrayed by Bruno Güttner, an actor about whom very little is known other than he was the son of Vittorio Güttner, a famous sculptor whose images of American Indians—his specialty—were shown at the Karl May Museum. The elder Güttner died unexpectedly in 1937 (the year *Hund* was released), and Bruno completed his father's last sculpture. According to one story, director Carl Lamac spotted Güttner working as an extra and, perhaps, cast him as the master detective because of his striking resemblance to Sidney Paget's drawings of Holmes for *The Strand Magazine*. Possibly Güttner was not much of a thespian or perhaps had a voice that didn't match his character because Lamac took the highly unusual step of having him dubbed by another actor, Siegfried Schürenberg. The latter had a distinguished stage career and a good number of film appearances in his own right, but probably made a small fortune dubbing American films for German audiences. He did voices for everyone ranging from C. Aubrey Smith to Cary Grant, but was best known as the voice of Clark Gable. M-G-M had him under contract in Berlin in the '30s and hired him again after the war, most notably to do Gable's voice for the 1953 German release of *Gone with the Wind*. (Please note that he does not sound anything like the Rhett Butler in *Hund*.) Schürenberg did dubbing for some 800 movies from Hollywood and elsewhere, but there's no record of him ever having dubbed a *German* actor other than here. For all that, the dubbing was smoothly done and is nigh imperceptible. Lamac was certainly right about how well Güttner's looks match the character, though his outfit—a black turtleneck, long leather coat, and tweed cap—aren't quite in keeping with the traditional image of the detective.

Siegfried Schürenberg continued to make movies well into the '60s and became identified with Edgar Wallace thrillers; Güttner, on the other hand, seems to have disappeared. There *was* a Bruno Güttner who was born in 1909 and killed in action in 1945. If he was our actor, he would have been only 27 years old when he played Holmes. While the actor in *Der Hund* certainly looks older than that, it's by no means impossible that he could have been 27. If he was *not* the same Güttner, then his fate remains a mystery that even Sherlock Holmes would find challenging.

The changes made to the Baskerville legend were not for the better, but the prologue sequence is still very effective. The camera glides across the banquet hall—catching glimpses of guests dancing and carousing, of Lady Baskerville and her lover Sir Bettam obscured for a moment by a curtain, a suggestion of sexual goings-on between some of the merrymakers—before finally settling on Lord Hugo's grim, frog-like countenance. Hugo gives the impression of degeneracy even though, unlike the character in the book, he doesn't kidnap and attempt to debauch a young maiden. More importantly, though, there's no strong sense of the supernatural in evidence anywhere. The hound doesn't materialize on the moors as an avenger from hell; instead, he's the family dog, and we see a portrait of Sir Hugo posing with the animal. His turning on his master is certainly somewhat unexpected, but that could be explained rationally enough if we assume the animal was attached to Lady Baskerville, and not the evil Hugo. In any case, the tale really doesn't seem like something that would inspire family curses.

The hound's cries are undoubtedly unsettling. The "traditional" howl is supplemented by different animal growls (one of them sounds as if it were being played backwards), and the effect is appropriately eerie and unearthly. The actual dog is described in the book as a combination mastiff and hound, but we're not sure what type of canine is running around in the film. Rather than being the usual Great Dane, he's a medium-sized but fast-moving animal that appears to be encased in some kind of hairy coat. He is shown only briefly (once in pursuit of the convict and again, later, while chasing Lord Henry) and, in a few shots, resembles some kind of wild boar (*Das Schwein von Baskerville?*) In the brief close-up before he is shot, he looks like he's wearing a beard. In fairness, though, it's hard to think of any of the film versions in which the hound is *not* something of a disappointment.

Carla von Stackelberg's script (this appears to be her only credit) makes Beryl the main red herring, but she's played with such intelligence and sex appeal by Alice Brandt that it would not have been a let-down had she turned out to be the villainess after all. This was Brandt's first film, and she only made a few more before disappearing from the silver screen entirely. Biographical details are also elusive.

Curiously, the script reveals from the first very first that Barrymore is helping the convict (though we don't know his motives), rather than saving the fact as a surprise for later in the film. Suspicion is cast very briefly on Dr. Mortimer when he is shown with his pet Great Dane right after someone has shot at Lord Henry (actually the source of the gunfire is never explained), but Laura Lyons and her unpleasant father are omitted entirely, so the list of suspects in the film is pretty short.

One might argue that the depiction of Stapleton by Erich Ponto is something of a cheat. The character functions mostly as comic relief: complaining about women, singing a tune to the fish he's frying, and fussing with his spectacles. He's older than the character in the book, but there, at least, we're given some indication that the man is not entirely harmless when he briefly flies into a rage when Henry courts Beryl. In the film, though, Beryl really is Stapleton's *sister*, not his secret and abused spouse. Ponto's playing the part for laughs (per Lamac's direction) doesn't quite prepare the viewer for his villainy in the closing scenes. Still, although Ponto often played comic roles, he occasionally went over to the dark side. In *Liebe, Tod und Teufel* (*Love, Death and the Devil*), a 1935 adaptation of Robert Louis Stevenson's "The Bottle Imp," Ponto played the sinister Chinaman who sells the hero the cursed bottle. The actor is perhaps best known to general audiences for his portrayal of one of Harry Lime's decadent friends in *The Third Man* (1949).

Peter Voss's Lord Henry is older and more sophisticated than the usual portrayals of the brash young Baskerville heir. Voss plays the part with just a touch of Teutonic arrogance, although he's certainly less pompous than Christopher Lee in the Hammer version, wherein viewers would have not been too sorry if Lord Henry had ended up as dog chow. After some work on the stage, Voss made his film debut in a supporting role in Richard Eichberg's 1925 *Liebe und Trompetenblasen*. He worked steadily in the Sound Era—often appearing with Hans Albers—but never became a star. He did, however, contribute one memorable performance, that of Death in Frank Wysbar's *Fährmann Maria*. In that 1936 thriller, he portrays the Grim Reaper as a kind of heartless Prussian bureaucrat, one focused on doing his job and impervious to pleas for mercy (which was pretty apropos, considering the times). Particularly striking is the macabre sequence where Death dances with Maria (Sybille Schmitz) in the village square as she tries to distract him from claiming her sick lover. Voss was drafted in 1943, a somewhat surprising fact in that actors were spared conscription more often than not (and considering that Voss was 52 at the time). He was a prisoner of war for a while, but later was able to resume his stage and (minor) film career.[4]

Fritz Rasp as Barrymore steals almost every scene he's in. When Sir Charles (played with an air of sad dignity by Friedrich Kayßler) tells him to get some flowers to brighten up the table dinner for Beryl, Rasp's acid, skeptical tone when he responds, "Flowers?" makes it sound as though he can't bear to hear the word tripping over his tongue. Rasp, like so many of his fellow film actors, was trained for the stage and was taught to be contemptuous of the movies, but when stage great Albert Bassermann made *Der Andere* in 1913, such prejudices quickly crumbled. Rasp commented on different styles of acting in an interview conducted by Hans-Michael Bock and Rudolf Körösi for television in 1972, toward the end of the actor's life:

> Back then most actors came from the stage. But film had other rules, for optical and audible rea-

sons. In film one can talk silent in a close up which isn't possible on the stage. There the audience is farther away. So it looks unnatural in the facial expression on the stage if you try talking soft. In the beginning of the talkies most actors had problems with that change. Expression is the most important thing in the movies, it's basic. I tried to internalize the role, and so almost automatically I got a different expression, the real voice. It was like a metamorphosis, not an adjustment. Kind of an auto-suggestion. One cannot sustain this tension for a long time on stage, but in the movies it goes shot after shot, lap after lap. So it appears true, not staged.

Rasp was usually cast in villainous roles and this perhaps was something of a deliberate choice as he had been given advice in the '20s to avoid comedies: "Mr. Pabst or Mr. Lang would say 'If you participate in that type of movie, I cannot hire you.'" With respect to the Silent Era, Rasp is best remembered as the sinister henchman of Joh Fredersen in *Metropolis* and as the vile seducer of Louise Brooks in *Diary of a Lost Girl*, as well as for his hissable roles in *Woman in the Moon* and *The Loves of Jeanne Ney*. When sound caught on, Rasp's sinister, purring delivery of lines served him in good stead as the parricide Smerdyakov *The Murder of Dmitri Karamazov* and the bank robber in *Emil and the Detectives*. His long career extended right into the '70s.

*Der Hund von Baskerville* premiered in two Berlin theaters on January 12, 1937. There were no German reviews simply because Dr. Goebbels had, in the words of David Hull Stewart, "abolished the critics" (although German reviewers were later allowed to critique non–German films). That was not yet the case in Austria where the writer for the *Neue Freie Presse* commented that Lamac had created a virtual "Witches's Sabbath" of suspense and had drawn excellent performances from his cast (April 4, 1937). The *Österreichische Film-Zeitung* praised Lamac for "creating the proper atmosphere of mystery and the uncanny" (April 9, 1937), even if the scribe for *Die Wiener Zeitung* disagreed, lauding the camerawork but describing Lamac's direction as only "fair" and the acting uneven (April 4, 1937).

When Hitler came to power in 1933, Lamac switched his base of operations to Vienna. By 1937, though, no independent company could operate in Germany because the whole film industry was slowly being nationalized. After the demise of his company, Lamac emigrated to the Netherlands, then to France, and finally to Britain. In 1952 he returned to Germany to make one final picture, *The Thief of Bagdad*.

*Hund* also marked the last time the lovely Hanna Waag (Lady Baskerville) appeared on the screen. She was married to the Jewish set designer, Rudolf Bamberger, and the two fled to Luxembourg to escape the Hitler terror. Rudolf's brother director, Ludwig Berger, survived the war, but Rudolf was eventually arrested and died at Auschwitz.

Perhaps ironically, *Der Hund von Baskerville* was one of Hitler's favorite films and even found a place in his private collection.

# *Císařův Pekař a Pekařův Císař*
# (*The Emperor's Baker, the Baker's Emperor*)

Ceskoslovenský Státní Film—1951[1]—4062 meters/144 minutes as a two-part Czech release (80 minutes and 64 minutes); 3065 meters/112 minutes as a feature-length Czech release; 110 minutes (U.S. release version)

**Cast**: Jan Werich as Rudolf II and Matew, the baker; Marie Vášová as Countess Katharina Strada; Nataša Gollová as Catherine (Sirael); Bohuš Záhorský as Chancellor Lang; Jiří Plachý as Edward Kelley; Zdeněk Stěpánek as Marshall Russworm; František Filipovský as the Court Astrologer; František Černý as Scotta; Václav Trégl as the Emperor's Servant/Confidant; Miloš Nedbal as the Court Physician; Bohuš Hradil as Tycho de Brahe; František Holar as the Commander of the Guard; Vladimir Řepa as the Bakery Owner; Lubomir Lipsky as the Alchemist; Theodor Pištěk as Portreeve; Bohumil Bezouška as Hans Von Aachen (the painter); Felix Le Breux as Bourgeois Delegation; Josef Kemr as the Alchemist breaking the lead atom; Fanda Mrázek as Halbardier; Ota Motyčka as the Scribe; Miroslav Svoboda as the Master of Ceremonies; Jan S. Kocár as Alchemist 1; Miloš Kopecký as Alchemist 2; Eliska Kuchařa as the Gardener; Josef Hlinomaz as the Journeyman; Alois Dvorský as the Man in front of the Bakery; Jana Werichová as Girl 1; Eva Jiroušková as Girl 2; Gustav Hrdlička as Barbier 1; František Miroslav Doubrava as Barbier 2; Marie Nademlejnská as Woman in front of the Bakery; Vladimir Svitáček as the Juggler; Ladislav Rychman as the Man with the Writing Desk; Věra Chytilová as Lady-in-Waiting 1; Anna Pitašová as Lady-in-Waiting 2; Jaroslav Vlk as the Stripling; Antonín Soukup as the Baker; Václav Švec as the Servant; Antonín Jirsa as the Doctor's Assistant; Martin Raus as the Servant with the Vase(s); Emanuel Kovařík as the Chamberlain; with Hynek Němec, Viktor Pejsar

**Credits**: *Director*: Martin Frič; *Screenplay*: Jiří Brdečka and Jan Werich; *Art Director*: Jan Zázvorka; *Set Decoration*: Vladimir Macha and Vladimir Slepicka; *Cinematographer*: Jan Stallich; *Original story*: Jiří Brdečka and Jan Werich; *Film Editor*: Jan Kohout; *Costume Design*: Vladimir Synek and Jiří Trnka; *Makeup*: Gustav Hrdlicka; *Production Manager*: Ladislav Ters; *Sound*: František Cerný; *Special Effects*: Jaroslev Horejc; *Music*: Julius Kalaš and Zdeněk Pter; *Music Department*: Filmov ý Symfonický Orchestr; *Conductor*: Milijov Vzelac

There aren't too many *famous* fantastic figures that pre-dated the Golem in the "What's Who?" of horror-film history. We're not talking about generic witches or ghosts or devils here; we're referring to the cinematic incarnations of "classic" blood-chillers who owed their specific infamy to myth or literature. In the first filmed version of Victor Hugo's *Notre Dame de Paris* (*Esmeralda*, 1906), for example, Quasimodo's screen-time was but a part of the ten minutes Alice Guy Blanche's vision took to unreel, but the renowned bell-ringer was already a recognizable force to be reckoned with. Likewise, Stevenson's Dr. Jekyll and Mr. Hyde could be found transforming (and barnstorming) as early as 1908, and 1910 had introduced a fairly offbeat rendition of the Frankenstein Monster to nickelodeons and nascent movie houses, courtesy of the Edison Studios. Sure, there were adaptations of stuff by Pushkin, Du Maurier, Haggard, and Poe—and innumerable nameless sprites, spell-casters, and semi-satans—but of the iconic characters that would recur, alone or with others, during the subsequent decades ... fewer than a handful took their maiden voyage before Rabbi Löw's mystical clay man traversed the beaded screen in 1914.

The earliest Golem movies—the Paul Wegener canon—turned variously on the conceits that (a) the Golem is up and about, and he's not happy!, (b) there's talk that some Rabbi is building a Golem, so watch out, Habsburgs!, (c) the Golem is up and about again, and he's not happy! Allowing for only the slightest of exaggeration, that's pretty much how Herr Wegener introduced his soon-to-be-infamous character to the cinematic world. Dwindling sources of funding and increasing displays of aggression in the mid–1910s meant the first film based on the Löw legend would have to take place in the present day, so conceit *a* played out sans everyone bedecked in period costumes and without costly reconstructions of shops and streets and neighborhoods from some 400 years earlier. *Some* explanation of what in blazes was going on was necessary for the viewer, of course, but sketchy details allow for unpredictable events. Thus, in a nutshell, *Der Golem* chronicled the peregrinations of a mystical figure who finds itself literally out of sync with the then-modern times.

Golem the Second, i.e., *Der Golem, wie er in die Welt kam*,[2] was set with one eye to historicity, and the other to invention and purposeful vagueness. Conceits *b* and *c* are the operating system of this 1920 "prequel." The legend maintains that Rabbi Judah Löw ben Bezalel constructed the Golem in response to the persecution of the Jews by the Habsburg monarchy in the 16th century. Rabbi Löw was a real-life human being—the first lady of the United States, Michelle Obama, visited his gravesite in Prague's Old Jewish Cemetery in 2009—and the Rabbi himself died in 1609. Of necessity, then, the Golem had to have been magicked together toward the end of the

**The actual gravesite of Rabbi Judah Löw ben Bazalel, in the Old Jewish cemetery, Prague.**

16th century. On the Habsburg throne during that crucial time—at least per the PAGU feature—was the Emperor Lahois, a personage as resoundingly unreal as the Golem, itself. Because the Habsburgs had pretty much died out by the end of the 19th century, we have to assume that scenarists Wegener and Henrik Galeen would have run little risk of libel litigation from the great-great-grandchildren of Rudolf II, the honest-to-God Habsburg emperor who *was* on the throne when all of this Golem mishegas was supposed to have taken place in an alternate universe.³ They went with "Lahois" anyhow.

Movie-wise, there was a total Golemic drop-off during the years 1920 and 1936, that is, between the time that Paul Wegener's arguably most renowned picture was released and Julien Duvivier received the go-ahead from Prague's A.B. Barrandov Film to produce another take on that city's most colorful celebrity. Like Wegener's 1920 picture, Duvivier's *Le Golem* (filmed in French only, despite being designed and shot in Czechoslovakia) exists in its entirety, with the original-release print and the reissue print both available on DVD and the like. The reason for our drawing this to the readers's attention is that, in the original release print, the scenarists credited for the screenplay were Monsieur Duvivier and André-Paul Antoine, and their source materials were listed as "the Prague legend" and "the novel by Gustav Meyrink."⁴ While researching the Martin Frič two-parter for this essay, we purchased a DVD of the 1936 film and discovered—serendipitously—that we were watching a print of the reissue. There was virtually no difference between the two prints to be found in the body of the story, but the scenario screen displayed an interesting variation from the original:

> "Scenario de André-Paul Antoine et Julien Duvivier, inspiré par la célèbre légende de Prague, et par Wookovec et Werich"

And just who were these men, Wookovec and Werich? Their roots are to be found in an artistic movement that came into being in the years immediately following the Russian Revolution and the Czechoslovak Rebellion.

> *Devětsil*, founded in 1920 in Prague [was] an association of young, predominantly Marxist, poets, critics, musicians, architects, and painters [who] represented the Czech Avant-garde movement of the twenties.... In 1925, *Devětsil* created its Liberated Theater [Osvobozené divadlo], which became one of the foremost stages of experimental productions.⁵

More than a few members of *Devětsil* found its "predominantly Marxist" ideology to be irreconcilable with a stylistic school that self-described as an "Avant-garde movement."

> In the mid-twenties, some members of *Devětsil* took a critical stand against Soviet art. Jiří Voskovec, while a high school student in Dijon, had rejected its propagandistic tendency already in 1925.... *Vest Pocket Revue* [1927], a play by Voskovec and his friend, Jan Werich [referred to by the acronym V+W], opened a second phase of the Liberated Theater. Soon this became the most popular theater in Czechoslovakia between the wars.⁶

Jiří Voskovec (aka "Wookovec") and Jan Werich (V+W) quickly became two of the country's most celebrated actors, comedians, and playwrights affiliated with the Liberated Theater, and their works ranged from parodies of revues—like *Vest Pocket Revue* and 1929's *Fata Morgana*—to plays that were

**The ultimate fate of the Golem: a baker's oven. Courtesy Naŕodní filmový archiv.**

more openly critical of the current social mores, even if tempered somewhat by humor and exaggeration—like 1931's *Golem*. By the end of the '20s, *Devětsil* was dissolved and a good number of the Prague Avant-garde turned to Surrealism, the next artistic spoke in the wheel. Nevertheless, as artists began to encounter more political pressure from the Soviet Union, the Surrealist movement also collapsed, and the linguist Roman Jakobson, Voskovec, and Werich fled Czechoslovakia. Some years later,

> Voskovec, who briefly returned to Prague, left for the United States and became there an acclaimed Shakespearean actor. Werich stayed in Prague, but was unable to have his own theater until the mid-fifties. One of the stagehands there was Václav Havel, the future playwright turned president.[7]

For a brief recap of V+W's play *Golem*, we turn to film and theater historian Veronika Ambros:

> Set in Prague at the court of Rudolf II, the action takes place at a carnival night of 1600 [and] the emperor wants to celebrate the occasion bt reviving the golem. According to V+W, Rabbi Löw provided the golem with just a modicum of brain. Chancellor Lang and the alchemist Scotta stole the statue from the synagogue and hid the magic shem...
> Břeněk, an stronomer who created the artificial woman Sirael, exposes their plot.... The crazy comedy ends well: Scotta and Lang are banished, and Sirael, whom the emperor tried to teach how to love, marries her creator in a modern Pygmalion fashion. The revived golem, in the end, becomes the emperor's drinking companion.[8]

Several of these elements will be recognizable in *The Emperor's Baker, the Baker's Emperor*, as is the fact that the emperor wishes to possess the Golem, not from fear of retribution for his treatment of the Jews—the Jews are scarcely mentioned—but because he is a collector of art and trinkets. Interestingly, Ambros points out that it is for similar reasons that Rudolf wishes to possess Sirael, whose name V+W formed from an anagram of Israel and as an allusion to Surreal, and, in quoting an essay[9] on *Golem* by Czech writer Jan Mukařovský, she reveals how the two actor-playwrights drew attention to the

**Director Martin Fric runs lines on set with the Golem. Courtesy U Golema Restaurant, Prague.**

narrative via "gestures, dance, song, and other means of expression."

V+W's *Golem* ran for 186 performances and was considered a great success.

Come 1936, the Third Reich was amassing power, Germany's neighbors were becoming nervous, and the descendants of the Jews who had looked to the Golem for succor in an earlier era were finding themselves repressed and persecuted once again. It was against this background that Julien Duvivier decided to film his version of the Golem story; Rudolf would still be on the throne—it would not be wise to set *this* tale of a Jewish juggernaut in contemporary East-central Europe—and a successor to Rabbi Löw would revive the Clay Man to provide respite for the Chosen People.

Again, the most succinct way to set the stage for *Le Golem* would be to quote Veronika Ambros:

The success of V+W's *Golem* prompted the French director Duvivier to commission the duo to write a screenplay for him. However, he eliminated the characters from the screenplay he had received, and he altered the genre as well as the focus of the original. Nevertheless, he kept parts of the text without acknowledging his debt, which unleashed another legal golem battle—won by the Czech artists in the end.[10]

Audiences familiar with the 1936 *Le Golem* will thus recognize that the palette on which V+W had painted their clay vision in 1931—a comic turn on love, greed, and social inequality—had, a mere five years later, been transformed into a depiction of fury, unbridled ambition, and unstoppable violence by the return of evil to the world and the desire of a filmmaker to offer some sort of symbolic hope. And the difference in screenplay credits between the original release print and the reissue version becomes clear.

*Císařův Pekař* (*The Emperor's Baker*), the longer of the two features, is primarily exposition.

> The Emperor Rudolf II, a whiny, wasteful megalomaniac, is surrounded by sycophants and "scientists"—in reality, con men and charlatans—paid handsomely to discover how to turn lead to gold, restore the emperor's youth, and so forth. Rudolf has been squandering his empire's resources in pursuit of such "occult knowledge," while his poverty-stricken subjects do not have enough bread to ensure their survival. His chief obsession, though, is the Golem, the one mystic commodity he has been unable to locate to add to his abundant store of artistic possessions, most of which are apparently fakes. As the film opens, imperial troops led by Marshall Russworm knock down the doors of the Synagogue and proceed to search the premises for the clay giant. They find nothing and Russworm later confides to Chancellor Lang, "I don't think there ever was a Golem."
>
> Awareness of the emperor's ongoing quest has even made its way down to the village, where Matew the baker provides a curious boy with the backstory of the Golem:
>
>> Once there lived a scholarly rabbi in Prague, Rabbi Loew. And he discovered that enormous power lay hidden in matter, even in common clay. So he molded a huge figure out of clay. And he named it Golem. And using a rather queer device called the shem ... the rabbi brought the Golem to life and with it, the enormous power hidden in the Golem.... One day, Rabbi Loew forgot about the Golem. And the big fellow began to smash everything in his way. He might have destroyed the whole world, so the Rabbi made the Golem lifeless and buried him somewhere—no one knows where.
>
> The long line of villagers outside the bakery is told that there isn't enough flour for them *and* for the special order of "nice and crispy" rolls placed by the palace, but Matew freely hands out what they have after the court astrologer—who has stopped by to shake down the bakery owner for money—grabs some bread for himself and runs out, chased by the owner. "When two thieves chase each other," he tells them, "the honest folk can relish."
>
> Back at the palace, the opulent salons are filled with courtiers—male and female—waiting to cater to Rudolf, who has awakened with a toothache. As he is dressed, the emperor is handed a vase to smash, as he has servants who attend to his every whim, even going so far as to provide endless series of vases to destroy. Chancellor Lang informs Rudolf that the Golem has still not been found, and Scotta, the Italian court alchemist, reports that the elixir of youth he has been trying to brew is not yet ready. This does nothing to improve the emperor's humor; nor does the news that the emissary from his brother, Matthias, has been waiting for three months for an audience. There is a protracted humorous bit here as Scotta rubs some "cleaning agent" of his own invention on the floor, causing any number of important folk to fall on their behinds.
>
> At table—where he waves off platter after platter of succulent dishes—Rudolf demands that Lang *summarize* the important events of the day. "Tell us only what needs *not* be done and leave out what needs to be done." [This refusal to attend to detail is a plot pivot waiting to be revealed.] The emperor orders Matew the baker to be arrested and imprisoned for giving away the rolls meant for the palace, and we watch as soldiers toss the baker into the lowest level of the dungeon.
>
> Cut to the emperor's bedroom, where he is awakened by the sound of a military march. Soldiers rush in. "It's Master Edward Kelley," they announce. "The doctor of black and white magic, an alchemist, and an occultist. You have invited him yourself." As Lang, Russworm, and Scotta meet Kelley—it appears that Kelley and Scotta are already acquainted—soldiers unload the magician's baggage in a basement apartment that shares a wall with Matew's cell. Kelley, after opening a trunk to reveal a young woman whom he will later "create magically" for the emperor's pleasure and then providing her with some food, leaves to consult with Rudolf. The woman, named Catherine, becomes acquainted with Matew after the baker's hand reaches up through a hole on the floor in search of the food he has smelled.
>
> While this is going on, Rudolf takes Kelley on a tour of his "C.I.A. [Central Imperial Alchemist] Laboratorium," where chicanery of all sorts is being perpetrated because of the emperor's scien-

tific naïvete. [We learn that Rudolf is in danger of bankrupting the empire by continually funding these "experiments" and by acquiring fraudulent works of art, instead of supporting the common people. He has, in fact, been borrowing huge sums of money from Lang. How Lang has obtained enough money of his own to finance the Habsburg Empire is never revealed.] The court astrologer, trying to placate a furious Rudolf [the elixir of youth is still not available], says that a mandrake root is necessary to complete the formula. The emperor orders Scotta and the astrologer to meet with him that night at Gallows Hill. They do, there's some low-comic business as they attempt to find a mandrake root, and Scotta falls down a deep hole and into a cave. When the emperor and the astrologer go to help him, the three come upon the inert form of the Golem.

Cut to a short scene in which Russworm, Kelley, and Lang are plotting to use the Golem to their own ends.

Cut to the emperor, seemingly drunk, talking to the Golem, which has been moved to the royal study. "The Moon has orbited the earth two times, Golem, and we are running short of breath too quickly to keep persuading you. What do you want? We offered you fame and power. We offered you our friendship. We promised the Earth to you. And you are as silent as stone." Rudolf keeps this up for a bit—he even shows a painting of the Golem with Rabbi Loew that he has collected—and throws his wine glass at the clay giant. Finally, out of patience, he fires a cannon at the Golem, which slowly falls over. Alarmed courtiers come running, as does Kelley, who tells Rudolf, "The constellation of the stars is unfavorable for reviving the Golem. It is most favorable for the creation of Sirael."

Cut to Catherine and [through the wall] Matew, who have been flirting all this time. When Kelley tells the young woman the time has come for him to "create" her, she refuses at first. As the magician readies his apparatus, Catherine slips her handkerchief to Matew.

There is great and multifaceted entertainment soon thereafter at the court theater, including jugglers and acrobats, but the high point is Kelley producing Catherine as Sirael from a sarcophagus-like box. The emperor is impressed and announces his just-formulated plan to mate the beautiful spirit with the Golem. "We shall betroth them and their union will give birth to a new being. It will inherit charm from Sirael and might from the Golem." Kelley places the young woman back into the box, and thence she exits back into the room adjoining the dungeon. "If he touches me," she says to Matew, "I'll hit him with something, emperor or not."

The next scene finds Sirael [standing in the sarcophagus] in the emperor's study. As he attempts to teach this new being to speak, the Countess Strada—the emperor's love interest—comes sliding out in a chair from behind a secret panel in the wall. Some comedy ensues as she slides back in and out, and Kelley returns to retrieve Sirael. Rudolf orders him to revive the Golem.

After a brief scene in which she smuggles food to Matew, Catherine [as Sirael] is back with the emperor, who maintains he will now teach her to dance. As they move to music from a chamber orchestra, Rudolf pulls her onto his bed. "In the darkness," he murmurs, "you shall see the rise of the Age of Rudolf." When Sirael replies that she smells rum on his breath, the emperor throws a tantrum. The young woman runs out and Lang enters to inform Rudolf that Mattias's emissary has now been waiting for four months. As Rudolf speaks to the emissary, he says in aside to Kelley, "You and Sirael may go stuff yourselves," and he tells the magician that if he doesn't revive the Golem, he'll return to England "in two pieces." When Kelley disappears right in front of Rudolf's eyes, the emperor admits, "That wasn't a bad trick at all."

Mattias's emissary hands Chancellor Lang one half of Mattias's royal seal and tells him whoever has the other half can "give orders." Lang joins up with Kelley and Rosswurm, who are in the emperor's study, with the Golem. When Kelley produces the other half of the royal seal, the three men begin to plot how to "remove His Imperial Majesty by fair means." Since Rudolf will sign anything Lang hands him without reading it, they plan to hand him an abdication order. In the

**Jan Werich was the first actor cast as Ernst Stavro Blofeld in *You Only Live Twice*; he was later passed over in favor of a distinctly more unpleasant-looking Donald Pleasence.**

midst of all this, Russworm—who has been poking around the Golem—finds what appears to be a ball. They place this in the forehead of the Golem and, as the cloth that covers the clay giant burns away, the Golem stands erect, its eye sockets filled with flames. Hurriedly, the men remove the ball—the *shem*—and all activity ceases. As the men argue over who will be in charge of the Golem, they drop the shem and a dog picks it up and runs out of the room.

We cut to the emperor's grand library, where he and his confidant reminisce about the romantic adventures they had with beautiful young women so many years in the past. The men agree to "leave it all behind" and—fortified with Scotta's elixir of youth—they plan to head to Brandejs. When told by Scotta that the elixir is "sticky," Rudolf—his toothache having returned—gives him until midnight to get it right, or off with his head.

Deep below the palace, Catherine has told Kelley that she and Matew are in love. Kelley muses that the emperor might help Matew if Sirael were more affectionate. While this is transpiring, Matew accidently trips a trapdoor and is now swimming about in an underground sewer.

*"This is how Matew, the Emperor's Baker ends, only to re-emerge in the second part of the film as the Baker's Emperor."*

### *Pekařův Císař* (*The Baker's Emperor*)

At midnight, Rudolf drinks the elixir of youth, as Scotta grabs his bags and tries to exit, only to find a hooded executioner behind each door. Meanwhile, the imperial servants pour the excess of the emperor's bathwater into a drain, and we see the water fall a distance onto the head of Matew, who is trying to find his way out of the sewer below. He does so, climbing up through the drain and into Rudolf's bubble bath. Now sporting the beard he has grown during his quite brief imprisonment, the red-headed Matew is [presumably] the spitting image of a younger Rudolf. When they return to bathe and dress him, the servants are amazed: "He either really got younger or all rusty."

Some moments later, a robed Matew wanders into a room where an identically robed Rudolf is napping. When he awakens, Rudolf goes to a full-length mirror to check on the effects of the elixir. Matew, having broken the mirror, stands behind it, and we have a replaying of the Marx Brothers's famous scene from *Duck Soup*. Convinced that he is younger, the emperor and his confidant head off in a carriage for romantic capers in Brandejs. Moments later, Scotta and Countess Strada accompany the imperial dentist as he seeks to ease Rudolf's toothache. The dentist is astonished—"His molars have grown back again!"—and the countess has the men take "Rudolf" to his bedroom and then follows, having drunk some elixir herself. After a short bit of tussling in the bed, the countess faints, and Matew takes stock of the situation. "If I tell them that I'm the emperor's baker, they'll kill me. On the other hand, if I become the baker's emperor, I can find Catherine and get even with that magician. I'll sleep on that."

[From this point on, the real emperor will be referred to as "Rudolf," while Matew will be called by name or referred to as "the emperor." Apologies in advance.]

Following a quick cut to Rudolf's driverless carriage in the country the next morning, we see Matew [as Rudolf] enter the breakfast room to the astonishment of everyone—"It's a miracle." Not only is the emperor younger, but he's also much more polite—no vase breaking here—and he asks each of the ladies in waiting, "Are you Catherine?" He has Lang tell Kelley to produce Sirael and then walks through the art gallery, where he sees the Golem: "If we could bring it to life, we could save a lot of work and trouble for a good many people." As the usual crowd of con men and sycophants approach the emperor, he cuts each off at the knees, and then announces, "The Emperor's TITBIT Bakery will be handed over to the apprentices." As Matew has everyone sit and actually eat one of the opulent meals that Rudolf usually waves away, Lang produces the planned order of abdication, convinced as he is that "the emperor" will sign anything he's given without reading it. Matew does read it—every word—and extorts an enormous bribe from Lang to tear it up and not have the chancellor executed. He then orders, "The imperial granaries will be open to the benefit of all people. And give bread to the poorest for free."

**Only in Prague can you buy a box of Golem chocolates, all shaped like the life-giving SHEM.**

**The painting of Rabbi Löw and his Golem, hanging on the wall of the Emperor's study.**

Later, Russworm threatens to stab the emperor, but cannot do so as King Mathias wants his brother removed from the throne by "fair means." Together with Lang and Kelley, the military man plans to poison Rudolf's wine at lunch. Kelley then brings Sirael into Matew's presence for the emperor's "lesson." Catherine tells the emperor that she's a normal woman and that she is in love with a baker she's never seen. When Matew—who doesn't reveal who he is—tries to kiss her, she slaps him and runs out of the room.

Come lunch, the plotters are astounded when the emperor shows up with the court astronomer, ladies in waiting, wall painters, house servants, and several hundred townspeople. The crowds are sent to the cellar to eat, and Matew—not realizing what he has in his hand—tosses the shem to a little dog. The plotters, seeing what the dog is playing with, fight over the shem, but the emperor takes it from them. In the interim, the astrologer, using the wine chalices to illustrate the movement of planets around the sun, mixes them up; inasmuch as the emperor's chalice had been poisoned, this screws up their plans. The men, forced to drink a toast to the astrologer, drink up and run out of the room.

Scotta returns with the crowd, all of whom have eaten well. He takes the emperor to his alchemist's lab where, after an assistant pronounces an elixir "Yummy al Aqua," the emperor corrects him: "Sliwowitz! Let everyone taste it and have a good time!" As Matew walks about the lab, the sundry charlatans begin to speak of their "experiments." Matew cuts them short:

> You are fiddling with utter nonsense. Forget about all this and come up with something useful for a change. Something that would soften a woman's palms after a day of hard work, skin smooth as velvet, their hair silky—teeth as white as pearls, cheeks ripe as peaches...

This leads into Matew's singing as he walks about the lab ["When we all give what we have to everyone, everything will belong to us all"], and everyone soon is dancing.

Cut to the four plotters [now including the astrologer], who agree to meet the following morning at 8:00 a.m. with a plan to revive the Golem and do away with the emperor. They depart, only to have three return [no Kelley] moments later, agreeing to meet at 7:00 a.m. After they leave again, two return and change the meeting time to 6:00 a.m. After this shtick with the plotters, Scotta, Matew, and the dog appear through a secret door, and Scotta and Matew share confidences: Scotta is not Italian, but was born in a village near Prague, while Matew owns up to being Matew.

They move through another secret door and, while standing in the art gallery in front of the Golem, they examine the little ball, which bears the inscription "Shem Ham Forash." Putting the ball into the Golem's forehead, they watch as the lights go on and the smoke pours out.... The clay giant ambles toward the men, knocking over statues as it advances. Matew cries out, "Halt! Look what you've done!" and the Golem stops. The men determine that the Golem obeys the person who brings it to life; they then remove the shem. "It's steaming hot," Matew observes, and both men realize that Lang, Russworm, and the others also know what the little ball controls.

Meanwhile, Kelley informs Catherine that they're about to kill her Matew, something she can prevent by holding a poisoned rose under the emperor's nose. After a quick cut, we see Catherine and the emperor in his study. The two battle a bit—she hands him the rose; he pulls out a handkerchief—before he reveals who he is to her. At that point, Kelley enters, flinging a knife at Matew. The men fight, Kelley grabs the shem and makes for the door where, providentially, a courtier holds the poisoned rose under the magician's nose; he drops, and Matew, Catherine, and Scotta [with the shem] run into the hall, where they're confronted by the remaining plotters. Scotta and Catherine escape through a secret door, but Matew—too big to make it through—is taken [the shem in his mouth] to the torture chamber to be placed on the rack.

While Scotta is rounding up the townspeople—"They want to torture Matew Kotrba!"—a comedy of incompetence plays out in the torture chamber. Matew inadvertently spits out the shem while laughing, and the astrologer grabs the ball and flees, locking Lang, Russworm, and the others in the torture chamber. Lang and Rosswurm break out as Matew unties himself. "Don't mess with the Golem!" he yells, as the townspeople storm the palace.

As the astrologer places the shem in the Golem's forehead, he is stabbed in the back by Lang, who is then run through by Russworm. The Golem, smoking furiously, moves on the military man, who cries out:

> Golem! Golem! I will place you at the head of a mighty army! And for me you will win the greatest war the world has ever seen. Together we will be victorious! Make war! We will destroy, crush, overthrow, and conquer and rule the whole world!

The Golem, however, will not be halted. The fire from his eyes totally vaporizes Russworm. Looking down momentarily at his handiwork, the clay giant crashes through the wall and into the hallway that is filled with angry townspeople; the Golem fires a ball of flame from its eyes and pandemonium breaks out. Scotta throws some of his cleaning agent on the floor, and the Golem falls. Just at this moment, Matew enters the scene and removes the shem from the clay giant's forehead. The baker stops the villagers from destroying the Golem—he tells them the clay giant can be useful—and he and Catherine embrace.

In the meanwhile, Rudolf has returned to the place and is not pleased with the devastation he sees. Matew tells him that he'll explain everything, but quietly gives the shem to Catherine and whispers, "If I'm not back soon, come for me with the Golem." Following a quick cut, Rudolf offers to forgive Matew if the baker will rule for him "now and then"; Matew declines—if he did step in, he explains, he'd have to tell the Countess Strada where the emperor has been and what he's been up to—and then says that he's leaving, and he's taking the Golem with him. Rudolf accedes.

The final scene takes place in the TITBIT bakery, where the Golem has been installed as the ultimate bread-baking oven. If this works, Matew announces, "there will be especially nice and crispy rolls for us all." The film ends with a reprise of the song.

As should be obvious from the synopsis, the two-parter *Císařův Pekař a Pekařův Císař* is more a period comedy-drama (with much more emphasis on the former element) than a fantasy film. The Golem has only a few minutes of footage wherein it is active, and the character is played not by an actor, but, rather, by a piece of genuine statuary that is shuffled across the floor from behind. The main theme of the pictures, of course, is not the revivification of Rabbi Löw's mystic creation; for Rudolf, the Golem is just another curiosity to be added to his accumulations. The gorgeously mounted productions are meant to endorse the comradely tendencies found in the common man (all of the villagers—including Matew, of course—look out for each other) as opposed to the egocentric drive of monarchies and empires ... and, really, any non-socialistic societies operating at the outset of the 1950s. Charity, support, courtesy, common sense, compassion: all are to be found only among the proletariat. The "ruling class" is rife with greed, corruption, vanity, treachery, indifference, and invincible ignorance, and so it's little wonder that a giant made of clay cannot relate to humans such as these.

V+W's eponymous Liberated Theater effort was considered, at the time, to be a "Jazz Revue." Per Czech theater historian Jarka M. Burian, this sort of presentation

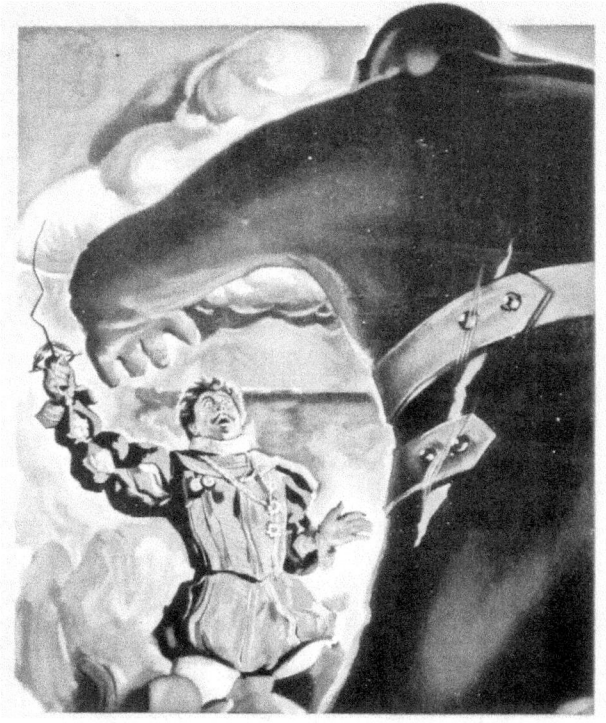

**Poster art depicting the Golem quelling the last element of the attempted coup d'état.**

quickly became popular, and—in form, at least—fairly well structured:

> [It was] an entertainment in two parts with a reasonably firm plot line that incorporated at least one multi-character scene of broad farce comedy, some half-dozen song and dance numbers growing out of the main action, and two or three relatively independent forestage interludes by Voskevec and Werich.[11]

*Golem* was one of a dozen and a half or so such soirees concocted and performed by V+W and company, but whereas earlier efforts had avoided political satire and had been largely escapist in nature, that changed in 1931. Again, per Burian:

> A critical sociopolitical event occurred [in Czechoslovakia] in November 1931 when groups of demonstrating unemployed workers in the northern Bohemian area of Fryvaldov were fired upon by police and military units. Voskovec and Werich, along with countless other artists and intellectuals, were appalled and outraged.[12]

It was during the run of *Golem* that the Fryvaldov incident occurred, and the theatrical piece that would, in part, be incorporated into the 1936 Czech genre feature marked the last romantic-comedy Jazz Revue that V+W would write. Per historian Peter Hames,

> [V+W were] brought together by a shared interest in American westerns and Mack Sennett comedy, Voskovec referred to the American slapstick comedians as "our Stanislavskys." Their mixture of circus, jazz, vaudeville and dadaism gave birth to what the novelist Josef Škvorecký described as "a kind of intellectual-political musical."[13]

In light of all this, it's easy to see why Martin Frič's rendition of V+W's paean to common humanity is much closer to being a musical-comedy remake of Duvivier's vision than any sort of spirited follow-up to either of Wegener's signature pieces.

Of the many cast members of *Císařův Pekař a Pekařův Císař*, only Jan Werich's name might ring the faintest of bells for American audiences. Werich was born in Prague in February 1905, when it was part of the Austro-Hungarian Empire, and died there on Halloween, 1975, when the city was nestled, quite simply, in Czechoslovakia. "W" had almost 30 writer's credits in the film and television media, and nearly three dozen appearances in Czech films. He had a small roll in Val Guest's 1968 British crime drama, *Assignment K*, but almost made it into the English-language cinema big-time a year earlier, when he was initially cast as Ernst Stavro Blofeld in *You Only Live Twice*. According to www.pleasence.com, director Lewis Gilbert and producer Albert Broccoli first laid eyes on Werich on location, and the two found the Czech actor "too benign" for the part; Donald Pleasence was brought in to replace Werich, and the rest is Bondian history.

Martin Frič was one of those cinematic Jacks-of-All-Trades, working as director, writer, actor, miscellaneous crew member, etc., in the course of an almost 40-year-long career. Like Werich, Frič (1902–1968) was born and died in different-era Pragues, and he directed V+W in *Svět Patří Nám* (*The World Is Ours*), a 1937 picture written by the long-time partners. During the Second World War, the director helmed—as Martin Fritsch—several films in Germany, and—as Mac Frič—acted in his own right in 17 movies, including Elektafilm's *Lelicek in the Services of Sherlock Holmes* (1932), in which he played Sherlock. While his body of work may not resonate with Americans, he did direct a trio of literary classics: the first sound version (1931) of Jaroslav Hašek's classic comic novel *The Good Soldier Švejk*; Gogol's *The Inspector General* (*Revizor*); and a Czech-Polish version of Ilf and Petrov's *The Twelve Chairs* (*Dvanáct křesl*, both 1933).

*Císařův Pekař a Pekařův Císař* celebrates both the quackery that passed for science in the Pre-Enlightenment Age and its equally absurd partner, "magic," represented herein by everything from astrology to stage conjuring. These two "fonts of knowledge" are pointedly contrasted with the common sense and selfless spirit of camaraderie evinced by anyone and everyone *not* connected somehow with the Hapsburg court. Throughout most of the attendant nonsense, the Golem is regarded by those in power as an awe-inspiring figure, although its ties to Judaism's mystical side are mentioned not at all. With the narratives thus chiefly concerned with contrasting a pompous, wasteful, and incompetent monarchy with the savvy and generosity of the common man, Rabbi Löw's creation doesn't even merit mention in the pictures's titles.

As with the 1920 and 1936 "versions," the monies allocated to set and costume design and art direction are there on the screen; the big differences lie in the splendid use of color here and the fact that the magnificence of the physical palette of the film(s) under discussion was intended not to be admired, but rather to be viewed askance by contemporary Eastern European–bloc audiences. Physically, these companion features are gorgeous to behold, but one must ask why, for a movie espousing what are at least Socialist principles under the guise of a late 16th-century fantasy, more money than may have been regarded as seemly was spent on the set-up (Rudolf II and his court) than on the pay-off (the Golem). With the dramatic climax finding the clay giant seemingly considering the fate of the Empire—its glowing eyes are exuding steam at a wondrous pace—shouldn't a bit more thought have gone into the character, itself? Aficionados recalling the humanity of a Paul Wegener or even a Ferdinand Hart might initially be taken with the design of the fearsome clay giant, but its herky-jerky movements, its almost comic falls (and the physically impossible way in which it regains its "feet"), and its display of consciousness effected only via smoke and lighting effects put it squarely in the midst of all the balderdash foisted on Rudolf by virtually half the principal cast.

Duvivier's *Le Golem* (from a script by Voskovic and Werich) had an extremely similar scene. (See Soister, *Up from the Vault*, p. 196.)

Balderdash or not, the Golem—at least the iteration found in *Císařův Pekař a Pekařův Císař*—is not only alive and well in contemporary Prague, but is a step above being a cottage industry.

> True to form, [the Golem] is once again experiencing a revival and, in this commercial age, has spawned a one-monster industry.
> There are Golem hotels; Golem door-making companies; Golem clay figurines [made in China]; a recent musical starring a dancing Golem; and a Czech strongman called the Golem who bends iron bars with his teeth. The Golem has even infiltrated Czech cuisine: the menu at a non-kosher restaurant called the Golem features a "rabbi's pocket of beef tenderloin."[14]

Whether *Times*'s reporter Dan Bilefsky was kidding or not about Golem figures made in China, the estate of Jaroslav Horejc—the sculptor who designed and crafted the Golem figure for *Císařův Pekař a Pekařův Císař*—was even then embroiled in what would be a five-year court battle over legal rights to the image and likeness of that particular clay giant. Prague's Municipal Court would rule that the design was the intellectual property of the Horejc family, and even ruled, "Prague's Wax Museum, which has featured two of the figures on its premises, would have to pay 50,000 crowns in damages."[15]

Back in January 1955, the U.S.-release version of Martin Frič's epic was screened—once only, courtesy of Artkino Pictures—the "official" distributor of Soviet pictures to North and South America between 1940 and 1980—at New York's Stanley Theatre. While there exists no record of attendance at the screening, an opinion of the U.S. release version itself by critic H.H.T. for the *New York Times* is extant. In a nutshell,

> pictorially, this Czechoslovak State Film Studios production could hardly be improved. It boasts a well-chosen cast, a flavorsome musical score [by Julius Kalas]; the tasteful settings and costumes literally glow in the first-rate color. Nearly every scene suggests a period painting come to life. But it takes the film, a frank comedy version with serious overtones, a tedious half-hour to do so.... Audiences who come expecting a reprise of the somber Harry Baur masterpiece, "The Golem"—look out! But at the risk of arousing that monster and discounting thirty minutes of dead wood, to us this sprightly, operetta-like sermon is reasonable and palatable.[16]

Once they had entered the country, the sundry bakers, emperors, and golems had a slightly easier time of it. The U.S.-release version was passed along—usually from one film archive or collectors's club to another—and the picture drew limited (but very appreciative) audiences. Due to the efforts of organizations such as these, the two-part original eventually turned up and was made available to those willing to look for it. The Czechoslovak Society of Arts and Sciences New York, for example, screened the two-parter as a Halloween Screening in 2011, and, on the very day income taxes were due in 2014, Golem seekers living in or near our nation's capital were treated better than their "Greater Metropolitan Area" ancestors when a special showing of *Císařův Pekař a Pekařův Císař*—again, as a two-parter—was advertised by the Embassy of the Czech Republic, no less. Between its mid–1950s U.S. premiere and the second decade of the new Millennium, as the Soviet Union collapsed and home-viewer technologies first emerged and then consistently improved, the film—in almost *any* version—has become more readily available to any and all willing to expend the ergs to search out W's clay giant.[17]

As we wrote above, in April 2009, Michelle Obama visited the gravesite of Rabbi Judah Löw ben Bazalel in Prague's Old Jewish Cemetery. What her entourage of reporters did *not* disclose was whether the First Lady then poked about the attic of the Old-New Synagogue for the rabbi's spiritual son.

# Chapter Notes

## Der Tunnel; Transatlantic Tunnel

1. *New Castle Morning Herald and Miner's Advocate* (New South Wales), April 25, 1914.
2. The picture is not mentioned under any of these titles in Gerhard Lamprecht's massive *Deutsche Stummfilme* series.
3. Reinhold Hanisch, *I Was Hitler's Buddy*, p. 242. Said book was never published; when Hitler heard of the venture, Herr Hanisch was arrested and subsequently died of "natural causes." Somehow, the *New Republic* magazine got hold of the manuscript and published excerpts in its April 5, 1939, issue.
4. The January 9, 1934, *Variety* review of the French iteration claimed that the studio was planning an English-language version as well.
5. Full details may be found in Mary Kiersch, *Curtis Bernhardt: Directors Guild of America Oral History*, pp. 58–59, 60–61.
6. *Sunderland Daily Echo and Shipping Gazette*, July 6, 1935.
7. Curt Siodmak, *Wolf Man's Maker*, p. 177.
8. *Ibid.*, p. 182.
9. *Film Daily*, January 2, 1936.
10. Ward Marsh, *Cleveland Plain Dealer*, December 16, 1935.
11. Norbert Lusk, *Los Angeles Times*, November 3, 1935.
12. P.A.S., *Yorkshire Post and Leeds Intelligencer*, November 12, 1935.
13. *Sydney Morning Herald*, June 15, 1936.

## Sherlock Holmes

1. *Really* short nowadays; only 18 feet of 16mm from a paper print survives at the Library of Congress.
2. Kemp Niver, *Motion Pictures from the Library of Congress Paper Print Collection, 1894–1912*, p. 87.
3. Both films may have been filmed as long as two years prior to the dates given, which reflect their registration at the LoC.
4. There were seven made-for-TV films that hit the small screens between 2000 and 2004, featuring Matt Frewer, Richard Roxburgh, James D'Arcy, and Rupert Everett. All enjoyed immediate acknowledgment, few enjoyed critical approbation, and only one actor—Frewer—played Holmes more than once. Frewer (and Kenneth Welsh as Watson) essayed a four-picture package for Muse Entertainment Enterprises; the films were aired on the Hallmark Channel.
5. Intriguingly, so did future Holmes impersonator Peter Jeremy William Huggins, who changed his name *to* Brett—Jeremy Brett—in reaction to *his* father's disapproval.
6. Robert W. Pohle, Jr., and Douglas C. Hart, *Sherlock Holmes on the Screen*, p. 73.
7. As quoted in Michael Pointer, *The Sherlock Holmes File*, pp. 41–42.
8. It *may* have been Michael Strange's *Clair de Lune*, based on Victor Hugo's *L'Homme qui rit*; however, the Broadway production lasted but eight weeks and closed in July 1921.
9. The eponymous seven-reel feature, thought lost for decades, was recently rediscovered at the Cinémathèque Française.
10. Hank Mann did a short spoof for Arrow, Conrad Veidt appeared as Dr. Warren and Mr. O'Connor in *Der Januskopf*—Murnau's royalty-free "adaptation"—and contemporary critics warned potential ticket-buyers not to confuse the Goldwyn picture with the Pioneer five-reeler, which updated the setting to contemporary times and presented Sheldon Lewis's Hyde largely as a poorly dressed pyromaniac.
11. Suzanne Sexton, *New York Morning Telegraph*, May 14, 1922.
12. *New York Times*, May 8, 1922.
13. *The AFI Film Catalog* lists the premiere print at an even 8,200 feet, while the *Film Daily* assessment is more specific at 8,156. The "published" footage length of the general-release prints was likewise rounded up (or down).
14. Pohle and Hart, *Sherlock Holmes on the Screen*, pp. 100–101.
15. This observation—ours—based on our viewing the KINO DVD. Kevin Brownlow has suggested the lighting in this scene may appear dim either due to poor lab work on the reduction print and/or to the fact that Albert Parker said the scene was tinted red in the original.
16. Margot Peters, *The House of Barrymore*, pp. 226–227.
17. In their requisite *The Films of Sherlock Holmes*, Chris Steinbunner and Norman Michaels aver that there were also "actual days of shooting in Switzerland" (p. 18). The only scenes in the restored print that bear evidence of this are Barrymore-less and concern the fate of Rose Faulkner.
18. Peters, *The House of Barrymore*, p. 227.
19. James Kostsilibas-Davis, *The Barrymores*, p. 35.
20. William K. Everson, *The Detective in Film*, p. 10.
21. The BFI Reuben Library indicates that the 35mm print of *Moriarty* that unspooled at the trade screening (January 25, 1923) and for general release (four days later) ran 8,000 feet. This would seem to indicate that M-G-M had exported its original cut and that a bit of trimming was done locally.
22. MGM's vault 7 fire didn't receive much attention from the "civilian" press, for whom it meant little more than yet another relatively minor conflagration. As a favor to the authors of this book, author/film historian/AFI employee Robert Dickson did some research on whether the *industry* press made more precise details—such as an inventory of the incinerated titles—available at that time to those for whom the cinema was their passion and livelihood. The rather startling results of Mr. Dickson's research: "Unable to find anything [apart from regular press mention] on MGM fire in '67." Wow!

23. Everson, *The Detective in Film*, p. 9.
24. *New York Times*, January 21, 2000.
25. Unless otherwise cited, quotations from Mr. Brownlow were taken from emails he exchanged with the authors of this book.
26. "The [Carey Salt] Mine is the unlikely location of all MGM fine grain prints and the central distributor to all television networks of MGM film footage." *Salinas (Kansas) Journal*, 5 August 1979, p. 30.
27. The eminently readable, vastly opinionated, refreshingly non-academic ("no semiotic obscurities") James Card, *Seductive Cinema: The Art of Silent Film*, pp. 294–295.
28. We feel justified in positing this scenario as, in an email to us, Mr. Brownlow wrote that Everson "had to assure Card ... that I was trustworthy[!]."
29. George C. Warren, *San Francisco Chronicle*, November 21, 1922. Emphasis added.
30. That was cleared up fairly quickly. The May 14, 1922, *Film Daily* did praise von Seyffertitz as being "excellent in a character not unlike Barrymore's own Dr. Hyde [sic]."

## *The Sky Ranger* (*The Man Who Stole the Moon*)

1. Kalton C. Lahue, *Continued Next Week: A History of the Moving Picture Serial*, p. 3.
2. See John T. Soister, *Up from the Vault*.
3. Lahue, *Continued Next Week*, p. 94.
4. Well, not quite. Honesty compels us to report *All Aboard for the Moon*, a 1920 American production. Still, it was but a one-reel cartoon, directed by Max (Popeye) Fleischer for the J.R. Bray Studios.
5. See Steve Joyce's coverage of *Mars* in John T. Soister and Henry Nicolella with Steve Joyce and Harry H. Long, researcher/archivist Bill Chase, *American Silent Horror, Science Fiction and Fantasy Feature Films, 1913–1929*, Vol. I, pp. 386–388.
6. Our discussion of early cinematic space travels is continued in our essay on *Just Imagine*.

## First Looks: *Das grinsende Gesicht*; *Die Insel der Verschollenen*

1. Number 183, September 1920. *Paimann's Film List* was an Austrian journal founded in 1916. Any film that played in Austria was given a brief synopsis and a rating.
2. The 1909 one-reel version of the novel—produced by Pathé—is MIA.
3. A television adaptation of *Le Docteur Lerne* was done in France in 1983.

## *The Monkey's Paw*; *Sweeney Todd*

1. Footage as reported in the October 20, 1923, *Exhibitor's Herald*. Denis Gifford's *The British Film Catalogue* has it at 5,700 feet.
2. In 1929 *The Beetle* was adapted for the stage in London and, while some found it superior to Hamilton Deane's *Dracula*, the box-office receipts told a different story.
3. The IMDB lists a UK 1919 film version, but gives neither cast nor credits. This is likely to be a mistake as no such film appears on the BFI website or is listed in Denis Gifford's very thorough *British Film Catalog*.
4. Casual research indicates that a "penny blood" is not the same as a "penny dreadful." Arguing over such as this is roughly comparable to arguing over just what constitutes a "B" movie.
5. Research has yet to uncover the identity of the author of this serial, although the names Thomas Peckett Prest and James Malcolm Rymer usually top the speculative list.
6. For an exhaustive—and exhausting—account of the demon barber's literary life, see Robert Mack's *The Wonderful and Surprising History of Sweeney Todd*.
7. Michael Kilgariff, *The Golden Age of Melodrama*, p. 267.
8. Jeffrey Richards, *The Unknown Thirties*, p. 147.
9. Mack, *The Wonderful and Surprising History of Sweeney Todd*, p. 230.

## *The House Without a Key*

1. John T. Soister and Henry Nicolella with Steve Joyce and Harry H. Long, researcher/archivist Bill Chase, *American Silent Horror, Science Fiction and Fantasy Feature Films, 1913-1929*.
2. Gary J. Svehla and Susan Svehla, eds., *Boris Karloff*.
3. See Soister, *Up from the Vault*.
4. *Harvard College Class of 1907 Twenty-Fifth Anniversary Report*, p. 43.
5. Yuante Huang, *Charlie Chan: The Untold Story of the Honorable Detective and His Rendezvous with American History*, p. 119.
6. *Motion Picture News*, November 27, 1926.
7. Jon Tuska, *The Detective in Hollywood*, p. 106.
8. *Ibid.*
9. Full coverage on this enjoyably bizarre production is found in Soister, *Up from the Vault*.
10. www.fandango.com/GeorgeKuwa/biography/p39667.
11. *Honolulu Star Bulletin*, July 7, 1928.
12. Ken Hanke, *Charlie Chan at the Movies*, p. 112.

## *Forgotten Faces*

1. *The AFI Catalog* mistakenly reports that the film follows the short story on Lilly's fate and has her getting arrested for shooting Harry. Apparently the writers of *Forgotten Faces* felt that was letting her off too easy, but it obliges Harry to give a rather casuistic interpretation of his promise to the warden not to hurt Lilly.
2. *Motion Picture World*, May 5, 1928.
3. *Till We Meet Again*, another 1936 film teaming Marshall and Gertrude, was also sometimes known as *Forgotten Faces*.
4. Humor was scarcely Dupont's strong point though some find his *Neanderthal Man*, made during the nadir of his career, pretty funny.
5. Bosley Crowther, *New York Times*, April 17, 1942.

## *Men Must Fight*; *High Treason*

1. *Daily News* (Perth, Western Australia), November 19, 1928.
2. For coverage of the silent version of *High Treason* see Soister, *Up from the Vault*.
3. *High Treason* program notes by Jack Theakston, Capitolfest, 2014.
4. *Motion Picture News*, October 18, 1930.
5. Sample lyrics: "March on to Peace, Fulfil Humanity's Call, The martial cry of war must die." Well, is this any worse than "Give Peace a Chance"?
6. The winsome Ms. Ray often played urchins in the

thirties, most notably in Conrad Veidt's *Passing of the Third Floor Back*. She later became a writer and scripted the 1956 British TV sci-fi series *The Strange World of Planet X* which was turned into the film *Cosmic Monster* (1958).

## Les Fantômes de Paris: *The Phantom of Paris*; *Chéri-Bibi*

1. See our coverage of the film in our silent genre features encyclopedia, *American Silent Horror, Science Fiction and Fantasy Feature Films, 1913–1929*, Vol. I.
2. Michael F. Blake, *Lon Chaney: The Man Behind the Thousand Faces*, p. 308.
3. Ibid., p. 352.
4. Michael F. Blake, *A Thousand Faces: Lon Chaney's Unique Artistry in Motion Pictures*, p. 272.
5. What's in a title? The Sunday, September 12, 1926, edition of the *New York Times* contained a review for Gaston Leroux's *Murder in Paris: The Phantom Clue*, which had just been published by New York's The Macaulay Company. Not Chéri-Bibi, though, but Joseph Rouletabille.
6. Simon Louvish, *Keystone; The Life and Clowns of Mack Sennett*, p. 246.
7. Except for Chaney himself: "On June 21 [1929], Lon is diagnosed as 'incapacitated.' He makes out his Last Will and Testament two days later." Blake, *Lon Chaney; The Man Behind the Thousand Faces*, p. 314.
8. Per Heinink and Dickson's *Cita en Hollywood* (pp. 104–105), Paramount also filmed a Japanese version of *Paramount on Parade* in Hollywood that year. Per the authors, utilizing French studios, Paramount filmed additional foreign-language versions, including German, Swiss, Danish, Polish, Czech, Serbian, Hungarian, Romanian, Dutch, and Italian.
9. The picture also had a French-language counterpart, *Le metteur en scène*.
10. For the full run-down on this, please see our article, "The Spanish Man of a Thousand Faces," in *Van Helsing's Journal* 7.
11. Harry Waldman, *Missing Reels: Lost Films of American and European Cinema*, p. 220.
12. As quoted by film historian Don G. Smith, "In 1936, Boris Karloff referred to *The Black Room* as 'my favorite picture so far'" (*Boris Karloff: Midnight Marquee Actors Series*, p. 129). Smith continued, "Consider for a moment that he had already done *Frankenstein*, *The Old Dark House*, *The Mummy*, *The Ghoul*, *The Black Cat*, and *Bride of Frankenstein*. I believe Karloff was right. In fact, I would rate Boris Karloff's performance in *The Black Room* the best of his career."
13. The picture is considered to be lost as we write this.
14. *Variety*, December 22, 1954.
15. Waldman, *Missing Reels*, p. 193.
16. The AFI Catalog lists the production dates for *The Phantom of Paris* as "17 February—late March, 1931," which means that the Spanish version had probably wrapped before the U.S. version began shooting.

## Just Imagine

1. *Los Angeles Times*, October 19, 1930.
2. We also hasten to remind interested readers that extensive coverage of *Radio Mania* and *A Message from Mars* may be found in our two-volume encyclopedia, *American Horror, Science Fiction and Fantasy Feature Films, 1913–1929*.

3. The best overview remains Bill Warren's magnificent *Keep Watching the Skies*.
4. "A rousing banquet ... one of the finest routined musical numbers yet presented to the screen." *Exhibitors Trade Review*, November 22, 1930. This, J's "farewell party."
5. *Variety*, November 26, 1930.
6. *The Daily Reporter*, October 21, 1930.
7. The *Exhibitors Trade Review*, cited above, also opined, "The picture at times seems ... like skits from a revue that have been continuized [sic] and knit together...."
8. *New York Times*, November 23, 1930.
9. *Los Angeles Times*, October 18, 1930.
10. We are in possession of a xerox copy of the article which, unhelpfully, has no top- or bottom-border information other than the page numbers, 52 and 98. Mr. Belfrage frequently wrote for *Film Daily*.
11. "Dutch" comics were a staple in Vaudeville, and silent slapstick comedies were populated with funnymen who crossed over into the pictures (and frequently crossed back); check out Mack Sennett's roster.
12. Ibid., p. 98.
13. *Harrison's Reports*, November 29, 1930.
14. www.jewishvirtuallibrary.org.
15. Evelyn Gerstein, *Theatre Guild Magazine*, December 7, 1931.

## *Fog*; *Terror Aboard*

1. Frank Bernds, *Mr. Bernds Goes to Hollywood*, pp. 214–215.
2. In Danny Peary's *Close-Ups* (1985), writer Sidney Salkow, who worked with Lombard on *Supernatural*, gives a very funny account of her behavior on the set.

## *The Horror*: The Patchwork Cinema of Bud Pollard

1. Nor was Bud related to diminutive comic actress Daphne Pollard or to director Harry Pollard. Daphne and Snub were not related either, but took the name Pollard from the Pollard Lilliputian Opera Company, a vaudeville children's company in which they had both appeared.
2. Will Morrisey, *On a Shoestring*, pp. 279–280.
3. The April 3, 1931, *Film Daily* noted that "Bud Pollard is synchronizing and cutting a 10-episode serial starring Jack Hoxie and Marion Sais. The picture will be released shortly by Guaranteed Pictures Corp." The title of the serial isn't given, but it might have been the 1927 *Heroes of the Wild* (though Sais isn't in it). We have not found anything definite on this, even whether the feature version was ever released as planned.
4. There are two other movies with the same title: a 1931 film made up of clips from different sleazy productions (including the aforementioned *Trial Marriage*) and a 1939 Columbia thriller.
5. Some sources mistakenly claim the film was exhibited under this title.
6. His stage name was sometimes misspelled as "Rabold" and "Raja."
7. Mark Walker, *Ghostmasters*, p. 37.
8. Presumably she was a stripper. Pollard seemed to have a thing for girls and snakes. Years later he tried to do a film version of the life of snake dancer Zorita.
9. George Turner and Michael Price, *Forgotten Horrors: The Definitive Edition*, pp. 94–95.
10. Richard Kozarski, *Hollywood on the Hudson*, p. 303.
11. In 1935 Pollard announced he would be working

with Margaret Sanger to do a movie titled *Birth Control* based on the play *The State Forbids*. This did not happen.

## Return of the Terror

1. *Charleston* (West Virginia) *Gazette*, August 9, 1933.
2. *Syracuse* (New York) *Herald Journal*, August 26, 1934.
3. *Oakland* (California) *Tribune*, March 29, 1934.
4. *Los Angeles Times*, June 29, 1934.
5. *Cleveland* (Ohio) *Plain Dealer*, July 13, 1934.
6. *Los Angles Times*, June 29, 1934.

## Death Takes a Holiday

1. *New York Times*, November 24, 1929.
2. *The American Film Institute Catalog: Feature Films, 1931–1940*, pp. 516–517.
3. Deborah C. Peterson, *Fredric March: Craftsman First, Star Second*, p. 78.
4. And the Swedes. In 1920, Victor Sjöstrm's *Körkarlen* (*The Phantom Carriage*) had Death at the reins of the titular barouche.
5. In ancient China, mourners dressed in *white* to denote their loss.
6. Aka, *The Scarlet Empress*.
7. *New York Times*, November 19, 1933.
8. Peterson, *Fredric March: Craftsman First, Star Second*, pp. 77–78.
9. *Variety*, February 27, 1934.
10. Gracias to David Wilt and *The Mexican Filmography: 1961–2001*.

## Hispanic Horrors

1. Juan Bustillo Oro, *Vida Cinematográfica*, p. 144.
2. In his retelling of *Rostro*'s original plotline in *Vida*, Bustillo Oro reveals that Montes (Mon*ter* in the original) and Engracia both die of cardiac arrest, brought on by more of Forti's drugs.
3. Wilt, *The Mexican Filmography: 1916–2001*, p. 28.
4. Bustillo Oro, *Vida Cinematográfica*, p. 146.
5. *Ibid.*, p. 147.
6. Lisa Jarvinen, *The Rise of Spanish-Language Filmmaking*, p. 31.
7. Rogelio Agrasánchez, Jr., *Miguel Zacarías: Creador de estrellas*, p. 40.
8. Agrasánchez was present when Zacarías credited Alejandro Galindo—onscreen as the adaptor—with the original story, as well. Dada, a producer who financed a number of films, usually asked for a story credit in return. Also a composer, some of Dada's films (like *Baúl*) would feature his songs.
9. Fairly early on in the proceedings, as René Cardona and Esther Fernández are pounding wildly away at the piano in the drawing room, we espy the clapboard being withdrawn hastily from the scene. Even Ed Wood might have called for a second take following something like that.
10. Emilio García Rivera, *Historia Documental del Cine Mexicano*, Vol. I, pp. 218–219.
11. *Ibid.*
12. H.T.S., *New York Times*, November 30, 1937.
13. If the nationality of Naschy's wolfman caught you up short, please repair immediately to the actor's autobiography, *Memoirs of a Wolfman*, for more detail on this fascinating character created by a fascinating individual.
14. *Nadie Inquietó Más*—"Nobody Disturbed/Disquieted More," said Spanish title built on his initials.
15. *La Cosa* 23 (October 1997).

## Der Hund von Baskerville

1. The information on the plot of the Oswald-Philipp play is from Benedikt Grawe's 2013 dissertation for the University of Vienna on Oswald and his part in the different versions of "The Hound of the Baskervilles."
2. *Das einsame Haus* (1914), *Das Dunkle Schloß* (1915), *Das unheimliche Zimmer* (1915), *Die Sage vom Hund von Baskerville* (1915), *Dr. MacDonalds Sanatorium* (1920), and *Das Haus ohne Fenster* (1920).
3. While still extant, the film is seldom seen outside the confines of the British Film Institute.
4. Voss, who died in 1979, is sometimes credited with appearing in the 1991 horror comedy *My Lovely Monster*. Unless he had his own Ferryman Maria saving him from the Grim Reaper, this is almost certainly a mistake and it is a different Peter Voss who appears in the film.

## Císařův Pekař a Pekařův Císař (The Emperor's Baker, the Baker's Emperor)

1. The release date here is taken from the website www.csfd.c2/film/3094. The IMDB has the original Czech release as 1952.
2. We are purposefully not including in this discussion Wegener's *Der Golem und die Tanzarin*, a 1917 comic treatment or the unmade (but not unpublicized) *Alraune und der Golem*.
3. Please see our less tongue-in-cheek and more comprehensive coverage on both Wegener Golem films in our volume *Many Selves: The Horror and Fantasy Films of Paul Wegener*.
4. A detailed overview of *Le Golem* based on this original-release print may be found in Soister, *Up from the Vault*, pp. 186–198.
5. Marcel Cornis-Pope and John Neubauer, *History of the Literary Cultures of East-Central Europe*, Vol. II, pp. 178–179.
6. *Ibid.*, p. 180.
7. *Ibid.*, p. 182.
8. Veronika Ambros, "How Did the Golems (and Robots) Enter Stage and Screen and Leave Prague?" *History of the Literary Cultures of East-Central Europe*, Vol. IV, p. 318.
9. "Dramatic Figure."
10. Ambros, "How Did the Golems (and Robots) Enter Stage and Screen and Leave Prague?" p. 319.
11. Jarka M. Burian, *Leading Creators of Twentieth-Century Czech Theatre*, p. 28.
12. *Ibid.*, p. 29.
13. Peter Hames, *Czech and Slovak Cinema: Theme and Tradition*, p. 34.
14. "Hard Times Give New Life to Prague's Golem," *New York Times*, May 10, 2009.
15. Czech Radio 7, Radio Prague, www.radio.cz.
16. *New York Times*, January 10, 1955.
17. As of this writing, free (as a 101-minute HD feature on YouTube); cheap—but in Czech only—on amazon.com. Plus available from the usual suspects.

# Bibliography

Agrasánchez, Rogelio, Jr. *Mexican Movies in the United States*. Jefferson, North Carolina: McFarland, 2006.

_____. *Miguel Zacarías: Creador de estrellas*. Guadalajara, México: Archivo Fílmico Agrasánchez, 2000.

Alonso, Harriet Hyman. *Robert E. Sherwood: The Playwright in Peace and War*. Amherst: Massachusetts Press, 2007.

Alpert, Hollis. *The Barrymores: The Full, Fascinating Story of Ethel, Lionel, and John—The Royal Family of the American Theater*. New York: Dial Press, 1964.

Ambros, Veronika. "How Did the Golems (and Robots) Enter Stage and Screen and Leave Prague?" *History of the Literary Cultures of East-Central Europe*, Vol. IV. Amsterdam: John Benjamins, 2004.

Benson, Michael. *Vintage Science Fiction Films, 1896–1949*. Jefferson, North Carolina: McFarland, 1985.

Bergfelder, Tim, and Christian Cargnelli. *Destination London: German-Speaking Emigres and British Cinema, 1925–1950*. Oxford: Berghahn Books, 2013.

Berlin, Howard M. *The Charlie Chan Film Encyclopedia*. Jefferson, North Carolina: McFarland, 2000.

Bernds, Frank. *Mr. Bernds Goes to Hollywood*. Lanham, Maryland: Scarecrow Press, 1999.

Biggers, Earl Derr. *The House Without a Key*. Chicago: Academy Chicago, 2008.

Blackbeard, Bill. *Sherlock Holmes in America*. New York: Harry N. Abrams, 1981.

Blake, Michael F. *The Films of Lon Chaney*. Lanham, Maryland: Vestal Press, 1998.

_____. *Lon Chaney: The Man Behind the Thousand Faces*. Vestal, New York: Vestal Press, 1993

_____. *A Thousand Faces: Lon Chaney's Unique Artistry in Motion Pictures*. Vestal, New York: Vestal Press, 1995.

Brownlow, Kevin. *The Parade's Gone By...* New York: Alfred A. Knopf, 1968.

_____, and Cy Young. *David Lean: A Biography*. New York: Macmillan, 1996.

Burian, Jarka M. *Leading Creators of Twentieth-Century Czech Theatre*. London: Routledge, 2002.

Bustillo Oro, Juan. *Vida Cinematográfica*. Distrito Federal (Mexico City): Cineteca Nacional, 1984.

Butler, Ivan. *Silent Magic: Rediscovering the Silent Film Era*. New York: Ungar, 1988.

Card, James. *Seductive Cinema: The Art of Silent Film*. Minneapolis: University of Minnesota Press, 1994.

Cherchi Usai, Paolo. *Burning Passions: An Introduction to the Study of Silent Cinema*. London: BFI, 1995.

Connor, Edward. "The 6 Charlie Chans." *Films in Review* 1 (January 1955).

Cornis-Pope, Marcel, and John Neubauer. *History of the Literary Cultures of East Central Europe*, 4 vols. Volumes. Amsterdam: John Benjamins, 2004.

Davies, David Stuart. *Holmes of the Movies: The Screen Career of Sherlock Holmes*. New York: Bramhall House, 1976.

Douglas, Drake. *Horrors*. Woodstock, New York: Overlook Press, 1989.

Everson, William K. *American Silent Film*. New York: Da Capo Press, 1998.

_____. *The Detective in Film: A Pictorial History of the Screen Sleuth from 1903 to the Present*. Secaucus, New Jersey: Citadel Press, 1972.

García Rivera, Emilio. *Historia Documental del Cine Mexicano*. Guadalajara, Mexico: Universidad de Guadalajara, 1998.

Gifford, Denis. *The British Film Catalogue, 1895–1985*. New York: Facts on File, 1986.

Grange, William. *Historical Dictionary of the German Theater*. Lanham, MD: Scarecrow Press, 2006.

Grawe, Benedikt. "Der Hund von Baskerville—Auf der spur eines verschollenen Film." Doctoral dissertation, University of Vienna, 2013.

Gredhill, Christine. *Reframing British Cinema: 1918–1928*. London: British Film Institute, 2003.

Haining, Peter, ed. *The Sherlock Holmes Scrapbook*. New York: Clarkson N. Potter, 1974.

Hames, Peter. *Czech and Slovak Cinema: Theme and Tradition*. Edinburgh: Edinburgh University Press, 2009.

Hanke, Ken. *Charlie Chan at the Movies: History, Filmography, and Criticism*. Jefferson, North Carolina: McFarland, 1989.

Hardy, Phil, ed. *The Encyclopedia of Science Fiction Movies*. Minneapolis: Woodbury Press, 1986.

Heinink, Juan B., and Robert G. Dickson. *Cita en Hollywood; antología de las películas norteamericanas habladas en español*. Bilbao, Spain: Ediciones Mensajero, 1990.

Huang, Yuante. *Charlie Chan: The Untold Story of the Honorable Detective and His Rendezvous with American History*. New York: W.W. Norton, 2010.

Jarvinen, Lisa. *The Rise of Spanish Filmmaking: Out from Hollywood's Shadow, 1929–1939*. New Brunswick: Rutgers University Press, 2012.

Kellermann, Bernhard. *The Tunnel*. London: Hodder and Staughton, 1915.

Kiersch, Mary, interviewer. *Curtis Bernhardt: Directors Guild of America Oral History*. Metuchen, New Jersey: Scarecrow Press, 1986.

Kilgariff, Michael. *The Golden Age of Melodrama.* London: Mosby-Wolfe, 1974.

Kobler, John. *Damned in Paradise: The Life of John Barrymore.* New York: Atheneum, 1977.

Kostsilibas-Davis, James. *The Barrymores: The Royal Family in Hollywood.* New York: Crown, 1981.

Kozarski, Richard. *Hollywood on the Hudson.* Piscataway: Rutgers University Press, 2004.

Kreimeier, Klaus. *The Ufa Story.* New York: Hill and Wang, 1996.

Lahue, Kalton C. *Continued Next Week: A History of the Motion Picture Serial.* Norman: University of Oklahoma Press, 1964.

Lamprecht, Gerhard. *Deutsche Stummfilme, 1915–1916.* Berlin: Deutsche Kinemathek Berlin, 1969.

Lennig, Arthur. *The Immortal Count: The Life and Films of Bela Lugosi.* Lexington: University Press of Kentucky, 2003.

Louvish, Simon. *Keystone: The Life and Clowns of Mack Sennett.* London: Faber and Faber, 2003.

Lukins, Jocelyn, ed. *The Fantasy Factory Lime Grove Studios, London 1915–1991.* London: Venta Books, 1996.

Mack, Robert L. *The Wonderful and Surprising History of Sweeney Todd.* London: Continuum, 2007.

Mitchell, Charles P. *A Guide to Charlie Chan Films.* Westport, Connecticut: Greenwood Press, 1999.

Morrison, Michael A. *John Barrymore: Shakespearean Actor.* New York: Cambridge University Press, 1997.

Morrissey, Will. *On a Shoestring.* Santa Barbara: Willdon Paul, 1955.

Naschy, Paul. *Paul Naschy: Memoirs of a Wolfman.* Baltimore: Midnight Marquee Press, 2000.

Nicolella, Henry, and John T. Soister. *Many Selves: The Horror and Fantasy Films of Paul Wegener.* Duncan, OK: BearManor, 2012.

Niver, Kemp. *Motion Pictures from The Library of Congress Paper Print Collection 1894–1912.* Berkeley: University of California Press, 1967.

Nowlan, Robert A., and Gwendolyn Wright Nowlan. *The Films of the Eighties.* Jefferson, North Carolina: McFarland, 1991.

Okuda, Ted. *The Monogram Checklist.* Jefferson, North Carolina: McFarland, 1987.

Peters, Margot. *The House of Barrymore.* New York: Alfred A. Knopf, 1999.

Peterson, Deborah C. *Fredric March: Craftsman First, Star Second.* Westport, Connecticut: Greenwood Press, 1996.

*The Picturegoer's WHO'S WHO and Encyclopedia of the Screen Today.* New York: Gordon Press, 1977.

Pitts, Michael R. *Famous Movie Detectives.* Metuchen, New Jersey: Scarecrow Press, 1979.

Pohle, Robert W., Jr., and Douglas C. Hart. *Sherlock Holmes on the Screen.* New York: A.S. Barnes, 1977.

Pointer, Michael. *The Sherlock Holmes File: The Many Personae of Sherlock Holmes on Stage, in Film, and in Advertising.* New York: Clarkson N. Potter, 1976.

Power-Waters, Alma. *John Barrymore: The Legend and the Man.* New York: Julian Messner, 1941.

Quirk, Lawrence J. *The Films of Fredric March.* New York: Citadel Press, 1971.

Rhodes, Gary Don. *Lugosi.* Jefferson, North Carolina: McFarland, 1997.

Richards, Jeffrey, ed. *The Unknown 1930s: An Alternate History of the British Cinema 1929–1939.* London: I.B. Tauris, 1998.

Saunders, Thomas J. "Film and Finance in Weimar Germany: The Rise and Fall of David Schratter's Trianon-Film 1923–1925." *Film History: An International Journal* 23, no. 11 (2003).

Schickel, Richard. *D.W. Griffith: An American Life.* New York: Simon & Schuster, 1984.

Sigoloff, Marc. *The Films of the Seventies.* Jefferson, North Carolina: McFarland, 1984.

Sims, Dorothy Rice, and Valentine Williams. *Fog.* New York: Washington Square Press, 1933.

Siodmak, Curt. *Wolf Man's Maker.* Scarecrow Filmmakers Series. Ann Arbor: Scarecrow Press/University of Michigan, 1997.

Slide, Anthony. *Nitrate Won't Wait: A History of Film Preservation in the United States.* Jefferson, North Carolina: McFarland, 1992.

Smith, Don. G. "The Black Room." *Boris Karloff: Midnight Marquee Actors Series.* Gary J. and Susan Svehla, eds. Arlington: Midnight Marquee Press, 1996.

Soister, John T., and Henry Nicolella with Steve Joyce and Harry H. Long, researcher/archivist Bill Chase. *American Silent Horror, Science Fiction and Fantasy Feature Films, 1913–1929.* Jefferson, NC: McFarland, 2012.

Soister, John. *Up from the Vault.* Jefferson, North Carolina: McFarland, 2004.

Steinbrenner, Chris, and Norman Michaels. *The Films of Sherlock Holmes.* Secaucus, New Jersey: Citadel Press, 1978.

Strickland, A.W., and Forrest J Ackerman. *A Reference Guide to American Science Fiction Films*, Vol. I. Bloomington: T.I.S. Publications, 1981.

Turner, George, and Michael Price. *Forgotten Horrors: The Definitive Edition.* Baltimore: Midnight Marquee Press, 1999.

Tuska, Jon. *The Detective in Hollywood: The Movie Careers of the Great Fictional Private Eyes and Their Creators.* Garden City, New York: Doubleday, 1978.

Vondereau, Patrick. *Bilder vom Norden: Schwedisch-deutsch Filmbeziehungen, 1914–1939.* Ann Arbor: University of Michigan, 2007.

Waldman, Harry. *Missing Reels: Lost Films of American and European Cinema.* Jefferson, North Carolina: McFarland, 2000.

Walker, Mark. *Ghostmasters.* Boca Raton: Cool Hand Communications, 1994.

Warren, Bill. *Keep Watching the Skies! American Science Fiction Movies of the Fifties.* Jefferson, North Carolina: McFarland, 1982, 1986 (rev. ed., 2010).

Wilt, David. *The Mexican Filmography: 1916–2001.* Jefferson, North Carolina: McFarland, 2004.

Wlaschin, Ken. *Silent Mystery and Detective Movies: A Comprehensive Filmography.* Jefferson, North Carolina: McFarland, 2009.

# Index

Numbers in **bold** indicate illustrations

*Abbott and Costello Meet Frankenstein* 189
*About Trial Marriage* 156
*Abraham Lincoln* 122
*Accident* 16
*The Active Life of Dolly of the Dailies* 43
Adams, Maud 100
*The Admirable Crichton* 60
Adrian 107
*The Adventures of Kathlyn* 43
*The Adventures of Mark Twain* 186
*The Adventures of Mr. Pickwick* 71
*The Adventures of Peg O' the Ring* 43
*The Adventures of Sherlock Holmes* (1905) 20
*The Adventures of Sherlock Holmes* (1921) 21
*Aelita* 127
Agrasánchez, Rogelio, Jr. 196–197, 198
*Ahí está el detalle* (*There's the Detail*) 192
*Die Ahnfrau* (*The Ancestress*) 53
Albers, Hans 206, 211
Albertson, Frank **129**, 136, 137
*The Alfred Hitchcock Hour* (TV series) 92
*Algol* 47
*Alice in Wonderland* 158–159
*Allá en el Rancho Grande* 198
Allain, Marcel 113
Allan, Hugh 85
Allen, Steve 150
Ambros, Veronika 216
*America Speaks* 166
*American Psycho* 62
*An American Tragedy* 109
*The Ancient Mariner* 112
*Der Andere* (*The Other*) 211
Anderson, Maxwell 181, 183
*Andy Hardy's Blonde Trouble* 51
*Anna Karenina* 186
*Anthony Adverse* 186
Antoine, André-Paul 215
*The Ape* 201
Apana, Chang 84, 89
Arbuckle, Roscoe "Fatty" 151
Arenas, Miguel 201
*Die arge Nonn* (*The Evil Nun*) 53
Arliss, George 16
Armengod, Ramón 201
*Armored Vault* 61
*Arsenic and Old Lace* (play) 200
*Assignment K* 222

Arvidson, Linda 32
*As the Devil Commands* 174
Ashwell, Lena 64
Asimov, Isaac 1
Astor, Mary 174
*The Atomic Submarine* 86
Atwill, Lionel 122, 137, 148
Auer, Mischa 136, 137–138
Aumont, Jean-Pierre 123
Ault, Marie 64
*The Awful Dr. Orloff* (*Gritos en la noche*) 189

Baber, Vivianne 159
*Back to the Future* 51
Baclanova, Olga 5, 57, 94–96
Bacon, M.R. 103
Baker, George 92, 93
*The Baker's Emperor* 5, 44, **215**, 216, 219–224, **223**
Balshofer, Fred J. 151
Bamberger, Rudolf 212
Bancroft, George 95
Banks, Leslie 15
*El barón del terror* (*The Brainiac*) 189
Barrat, Robert 174
*The Barretts of Wimpole Street* 185–186
Barrymore, John 4, 22–23, **22**, **24**, **26**, 27, 28, **28**, **29**, **31**, 32, 33, 83, 185
Barrymore, Lionel 27, 118, 137, 187
Barzini, Luigi 91
*The Basilisk* 63
Bassermann, Albert 211
*Batman and Robin* 86
*The Battle Cry of Peace* 108
*El baúl macabro* 5, 188, **192**, 193–198, 201
Bava, Mario 189
*Beau Brummel* (character) 23
*Beau Geste* 147
*Bedazzled* 67
Beecher, Janet **106**
Beery, Wallace 186
*The Beetle* 63
*Behind That Curtain* 83, 84
*Behold the Man* 86
Behrendt, Hans 60
*The Bells* 33
*The Beloved Rogue* 83
ben Löwe, Rabbi Judah 214, **214**, 216, **220**, 221, 223, 224
Bennet, Spencer Gordon 4, 51, 82, 85, 86, **89**

Bennett, Leila 147
Berger, Ludwig 212
Berkeley, Busby 131
Bernds, Frank 144
Bernhardt, Kurt 14
Bert, Flo 135
*The Best Years of Our Lives* 186
*Beware* 166
*The Big City* 116
*The Big Parade* 120
*Big Timers* 166
Biggers, Earl Derr 4, 83, 84, 88, 89, 90
Binyon, Claude 145
*The Birth of a Nation* 135
*Birth of a Star* 167
*The Bishop Murder Case* 33, 121
*The Black Book* 85
*The Black Camel* 90, 137
*The Black Cat* 168
*The Black King* 159
*Black Moon* 168
*Black Orchids* 121, 122
*The Black Room* 119
*Black Sunday* (*La Maschera del Demonio*) 189
*The Black Swan* 62
*Blackhawk* 51
*Blackmail* 101, 205
Blackwell, Carlyle 205
Blackwood, Jack 153
*Blood and Roses* (*Et Mourir de Plaisir*) 189
Bogart, Humphrey 50
*La Bohème* 120
Bois, Curt 154
Boland, John 192
*A Bolt from the Sky* 46
Bond, Christopher 4
*Bondage* 159
Borcosque, Carlos **114**
*Born to Kill* 105
Borzage, Frank 136
Bosworth, Hobart 83
*The Bottle Imp* (story) 64, 211
*The Bottle Imp* 87
*Bound and Gagged* 85
The Bowery Boys 122
Brandt, Alice **204**, **208**, 210–211
*The Brass Bottle* 33
Braughan, E.A./Braughan, G.A. 71
Breen, Joseph 174, 180
Brendel, El 4, **128**, **129**, 135–136, 137
Bretherton, Howard 172, 173–174
Brian, Mary 144
*Broadway* 148

**231**

*Broadway Danny Rose* 150
Broccoli, Albert 222
Brody, Louis 61
Brook, Clive 28, 94, 95, **95**, 96, 117
Brooks, Louise 212
Brown, Joe E. 137
Browning, Tod 93, 114, 116, 121, 137, 161, 179
Brownlow, Kevin 20, 23, 29–32
Bruce, Nigel 28
Burian, Jarka M. 221–222
Burton, Fred 93
Burton, Tim 58
*Bury the Dead* (play) 105
Busquets, Joaquín **189**, **190**, 191, 192, 198
Bustillo Oro, Juan 138, 189, 192–193
Butler, David 125, 126, 135
Butler, Frank 145
Butt, Johnny 64

C. Auguste Dupin (character) 20, 113
*The Cabinet of Dr. Caligari* 3, 52, 60, 62
*Calamity Jane* 135
*Cally's Comet* 46
*The Canary Murder Case* 33
Cantor, Eddie 132
Canutt, Yakima 149
*Cappy Ricks* 137
Caprice, June **35**, **36**, **38**, **49**, 50
*Caprice of the Mountains* 50
Captain Ahab (character) 23
*Captain January* 135
*Captain Video* 86, 135
*Captain Z-Ro* (TV series) 135
*Car 54, Where Are You?* (TV series) 149
Card, James 29, 30–32
Cardona, René **191**, 192, 193, **193**, 195, 198, 200
Carney, "Uncle Don" 159
Carter, Lin 1
Casella, Alberto 179, 180, 181, 183, 186
*The Cat and the Canary* (1927) 82, 121
*The Cat and the Canary* (1939) 184
*The Cat Creeps* 121
*Cat People* 64
*Catherine the Great* 184
*Cavalcade* 96, 105
Chandler, Helen 137
Chaney, Lon 52, 62, 113, 114–118, 119, 120, 121, 122, 123, 137, 161, 198, 200
Chaney, Lon, Jr. 137
Chaplin, Charlie 31
Charlie Chan (character) 3, 82, 84, 88
*Charlie Chan at the Opera* 83
*Charlie Chan at the Racetrack* 185
*Charlie Chan Carries On* 4, 82, 83, 84, 137
*Charlie Chan in Honolulu* 90
*Charlie Chan's Murder Cruise* 87
*Le Chauldron Infernal et les Vapeurs de Fantasmatiques* 113

*The Cheat* 83
Chéri-Bibi (character) 5
*Chéri-Bibi* 110, **111**, **112**, **113**, **114**, 114, 117–119
*Chéri-Bibi* (1938) 123
*Chéri-Bibi* (1955) 123
*Chéri-Bibi et Cécily* (novel) 114, 117, 123
Child, Richard Walburn 91, 92, 93, 98
*Chinatown Charlie* 87–88
*Chinatown Nights* 162
*The Chinese Parrot* 4, 83, 85, 87
Christie, Agatha 67
Christie, Al 151
Christopher Columbus 186
*Císařův Pekař* see *The Emperor's Baker*
*Cleopatra* 122
*The Clubfoot Mysteries* (stories) 140
*C'mon, Let's Live a Little* 135
*The Cock-Eyed World* 135
Cody, Lew 118
Colbert, Claudette 122
*College Humor* 145
Columbus, Christopher 166
Comathiere, A.B. 159
*El comediante* 119
*The Comet* 46
*Comets* 43
*The Comet's Come-Back* 46
Compton, Betty 95
Conan Doyle, Sir Arthur 5, 20, 21, 22, 32, 46, 146, 164, 202, 203, 209
*Condemned to Live* 137
*A Connecticut Yankee in King Arthur's Court* 135, 137
Coogan, Jackie 153
Cook, Donald 144
Cooper, Frank B. "Jack" 151, 158
Córdoba, Irma **197**
Corelli, Marie 32
*The Corpse Vanishes* 201
Cortázar, Ernesto 187
Cosmo Topper (character) 33
Costello, Lou 149
*Coup d'État* (novel) 123
*Cow Pasture Pool* 153, 154
Crabbe, Buster 137
*Cradle Song* 183
*The Crawling Hand* 185
Crespo, José 118
*The Crime of Dr. Forbes* 174
Criswell, Jeron 161
Crosby, Bing 135, 151, 167
Crosland, Alan 116
*Crossed Trails* 87
Cumberbatch, Benedict 21
*Curlytop* 87
Curry, Joe **39**, **44**, **47**
*Curse of the Demon* 64
Cushing, Peter 137

Dada, Jorge 197
Dalio, Marcel 123
Daly, Arnold 64
*Dance Hall Dames* 162, 163, 165
*Danger* (play) 71
*Danger Man* 155

*A Dangerous Woman* 95
Daniels, Doris 159
*The Dark Angel* 186
*The Dark Star* 33
Dary, A. Homer 157
*Daughter of Don Q* 51
*Daughter of the Dragon* 88
Daw, Marjorie 153
Day, Doris 135
*A Day at the Races* 137
*The Day Mars Invaded Earth* 185
*The Day the Earth Stood Still* 125
*The Dead March* 166
*Dead Reckoning* 144, 145
*The Death Kiss* 3
*Death of a Cop* (TV episode) 92
*Death of a Salesman* 186
*Death Takes a Holiday* (musical) 187
*Death Takes a Holiday* (play) 186
*Death Takes a Holiday* 5, 148, 168, 176–187, **180**, **181**, **182**, **185**
Delacroix, Lucienne **56**
*Deluge* 50
DeMille, Cecil B. 83
Dempster, Carol 32
Denny, Reginald 143, 144
Depardieu, Jean 58
Darbyshire, Iris 75
DeShannon, Jackie 135
de Silva, Nina 158
*Destry Rides Again* 137
De Sylva, Brown, and Henderson 126, 131, 132, 133, 135, 138
Dessauer, Siegfried 9
*Destiny* 61
*Devětsil* 215–216
*The Devil Bat* 192
*The Devil Doll* 137
*The Devil-Stone* 33
*Diabolique* 91
*The Diamond from the Sky* 46
*Diary of a Lost Girl* 16, 212
*Dick Tracy vs. Cueball* 122
*Dick Tracy's Dilemma* 122
Dickens, Charles 56, 69
*Die Frau im Mond* 46
Dieterle, William 52
Dietrich, Robert A. 60
*Diplomaniacs* 137
Dix, Richard 15, **16**, 18
*The Docks of New York* 95
*Dr. Jekyll and Mr. Hyde* (novel) 213
*Dr. Jekyll and Mr. Hyde* (1920) 123
*Dr. Jekyll and Mr. Hyde* (1932) 179
*Dr. Jekyll and Mr. Hyde* (1941) 123, 185
*Le Docteur Lerne* (novel) 59, 60
Dr. Mabuse (character) 156
*Dr. Trimble's Verdict* 63
*Doctor X* 168
Dominik, Hans 8
Don Juan (character) 23
Donlevy, Brian 98
*Dorian Gray* (play) 161
*Dos monjes* (Two Monks) 192
*Double Door* 148, 168, 185
*Down Memory Lane* 150
Downey, Robert, Jr. 21

*Dracula* (novel) 63, 139
*Dracula* (play) 71
*Dracula* 122, 137, 179, 203
*Drácula* 88, 191
*Drácula otra vez* (*Dracula Again*) 201
*Drakula halála* 57
Dreier, Hans 184
Dreyer, Carl 57
*Drums O' Voodoo* 149
Dumbrille, Douglas 98
Duncan, Bud 150, 151
Duncan, Mary 96
Dupont, E.A. 97, 98
Durante, Jimmy 132
Duvivier, Julien 113, 123, 215, 216, 222
*Dvanáct křesl* (*The Twelve Chairs*) 222
Dwan, Allan 88

Earles, Harry 116
Eck, Johnny 161
Eddy, Nelson 137
Edward Scissorhands (character) 58
Eichberg, Richard 211
*Eleagabal Kuperus* (novel) 53
*Elementary* (TV series) 21
Elvey, Maurice 14, 15, 16, 18, 101, 104
*Emil and the Detectives* 212
Emory, Gilbert 106
*The Emperor's Baker* 5, 44, **216**, 216, 217–224
*En cada puerto un amor* 118
*Eran trece* 4
Esmeralda (character) 198
*Esmeralda* (1906) 213
Esper, Dwight 156
*Estrellados* 118
Evans, Madge 15
Everett, Francine 166
Everson, William K. 28, 29–32, 33, 83
*The Evil Eye* 161
*Experience* 161
*The Exploits of Elaine* 43, 50
*The Eyes of Hell* 189

*Fährmann Maria* 60, 211
Fairbanks, Douglas 88
*The Family Stain* 86
*Fantasma* 113
*El fantasma de la opera* 201
*El fantasma de la opereta* 201
*El fantasma del convento* (*The Phantom of the Convent*) 192
Fantomas (character) 113
*Fata Morgana* (play) 215
Fawcett, L'Estrange 101
*Fear* 62
Fegté, Ernst 184
Felix, Seymour 132
Fenton, Leslie 83
Fernández, Esther **192**, **193**, 198
Fernández, Severo **195**, **197**
Ferris, Walter 179, 183
Fields, W.C. 32, 137
Fields, Stanley **142**, 148

*Fifty Candles* (novel) 84
*The Final Problem* (story) 202
Fine, Larry 137
*The Fire Detective* 85
*First Men in the Moon* (novel) 46
Fischbeck, Harry 147
*Flesh and Fantasy* 123
*Flesh and the Devil* 120
Fletcher, Bramwell 136
*Flight Plan* 148
*The Florentine Dagger* 123
*Fog* (story) 139–140, **140**
*Fog* 5, 139–144, **141**, 145, 148
*Fog Island* 122
*Follow Thru* (play) 132
Folsey, George 104
Fook, Lee 89
Ford, Henry 129, 136
Ford, John 135
*Forgotten Faces* 5, 91–98, **95**
*Forgotten Faces* (1936) 97
*Forgotten Men* 157
*The Fortieth Door* 85
Foster, Preston 98
Fox, Finis 153
*F.P. 1 Doesn't Answer* 13
*Framed* 162
Francis, Helen 166
Franco, Jesús 189
Frank, Consuelo **198**
*Frankenstein* (1910) 43, 111
*Frankenstein* (1931) 101, 179
*Frankenstein, el vampiro, y cía* 189
*Frankenstein's Bloody Terror* 189
*Die Frau im Mond* 127
Frazer, Robert 87
*Freaks* 5, 121, 161
*Free and Easy* 118
Freeman, Helen **141**, 143, 144
Freeman, Martin 21
Fregues, Nicolás **195**
Fresney, Pierre 123
Fric, Martin 216, 222, 224
*From the Earth to the Moon* (novel) 46
*La fruta amarga* 118
Fu Manchu (character) 117
Fuller, Mary 43

Gabin, Jean 14
Gable, Clark 105
Gabor, Eva 167
Gad, Urban 60
*Galas de la Paramount* 117, 118
Galeen, Henrik 215
*Games* 91
Gance, Abel 105, 166
Garbo, Greta 50, 120, 121, 122
García Riera, Emilio **197**
Gardin, Marc-André 57
Garrick, John **127**, **129**, 137
Garvey, Marcus 159
*Gaslight* 91
*The Gay Deceiver* 119
*General Spanky* 109
*A Gentleman after Dark* **96**, 98
*Genuine* 12, 61
George, Heinrich 61
*The Ghost Breakers* 184

*The Ghoul* 161, 168
Gibson, Wynne 145
Giglio, Clemente 159
Gilbert, John 5, **115**, **118**, 120–121, **120**, **121**, 123
Gilbert, Lewis 222
Gilbert, Ruth 158
Gill, Basil -104
Gillette, William 3, 4, 21, 32–33, 202–203
*The Girl from Child's in 1950* (play) 165
*Girls for Sale* 152, 157
*Gloria's Romance* 43
*G-Men vs. the Black Dragon* 51
Godard, Jean-Luc 197
Gogol 222
Goldberg, William 160
*Golem* (play) 216
*Der Golem* 1, 62, 214
*Le Golem* 113, 215, 216, 217
*Der Golem, wie er in die Welt kam* 214
*Gone with the Wind* 210
*The Good Soldier Švejk* 222
Goodwin, Thomas **49**
Goofy Tone (aka *Goofytone*) Films (vaudeville act) 151, 158
*Goofy Movies* 158
*Goofytone Newsreel* 158
Gordon, Julia Swain **92**
Gordon, Ruth 186
*Grand Torino* 92
Grant, Cary 144, 145, 210
Grassby, Bertram 84
Gray, Shirley **142**, 145, 146
*The Great Houdini* 137
*The Green Archer* 51, 85
*The Green Jade* 162
Gregor, Nina **56**, 57
Grey, George Arthur 85
Griffith, D.W. 15, 32, 135, 161
*The Grinning Face* see *Das grinsende Gesicht*
*Das grinsende Gesicht* 4, 52–58, **53**, **54**, **55**, **56**, **57**, 61
Gründgens, Gustav 13–14, **13**, 15
Guarracino, Umberto 61
Guest, Val 222
Güttner, Bruno 28, **204**, 209–210
Güttner, Vittorio 209
Guy Blanche, Alice 213

Haack, Käthe 47
Haley, Jack 132
Hall, Jon 86
Halliday, John **143**, 144, 147–148, 174
Ham and Bud 150
Hameister, Willy 60
Hames, Peter 222
Hamilton, Betty 165
Hamilton, Lloyd 150
Hamilton, Neil **142**, 145, 147
Hamlet (character) 4
*Hamlet* (play) 27, 33
*The Hands of Orlac* (novel) 59
Hanke, Ken 83, 90
The Hanlon Brothers 113

*Hannah and Her Sisters* 137
Harding, Warren 91
Hardwicke, Sir Cedric 187
Harryhausen, Ray 123
Hart, Ferdinand 223
Hartmann, Paul 14
Hašek, Jaroslav 222
Hatton, Rondo 198, 201
*The Haunted Grange* (story) 32
*Das Haupt der Medusa* (*The Head of Medusa*) 54
*Hawk of the Hills* 85, 88
*Häxan* 167
*Hay que matar a Drácula* (*Dracula Must Be Killed*) 201
Hayakawa, Sessue 83
Hayes, H. Manning 64, 67
Hayward, Lydia 64
*The Hazards of Helen* 43
*He Who Gets Slapped* 120
Hearst, William Randolph 93
Heinlein, Robert 1
*Held for a Ransom* 20
*Heliotrope* 92–93, **92**
*Hell Divers* 105
*Her Soul for Sale* 157
*La herencia macabra* (*The Macabre Legacy*) **198**, 201
Hersholt, Jean 121–122
Herzka, Julius 57
Heywood, Donald 159
*High School Hero* 135
*High Treason* 3, 5, 15, 16, 99–105, **100**, **101**, 106, 107, 132
*High Treason* (play) 101–102
*Hilde Warren and Death* (*Hilde Warren und der Tod*) **179**, 180–181
Hill, Ethel 142
*Hill's Valley* 87
*Himmelskibet* 126
Hinds, Samuel S. 144
*Historias para no dormir* (*Stories to Keep You from Sleeping*) (TV series) 201
Hitchcock, Alfred 74, 205
Hitler, Adolf 13, 160, 201, 212
Hobart, Rose 179
Höbling, Franz **55**, **56**, 57, **57**
Hoffman, Otto **180**
*Hoffmann's Tales* (*Hoffmans Erzählungen*) 53
*Hold Everything* (play) 132
*Hold That Ghost* 137
Holden, Gloria 98
Holmes, Phillips 109
*El hombre y la bestia* 201
*L'Homme qui rit* (novel) 52, 57
*Homunculus* 60
*Honeymoon Ranch* 87
*Honor Bright* (TV episode) 92
Hope, Bob 135
Hopkins, Anthony 182
Hopkins, Miriam 98
Hopper, Hedda 96
Horejc, Jaroslav 223, 224
*The Horror* 5, 149, 150, 152, **155**, **156**, 158–159, 161–165
*Hot for Paris* 135

*The Hound of the Baskervilles* (story) 202, 203
*The Hound of the Baskervilles* (1921) 101, 205
*House of a Thousand Candles* 109
*The House of Hate* 50
*House of Horrors* 185
*The House Without a Key* 3, 4, 6, 50, 51, 76–90, **84**, **86**, **89**
Howard, Leslie 169
Hugo, Victor 52, 56, 58, 213
*The Human Beast* (aka *Jumen*; Japanese release title for *The Horror*) 163
Hume, Benita **101**, 103, 104
*The Hunchback of Notre Dame* (1923, 1939, 1956) 52, 82, 115, 185
*Der Hund von Baskerville* (1929) 205
*Der Hund von Baskerville* (1937) 5, 6, 12, 28, 202–212, **204**, **207**, **208**
*Hungarian Rhapsody* 103
Hunt, J. Roy 96
Huntley, G.P. Jr. 185
*A Huntress of Men* 82
Huston, Walter 16, 122
Hutchison, Charles 155
Hyams, Lila **118**, 121
Hymer, Warren 137, 198

Ibáñez Menta, Narciso 194, **194**, **196**, 200–201
Ibáñez Serrador, Narciso "Chicho" 201
*Idiot's Delight* (play) 105
*If You Believe It, It's So* 153
*L'Île d'épouvante* 59, 60
Ilf and Petrov 222
*I Married a Witch* 184, 185
*The Immoral Mr. Teas* 167
*Impetuous Youth* 57
*The Indians Are Coming* 87
*Inherit the Wind* 186
*Die Insel der Verschollenen* 4, 58–61, **59**, **61**, 205
*The Inspector General* 222
*Interference* 96
*Invasion* 166
*La invasión de los vampiros* 189
*The Invisible Man* 168
*The Invisible Ray* 87
*The Island of Dr. Moreau* (novel) 4, 52, 58, 59, 60
*Island of Doomed Men* 87
*Island of Lost Souls* 52, 59, 60, 61, 121, 144, 145, 146, 148
*It Came from Beneath the Sea* 123
*It Happened in Harlem* 166
*It Happened One Night* 50
*It's Great to Be Alive* 138

*J'Accuse* 105, 166
*The Jack Rider* 155
Jackson, Thomas B. 148
Jacobs, W.W. 4, 63–64, 66
Jacques, Norman 156
Jakobson, Roman 216
Janney, William 148
Jannings, Emil 47
*Der Januskopf* 58

*The Jazz Singer* 75, 114
*Jengo* (documentary) 158
*Jesse James under the Black Flag* 155
John, Georg **179**, 181
*John the Drunkard* 163
Johnson, Noble 61
Jolson, Al 116
Jordan, Louis 166
Jory, Victor 92, 197
Joseph Rouletabille (character) 113–114
*Jud Süss* 61
*Jungle Killer* 158
*Just Imagine* 4, 51, 125–138, **126**, **127**, **128**, **129**, **130**, **131**, **133**, 193

Kaiser-Titz, Eric 61, 205
Kaiser Wilhelm 203
*Kamaradschaft* 17
Karl, Roger 113
Karloff, Boris 1, 50, 75, 87, 119, 122, 161, 185, 200, 201
Kaye, Danny 167
Kayssler, Friedrich **10**, 12, **207**, **208**, 211
Keaton, Buster 118, 205
Keel, Howard 135
Keighley, William 173
Keith, Ian 122, 123
Kellermann, Bernhard 7, 8, 9, 14
Kennedy, Edgar 83
Kennedy, Robert 125
Kenton, Earle 144
Kesselring, Joseph 200
*Killer Aboard* 145
*Killer Ape* 86
King, Leslie **153**, **155**, 158–159, 161
King, Martin Luther 125
King Kong (character) 107
*King of the Damned* 15
*The King of the Kongo* 87
*King of the Wild* 87
*King of the Zombies* 58
*Kings of Laughter* 162
*Kiss of Death* 92
Knowles, Patric 123
Kohler, Fred 96
Kotsonaros, George 121
Kortner, Fritz 57
Kruger, Alma **107**
Kubrick, Stanley 125
Kühne, Friedrich 204, 205
*Kukan: The Battle Cry of China* (documentary) 166
Kuwa, George 83, **86**, 87–88, 89
*Kurfürstendamm* 184

*Ladies They Talk About* 173
Ladrón de Guevara, María **112**
*Lady on a Barge* (stories) 64
Laemmle, Carl 82, 83, 114, 115, 145, 153, 179
Laemmle, Carl, Jr. 116, 179
Lahr, Bert 132
Lamac, Carl 205, 206, 209, 211, 212
Lamarr, Hedy 75
Lang, Charles 184
Lang, Fritz 46, 53, 61, 101, 127, 181, 212

# Index

LaRue, Jack **143**, 148
*Lass of the Lumberlands* 43
*The Last Man on Earth* 138
*The Last Moment* 139
*Laugh, Clown, Laugh* 116
Laughton, Charles 52, 121, 198
Laurel and Hardy 50, 118
Lauren, S.K. 105, 107
Law, Jude 21
Lawrence, Reginald 105, 107
*Lawrence of Arabia* 101
Lawson, John 64
Layton, Harry 153
Lean, David 101
*Leave It to Beaver* (TV series) 135
Lee, Christopher 1, 63–64, 211
Lee, Norman 71
*La Légende de Fantôme* 113
Lehman, Gladys 181, 183
Leisen, Mitchell 183, 184, 185
*Lelicek in the Service of Sherlock Holmes* 222
Leni, Paul 83, 85
Leonard, Benny 161
Leroux, Gaston 5, 113, 115, 121, 198
Levy, Fred 165
*Liebe, Tod und Teufel (Love, Death and the Devil)* 211
*Liebe und Trompetenblasen* 211
*Die Liebschaften des Hektor Dalmore* 184
*The Life Story of David Lloyd George* 15
*A Light in the Window* see *Una luz en la ventana*
*Lightning Hutch* 155
*The Lightning Raider* 50
*Lilith und Ly* 53
Lindsay, Margaret 169
Linow, Ivan 137
Lithgow, John 64
*Little Friend* 14
Liu, Lucy 21
Lloyd, Harold 154
*The Lodger* 74
Lombard, Carole 144, 145
*London after Midnight* 114
*Long Day's Journey into Night* (play) 186
*Look-Out Sister* 150, 166
López Chaflán, Carlos 198
*Lo que va de ayer a hoy (So Far from Yesterday to Today)* 138, 193
Lord Northcliffe 101
Lorraine, Harry 74–75
*The Lost World* 122, 126
*The Lottery Bride* 137
*Love* 120
*Love and Terror Aboard* 147
*The Love Boat* (TV series) 142
*The Love Comet* 46
*Love Island* 167
*The Loves of Jeanne Ney* 212
*Loving the Ladies* 103
Loy, Myrna 33, 136
Lubin, Bert 87
*Las luchadoras contra la momia (The Wrestling Women vs. the Aztec Mummy)* **196**

Lugosi, Bela 1, 61, 75, 90, 121, 122, 146, 147, 161, 189, 191, 193, 201
*Lunatic at Large* 162
Lüthge, Bobby E. 60
*The Lurking Peril* 50
*Una luz en la ventana* 2, 5, 188, **195**, **196**, **197**, 198–201

*Macabre* 91
*The Macabre Trunk* see *El baúl macabro*
MacDonald, Jeanette 137
MacIntyre, Diane 31
*Maciste in Hell* 61, 167
*Maciste in the Lion's Den* 61
*The Mad Genius* 87
*Madame Butterfly* 83
Maddow, Rachel 2
*Madrid en el año 2000* 138
Maisell, Lew 159
Mamoulian, Rouben 179
*The Man from Mars* 126
*Man-Made Monster* 137
*The Man Who Could Work Miracles* 14
*The Man Who Cried Wolf* 87, 122
*The Man Who Laughs* 52, 61, 95
*The Man Who Reclaimed His Head* 185
*The Man Without a Face* 85
*Der Mandarin* 53
*Manhattan Madness* 162
*Der Mann, der Sherlock Holmes War (The Man Who Was Sherlock Holmes)* 206
Manners, David 192
Manson, Ona 132
*A Man's Past* 122
*The Marble Heart* 86
*La marca del hombre lobo (The Mark of the Wolfman)* 189
March, Fredric 178, 179, 180, **180**, **181**, 181, 182, **183**, 184, **185**, 185–186, 187
*Maria Marten, or Murder in the Red Barn* (story) 68
*Maria Marten* 71
*Mark of the Vampire* 122, 147
Markham, Monte 187
*Married in Hollywood* 137
Marriott, Moore 4, **63**, 64, 66, 74–75
*M.A.R.S.* 126
Marsh, Mae 32
Marshall, Herbert 97
*The Martian* 4
The Marx Brothers 137
*The Mask* 189
*The Mask of Fu Manchu* 122
*The Masked Marvel* 86
*The Masque of the Red Death* (story) 181
Massary, Fritz 12
Massey, Raymond 28
*The Match King* 173
Matull, Kurt 9
Maude, Cyril 64
May, Joe 180
May, Mia **179**

Mayer, Louis B. 120
McConnell, Gladys 85
McCoy, Tim 87
McHugh, Frank 174
McLaglen, Victor 64
McQuade, Robert 144
*Meet Joe Black* 178, 182
Meinert, Rudolf 203
Melford, George 88
Méliès, Georges 46, 113
*Melody in Spring* 85
*Melting Millions* 85
*The Memoirs of Sherlock Holmes* (TV series) 21
*Men Must Fight* 5, 99, 105–109
*Men Must Fight* (play) 105, **106**, 106–107, **107**
Mendes, Lothar 14
Menzies, William Cameron 103
*The Merchant of Venice* (play) 57
*Merista the Dancer* 57
Merivale, Philip 179
*A Message from Mars* 47, 126
Messter, Oscar 180
*Metropolis* 16, 101, 181, 212
*Metropolitan Murders* 162
Metzner, Ernö 16–17
*México de mis recuerdos* (*Mexico of My Memories*) 192
Meyers, Russ 167
Meyrink, Gustav 215
*Michael* 57
Michael, Gertrude 97
Millarde, Harry F. 50
Miller, Jonny Lee 21
Miller, Marilyn 132
Miller, Walter 82, 85, 86–87
Mimieux, Yvette 187
*The Miracle* (play) 95
*Les Misérables* 186
*Missing Daughters* 156
*Mr. Hex* 122
Mister Moto (character) 185
*Mister Roberts* 33
*Mr. Wu* (play) 117
*Mr. Wu* 118
*El misterio del rostro pálido* 5, 188, **189**, 189–193, **190**, 198, 201
Mix, Tom 150
*A Modern Miracle* (documentary) 17
*The Monkey's Paw* (1915) 64
*The Monkey's Paw* (1923) 4, 62–68, **63**
*The Monkey's Paw* (1933) 3, 123
*The Monkey's Paw* (story) 63
*The Monster* (play) 71
*The Monster Walks* 137, 161
Montez, Maria 123
Montez, Nyrida **154**
Montgomery, Douglass **106**
Monroy, Alberto 193
*El monstruo no ha muerto (The Monster Hasn't Died)* 201
Monty Python 137
*The Moonstone* 164
Moonstruck 46
Moore, Victor 132
*Moran of the Lady Letty* 88

Morgan, Frank 132
Moriarty (character) 202
*Moriarty* 27, 28
Morosco, Oliver 88
Morrissey, Will 149, 150
*La Morte in vacanza* (play) 179, 183
Mosjoukine, Ivan 95
*Most* (play) 186
*Il mostro di Frankenstein* 61
*Moulin Rouge* 97
*Movie Maniacs* 50
*La muerte enamorada* (*Death in Love*) 187
*La mujer X* 118
Mukařovsky, Jan 216
*Der Müller und sein Kind* (*The Miller and His Child*) 53
*The Mummy* 136
*El mundo de los vampiros* (*World of the Vampires*) 189
*The Murder of Dmitri Karamazov* 212
*Murder in the Private Car* 168
*Murders in the Rue Morgue* (story) 20
*Murders in the Rue Morgue* (1914) 111
*Murders in the Zoo* 145, 185
Murnau, F.W. 111, 139
*The Music Man* 153
Mussolini, Benito 91
*My Man Godfrey* 96, 138
Myers, Harry 87
*The Mysteries of Myra* 43
*The Mysterious Island* 112, 126
*The Mystery Mind* 50
*Mystery of Marie Roget* 123–124
*The Mystery of the Marie Celeste* 146
*The Mystery of Mr. X* 122
*The Mystery of the Ghastly Face* see *El misterio del rostro pálido*
*Mystery of the Wax Musuem* 168
*The Mystery of the Yellow Room* (novel) 113

*Nachtgestalten* 53, 184
Nagel, Conrad 96
Naish, J. Carroll 174
*Narciso Ibáñez Menta presenta* (TV series) 201
*Narciso Ibáñez Serrador presenta a Narciso Ibáñez Menta*(TV series) 201
Naschy, Paul 5, 189, 200
Negri, Pola 95
Neill, Roy William 95
Nerz, Louis 57
*Der 9 November* (*The 9th of November*) (novel) 14
Neuss, Alwin 204, 205
Nick Charles (character) 33, 50
Nielsen, Asta 60
*Night of Terror* 175
*Night of the Living Dead* 1
*Night Owls* 118
*Nightmare* 91
*Ninotchka* 50
Nixon, Marian 83

*Non-Stop* 148
Noriega, Manuel 193, **193**
Northcote, Sidney Webber 64
Norwood, Eille 21–22, 205
*Nosferatu* 3, 53, 58, 62, 112, 139
Nostradamus 192
*Notre Dame de Paris* (novel) 213
*Nouvelles Aventures* (stories) 123

Obama, Michelle 214, 224
Oboler, Arch 187
O'Brien Moore, Erin **106**
O'Connor, Robert Emmett 174
Odemar, Fritz **204**, 209
Ogle, Charles 43, 113
*Oh! Calcutta!* (play) 165
O'Hara, Maureen 198
Oland, Warner 50, 82, 83, 84, 85, 86, 88, 90, 117
*The Old Dark House* 168, 200
Oliver, Edna Mae 138
*Oliver Twist* 101
*On a Shoestring* (book) 150
*On Borrowed Time* 187
Ondra, Anny 205
*One Exciting Night* 32
O'Neill, Eugene 186
*Only a Jew* (play) 64
O'Reilly, Tex 87
*Orlacs Hände* 57
*Orphans of the Storm* 161
Ortiz, Natalia **190**, **191**
O'Sullivan, Maureen **127**, 136–137
Oswald, Richard 53, 203–204, 205
Otis, Joey 153
Owen, Harold 117
Owen, Reginald 28

Pabst, G.W. 17, 212
Pagano, Bartolomeo 61
*A Page of Madness* 163
Paget, Sindmey 209
*Pandora's Box* 16
*Paramount on Parade* 117
Park, E.L. 83, 84
Parker, Albert 22, 30, 31, 32
Parker, Louis N. 64
*Partners of the Sunset* 87
*The Passing of the Third Floor Back* 15
Patrick, Gail 183, 185
Patterson, Frederick 158
*The Patty Duke Show* (TV series) 135
*Peggy Sue Got Married* 136
*Pekařův Císař* 5, 44; see also *The Baker's Emperor*
Pemberton-Billing, Noel 100–102
Pereda, Ramón **192**
*The Perfect Crime* 96
*The Perfumed Trap* 93
*Perils of Our Girl Reporters* 43
*The Perils of Pauline* 43, 51, 82, 86
*Perry Mason* (TV series) 185
Peter Ibbetson 148, 184
*Phantasmes* 113
*The Phantom* 87
*The Phantom* Foe 85
*The Phantom from 10,000 Leagues* 185

*The Phantom of Paris* 5, 110, **115**, **116**, 116, **117**, **118**, 120–124, **121**, **122**
*Phantom of Paris* (*Mystery of Marie Roget*) 124
The Phantom of the Opera (character) 113, 189, 200
*The Phantom of the Opera* (1925) 3, 114, 116, **119**
*Phantom of the Opera* (1943) 124
*The Phantom Signal* 113
Philipp, Julius 203
Philo Vance (character) 33, 117
*Piccadilly* 97
Pichel, Irving 61, 174
Pickford, Mary 83, 153
*The Picture of Dorian Gray* (1916) 63
Pierce, Jack P. 57
*Pinocchio* 185
Pitt, Brad 182
Pitt, George Dibdin 69, 73
Pitts, ZaSu 137
*The Plague in Florence* (*Die Pest in Florenz*) 181
*Plan Nine from Outer Space* 3
*Play Ball* 85
Pleasance, Donald 222
Poe, Edgar Allan 111, 123, 124, 181, 198, 201
Pollard, Bud 5, 149–167, **150**, **151**
Pollard, Harry 153
Pollard, "Snub" 149, 153
Pompillo, Pedro **195**
Ponto, Erich **207**, **208**, 211
Porten, Henny 180
Powell, Eleanor 132
Powell, William 33, **95**, 96, 117, 136
*Première Aventures* (stories) 114, 123
Presenell, Robert 145
Price, Vincent 1
*The Prisoner of Zenda* 6
*The Private Life of Don Juan* 165
*Psychic Bidding* (book) 140
Pulido, Juan 158
*The Purple Monster Strikes* 51

Quasimodo (character) 198, 200
*Queen Christina* 121, 122
Quinn, Anthony 52

Raboid, Rajah 161
*Radio Mania* 126
Rains, Claude 124, 185, 187, 198, 201
*Ramar of the Jungle* (TV series) 86
Rasp, Fritz 205, **207**, **209**, 211–212
*Rasputin and the Empress* 108, 156
*Rasputins Liebesabenteuer* 156
Rathbone, Basil 5, 28, 33, 121
*The Raven* 75
Ray, Allene 82, 85, 87
Ray, René 104–105
*Red Lights* 168
Redman, Frank 50
Redman, George 67
Rehkop, Paul **204**
Reicher, Frank **172**, 174
Renard, Maurice 59
Rendel, Robert 28
Renoir, Jean 57

*El retorno del hombre lobo* (*The Return of the Wolfman*) 200
*The Return of Peter Grimm* 96
*The Return of Sherlock Holmes* (play) 22
*Return of the Phantom* (story) 115
*Return of the Terror* 5, 168–175, **172**
Reville, Alma (Hitchcock) 15
*Revizor* 222
*Rhodes of Africa* 16
*Richard Wagner* 10
*Richthofen the Red Ace of Germany* 156
Rin-Tin-Tin 87
*Rio's Road to Hell* **152**, 157
*Rip Van Winkle* 159
Rippert, Otto 181
Ritchie, Guy 21
Roach, Hal 118
Roach, Joseph Anthony 85
*The Road to Hell* 157
*The Road to Hollywood* 151, 167
*The Road to Mandalay* 83
*Road to Morocco* 135
Robertson, John S. 123
*The Rocky Horror Picture Show* 71
*Les Rôdeurs de l'Air* see *The Sky Ranger*
Rogell, Albert 143, 144
Rogers, Will 132, 135, 137
Romero, George 1
Romero, Manuel 200
*Room Service* 137
*Rosalie* (play) 132
Rose, Arthur 22
Ross, Joe E. 149, 167
Rothauser, Eduard 9
Rotman, Ernst **208**
Roulien, Raul 138
Rowson, Harry 71, 73
*The Royal Family of Broadway* 185
Ruggles, Charlie **143**, 144, 147
*The Rules of the Game* 57
*Runaway Jane* 43
Ruth St. Denis Dance Company 32

*La saga de los Drácula* (*The Dracula Saga*) 201
*The Saint's Double Trouble* 87
Salazar, Abel 189
*Sally of the Sawdust* 32
*Salome* (play) 100
Sandrino, Oreste 159
Sanger, Margaret 165
*Scandals* (play) 132
Schertzinger, Victor 94, 96
Schmelling, Max 205
Schmitz, Sybille 211
Schneer, Charles H. 123
Schratter, David 153, 154
Schulberg, B.P. 179
Schürenberg, Siegfried 210
Scott, Rey 166
*The Sea Beast* 83
Seitz, George B. **35**, **36**, **38**, **47**, **49**, 50–51, 85, 86, 87
Selwyn, Edgar **107**
Selznick, David 109
Semels, Harry **39**, **44**, 50, 51

Sennett, Mack 145, 150, 151
*Seven Keys to Baldpate* (novel) 84
*Seven Seas* 114
*Sevilla de mis amores* 118
*Sex Madness* 156
*The Shadow* 86, 197
*The Shadow of the Sea* (*Der Schatten des Meeres*) 180
*Shadow of the Thin Man* 50
Shakespeare, William 57
*Shanghai Express* 96
Shanor, Peggy **44**, **47**, 50
Shary, Dory 142, 144
Shaw, George Bernard 64
Shaw, Irwin 105
*She* 63, 112
Shearer, Norma 105
Shelley, Mary 46, 198
*Sherlock* (TV series) 21
Sherlock Holmes (character) 96, 113, 117, 164, 202
*Sherlock Holmes* (1916) 3–4
*Sherlock Holmes* (1922) 2, 4, 20–33, **22**, **24**, **26**, **28**, **29**, **31**
*Sherlock Holmes* (2010) 21
*Sherlock Holmes and the Great Murder Mystery* 20
*Sherlock Holmes Baffled* 20
Sherman, Lowell 144
Sherwood, Robert 105
*Shielding Shadow* 161
Shock Theater 1
*Shooting Big Game with a Camera* (documentary) 158
Siff, Manuel 145
*The Sign of Four* (story) 164
*Sign of the Cross* 122
Simmons, Ira 162
*Simple Simon* (play) 132
Sims, Dorothy Rice 139–140, 142
Sinclair, Irene 32
*Singin' in the Rain* 118
*Sinister Hands* 161
*Sinners in Silk* 121
Siodmak, Kurt 13, 14, 16, 18
Skipworth, Allison 137
*The Sky Dragon* 82
*The Sky Hawk* 137
*The Sky Ranger* 2, 4, 34–51, **35**, **36**, **37**, **38**, **39**, **40**, **41**, **43**, **44**, **47**, **49**
Slaughter, Todd 4, 73, 74
Sloane, Paul 144
Smith, Basil 164
Smith, C. Aubrey **16**, **116**, 123, 210
Smith, Frank Leon 45, 47, 82, 83, 85
Smith, Pete 158
Smolowa, Sybill 9
*So This Is London* 136
Sojin, Kamiyama 83
*Something to Live For* 97
*Son of Kong* 168
Sondheim, Stephen 4, 75
*Song o' My Heart* 137
Sorel, Jean 57
*The Sorrows of Satan* (1917) 63
*The Sorrows of Satan* (1926) 32, 112, 147
*The Soul of Kura San* 87

Souvestre, Pierre 113
Sparks, Ned 198
*Sparrows* 33
Standing, Sir Guy **180**, 182, 183, 185
Stephenson, Henry 144–145
Stevenson, Robert Louis 22, 64, 211, 213
Stifter, Magnus 9
Stoker, Bram 63, 139
Stone, George E. 174
Stone, Lewis 108, **115**, 122
*The Story of Temple Drake* 148
*The Strange Affair of Uncle Harry* 62
*Strange Holiday* 187
*Strange Women of the World* 162
*Strike Me Pink* (play) 132
*The String of Pearls* (story) 68, 69
Strobel, Karl 53
Stuart, Gloria 138
*The Student of Prague* 60
*A Study in Scarlet* (novel) 20
*Su última noche* 118
*The Suicide Club* 63
Sullivan, C. Gardner 107
Summerville, Slim 83
*Sumurun* 16
*Sunken Silver* 51, 85, 86, 87
*El superloco* (*The Super Madman*) 192, 201
*Superman* 86
*Superman and the Mole Men* 184
*Supernatural* 145
*Svět Patří Nám* (*The World Is Ours*) 222
*Sweeney Todd* (1928) 4, 62, 68–73
*Sweeney Todd* (1928) (play) **70**
*Sweeney Todd* (1936) 73
*Swiss Miss* 50
Sydney, Basil **16**

Talbot, Lyle 172, **172**, 173, 174
*Tall, Tan, and Terrific* 166
*Tangled Lines* 86
*Tarzan, the Ape Man* 123
*Tarzan the Fearless* 137
*Tarzan's New York Adventure* 50
Taylor, Kent 183, 185
*Te quiero con locura* (*I'm Crazy About You*) 192
Teasdale, Vera **143**
*Tell It to the Marines* 118
Temple, Shirley 135
*The Terrible People* 85
*The Terror* (novel) 171
*The Terror* 121, 168, 169, 170–171, **171**, 174
*Terror Aboard* 5, 139, **142**, **143**, 144–148, 174
Terry, Harold 22
Thalberg, Irving 109, 115, 116
*That Man from Tangier* 33
*That Royle Girl* 32
Thew, Harvey 145
*The Thief of Bagdad* (1924) 83, 112, 126
*The Thief of Baghdad* (1952) 212
*The Thin Man* 96, 136
*Things to Come* 17, 103, 105

*The Third Man* 211
*The Thirteenth Chair* (1929) 121
*The Thirteenth Chair* (1937) 122
*This Island Earth* 104
Thomas, Augustus 123
Thomas, Danny 92
Thomas, Jameson 104
Thorndyke, Sybil 75
Thorry, Juan Carlos **195**, **197**, 200
*Thou Shalt Not Kill* (aka *O Festino o la Legge*) 159
*Three Cheers* (play) 132
*Three Little Beers* 50
The Three Stooges 50
*Thunder* 117
Tierney, Edward 149
*The Tiger Woman* 86
*Tillie and Gus* 137
*Times Have Changed* 87
Todd, Arthur L. 174
Toler, Sidney 82, 90
*The Toll House* (story) 63
*The Toll of the Sea* 83
Tom Sawyer (character) 73
*Topper* 33
*Tower of Lies* 122
*Traffic in Souls* 157
*Transatlantic Tunnel* 7, 14–17, **16**, **17**, 18–19, 123
Travers, Barry 145
*Trial Marriage* 156
*The Trial of Mary Dugan* 57
*Trifling Women* 122
*Trilby* (novel) 53
*Trilby* (1914) 63
*A Trip to Mars* 46, 126
*Trip the the Center of the Moon* 46
*A Trip to the Moon* 46
*Der Tunnel* (1915 film) 3, 7–14, **10**, **12**
*Der Tunnel* (1915 film, aka *Das Riesenprojekt, Der Schienenweg unter dem Ozean*) 9, **9**, **11**
*Der Tunnel* (1933 film) 13–14, **13**, **15**
*Der Tunnel* (1935 film) 14–17
*Der Tunnel* (novel) 7–9
Turpin, Ben 149
*The Twilight Zone* (TV series) 135
*2001: A Space Odyssey* 125, 132

*The Unholy Three* 116, 117, 137
*The Uninvited* 184
*The Unknown* 114
*Up the Ladder* 16
*The Utah Kid* 87

V+W 215, 216, 221, 222
Vadim, Roger 189
Valentino, Rudolph 88, 120
Vallentin, Hermann 12
*Valley of the Zombies* 122
Van Dine, S.S. 33
Van Sloan, Edward 138, 185
*The Vanishing Shadow* 87
*Varieté* 97

Vee, Bobby 135
Veidt, Conrad 1, 14, 15, 53, 57, 83, 122, 184
Veldtkirch, Rose 12, **12**
Venable, Evelyn 178, 180, **181**, 183, 185, **185**
*The Ventures of Marguerite* 43
*Der vergiftete Strom* 60
Verne, Jules 7, 46, 132
Verne, Michael 7
Vernon, Bobby 145
Vernon, Maurice 117
*Vertigo* 96
*Vest Pocket Revue* (play) 215
*Victims of Persecution* 160, 165
*Vida de Noche* 158
Vidor, King 149
Viertel, Berthold 14–15
Vilches, Ernesto **112**, **113**, **114**, 117–120, 121
Villarías, Carlos **191**, 191, 192, 193, 201
Villiers-Stuart, Eileen 100
Vinson, Helen 179
*Voice of the Jungle* 158
The Volstead Act 129, 136
von Harbou, Thea 181
von Seyffertitz, Gustav 28, 29, **29**, 33, 121, 123
von Stackelberg, Carla 210
von Sternberg, Josef 95, 184
*The Voodoo Man* 3, 201
*Voodoo Tiger* 86
Voskovec, Jiří 215–216
Voss, Peter **204**, 211

Waag, Hanna 212
*Wagon Train* (TV series) 135
Wagner, Richard 156
Wallace, Edgar 168, 169, 171, 174, 175, 205
Wallace, Morgan **143**, 145
Warm, Hermann 10, 203
Warren, E. Alyn 83
Warren, Eda 147
Wauer, William 9–10
*The Way of a Man* 87
*The Weary Death* (*Der Müde Tod*) 181
Wegener, Paul 53, 60, 214–215, 223
Weissmüller, Franz **54**
Weissmuller, Johnny 86, 136, 137
Well, H.G. 4, 46, 52, 58, 59, 101
*The Well* (story) 63
Wells, Jacqueline 137
Welles, Orson 45
*The WereWolf of London* 46, 124
Werich, Jan 215–216, **217**, 222
Wessel, Horst 14
West, Walter 71, 73
*West of Zanzibar* 114
Whale, James 101
*What Happened to Mary?* 43
*What Women Give* 105
Wheeler, Charlie 154

Wheeler, Hugh 4
Wheeler and Woolsey 137
*When Clouds Roll By* 88
*When the Sleeper Wakes* (novel) 101
*A Whiff of Heliotrope* (story) 91, 93, 97
*While Paris Sleeps* 120
*While the City Sleeps* 116
*The Whispering Chorus* 33
White, George 132
White, Marjorie **129**, 137
White, Pearl 43, 50, 51
*White Cargo* 75
*The White Sister* (play) 159
*White Zombie* 3, 87
*Whoopee* (play) 132
*Wicked* 88
Wilde, Oscar 100
Williams, Valentine 139, 140, 142
*The Willow Tree* 87
*Wings* 135
Winters, Roland 82
Wiren, Myra Page 186
Wiren, Oscar B. 186
Wiseman, Joseph 187
*The Witching Hour* 123, 148, 168, 185
*Who Will Marry Mary?* 43
*The Wizard* 33, 121
*The Wizard of Oz* 62
Wolheim, Louis 26
*Woman Haters* 137
*Woman in the Moon* 212
*Woman in the Window* 62
*A Woman of Affairs* 120
*Womanhood, the Glory of a Nation* 108
*The Women's House of Rio* (*Das Frauenhaus von Rio*) 156, 157
Wong, Anna May 83, 85
Wontner, Arthur 28
Wookevec see Voskovec, Jiří
*Words and Music* 137
Wright, Humberston 104
*Wu Li Chang* 118
Wynn, Ed 132
Wynyard, Diana 105, 108–109, **108**
Wysbar, Frank 211

Yaconelli, Frank 183
*Years Ago* (play) 186
*The Yellow Cameo* 85
*Yiskor* 160
*You Can't Take It with You* 137
*You Only Live Twice* 222
Young, Roland **24**, 27, 33

Zacarías, Miguel 196–197, 198
Zacherley, John 1
*The Zane Grey Theater* (TV series) 92
Zola, Emile 56
*Zorro's Black Whip* 51
Zucco, George 122

www.ingramcontent.com/pod-product-compliance
Lightning Source LLC
Chambersburg PA
CBHW081551300426
44116CB00015B/2837